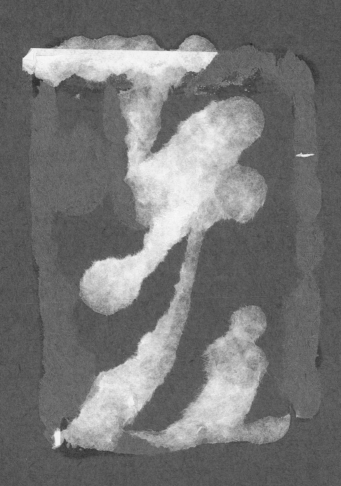

Managing Change
in
Educational
Organizations

SOCIOLOGICAL PERSPECTIVES, STRATEGIES,
AND CASE STUDIES

Compiled and Edited by

J. Victor Baldridge
Stanford University

and

Terrence E. Deal
Stanford University

With the assistance of

Mary Zieg Ancell

A book related to the work of the
Stanford Center for Research and Development in Teaching.

McCutchan Publishing Corporation
2526 Grove Street
Berkeley, California 94704

ISBN: 0-8211-0128-5
Library of Congress Catalog Card Number: 74-24479

Printed in the United States of America

Acknowledgments

We wish to express our thanks to the contributors who not only gave permission for the use of their work but also cooperated in the task of adapting their previously published material to fit the needs of the volume. (The permission of the respective copyright holders is acknowledged at the appropriate places.)

In preparing this volume we examined many more articles than could possibly be included. We believe the final product properly reflects both the role of the pioneers in the study of innovation and change and the developments of the last ten years.

We were especially impressed, when making our final selection, with the number of articles that came from federally funded research and development centers. Over half of the material in this book was supported by such institutions, an outcome that was not intentional. We undertook our search of over three hundred articles in order to identify and select exemplary work in educational innovation, not to emphasize work done at research and development centers. Contributions from staff members of the Stanford School of Education's Stanford Center for Research and Development in Teaching (Chapters 1, 5, 6, 7, 13, 19, 22, 23, and 25) and those from the University of Oregon's Center for Educational Policy and Management, formerly CASEA (Chapters 8, 9, 10, 14, 17, 20, 24) testify, however, to the importance of the work of these institutions.

Educational research and development, now supported in large part by the National Institute of Education, is presently being challenged. Criticism in part reflects a perception on the part of legislators, administrators, and teachers that such activities have not contributed substantially to the solution of educational problems. This book, we believe, demonstrates that educational research and development activities have indeed provided valuable assistance for school administrators wrestling with the problems involved in changing schools.

J. Victor Baldridge
Terrence E. Deal

Contents

Contributors

Abbott, Max G., Center for Educational Policy and Management, University of Oregon

Baldridge, J. Victor, Office of the Vice President for Academic Affairs, California State University, Fresno

Bennis, Warren G., University of Cincinnati

Bernstein, Marilyn, current information not available

Bredo, Anneke E., Stanford Center for Research and Development in Teaching, Stanford University

Bredo, Eric R., Stanford Center for Research and Development in Teaching, Stanford University

Carlson, Richard O., Center for Educational Policy and Management, University of Oregon

Charters, W. W., Jr., Center for Educational Policy and Management, University of Oregon

Chesler, Mark, Department of Sociology, University of Michigan

Clark, Burton R., Department of Sociology, Yale University

Cohen, Elizabeth G., Stanford Center for Research and Development in Teaching, School of Education, Stanford University

Deal, Terrence E., Stanford Center for Research and Development in Teaching, Stanford University

Giacquinta, Joseph B., School of Education, New York University

Gross, Neal, Graduate School, University of Pennsylvania

Hampson, David H., National Institute of Education, Washington, D.C.

Jones, John E., Center for Educational Policy and Management, University of Oregon

Kahn, Robert, Department of Psychology, George Washington University

Katz, Daniel, Institute for Social Research, University of Michigan

Keith, Pat M., Department of Sociology, Iowa State University

Lippitt, Ronald, Institute of Social Research, University of Michigan

Lortie, Daniel C., Midwest Administration Center, University of Chicago

Meyer, John W., Stanford Center for Research and Development in Teaching, Department of Sociology, Stanford University

Miles, Matthew B., Center for Policy Research, New York, N.Y.

Packard, John S., Center for Educational Policy and Management, University of Oregon

Pellegrin, Roland J., Department of Sociology, Pennsylvania State University

Runkel, Philip J., Center for Educational Policy and Management, University of Oregon

Schmuck, Richard A., Center for Educational Policy and Management, University of Oregon

Scott, W. Richard, Stanford Center for Research and Development in Teaching, Department of Sociology, Stanford University

Sieber, Sam D., Institute of Applied Social Science, Columbia University

Smith, Louis M., Department of Education and Psychology, Washington University

Wacaster, C. Thompson, Abt Associates, Inc., Cambridge, Mass.

1 Overview of Change Processes in Educational Organizations

J. Victor Baldridge
Terrence E. Deal

Change or innovation is a topic constantly discussed in the educational world. Schools, colleges, and universities are always changing, either by deliberate design or by whim or fate. Students, faculty members, administrators, and the general public are concerned about the ability of educational organizations to adapt in the face of new demands, and, as a consequence, the careers of educational administrators reflect their ability to stimulate and manage change. Being known as an "innovative" administrator often assures promotion within an organization and movement from one organization to another.

Most change management is largely based on intuition and seat-of-the-pants strategy. Certainly there are no valid, tested scientific principles of change. Stimulating and managing change could, however, be less an intuitive process if knowledge based on social science research and the experience of practicing change agents were applied. At least three things are needed to understand change processes in educational organizations: a comprehensive *organizational perspective,* that is, an understanding of crucial organizational subsystems and processes involved in innovation; familiarity with *strategies* that can be used to cause and support educational changes, such as leadership dynamics, the role of change agents, the dynamics of organizational politics, and the use of program evaluation processes; and *practical experience* with the dynamics of educational change, either from actually administering a changing institution or from gaining

Adapted from R&D Memorandum No. 126, "An Organizational View of Educational Innovation," published by the Stanford Center for Research and Development in Teaching. This research was conducted at the Center pursuant to contract NE-C-00-3-0062 with the National Institute of Education, Department of Health, Education, and Welfare.

1

vicarious experience through case studies of actual attempts to change educational organizations.

The articles in this book deal with all three elements—comprehensive perspectives, change-oriented strategies, and practical experience through case studies—involved with change and innovation at both the elementary-secondary level and that of higher education. Because the articles apply to broad spectrums of education and general organizational dynamics, those written about higher education also relate to change processes in secondary and elementary schools, and vice versa. Many of the articles, since they are from the research tradition, use the social sciences to investigate change. In addition, a number of practice-oriented articles describing the experiences of applied administration are included to complement and broaden those from a research orientation. The perspectives on organizational change and innovation presented here provide the frame into which succeeding chapters are set.

Difficulties in Applying Research to Administrative Practice

The prevailing climate in education favors innovation over maintaining the status quo. This climate nudges even the most conservative educational administrator, whether he be motivated by job satisfaction, career enhancement, or job security, toward changing any aspect of an institution in order to claim the title "innovator." As such efforts often cause unavoidable problems or give rise to formidable obstacles, the question often asked is, "What do I do now?" School principals, superintendents, headmasters, and college and university presidents often look to the social and administrative sciences for answers or aid. There is unlimited opportunity to locate books, monographs, articles, and essays—all dealing in some way with adoption, implementation, or support of innovation. In fact, there is a long and distinguished history of such research done by anthropologists, psychologists, sociologists, economists, and social psychologists. This history, coupled with a continuing interest in innovation on the part of social scientists, has produced an enormous body of literature that continues to grow at a staggering rate. Everett Rogers reviewed over five hundred articles in the area of innovation diffusion in 1962. Nine years later, over fifteen hundred articles were examined in a revised edition (Rogers and Shoemaker, 1971).

As changing social and economic circumstances press nearly all social institutions to change policies and programs, the body of innovation studies continues to grow not only in size but in scope. The attention of the social scientist has expanded from factors that promote or discourage innovation to include factors that maintain innovation and evaluate whether social inventions are accomplishing their intended purpose. Schools, particularly, have been studied as they have integrated the races, modified curricula and instruction, or altered the work arrangements of teachers. The entire range of the innovation process, from invention to implementation and assessment, is presently being scrutinized by representatives of the various social science disciplines. Indeed, for the administrator seeking solutions to perplexing problems of how to produce change or support new programs, there is an abundance of scholarly literature.

In spite of the sheer volume of material, however, there is a general consensus, particularly among educational administrators, that research has not produced practical assistance in proportion to its enormous volume. They feel that much innovation research is not applicable to the important problems of administering change for several reasons.

Individualistic bias. Until recently most of the research on innovation diffusion has been individualistic. Studies have focused on a single technical invention (a new fertilizer, a new medicine, a new curriculum), and the factors that cause an individual user (farmer, physician, teacher) to adopt or reject it. Quite often, the individual characteristics of the adopter receive most of the attention: What type of farmer will adopt a new fertilizer? What kind of physician will start using a new drug? What personal characteristics cause teachers to accept or reject a new approach to instruction?

Not only is the adopter always an individual, but the factors that produce innovative outlooks or behaviors are typically individualistic. For example, are the adopters young or old, rich or poor, leaders or followers? Is their social status high or low? Are they at the center of a communications network or isolated? Do they have a traditional or a modern outlook? (See Rogers and Shoemaker, 1971.)

Neglect of organizational features. Despite the fact that most major social inventions are used by organizations rather than by individuals, complex organizations and their innovation problems are rarely treated in the diffusion literature. Educational innovations are examples of social inventions adopted primarily by complex organizations, not by individuals. Even when an individual teacher might be considered the adopter, the fact that a teacher is firmly enmeshed in the social system of the school carries strong organizational implications for both the adoption and maintenance of new instructional techniques. Unfortunately, the literature on innovation provides little help for administrators who must confront innovation in its organizational context. In fact, Rogers' monumental study of innovation (1962) summarized the conclusions of the research in fifty-two major propositions, *not one of which referred to a complex organization as the innovation adopter or to organizational features as affecting the process.* The revised version (1971) is no better in dealing with organizational factors.

Stress on nonmanipulable factors. Another characteristic of innovation research that has weakened its usefulness for administrators is that it has not stressed manipulable factors. The individualistic bias has emphasized individuals and personal characteristics as important determinants of the spread and adoption of important social inventions. A result of this emphasis has been to conclude, for example, that young, inexperienced teachers from middle-class families are more likely to adopt new instructional practices.

It is readily apparent that none of these characteristics is directly manipulable. Administrators cannot make teachers younger or control their social origins. They can give them opportunities to gain more experience, but this is an expensive, time-consuming process. Research and past experience both stress the difficulties involved in changing people—their outlooks, values, or habits. Through hiring and firing practices, administrators can control the kinds of individuals who participate in an organization. But teachers—tenured or otherwise—are almost impossible to fire, and decreasing enrollments reduce the possibility that new teachers with "innovative" characteristics can be selected into the organization.

In short, the social psychological bias in innovation research has produced conclusions that point to administrative efforts to change individuals as being a way of stimulating the adoption of new practices. Because schools are particularly limited in terms of adding new teachers or firing old ones, innovation research has encouraged the development of people-changing strategies such as T-groups, sensitivity training, and laboratory groups. But, as a recent article by Bowers (1972) points out, these strategies have not been particularly effective. The administrator is, therefore, still in the almost impossible position of trying to manipulate people to bring about structural changes. The research emphasis in innovation diffusion has not been of much help to the administrator facing problems stemming from innovation.

Neglect of policy implications. Another weakness of innovation literature is that many social scientists have not focused sharply enough on policy questions or developed policy implications from their studies. The problems selected for inquiry are largely disciplinary in origin. Psychologists have studied the personality characteristics of innovators; anthropologists, the kinship patterns of innovators; sociologists, the position of innovators in social networks. The goal of this discipline-based research is not to solve the practical problems of innovation; rather, it is to advance the development of the discipline. Administrators looking for solutions to problems of managing innovation find, instead, scholarly treatises written in the appropriate academic jargon with the popular conclusion: "More research is needed." The research has an academic- rather than a problem-oriented focus.

In the field of education, research and development centers were established expressly for the purpose of doing problem-oriented or policy research. There is, however, a significant gap between the reach and grasp of the centers (Baldridge, 1973). Many have continued to sponsor academic-oriented research under the guise of the problem-oriented banner. Others have sponsored problem-oriented research without appropriate roots in disciplines, adequate research design, or appropriate methodological considerations. Either practical implications have not been developed from important research studies, or unimportant research has unduly influenced the development of administrative guidelines and policy. Very few policy documents on innovation have been placed in the hands of administrators to help them as they labor to change schools. Where guidelines have been available, as we pointed out previously, they invariably provide the administrator with recommendations for action that are outside his span of control.

Overcommitment to a specific strategy, or the "black bag" problem. Innovation research has again fallen short of administrative expectations because it has failed to test, systematically, alternative strategies for causing or controlling educational innovation. Instead, there has been a regrettable tendency to seize on a few narrow perspectives and then to apply them willy-nilly regardless of the organization's real need. The narrow perspectives of the "human relations-organizational development" school have been seized on by most educational consultants and "change agents" and developed into specific strategies for producing change in schools and school systems. Once developed, the strategies are placed in a consultant's black bag, endowed with magical powers, and sold at a premium to school principals and superintendents who need assistance in overcoming organizational resistance to new educational ideas.

To be sure, some narrow perspectives may produce the intended

effects and may indeed result in the adoption and successful implementation of new curricula, instructional techniques, teacher work
patterns, or new approaches to decision making. Because innovation
research has seldom carried the process of inquiry to the stage of ex-
perimentally testing several change strategies, we can never be sure
whether it is the consultant, the strategy, the "Hawthorne effects,"
or any of several other explanations that might ostensibly have
produced changes caused by the contents of the "black bag." Without careful testing of a variety of approaches, administrators can
become wedded to simplistic, narrow strategies of change.

In a sense we are suggesting a shift in overall orientation to the
problem of innovation in organizations. The terminology alone pulls
us in the wrong direction, for the "adoption of innovations" induces
thoughts of a commercial distribution of products from a manufacturer to a potential buyer. With that perspective, the research and
development community may be tempted to huckster particular
products, and, in the urgency to sell, they may overlook the need to
build problem-solving capacity into the organizations they are serving. Researchers, developers, administrators, and educators have seldom created an innovative environment where alternatives could be
considered and options explored.

Donald Campbell has perceptively commented that the tradition
of social innovation that ties it to particular products and techniques
has led to social waste, forcing the defense of innovations that did
not deserve defending. Campbell argues, instead, for a risk-taking
approach to solving social problems, where a variety of innovations
and techniques can be explored.

If the political and administrative system has committed itself in advance to the
correctness and efficacy of its reforms, it cannot tolerate learning of failure. To
be truly scientific we must be able to experiment. We must be able to advocate
without that excess of commitment that blinds us to reality testing. . . .

One simple shift in political posture which would reduce the problem is the
shift from the advocacy of a specific reform to the advocacy of the seriousness
of the problem, and hence to the advocacy of persistence in alternative reform
efforts should the first one fail. The political stance would become: "This is a
serious problem. We propose to initiate Policy A on an experimental basis. If
after five years there has been no significant improvement, we will shift to Policy
B." By making explicit that a given problem solution was only one of several
that the administrator or party could in good conscience advocate, and by having ready a plausible alternative, the administrator could afford honest evaluation of outcomes. Negative results, a failure of the first program, would not
jeopardize his job, for his job would be to keep after the problem until something was found that worked [Campbell, 1972, page 189].

We must not be in the business of disseminating a particularly exciting new product; we must be in the business of creating organizations with built-in capacities for assessing needs and creating viable alternatives. The adoption of any specific innovation is a sideline activity that must not consume our energies. Our continuing enterprise should be the building of flexible organizations responsive to environments, organizations with reserves of expertise and resources to sustain long-range problem solving.

Problems with Using Research for Change: A Summary

The profusion of innovation research has not been particularly useful for administrators as they are changing, reforming, or installing new ideas in educational organizations. This gap between the research and administrative action stems from several characteristics of the innovation research: an individualistic perspective tends to ignore the fact that most social inventions are adopted by organizations, not individuals; there has been a focus on factors that are difficult or impossible for an administrator to control; the policy implications of much innovation research are not spelled out; alternative strategies for change that result from the research are not adequately tested; consultants have discouraged an experimental problem-solving approach by promising simple solutions from their "black bag" of tricks.

Goals of the Book

Despite weaknesses of research and a lack of communication between research and practice, knowledge of research in organizational innovation is a necessary asset for administrators who must promote and successfully manage the diffusion and implementation of new educational ideas. Several characteristics of innovation research that make its application to administrative practice difficult have been highlighted, but the present crisis in education and the need to install new instructional practices and educational ideas still places a heavy responsibility on administrators to change schools. Changing an organization as complex as an elementary school, a public school district, or a university is very difficult. Administrators need more than personal skill and charisma; they need extensive knowledge of organizational behavior and of the process of organizational change.

In spite of its shortcomings, the literature on innovation and change can provide helpful guidance for administrators locked in the struggle of reforming educational organizations. The purpose of this book is to organize the literature on educational change and innovation so that it can be more readily applied to administrative practice. There are three principal goals: to broaden administrators' perspectives on educational change, providing more complex conceptual maps of the organizational factors that provide impetus for change, obstacles to change, and objects of change; to illustrate the various administrative strategies that can be used to change educational organizations; to show, through recent case studies, the complicated interlocking properties of complex organizations that make change such an incredibly difficult task.

Goal One: Broadening Perspectives on Educational Innovation

Our first objective is to question some common assumptions about educational change. This allows one to develop a broader perspective from which to view the issue.

Two Common Perspectives on Change: Invention and Diffusion

There are several problems in discussing change or innovation. First, the topic lends itself to easy trivialization; the most insignificant changes sometimes become objects of serious research. Thus, the literature is filled with minute details about small-scale projects, many of which failed—often a good thing! Here we are concentrating on changes that have major impact for the organization, that involve significant numbers of participants, that seriously affect how the organization achieves its goals, and that require large investments in terms of personnel, time, and money. There are other kinds of changes, but we have chosen to focus on what we consider to be serious organizational developments. This immediately eliminates a considerable block of literature.

A second problem arises from the complex and slippery terminology that is used in discussing the subject. In spite of the inconsistent terminology, progress can be made simply by showing some of the different approaches to the problem. It is useful to divide the literature into three categories: invention, innovation and diffusion, and basic organizational change.

The invention process. Invention is the process of developing new technologies and procedures for an organization. In the educational world this means new curriculum ideas, new procedures for teaching, or new methods of organization. The essence of invention is that a new procedure has been developed that was not previously available. One major source of new inventions in the educational world is the research and development activities of various federal laboratories and centers. In addition, local university, college, and public school systems work to invent procedures. One example of an educational invention would be a new computerized method of teaching mathematical skills. Invention is probably the least common of the various types of organizational change; it is rare, indeed, to develop really new products or procedures.

The diffusion process. For many years anthropologists, sociologists, organizational theorists, and social psychologists have been interested in the diffusion processes of technological and social inventions, an interest readily apparent from the many publications on the subject. The innovations studied cover a broad spectrum of social life: smallpox inoculations, educational innovations, agricultural inventions, child-rearing practices among American mothers, medical inventions, the introduction of modern machinery into underdeveloped nations. The diffusion of innovation continues to interest social scientists.

Much of the literature has concentrated on limited kinds of technological innovations. Often such innovations are highly technical, and effectiveness can be proved before dissemination. The payoff time is relatively short so the person adopting the innovation can decide whether or not to continue using it. Also, the innovation's technical efficiency can be readily evaluated. Finally, the decision maker is usually an individual or a small group, not a complex organization. Most major educational innovations are not so technically narrow or so easily put into effect. The decision base of a farmer is simpler than that of a teacher, a school, or a university. The farmer judges his innovation by the grain that grows. But how does a school judge whether its students have learned social studies better under a new system? How does a university evaluate its success at doing better research? The adopter of most educational innovation is a complex organization, which increases the complexity of the decision process and the multiple chains of command necessary to carry out a decision, and different analytic tools must be developed to understand the complex process of educational innovation.

The articles included in this volume were selected because they are concerned with organizational innovation where technologies are relatively unclear, where there are long-range payoffs, where evaluations might not be readily apparent, and where there are organizational rather than individual adopters. Throughout the book there will be examples of the diffusion of organizational innovations that meet the criteria outlined above.

Another Perspective on Change: Organizational Subsystems

Apart from invention and diffusion, there is a third and even more fascinating case of change that deals with basic transformations in the organization itself. It is a much more significant, far-reaching kind of change. Although a new technology or procedure may bring change in an organization, changes in basic authority structure, goals, and programs represent even more fundamental transformations.

As has been noted, one of the limitations of innovation research has been its individualistic bias. This individualistic view has had an important influence on administrators' conceptions of the change process, mainly through its contribution to the human relations approach to organizational innovation. The human relations approach has emphasized the importance of individual leadership in promoting change and has singled out the attitudes, characteristics, and outlooks of individuals as forces to be overcome if educational change is to be successful.

In contrast, our perspective on educational change and innovation is based on changing organizational factors. We resist the human relations tendency to place the burden for changing people on the administrator. Instead, we emphasize that educational change engages all the subsystems that together comprise complex educational organizations. These include the goals, the environment, the formal system or structure, and the technology of the organization, as well as individuals and groups in an informal system of relationships. These various organizational subsystems are related in systematic ways. Any subsystem can pressure another subsystem to change. A changing environment, for example, affects educational goals, technology, and the formal structure. A changing formal structure interacts with informal relationships.

A systemic map of organizational change is far more complex than the popular individualistic model. An educational administrator must be aware of a variety of organizational elements. These must be balanced, controlled, and manipulated to assure the success of an educational innovation.

In order to understand basic organizational change we first need to realize that organizations are such complex networks that it is almost impossible to study change processes without first examining the various subsystems. One of the most widely used taxonomies of organizational subsystems, proposed by Stanley Udy, Jr. (1965), is shown in Figure 1-1. It is composed of a number of parts: goals, environment, technology, formal structure, group and individual processes.

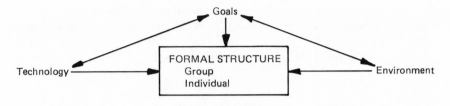

FIGURE 1-1
Organizational Subsystems
(from Udy, 1965)

Goals. Organizations are social systems set up to achieve specific goals. Often the goals are contradictory, opposed by various participants in the organization, and rather vaguely articulated. Nevertheless, it is true that institutional mission, goals, and objectives are critical starting points for many organizational changes, as articles by Clark and Sieber clearly demonstrate.

Environment. Organizational theorists are gradually realizing that many significant changes come from the environment. The environment consists of a broad collection of clients, suppliers, customers, government regulatory agencies, and a host of other organizations. No analysis of change can afford to neglect the strong influence of the environment for both promoting, supporting, or hindering change, as the case may be. Articles by Baldridge, Carlson, and Abbot underline the importance of the environment as an independent force in producing organizational change.

Technology. Every organization has procedures for carrying out its work. In industrial organizations there can be a great deal of technological hardware, including processes for production and assembly lines. Other kinds of organizations also have complicated technologies, although they may not involve such large amounts of hardware. In client-serving organizations such as hospitals and schools the technology consists of "treatment" activities for clients or patients. Research on organizational change in this area has typically looked at "sociotechnical" relations, that is, the social consequences of introducing some new work technology.

For educational organizations the "technology" is generally the instructional program. The main message for us is that the structure of an educational system is at least partly shaped by its technology—a deterministic argument very similar to that of the environmentalists. Educational technology has undergone rapid change in the past decade, both because of changed societal needs and because of the large amount of resources devoted to curricular and instructional improvement. The administrative implication of this line of research is that, when instructional changes occur, changes must also be made in the structure of the organization, or the program will not function well.

Formal structure. Every organization has a system for regulating its operation. A formal authority structure, a hierarchy of command, systematic decision processes, and reward processes are all part of the formal structure. Organizations frequently try to manipulate these characteristics in order to achieve their goals.

Research on academic organizations has revealed some important weaknesses in their basic structures. An examination of division of labor, coordination, decision making, and other structural patterns in schools and colleges, when they are compared to other organizations, reveals some inherent problem areas. Miles's article on the organizational "health" of schools follows this line of research. Structural properties are highly relevant in educational change, both as characteristics to be changed and as characteristics that change in response to either environmental or program pressures. This area is particularly important because, in managing innovation, organizational structure is most directly controlled or manipulated by the administrator. Structure is the prime administrative handle that provides leverage both for producing and adjusting to educational innovation.

Group-Individual. One of the major traditions of organizational research, called the "human relations school," has concentrated on informal relationships within an organization. Researchers within this tradition, usually schooled in social psychology, have stressed relationships between individual attitudes and morale and the informal structure of the organization, as well as group processes and group norms. Much of the literature on organizational change falls within this human relations school, as it is variously called. Each of these five subsystems will be discussed in more detail in articles related to one particular type of organizational change.

Subsystems and the Process of Change

It is important to realize several things about organizational subsystems and the change process:

Almost all of the major traditions of research on organizational change have focused on one subsystem at a time. Researchers who might examine organizational change as it relates to individual and group behavior are likely to ignore most of the other subsystems. Each group of studies presented here tends to overemphasize or accentuate the importance of a single perspective. Clark's article on organizational saga, for example, tends to ignore the organization's formal structure and technology. In the same manner, the Baldridge article on the relationship between innovation and organizational environments does not include individual goals. Generally, social scientists conducting research on educational innovation narrow their focus to the relationship between no more than two or three organizational subsystems. This reduced scope is essential when establishing scientific criteria for judging scientific, scholarly work.

Implementing an educational innovation, on the other hand, requires a broader outlook. An administrator must take all the organization's subsystems seriously. His primary goal is not an academic understanding of the relationships but the manipulation of goals, formal structure, or environment to allow the desired educational change. The educational administrator needs a broad organizational perspective and a general understanding of how the various organizational subsystems relate.

Each of the subsystems may be seen as an impetus for change, or as the unit that is being changed. The subsystem may be studied as either an independent or a dependent variable. For example, we might examine a change in educational goals to determine what impact that change had (independent variable). Or, on the other hand, we might examine changes in goals that are being produced by some other subsystem, such as a rapid change in the environment surrounding a college (dependent variable). In short, each subsystem can be viewed as either the thing being changed or the thing that is causing the change. It is important to keep these distinctions in mind because the study of educational change has often been confused when it was unclear whether the subsystem was being changed or was causing change.

A particular organizational subsystem is usually the beginning of practical change. Rarely does an organization try to change many activities at once. An organization trying to improve its activities will generally concentrate on one subsystem as a starting point for change, and improvement is usually piecemeal and gradual. For example, a school may try to make limited improvements in its teaching technology without having to deal with accompanying changes in authority structures and morale problems. Or it may focus on faculty morale and attitudes without dealing with the environment or the formal authority system. The normal practice is to begin making marginal improvements in one area and to adjust for the repercussions in other subsystems later. This brings up a final important point—the interconnectedness of the different subsystems.

Any change in an organization is likely to involve more than one subsystem. Organizational changes are complex, and the effects are interwoven throughout various subsystems. Goals cannot be changed without affecting group attitudes and technology; the environment cannot shift substantially without formal authority structures being seriously affected; major upheavals in individual or group morale certainly have repercussions on decision processes and other formal systems. In short, a change in one subsystem almost surely results in changes in other subsystems. Any strategy of research or any active program of organizational change must carefully analyze possible interconnections.

Each of these perspectives is a research tradition. Each focuses on certain organizational characteristics and relationships and tends to ignore or exclude others. In reality, however, the perspectives overlap, and all deserve the attention of the educational administrator concerned with innovation.

Goal Two: Studying Strategies in Educational Innovation

In addition to those readings that fit our goal of broadening administrative perspectives on organizational change, there is research that weighs the impact of administrative strategies designed to produce and manage educational innovation. Such strategies include leadership, evaluation, change agents, politics, and the use of research staff as a means of promoting organizational change.

Which of these strategies is effective in a change situation is contingent on a variety of factors. Following the section on perspectives, it is suggested that the selection of an administrative strategy in innovation should reflect what is changing and what is being changed. Program changes may require one strategy; environmental or structural changes, another. Beyond these general considerations, however, there are some specific characteristics of a good change strategy that provide a set of useful criteria in evaluating the research included in the strategy section.

Rule One: A Serious Assessment of Needs Is Necessary

To mention the requirement for careful needs assessment seems ridiculous. After all, is not all change preceded by such analysis? Unfortunately, this is not always the case. Various problems obscure the needs assessment stage of organizational change.

The "captured" administrator. All too often administrators develop their own pat diagnosis of what they think an organization needs, and, with the best of intentions, they apply that solution to every problem that arises. People often have axes to grind, and the old saying holds: "Give a little boy a hammer and suddenly the whole world needs to be hammered." Usually administrators adopt some preconceived solution that is very near to their own center of control and to the levers of power they can pull. This is not necessarily bad, for we all have a tendency to specialize and to concentrate our change efforts in our own sphere of activity. It may, however, lead to a persistent bias or the persistent neglect of the needs of the whole organization if an administrator can see no other solutions.

Consultants and their bags of tricks. The process of diagnosis is often circumvented by outside consultants who have preconceived solutions. We have already mentioned that many organizational consultants come with "black bags" filled with special techniques for resolving organizational problems. Consultants, too, are captives to the range of their skills and their special interests. Any organization hiring consultants should thoroughly explore the particular biases and procedures that they bring to the situation.

The "iceberg" phenomenon. Another problem that arises in the diagnosis process is the "iceberg" phenomenon. An adequate diagnosis may be done on an apparent problem that is only symptomatic of more serious ones. Very often the visible problem is no more than the tip of a deeper-seated problem. The overt symptom may be corrected, but the deep-seated problem may remain.

For this reason a comprehensive diagnosis of organizational problems is needed if any change is to be attempted. Experts from throughout the organization must participate in the diagnostic stage, for the definition of problems should not be limited to the world views of a few people. Symptomatic surface problems should be probed to determine whether there are more basic issues, and it is most important that the process take into account all the different organizational subsystems mentioned earlier—technology, structure, environment, and group processes. Difficulties in any of the subsystems may spin off so that the problem touches areas far from the original source.

Rule Two: Proposed Changes Must Be Relevant to the History of the Organization

Organizations have their roots deep in history; they have traditions and patterns of life that have evolved over a long period of time. It is important to realize that organizational change is always relative to a specific situation and to the unique circumstances of a given organization. Change simply cannot "take" if the history and tradition of the organization conflict with the proposed innovation. For example, in this period of tightened financial resources there is a demand for "efficiency" and "scientific management" in educational organizations. All too often, well-intended programs are undermined because there is little or no regard for the special conditions and historical procedures of educational organizations. Many changes that are potentially valuable must be severely modified if they are to mesh with the ongoing life of the organization. To be sure, assessing the fit between a new change and an organization's history and tradition up to that point is complex, but it is a task that must be done, and it must be done carefully.

Rule Three: Organizational Changes Must Take the Environment into Account

Organizational changes are almost never fully dictated by internal factors. The environment is a major impetus for change, for new environmental demands are a critical source of new ideas, new procedures, and new activities. Not only is change promoted by the environment, but changes made internally must also be supported by environmental connections. A change in student rules in a school district, for example, may be popular with both students and teachers, but totally opposed by the surrounding community. New accounting procedures for business firms may generate enormous hostility among clients because of their complexity. In short, there are two basic questions: What does the environment *need,* and what will it *support?* The answers to these two questions are often the key to substantial organizational change.

Rule Four: Serious Changes Must Affect Both the Organizational Structure and Individual Attitudes

We noted earlier that a prime problem with much organizational change literature is that it often focuses narrowly on individual attitudes. Although individual attitudes are obviously important, it is also important to stress that organizational structure must be changed to support any changes in attitudes. For example, let us assume we want teachers in a school to teach differently. One strategy would be persuasion—convincing the teachers that the change was important. We could, however, reinforce that persuasion by changing organizational features such as the sanction and evaluation process. If teachers got paid more for carrying out the new procedure, this would reinforce changes in their attitude. Attitudinal change is also encouraged by shifts in the authority structure, participation in decision making, and development of new technologies and procedures. In short, any change that requires a shift in the attitude of key personnel can be reinforced by changing the organizational structures that support and undergird those attitudes.

Rule Five: Changes Must Be Directed at Manipulable Factors

It makes no sense to plan organizational change around factors that simply cannot be changed, a statement that sounds almost tautological. It is remarkable how many times strategies are proposed that simply will not work. For example, in trying to implement school integration it was obvious that changing the attitudes of millions of people was virtually impossible, while actually changing the racial composition of the schools was more feasible. Either strategy would have promoted integration. Of the two factors, however, only one was actually manipulable in any reasonable sense—changing the racial composition.

This is one reason why we continually argue that individual attitudes are a weak basis for organizational intervention. Individual beliefs and opinions are almost nonmanipulable. They are almost impossible to change, and they remain essentially stable in spite of persuasion and preaching. Consequently, they can do little to advance serious organizational change.

Factors that are very difficult to manipulate include: major environmental relations, such as the nature of the organization's clientele (clients, customers, students, patients, or others); basic missions and fundamental goals; and attitudes, opinions, and beliefs of workers.

Examples of organizational features that are more readily manipulable include organizational rewards, evaluations, and sanction systems; administrative and departmental structure; personnel practices such as hiring, firing, and promotion policies; and technology and operational processes. Fertile imagination and careful thought will help to distinguish between factors that lend themselves to change and those that do not. Although this seems like a simple point, it is remarkable how many grandiose schemes for organizational change have been planned around factors that proved virtually impossible to change.

Rule Six: Changes Must Be Both Politically and Economically Feasible

It might be desirable to have sex education classes in a politically conservative community. Only the most foolhardy school administrators would propose such a drastic change where the environment was hostile, however. Not only is it important to make changes that will survive in the organization's environment, but it is also important to gauge political opposition from within. Powerful interest groups which fight proposed changes in an organization may have the clout to stop change. A vital part of any shrewd administrator's job is assessing what things will survive politically and what things will not. Often it is best simply not to try changes that are doomed to failure. If a change is so important that it must be done despite political opposition, however, it is critical that interest groups and coalitions be mobilized in support. Rational planning often completely disintegrates as a result of poor political strategy.

The political issue is frequently tied to the cost issue. Many plans fail because they simply are not viable in terms of what the organization can afford. All too often those who planned the changes simply do not take into account the financial cost to the organization. It is important to do some preliminary calculations long before time and money have been expended in order to avoid hard feelings and wasted energy. Usually this means expert advice and help, with a variety of opinions brought to bear on the issue.

It is important to remember that one of the most expensive costs is personnel time. Before the change is undertaken, there should be a careful assessment of available personnel, talent, and expertise. If necessary skills or appropriate personnel are not available and there is no prospect of obtaining them, the proposed innovation might as well be forgotten.

Rule Seven: The Changes Must Be Effective in Solving the Problems That Were Diagnosed

The most cost-effective plans involving the most manipulable factors in the finest of political environments will still fail if they do not solve the problem. The critical questions are: Will the proposed changes actually solve the diagnosed problems? Will they involve costs, in terms of money and personnel, that make sense to the organization? Will they provide a permanent solution? Can the changes be structured into the organization itself, or are they overly dependent on individual personalities?

Too often changes are proposed that meet all criteria except the effectiveness one. Changes may be based on real diagnosis, sensitive to both the environment and the organization's history, be arranged around manipulable variables, and be politically and economically feasible. Unless they actually solve the problem, however, they are a waste of time.

Effective Change Strategies: An Example of the Rules in Action

The rules for a good change strategy can be applied to a concrete case of major educational change: the drive for equality of educational opportunity in the public schools. Are the change rules outlined above useful for analyzing the solutions that were proposed to this important national problem?

Equality of educational opportunity was advanced as a national goal after the Supreme Court's *Brown* decision in 1954. In 1964 a huge research effort culminated in a government report, *Equality of Educational Opportunity,* often called the Coleman Report. This research conclusively verified that racial minorities were getting a much poorer education and were achieving at much lower levels than majority groups. The Coleman Report identified a number of factors as causes of this problem:

Fate control. Minority students did not feel that they were able to control their social destinies. As a consequence, they often reported that their motivation to learn in school was much lower than majority students who had been given so many more advantages in life. The minority students felt, realistically, that they had been cheated by their position in society and that no amount of hard work in school would reap them reasonable benefits.

Family background. A larger proportion of minority students came from broken homes than did majority children. In addition, minority students often came from families where achievement in school was neither highly valued nor effectively promoted.

Teacher quality. Schools with a predominance of minority students often had teachers who were less well prepared.

Segregation. Segregated schools were shown to have a number of harmful side effects, including lowered self-esteem and fewer middle-class role models.

Resource equalization. Because of discrimination by middle-class-dominated school boards, minority schools simply did not get the per capita expenditure for their pupils that middle-class schools got. It is a reasonable assumption that less money meant lower-quality education.

The Coleman Report, then, diagnosed the problem and found that low achievement, high dropout rates, and generally poor educational performance were characteristic of some minority groups. In addition, the research identified five factors as essential causes. How does each of these factors meet the test for a good change strategy? If we wanted to design a program of organizational change that would help solve the problems, which of the causes would we try to manipulate, and which changes would be likely to succeed in light of our change strategy rules?

Both fate control and family background share the same problems. They are effective variables. If we changed them it would certainly make a difference, but they cannot be readily manipulated. There is nothing we can really do, in the short run at least, about family background and pupil attitudes toward their general life environment. These two factors can probably be eliminated as effective strategies unless acceptable means of manipulation can be found.

The other three factors fare somewhat better under our rules. Teacher quality is a variable that meets most of the rules' requirements: it is a manipulable factor that we can do something about; it is probably an effective factor that would actually make a difference; it is politically feasible in light of the political muscle of teachers' groups; it is a change that would be supported by the environment. The major difficulty in manipulating teacher quality is the extremely high cost. Teachers' salaries account for the bulk of school system budgets, and to manipulate this factor in any serious manner might literally bankrupt half the school districts in the country. As a consequence, only marginal changes have been made in this area.

Integration meets many of the requirements of a good change strategy: integration is probably effective and would have impact on student learning; it is a variable that could be manipulated with the help of bussing and redistricting; it is probably a cost-effective measure that is well within the financial resources of most districts; it does affect the structure of the school system itself while it is changing individual attitudes. In spite of the many advantages, however, there are some obvious liabilities. The political cost of integration activities has always been phenomenal, and it is doubtful that the environment around most school districts is supportive of such attempts. In many ways, then, integration is a strategy that meets most of our tests, but, at the same time, carries with it serious liabilities.

Finally, resource allocation is also a mixed blessing. The equalization of resources under court-mandated plans emerging from decisions such as California's *Serrano* v. *Priest* should be relatively effective in producing changes in school opportunities for minorities. To be sure, there has been considerable debate about whether merely adding dollar resources actually changes pupil performance. Nevertheless, there is still a very strong commonsense appeal to arguing that equalizing money might help equalize other opportunities. Resource changes are moderately effective, manipulable, and usually financially feasible. Again, the liabilities are political. There has been strong opposition to equalizing school expenditures because it means a redistribution of money from wealthier areas into poorer ones, a procedure that invariably stimulates political opposition.

This example teaches us something about our rules for efficient change strategies. Several of the proposed solutions were impossible because critical variables simply could not be manipulated—fate control and family background being prime examples. Another factor that was on other grounds reasonable but faced stiff opposition because of its enormous costs was upgrading teacher quality. Finally, political costs are often, as they were in this particular situation, a major barrier—especially where integration and resource equalization are concerned.

From the illustration above, what do we learn about evaluating change strategies? First, any strategy has to meet the minimal requirements of effectiveness and manipulability. Without these characteristics there is no sense in making the effort. Second, almost any strategy has some liabilities, perhaps cost or political opposition. It is important, however, not to be so concerned about liabilities that we are paralyzed into inaction. The basic lesson, then, is to evaluate any strategy in terms of all these factors and then to act on the most feasible possibilities. Often a complex mixture of alternative strategies can help balance liabilities and maximize opportunities for effective change. It is because we believe that some changes will work that we have taken the trouble to assemble this book. Some instances where the various strategies are interconnected in the real world are vividly provided in the case study section.

Goal Three: Providing Case Studies of Educational Innovation

In our most optimistic frame of reference, we have organized studies of educational innovation and change so that administrators actively engaged in implementing new educational ideas can approach their task with new conceptions of organizations and new strategies for stimulating desired changes. In this final section we leave this optimistic plane and plunge instead into a pessimistic void. The several case studies, both of new organizations and of attempts to change the direction or form of established institutions, dramatically illustrate the difficulties involved in changing complex organizations. Although the probability of successful innovation may be increased when administrators have adequate conceptions of complex organizations and possess knowledge of well-tested change strategies, educational change is bought at a premium price, often at the expense of the educational administrator. The materials included here have been organized to assist administrators who are planning, or who are engaged in, reforming educational organizations. We feel obliged, however, to emphasize the barriers and pitfalls that clutter the course, which is meant to say that we did not promise you a rose garden.

All of the case studies document the complexities and difficulties involved in educational innovation. The titles of the studies reflect this pessimistic note. For new institutions, Deal offers an alternative postmortem for alternative schools; Wacaster discusses the "Life and Death of Differentiated Staffing." Smith and Keith dissect the anatomy of an educational innovation, and the titles of studies of established institutions sound equally ominous. For example, there is Gross, Giacquinta, and Bernstein's "Failure to Implement a Major Organizational Innovation." Packard's "Changing to a Multiunit School" sounds more hopeful, but, despite the title, the conclusion is essentially the same. Only Baldridge, in his "Organizational Change," presents a case study that reveals a quasi-successful attempt to alter the course of a major educational institution.

We have purposely included case studies that hammer home to educational administrators several important points about innovation and change. First, educational change is incredibly difficult. Second, educational changes are required, and that need is continuous in contemporary society. A new educational idea successfully installed is almost immediately obsolete, and a new innovation is soon required to take its place. Third, the various characteristics of educational organizations are interwoven, and, when administrators try to change one aspect of an organization, they must anticipate that all other organizational subsystems must be considered. Environment, program, structure, character, goals, subgroups, and individuals are part of a system. Changing one aspect of the system usually involves changing others if the innovation is to survive. Essentially we have no tricks to offer educational administrators committed to changing the fabric of schools; there is no magic bag of tricks with instant answers.

Our bias is heavily oriented toward the underlying "whys" of educational innovation and change, not necessarily toward schemes for "how to." We have organized these research studies to accomplish our three goals of broadening administrators' theoretical perspectives, providing examples of administrative strategies, and offering an opportunity to learn secondhand from the case studies of others who have tried to reform educational organizations. Once we can begin to understand the fundamental processes involved in innovation and begin to develop strategies with a reasonable probability of producing the desired results, we will be far along in the development of an administrative science.

This goal will never be reached until school administrators begin systematically to test a variety of approaches to innovation in schools, while social scientists begin systematically to record successes and failures and the conditions under which successful changes were produced. Our dedication is to the importance of the problems of innovation and change, not to specific solutions. This, then, focuses the theme of the book. In our most optimistic moments, we hope that it will introduce a new approach to change and innovation in schools, one that recognizes the difficulties of administrative efforts while simultaneously and persistently working toward the development of new and workable solutions.

References

Baldridge, J. Victor (1973). "The Impact of Individuals, Organizational Structure, and Environment on Organizational Innovation," R&D Memorandum No. 124. Stanford, Calif.: Stanford Center for Research and Development in Teaching.

_____, Deal, Terrence E., Johnson, Rudolph, and Wheeler, Jeanette (1973). "Improving Relations between R&D Organizations and Schools," R&D Memorandum No. 115. Stanford, Calif.: Stanford Center for Research and Development in Teaching.

Bowers, David G. (1973). "O.D. Techniques and Their Results in Twenty-three Organizations." *Journal of Applied Behavioral Science*, 9(January):21-43.

Campbell, Donald (1972). "Reforms as Experiments," in Carol H. Weiss, ed., *Evaluating Action Programs: Readings in Social Action and Education*. Boston: Allyn and Bacon.

Clark, B. R. (1972). "The Organizational Saga in Higher Education." *Administrative Science Quarterly*, 17(June):178-184.

Coleman, James S. (1966). *Equality of Educational Opportunity*. Washington, D. C.: National Center for Educational Statistics.

Rogers, Everett (1962). *Diffusion of Innovations*. New York: Free Press.

_____, and Shoemaker, F. Floyd (1971). *Communication of Innovations*. New York: Free Press.

Udy, Stanley (1965). "The Comparative Analysis of Complex Organizations," in James G. March, ed., *Handbook of Organizations*. Chicago: Rand McNally.

PART ONE
PERSPECTIVES

Individual and Small Group. Discussion of the various change perspectives begins with a focus on the individual and small-group approach. This approach, as has been noted in Chapter 1, is heavily influenced by psychological and social-psychological research and by studies of innovation diffusion in agriculture, rural sociology, and medicine. From this perspective, the individual is generally seen as adopting or rejecting new ideas. Attitudes toward innovation and change are seen as flowing largely from unique personal characteristics and personality traits but also as being heavily influenced by the values of an individual's peer group. This individual and small-group perspective has produced important insight into the process of innovation and change. Generalizations have been developed about individual innovators and the group conditions that produce innovative behavior. From this work we have learned, for example, that innovators are young, from wealthy backgrounds, cosmopolitan in outlook, opinion leaders, and divergent thinkers (Everett Rogers, *Diffusion of Innovations* [New York: Free Press, 1962]). We have also learned that innovations occur more frequently in groups that favor change, provide a supportive, trusting interpersonal atmosphere, and tolerate diversity (J. A. Watson, "A Formal Analysis of Sociable Interaction," *Sociometry,* 21 [1958] , 269-280).

The chapter by Daniel Katz and Robert Kahn, the only one included in this section, was selected because it does two things exceptionally well. First, the chapter systematically reviews the literature on individual and group strategies of organizational change. Katz and Kahn describe and compare seven approaches to change and innovation: information exchange, counseling and therapy, peer group influences, sensitivity training, group therapy within organizations, the use of feedback and discussion, technological innovation and structural change. In each of these sections supportive literature is reviewed, and examples of the use of the approach in actual organizations are provided. In the systemic change section, for example, Katz and Kahn discuss the Morse-Reiner experiment in which an organization changed the distribution of authority as a means of increasing morale and productivity. A final section discusses the general issue of change and stability in organizations, noting particularly that change can be produced either by internal strains and alterations or by larger environmental changes that alter the organization's input. Katz and Kahn argue that environmental changes are the most powerful influence on organizational change.

In addition to reviewing the literature, Katz and Kahn undertake a second important task—criticizing the "psychological fallacy," the myth that organizational change best occurs by changing *individual* attitudes and actions, which, in turn, will change the *organization*. Katz and Kahn emphatically reject this notion, persuasively arguing that long-lasting organizational change can be achieved only through the manipulation of *organizational* variables, such as authority structures, reward systems, technology, and environmental relations. Whether the reader agrees or disagrees, the Katz and Kahn debate with the dominant psychological approach to change makes fascinating reading for anyone who seriously wants to promote organizational innovation.

In line with the many examples of organizational change that Katz and Kahn provide, educational changes take place in an organizational context. Producing change or implementing innovation in schools usually, therefore, involves changing one or more parts of a complex organization. Administrative thinking dominated by the psychological fallacy can be seen as limiting the success of educational change or innovation. All organizational subsystems must be considered by an administrator making or adapting to educational innovation or change. The individual and small-group perspective is necessary, as are the other subsystems. It does not compete with other approaches; rather, it is quite compatible and complementary. There are, however, three primary reasons for challenging it. First, this perspective seems to have had a major, if not an overriding, influence on administrative approaches to innovation and change in schools. Second, like Katz and Kahn, we are not convinced that changing individuals or the norms of small groups results in systemic change. Third, the individualistic tradition may not offer many fruitful directions for school administrators.

In practice, changes or change strategies arising from the individualistic approach have often proved difficult to implement, and they do not provide a firm basis for developing administrative action or policy. In considering the sociological argument for a more systemic approach to change and innovation in schools, however, we must be careful not to replace the psychological fallacy with a sociological one. The individual and small-group perspective is necessary in promoting innovation and change; we stress criticism of that approach to encourage the simultaneous development of a more systemic approach to change and innovation in schools and colleges.

Goals and Saga. As academic administrators confront the task of educational innovation and change, inevitably they focus on educational goals. Accountability legislation, new student populations, programmed-budgeting systems, community needs assessments, and demands for alternatives to conventional education are among the issues that focus attention directly on educational goals. These goals are now established for nearly every college, school, and school district, often in consultation with local communities and service areas. Goals are frequently the targets of educational change, but they are just as often affected by changes in the organizational subsystems.

One of the pitfalls of the goals perspective is that goals are probably as hard to change as they are to study. All too often goals are diffuse and vague, especially in large, complex, fragmented organizations. They exist to provide general direction, to provide a base of social support, and to offer a symbolic rallying point for organizational participants. But, particularly in educational organizations, goals are often so lofty and abstract that they fail to indicate even general direction, to elicit social support, or to provide adequate orientation for the efforts of administrators, instructors, and students. Attempts to make goals more specific, however, often result in conflict because educational goals are hotly contested and because the process of setting goals provides a battleground for warring educational ideologies. Despite difficulties in studying educational goals, or of changing them, they are an important perspective in change and innovation, mainly because they provide a reason for the organization's existence and an anchor for the efforts of participants.

Goals are often lumped together with other characteristics or features that play a symbolic role in organizations. One such symbolic characteristic is "organizational saga." Like goals, the saga performs a symbolic function in an organization. It is the myth and belief system that explains why the organization exists and justifies the time and energy needed to keep the organization going. A saga is a set of beliefs, rooted in history, that claims unique accomplishment and is held with sentiment by organizational participants. This institutional belief system unites people inside and outside the organization. It provides a sense of mission, defines the organization's character, and provides a sense of identity for the participants. Not all organizations have strong sagas, but those that do are not just organizations—they are beloved institutions. As such, organizations with rich, deep-rooted sagas are extremely difficult, if not impossible, to change. All organizations have some degree of saga. Schools and colleges are no exception. Saga is a highly useful concept in studying or managing change and innovation.

Two chapters are included in the goals and saga section. The first, by Sam Sieber, focuses on the characteristics of public schools that distinguish them from other organizations. Two of these characteristics—professionalism and client control—are only touched tangentially in this book. Another characteristic—environmental vulnerability—is discussed in greater detail in the environment section that follows. The fourth characteristic that Sieber identifies as differentiating schools and colleges from other social systems is "goal diffuseness," a problem that has enormous consequences for innovation and change efforts. Sieber distinguishes between "terminal" and "instrumental" goals. Terminal goals specify ends; instrumental goals specify means. Terminal goal diffuseness reinforces the vulnerability of schools to outside forces by making it difficult to prove that schools are succeeding. Thus, goal diffuseness reinforces the insecurity of professionals by failing to provide a set of criteria by which to judge materials and practices. Since terminal goals are so highly diffuse, Sieber argues that an illusion of consensus is created that focuses undue attention on the instrumental goals—or daily classroom practices. It is these, he argues, that are most hotly contested. In short, diffuse terminal goals lead to an almost paranoid ritualization of daily routine, effectively undermining long-term change efforts.

The second chapter, by Burton Clark, develops the notion of "organizational saga" as it applies to colleges and universities—and by implication to other types of schools. Clark defines saga and then sets forth the conditions of its initiation and preservation. Saga is usually initiated by a charismatic leader in new organizations, decaying organizations, or organizations which, for special reasons, are ripe for evolutionary change. Once established, the saga is maintained by a small group of believers, special aspects of the educational program, the student subculture, the environment, and rituals, ceremonies, and the organizational climate. Clark offers three examples of colleges with strong organizational sagas.

Goals and sagas are critical administrative considerations in stimulating or managing organizational innovation. Goals are often the beginning target for change efforts, but their symbolic nature is often overlooked. One administrative strategy in change is to make goals more specific, which results in dissension and political contests. Another strategy is to replace old diffuse educational goals with new ones—equally diffuse. Only when these goals are operationalized does the illusion of consensus disappear and the resistance to the new direction become manifest. For these reasons, goals are often a difficult starting point for change.

Under some circumstances, particularly in times of crisis, it is possible to use a new saga, a new world view, as a tool for producing long-lasting change. In a crisis-charged organization an innovation may become institutionalized because its saga, its mythology, shifts rapidly. On the other hand, in organizations with strong existing sagas resistance to change will be unduly powerful; saga may be a real barrier to change. In either case, developing a sense of the prevailing saga—or the history, unique mission, and affective bond between the participants—may be a necessary administrative step before introducing a change to an educational setting.

Technology. Innovation and change in education during the past ten years has been concentrated in curriculum and instruction. Teaching strategies, instructional materials, how students are grouped for instruction, what is taught and at what levels—all aspects of teaching and learning have undergone major changes. As researchers have studied the impact of instructional innovation on other organizational subsystems, they have grouped specific changes under the more general sociological concept of "technology." Technology, as defined by social scientists, is the nature of work the organization performs—procedures, processes, and activities that accomplish its major objectives. In schools and colleges, of course, the main objective is learning, and the technology is the entire range of teaching and instructional activities conducted to accomplish this purpose.

Technologies change for several reasons: because the environment places new demands on the organization, because new technical inventions are developed, or because organizational participants themselves devise new ways of doing things. In education, all three of these forces have changed instruction. Society has increased its expectations, giving schools and colleges new and more varied responsibilities. New technical breakthroughs have produced such innovations as individualized instruction, modular scheduling, and programmed learning. And, with greater professionalization, faculty members are viewing students differently and have developed new ways to approach students in the classroom.

All of these changes have made instruction and educational technology more complex. As a result, students are seen as having a greater range of skills, abilities, and needs. A wider range of materials, activities, and other resources are required to match student diversity, and the knowledge required to link students with these resources is complex, which means that the kinds of decisions instructors must make have become increasingly sophisticated.

Several social scientists are presently trying to determine the results of these changes, often in terms of the impact that changing technology has on the structure of an organization. We have emphasized that organizational subsystems are interrelated and that changes in one area require changes in others. What, then, are the changes caused in the structure of educational work by instructional innovation?

The first study in this section, by Deal, Meyer, and Scott, reports the preliminary results of a study of the technology-structure relationship in 188 elementary schools located in 34 school districts. Their conclusion is that school organizations are doubly segmented. Each level—district, school, and classroom—operates independently of the other, which can produce major difficulties for the continued support of educational innovation. The Cohen-Bredo chapter is an intensive study of 16 schools from the larger sample used above. Cohen and Bredo focus on the structure-technology relationship by investigating teacher teams functioning at the classroom level. The internal structure of teams appears to be related to the instructional approaches: the more interdependent the team, the more sophisticated the approach to instruction.

What are the implications of such a perspective for educational administrators? Most importantly, planned changes in curriculum and instruction must be assessed in terms of the demands they will make on the structure of the organization. Innovations often require new roles, higher levels of coordination and problem solving, and increased interdependency among participants. Individualized instruction, for example, places considerable strain on the isolated organizational teacher in a single classroom which is, incidentally, the predominant pattern in most elementary schools.

A second, but somewhat more problematic, implication of the technological perspective is that changes in instruction and curriculum might be produced by changing aspects of school organizations. Organizing teachers into small interdependent work groups, or teams, may increase the individualization of instruction. The impact can, however, run either way: changes in technology may affect the social structure and work patterns of faculty members, or changes in social arrangements may foster or hinder new technologies.

Environment. A crucial, but often overlooked, factor in educational innovation is the environment in which a school district, school, or college carries out its primary functions of teaching and learning. The educational environment does not consist solely of parents, students, and the local community. It does include, among other elements, teacher unions; state, local, and even federal governmental agencies; other educational organizations; and the prevailing professional or educational climate.

Environments can be relatively homogeneous or highly diverse, relatively stable or excessively dynamic, changing continuously. Elements in the environment may agree on educational policies and practices or prove quite discordant. All educational institutions depend on their environments for financial support, clients, and a general endorsement of their effectiveness. For each of these dependencies, environments prove to be generous or stingy, hostile or friendly. They provide "bright students" or "trouble makers." Some environments heavily support educational innovation; others fight bitterly to prevent colleges, schools, or districts from changing.

In dealing with environments, educational organizations have two basic alternatives. They may attempt to control the environment, or they may adapt by changing internally. Public relations campaigns, political strategies, or attempts to insulate themselves from certain sectors represent attempts to control environments. Instructional and organizational innovations or basic structural changes represent attempts to adapt. In short, the educational setting of a school or school district can either facilitate or impede innovation.

The relationship between educational organizations and their environments is the perspective in this section. The chapter by Baldridge draws on three separate research studies to show that a school's environment is a more important predictor of innovation than the individual characteristics of teachers or administrators. Baldridge argues that school districts (or schools) in dynamic, heterogeneous environments reorganize and innovate in order to cope with external demands. In turn, the increased complexity of the internal system results in the development of new educational ideas and the adoption of innovative programs. Abbott's position is comparable to that of Baldridge. Abbott characterizes school environments as potent stimulators of educational innovation, both through instant organizational reaction and deliberate planned adjustment. He breaks the innovative process into three distinct phases: awareness, search, and implementation. For each phase he presents propositions relating organizational characteristics to conscious, deliberate change. For example, he predicts that the more "open" a school's climate, the more likely it is that the school will adopt instructional or administrative innovations and that these innovations will be implemented. Carlson singles out one aspect of the environment for special attention, examining the "admission rights" of clients—organizations either have the right to determine admission, or they do not. Clients can either elect to participate, or their participation is required. From the two dimensions, admission and participation, Carlson develops a typology of organizations. Organizations vary from "wild" to "domesticated," depending on the control both they and the client have over admission and participation. In "wild" organizations both the client and the organization hold decision rights; in "domesticated" organizations, neither does. Public schools, according to Carlson, are examples of "domesticated" organizations. As such, they are ensured environmental support without being required to modify their instructional or administrative practices. In contrast, private schools would be examples of "wild" organizations that are encouraged to maintain the tempo of the environment in order to secure clients.

Baldridge's case study of innovation at New York University (Chapter 22), which deals extensively with the impact of environmental changes on a university's goals, can also be read in conjunction with this section.

The administrative implications of this research perspective are straightforward. Since the environment is both a stimulator of and a barrier to innovation, its characteristics and dynamics must be constantly assessed by educational administrators. Once this assessment is made, deliberate, planned change can be assured either by changing the environment, adjusting to environmental forces, or organizing to deal with these forces.

Structure. While major changes have occurred in other organizational subsystems in education, the basic structural features of educational organizations have remained nearly the same. There have been several attempts to reorganize schools and colleges. At the district level, decentralization of authority through involving local schools has been attempted; at the school level, team teaching and differentiated staffing have been suggested as new ways to structure the work arrangements of teachers; at the college level, there have been several moves toward centralizing decisions at the state level. By and large, however, the basic organizational patterns in educational organizations have persisted despite attempts to restructure them.

Until now, organizational characteristics of educational organizations have been viewed both as a cause and a consequence of innovation. Baldridge, for example, located the impetus for change in the educational environment: Schools develop complex, specialized structures as they adapt to diverse, dynamic environments. In turn, organizational complexity results in higher adoption rates of innovative educational ideas. In contrast, Deal, Meyer, and Scott suggest that changes in instruction, or educational technology, have placed new demands on school organizations that must be met by corresponding structural changes if more sophisticated approaches to teaching and learning are to survive. Structure, from this perspective, is seen more as consequence than cause of innovation. In this section there is still a dual focus. Organizational structure is examined both as a cause of educational innovation and as a target of innovative reforms.

Within this section, organizational structure is defined in several ways. Traditional structural concepts are size, complexity, formalization, division of labor and specialization, interdependence, and authority. In addition, organizational processes such as communication, coordination, evaluation, and distribution of organizational rewards are often included. Structure can also be analyzed at several levels. In school districts, for example, structural patterns exist at the district, school, and classroom levels.

In the first chapter on organizational structure, Pellegrin compares the features of a group of traditional elementary schools with those of Wisconsin's multiunit schools. Essentially, the multiunit plan is an innovative approach developed by the Wisconsin R&D Center that both reorganizes the school and changes the nature of the instructional program. The comparison Pellegrin draws between the multiunit schools and the control schools illuminates some important structural features of schools. In most elementary schools many features reduce interdependence among teachers. First, teachers are dependent on the principal for successful performance of their teaching task instead of on other teachers. Second, in most elementary schools division of labor and specialization are low. Just two roles exist in the school: teacher and principal. Third, while teachers in most elementary schools are highly autonomous in their individual classrooms, they have little influence over schoolwide decisions. The structural reforms of the multiunit school—team teaching, an active instructional committee, and unit leaders who perform many aspects of the traditional principal's role—show promise of reducing some of those basic structural weaknesses. Next, Miles provides a diagnosis of the organizational "health" of schools. His main premises are that efforts at planned changes must take into account the health of the system and that the organizational characteristics of schools must be given as much of our attention as instruction, teaching, and learning. Miles lays out ten indicators of organizational health, many of which include some of the same structural features mentioned first by Pellegrin and later by Lortie. He then holds schools against the ten indicators of organizational health. From this comparison schools emerge as decidedly unhealthy. Miles concludes by suggesting some strategies that may restore the patient. Finally, Lortie provides an organizational analysis of schools. Like many other sociological studies in education, the Lortie chapter illuminates several weaknesses in school organizations. It focuses on the elementary school, showing how authority patterns, the distribution of rewards, and the flat career hierarchy of teachers create some basic organizational problems. Lortie then speculates about the potential of team teaching as a structural reform and as an innovation in teacher work arrangements.

Of all the perspectives on changes and innovation, research on the structural properties of schools is probably one of the most important for several reasons. Many educational administrators use only the "human relations," individual-oriented approach, a monopoly that has, we believe, impeded the progress of organizational reform in schools. Also, compared to other administrative subsystems, the structural properties of schools are most easily manipulated by the administrator. Finally, it is only through basic structural reorganization that schools will be able to set and accomplish desired goals; monitor, adopt, and influence the environment; and deal successfully with changes in educational technology. Team teaching, differentiated staffing, decentralization, and community participation are specific examples of structural reforms. Changing the structural characteristics and the work environments of schools is within the grasp of every educational administrator. The primary function of that role can be one of designing an appropriate work setting, taking into account the characteristics of environment, technology, and goals.

Individual and Small Group

2 Organizational Change

Daniel Katz
Robert Kahn

The major error in dealing with problems of organizational change, both at the practical and theoretical level, is to disregard the systemic properties of the organization and to confuse individual change with modifications in organizational variables. It is common practice to pull foremen or officials out of their organizational roles and give them training in human relations. Then they return to their customary positions with the same role expectations from their subordinates, the same pressures from their superiors, and the same functions to perform as before their special training. Even if the training program has begun to produce a different orientation toward other people on the part of the trainees, they are likely to find little opportunity to express their new orientation in the ongoing structured situation to which they return.

Almost all psychotherapy, including group therapy, suffers from this same weakness. Its immediate target is improved insight by the individual into his motivations. Even if individuals and small groups emerge from the therapeutic sessions with improved understanding of themselves and others, the effects of such individual change on social structures tend to be minimal. With respect to the supersystem of the nation-state, the same confusion of individual and system

Abridged version of Daniel Katz and Robert Kahn, *Social Psychology of Organizations* (New York: Wiley and Sons, 1966), ch. 13. Reprinted by permission of John Wiley and Sons, Inc.

functioning is often apparent. It was conspicuous, for example, in the objections to changing Negro-white relations by law. A common point of view was that individuals would have to change their attitudes and habits first. The fallacy in this position has been demonstrated by the revolution created by changes at the top of the legal structure, specifically the Supreme Court decision of 1954.

The confusion between individual and organizational change is due in part to the lack of precise terminology for distinguishing between behavior determined largely by structured roles within a system and behavior determined more directly by personality needs and values. The behavior of people in organizations is still the behavior of individuals, but it has a different set of determinants than behavior outside organizational roles. Modifications in organizational behavior must be brought about in a different manner.

Let us examine the individual approach in more detail. Its essential weakness is the psychological fallacy of concentrating upon individuals without regard to the role relationships that constitute the social system of which they are a part. The assumption has been that, since the organization is made up of individuals, we can change the organization by changing its members. This is not so much an illogical proposition as it is an oversimplification which neglects the interrelationships of people in an organizational structure and fails to point to the aspects of individual behavior which need to be changed.

Some psychoanalysts, for example, assume that wars are caused by the aggressive impulses of man and that, if we can lessen frustrations and redirect aggressive impulses, we can change the belligerent character of the state and eliminate war. Reasonable as this sounds, it has very little to do with the case. The finger that presses the button unleashing a nuclear warhead may be that of a person with very little repressed hostility, and the cabinet or state directorate behind the action may be made up of people who are kind to their families, considerate of their friends, and completely lacking in the psychopathology of aggression. They are merely carrying out their roles in a social system, and, unless these roles and the social structure which gives them definition are changed, we will still have wars. Yet we persist in attempting to change organizations by working on individuals without redefining their roles in the system, without changing the sanctions of the system, and without changing the expectations of other role incumbents in the organization about appropriate role behavior.

In short, to approach institutional change solely in individual terms involves an impressive and discouraging series of assumptions—assumptions which are too often left implicit. They include, at the very least, the assumption that the individual can be provided with new insight and knowledge; that these will produce some significant alteration in his motivational pattern; that these insights and motivations will be retained even when the individual leaves the protected situation in which they were learned and returns to his accustomed role in the organization; that he will be able to adapt his new knowledge to that real-life situation; that he will be able to persuade his co-workers to accept the changes in his behavior which he now desires; and that he will also be able to persuade them to make complementary changes in their own expectations and behavior.

The weaknesses in this chain become apparent as soon as its many links are enumerated. The initial diagnosis may be wrong; that is, the inappropriate behavior may not result from lack of individual insight or any other psychological shortcoming. Even if the initial diagnosis is correct, however, the individual approach to organizational change characteristically disregards the long and difficult linkage just described. This disregard we have called the psychological fallacy. In warning against it, however, we do not propose to commit a complementary sociological fallacy. We do not assert, in other words, that *any* alteration in human behavior can be brought about in organizations provided the process of change is initiated with due attention to organizational structure. The problems of change are too complex for such simplistic generalizations and require further specification.

Perhaps the best way of introducing such specification into problems of social change is to examine two separate aspects of the matter: the methods employed to bring about change, and the targets at which such methods are directed. Although a single method may be directed at different targets or at a sequence of targets, it can be argued that there is inherent in each method a primary or preferred target and a hypothesized linkage by which other targets may be reached. We shall discuss a primary target in relation to our presentation of each method of change.

These methods for bringing about organizational change include the direct use of information, skills training, individual counseling and therapy, the influence of the peer group, sensitivity training, group therapy, feedback on organizational functioning, and direct structural or systemic alteration. The primary target of change may be the individual as an individual personality, the interpersonal relationships between members of peer groups, the norms of peer groups, the interpersonal relationships between members of an organizational family, the structure of a role, the role relationships of some segment of organizational space, or the structure of the organization as a whole. The difficulty with many attempts at organizational change is that the changers have not clearly distinguished their targets and have assumed that the individual or group-level target was the same as the social structure target.

Information as a Method of Change

The use of information (merely supplying additional cognitive input) has a supplementary and supportive function for other methods of change, no matter what their target. It can give the rationale for an anticipated program of change and make clear what is expected of the individual, the group, or the organization as a whole. But it requires the use of other methods to produce the basic modification desired. The target of information may be a change in the individual's role; unless this change is legitimized with the invoking of penalties and rewards, the mere explanation of his new role is not likely to bring about new behavior. Information capitalizes upon the existing forces in a situation, and is not itself a prime mover. It produces change, therefore, only if the necessary motivation is forthcoming from other sources. One of the studies of the Survey Research Center (Kahn and Boulding, 1964), conducted in a company manufacturing household appliances, investigated the effects of the communication skills of foremen in presenting and explaining changes in methods and incentive rates. The initial and discouraging finding was that differing communication skills of foremen produced no significant differences in the response of workers. Further analysis revealed that the communication practices of the foreman made a difference in the behavior of the men if the foreman possessed a significant amount of power in the organizational structure. Among foremen who lacked such power, communication practices were negligible in their effects.

One exception to the statement that informational techniques are effective only in combination with some other motivational source should be noted. Techniques relying primarily on information giving are effective in ambiguous situations, where lack of information is the obstacle to appropriate performance. The individual accepts suggestions which clarify matters for him and give him a feeling that things are under control. In organizational settings, however, the patterns of expected behavior are more often clear than not.

Individual Counseling and Therapy

The realization that information can reinforce rather than redirect behavior has led to utilization of therapeutic devices for bringing about personality changes at a deeper level. Theory and research suggest the importance of dealing with basic motives in attempting to change the individual. Gordon Allport (1945, 1954) suggested that giving people insight into the psychological dynamics of prejudice toward other races and nations might be an effective way of restructuring their attitudes. Katz, Sarnoff, and McClintock (1956) demonstrated that prejudices toward Negroes could be changed momentarily by information, but that more lasting change resulted from giving people insight into their own motivation about prejudice. A number of industrial organizations have utilized consulting firms for therapeutic counseling of middle management personnel. Often the practice has not been to select out problem cases but to give all supervisory personnel at the intermediate level the benefits of a series of long sessions with a professional counselor.

The logic of therapy leads to social change by a long and doubtful route, as we have already implied. The assumption is that, if the individual is to change, he should first be removed from the social situation reinforcing his present behavior. In isolation from his former associates he can learn about himself, then learn to relate to his therapist, and finally to his former colleagues. Since there has been no corresponding change occurring in his colleagues, the changed personality of the subject encounters a series of shocks in attempting to try out his new *me* on his old colleagues. Even if he himself can maintain his personality change, it is unlikely to make a dent on the pattern of the organization.

The target of therapy is basically the personality of the individual. If he gains new insights, overcomes his insecurities, experiences his world as a less-threatening place, and hence perceives it more objectively, he should be able to relate to his fellows more effectively. The secondary target, then, of changing an individual's personality structure is the restructuring of his own role and his relationships with others in the organization. In extreme cases, such individual changes may help the functioning of the organization; sick people, or people with particular blind spots or psychological weaknesses, may no longer impede organizational functioning. The semiparanoid character after therapy may be capable of being integrated into his group, or into his organizational family. In less extreme cases, it is difficult to predict the carry-over of individual change to organizational targets. Nor is every organization so structured that it can absorb healthy, well-integrated personalities who express rather than inhibit their aggressions. Other things in the organization must change, too, or the rehabilitated individual may find himself outside the organization because of his rehabilitation.

There is, however, the occasional case in which personality conversion is achieved in the individual who is either the most powerful figure in the organization or who is close to the top in power position. Here, of course, the change achieved through individual therapy may have reverberations in the organization as a whole. Since such a person is in a position to introduce legitimized change in the organization through utilizing its authority structure, any real changes in his personality can have important organizational consequences. This is especially true in small organizations, where the other social forces maintaining a steady state are less imposing in their weight.

In summary, the difficulty with the use of personality conversion in changing organizations is twofold: (1) In general, the top officers of an organization tend to see counseling and therapy as more appropriate for their subordinates than for themselves. They do not have the time for it; nor, as successful operators, do they see the need. (2) Other organizational forces will tend to maintain the organization in a steady state. The manager who returns to his organization a relaxed and secure individual may still not be able to change the many subsystems and their mutually reinforcing relationships which tend to preserve the operating mode of the enterprise. A more precise theoretical statement would be that organizational properties are by definition systemic and their change calls for system change. The personality of the manager is not a system property or variable save in a small group which is organized around the idiosyncratic traits of the leader.

To these difficulties must be added the fact that therapy is not yet a very predictable tool for personality change. It varies in effectiveness, depending upon the patient and his problems, the therapist, the relation between the two, and the type of therapy utilized. Many people have undoubtedly benefited in some degree from therapy; others have not been changed appreciably, and some have changed for the worse. Research evidence on the effectiveness of therapy and the conditions under which it is effective is only now beginning to be gathered.

The Influence of the Peer Group

A third approach to producing individual change is through the influence of the peer group. This method has three advantages: (1) The behavior of associates does exert tremendous power over the individual. (2) Changing several people at the same status level in the organization introduces the possibility of continuing reinforcement of the behavioral changes. (3) The possibility of discovering an acceptable solution calling for change is greater in groups not inhibited by authority figures. Maier and Hoffman (1961) have demonstrated that the production of creative solutions to a problem increased when subjects' orientation to authority relations was low. There are serious limitations, however, in the organizational change which can be accomplished through peer group discussion and decision.

The target of group influence may be any one of a number of peer groups. It may be a group of first-line foremen or a cabinet of vice-presidents and managers. As with therapy, the creation of better relations in the peer group may not lead to the desired organizational change. A stronger peer group at the rank-and-file level may become more resistant to organizational needs, as the study of Seashore has demonstrated (1954). Moreover, the lower the group in the organizational structure, the less likely is any significant movement in the total structure. Maier (1952) has suggested the concept of area of freedom to indicate the amount of decision making possible at various hierarchical levels in the organization. The method of group discussion has been used predominantly at those levels where the area of freedom for decision making is smallest.

The peer group is a promising vehicle for intragroup processes of influence because equal status and power encourage full discussion, free decision making, and the internalization of the resulting decisions. Research evidence clearly establishes the effectiveness of such group discussion and decision making in changing behavior and attitudes where the individual is the target of the attempts to produce change.

Kurt Lewin and his followers were the first to demonstrate systematically the superiority of the group method over the usual informational approach in modifying individual behavior. Lewin's (1952) first experiment in changing food habits during World War II was directed at getting housewives to use unpopular foods such as beef hearts, sweetbreads, and kidneys instead of the more conventional cuts of meat. Six groups of Red Cross volunteers organized for home nursing were the subjects. Three groups received the usual lecture and three were involved in group discussion and decision. A follow-up of the women showed dramatic differences, with only 3 percent of the lecture groups serving the unpopular foods as compared with 32 percent of the discussion groups. . . .

An interesting application of group discussion and decision making to industrial problems is found in the work of Levine and Butler (1952). These experimenters were interested in getting supervisors to rate employees on the basis of performance alone. Previous studies had shown that such ratings were colored by knowledge of the grade and pay scale for the job. One group of supervisors was given information about the pitfalls of ratings in a lecture, followed by a question and answer period. In a second group the discussion method was employed, and a third group served as a control. The performance of employees was rated by an outside group of experts, and these expert evaluations comprised the criterion against which the supervisors' ratings were compared. Improvement in ratings occurred only in the group in which the discussion procedure had been utilized.

In . . . the above experiments the group method was used to influence the individual without respect to his further involvement in the group. Most of the individuals involved never saw one another again, though the group influence persisted over time. In other experiments, however, the group method has been used to change the norms of groups which continue as groups. Here the primary target is group norms rather than individuals. Bavelas (Lewin, 1947), for example, tackled the difficult problem of changing the informal norms of a work group with respect to productivity. Employees in a garment factory were given the problem of their production standards for group discussion and decision. Two other groups used as control groups also had discussion, but were under no constraint to come up with a group decision about a solution. The group which reached a decision about production goals was the only one to increase its productivity. . . .

The failure to affect the informal standards of the work groups is reminiscent of the studies at Western Electric. Mayo (1933) and his colleagues were able to improve the productivity of a group of girls who were removed from the floor of the factory; subsequent efforts to improve the productivity of men by setting them apart in a test room were unavailing, however. Though the wage incentive scheme contained a complicated group piece rate by which the faster workers contributed more to the earnings of the group than the slower workers, the pressures within the group were brought to bear on the faster rather than the slower workers. . . .

The degree of objective truth behind such workers' fears has too often been dismissed as unimportant, and emphasis has been placed upon the psychological fact that workers believe management to be capable of such behavior. It should be recognized that reductions in piece rates are not unusual and that historically workers, like other groups, have had to rely upon themselves for the preservation of their own interests. All groups tend to resort to protective devices for that purpose. . . .

The major factor conditioning the success of group discussion and group decision in changing group norms and individual behavior is the significance of the decisions for the people involved. One reason for the efficacy of the method is the involvement of people, the degree to which they can work out problems of importance to themselves and make decisions about their own fate. Workers are not generally as involved in making higher profits for management as they are in their own problems of making a living, achieving job security, and doing interesting work under good working conditions. The group discussion method, to be successful with hourly employees, must offer something of importance to them for decision making. Unless the area of freedom in the organization gives them some scope, the method may be ineffective or may actually boomerang. To be asked to invest time and energy in discussing trivial matters, while important issues are forbidden, can be infuriating.

Besides the major factor of influence in significant decisions, there are other factors which account for the effectiveness of group process. Discussion and decision about problems of importance invoke powerful individual forces of self-expression and self-determination. Not only are people discussing important matters, but each individual is given a chance to express his own views and to persuade others. Ideas that come from the outside, even if significant for personal welfare, are not as satisfying as the expression of a person's own ideas on the problem.

The peer group, especially without the presence of authority figures, can develop a warm, permissive atmosphere in which spontaneity is encouraged. People can not only contribute constructive suggestions, but [they] can [also] express specific grievances or ventilate their feelings about things in general. Such complaints can mutually reinforce one another and produce a negative organizational outcome. This generally does not happen if the group has freedom to make decisions of consequence to themselves. Less-aggrieved individuals will bring the discussion around to a positive orientation and even the more offended, having unburdened themselves of some of their troubles, may move in upon problems in a constructive fashion.

Since the solution emerging from group discussion is a group product, the individuals experience the satisfaction of being part of something greater than themselves. They have had a hand in creating it, but it is bigger than they, and knowing they are a part of it heightens their self-esteem.

Group interaction, as it reaches the point of decision, makes salient the group norm or consensus. Norms imposed from without may vary in clarity, visibility, and psychological nearness. After a discussion has finally reached consensus, the group norms are abundantly clear and psychologically real to the members.

Since the group has to come up with a decision if it is to be successful, members have to reach a point of crystallization in their own thinking and hence a self-commitment on the issues. Often when outside views are presented to us we may assent without reaching that genuine crystallization of our own views which represents self-commitment.

The self-commitment embodying the group decision is a public commitment. At the end, all members have stood up to be counted. This public visibility of their individual positions helps to freeze the outcome of the group process. It may account for the fact that the changes produced in the cancer education groups persisted for more than thirteen months. Public commitment should be even more potent in a group with a continuing life in which members mutually reinforce one another.

Finally, group discussion and decision is more powerful when its decision outcome is clearly stated in terms of a course of action. The changed beliefs are removed from the area of good intentions to the realities of everyday behavior. When the individual steps out of the group setting and is subjected to other sources of influence, he may not act on his newly acquired beliefs and attitudes unless they have been structured with a commitment to specific forms of behavior. . . .

The determinants of the quality of group problem solving have been systematically studied by Maier and Hoffman (1961). These investigators found that homogeneous groups (composed of members similar with respect to personality characteristics) produced fewer high-quality solutions than did heterogeneous groups (Hoffman and Maier, 1961; Hoffman, 1959). Presumably, diversity of approach among group members facilitates problem solving. In another experiment diversity of opinion was produced by strengthening the original position of rank-and-file members in opposition to their leaders (Hoffman, Harburg, and Maier, 1962). Moreover, some of the leaders were instructed to play their roles as foremen in a fashion considerate of group members; others were instructed to play a dominating role. The greatest number of integrative solutions occurred in groups led by considerate leaders with strongly convinced members; the fewest occurred in those groups led by considerate leaders and composed of members with weak convictions. The authors conclude that the conflict generated between the subordinate members and their leaders was productive of high-quality solutions because it made differences of opinion visible and stimulated consideration of several points of view. Pelz (1956) has also shown that scientific productivity is facilitated by an environment in which the scientist has contact with some people who do not resemble him closely in values and orientation toward problems.

When groups with formally designated leaders discuss problems, as in the experiments cited above, the character of the leadership is a significant factor in determining the quality of the solution. Maier (1950) has demonstrated that groups with leaders trained in democratic approaches achieve more inventive solutions than groups with untrained leaders. The training in this instance emphasized (1) having the group identify the nature of the problem; (2) keeping the discussion task oriented rather than personally oriented; (3) considering all suggestions; and (4) stimulating the group to analyze and evaluate completely all suggested solutions. . . .

Two basic assumptions in the original Lewinian method of group discussion and decision are not always made explicit but have profound implications: (1) The technique has been essentially limited to the peer group, to people who come together as equals with respect to formal authority and formal status. (2) People come into the group because of common interests of their own and not as formal representatives of other groups. They can disagree or even leave the group, without ramifying consequences.

The first assumption is important with respect to the power of the group influence generated. If authority or status figures are present, the spontaneous interaction of group members is inhibited. People are less free to work through their own feelings and ideas, and the resulting group decision may reflect less of their own constructive solutions and produce less internalization. A peer group does not lend itself readily to organizational structure in which the hierarchical principle is dominant. In fact, decision making by peer groups could not be carried out fully without genuine modification of the hierarchical principle. The dynamic of the peer group is in contradiction to the hierarchical principle.

The second assumption has received even less attention in Lewinian theory, which has been little concerned with the distinction between people playing formal roles and people acting as individual personalities. In many group situations, however, people represent the wishes of their constituents, or in some fashion serve as role representatives of other groups. Every legislative group is, of course, of this character, as is the mediation group composed of representatives from management and union.

The heads of departments in an industrial company, or in a university, or in government may have equal status in their group meetings, but each department head is constrained by the interests of his own constituency. University committees are frequently set up as peer groups and given problems of common university interest. Their members are supposed to act as citizens of the university. But often the member from the history department will have in the back of his mind the reactions of people in his own department, and the classical scholar will think in terms of how well he is representing the humanities. Organizational life means that many group meetings will bring together people from different sectors of organizational space, each subject to the influences of the particular sector from which he comes. A continuing problem in organizations is to produce a true peer group situation in which members leave behind their other role involvements and function only as citizens of the organization.

There are many situations in which the role of the individual is and should be paramount because of the nature of organizational structure. In such situations, the group meeting is a means by which needs and wishes of subgroups are given vigorous expression and compromises are achieved. The Lewinian group method presumes a solution which integrates rather than compromises the needs of the members; hence, the demand that the final decision be unanimous. With the representative group, the usual requirement is a majority vote and the commitment of the minority to abide by the majority decision until the next round of decision making. Representative groups may be legislative, mediative, executive, or administrative in character, and their common techniques are logrolling, trading concessions, bargaining, and compromise. This is the realm of *real* politics, and politics has been defined as the great art of compromise.

No substitute for this type of group process has been devised. The pure democracy of the small Lewinian group discussion and decision is not directly applicable to systems composed of many subgroups with distinctive functions, values, and interests. On the other hand, a monolithic authority structure which eliminates all group process is undesirable and, for that matter, impossible to achieve. The art of politics and of group process has not been eliminated from Soviet Russia. The solution to the dilemma of representative group process is not to abolish it, but to make it more truly representative and, in so doing, to establish the central membership character of citizenship in the organization.

Sensitivity Training: The Bethel Approach

The group process of Lewin for achieving agreement among peers on their own problems has been extended by his students to the technique of sensitivity training. Just as the individual has to be isolated from ongoing influences to learn about himself, so, too, must the group be separated from its usual environment. As the therapist leads the individual to express his own emotional conflicts, to become aware of them, to explore and to attain insight into his own motivations, so, too, is the group encouraged to express its emotions, to examine its activities, and to become aware of group process.

Since 1947 the National Training Laboratories has held sessions every summer at Bethel, Maine, for leaders from industry, government, universities, and other institutions. On this cultural island people leave behind their organizational roles and enter as peers, unrepresentative of their group memberships, into an exploration of group process and leadership. The frustrations in dropping their usual role supports and ingrained organizational techniques lead to a reexamination of methods of participating in groups and influencing other people.

The major device for such learning is the T group (training group). Each such group consists of approximately ten to sixteen people, including one or two trainers. The group is scheduled for one or two meetings each day over a period of two or three weeks. The meetings typically last for an hour and a half or two hours.

Each group begins without agenda, structure, division of labor, or rules of procedure. The people in each group are strangers to each other, brought together only by the common goal of learning more about themselves, the impact which they have on others, and the ways in which groups can become effective instruments for meeting the needs of their members. The absence of the usual props of officers, agenda, and Robert's Rules of Order creates an initial vacuum which is often quite uncomfortable. As the members struggle to fill this vacuum with meaningful activity and relationships, the trainer attempts to observe problems of communication, attempted seizures of power, misunderstandings, and other phenomena of interpersonal life. He communicates these observations to the group, whose members gradually begin to attend to such matters themselves and to check the accuracy of their own observations by describing them and asking for corroboration or correction from others. By this method (which is difficult to describe but most exciting and rewarding to experience) the members of the group attain increased sensitivity to their own behavior, the actions of others, and the nature of group development. Group members often emerge with a restructuring of their values about people and about their operations in group settings.

Powerful as this method is, its target is essentially the individual and not the organization. When the individuals return to their old structures, they step back into the same definitions of their roles. What is more basic, these roles are intimately related with a number of other organizational roles; the converted returnees may want to redefine their own way of functioning, but the expectations of superiors, subordinates, and colleagues have not changed; nor has there been a change in organizational sanctions and rewards.

If the person who has undergone change happens to be the head of an organization or a major unit of an organization, then organizational change may ensue. But there is no guarantee of significant organizational change even in such an instance. The old methods of operation have forces behind them other than the personal style of the leader, and these, too, must change to ensure system change. Sometimes such changes are beyond the power of the organizational head. Sometimes they are possible, but require skills and methods beyond those the chief learned in the laboratory training experience.

In recent years the activities of the National Training Laboratories have greatly expanded, and the methods pioneered by Bradford and his colleagues have been adopted by many organizations and individuals. Laboratory or sensitivity training sessions are conducted under various auspices on a continuing basis in many different locations throughout the country. In addition, many innovations have been introduced and given some research evaluation (Bradford, Benne, and Gibb, 1964). The most important of these, for our present purpose, is the closer linking of the T group to the realities of specific organizations. This is achieved in part by dealing specifically with problems of organizational change as adjunct curriculum. A more dramatic innovation has been the use of the T-group procedure with people who are members of the same organization, whether company, school, or labor union. Such a group may consist entirely of peers, or of people at different levels in the organizational family, such as a superior and his immediate subordinates.

It is perhaps too early to attempt an evaluation of these variations on the T-group theme. Certainly they offer increased power with respect to generating organizational change, and to the maintenance of changes begun within the group. On the other hand, the role relationships which members bring into the T-group setting add to the initial difficulties of launching the training process and may continue to impede it. The organizational T group, in short, is a promising development, but its properties and potentialities require continuing exploration and research evaluation.

The relationship of sensitivity training to group therapy has often been discussed (and as often left unresolved). There is sufficient variation among practitioners of the laboratory method of training and among group therapists to make difficult any estimation of the degree of relationship or separation between the two.

Our own view is that laboratory training is not basically therapeutic in theory or in practice. Laboratory training does not aim at the resolution of unconscious conflicts within the individual but at a fuller perception of his behavior and the behavior of others. The content of the discussion in the T group, and especially of the comments of the trainer, is consistent with these aims. The comments are strongly oriented toward interpersonal processes as they are directly observable in the group; inferences about the motives and internal conflicts of others are not encouraged. Each member comes to understand that he is expert and can talk well about how he feels or what he sees, but that he is on questionable ground when he attempts to make inferences about the motives of others.

As we have noted, the differences among trainers are great, and the distinction between cognitive learning and therapy is not absolute. The distinction is easy to observe, however, if we contrast the training procedures of the National Training Laboratories with those of Elliott Jaques and his former colleagues at the Tavistock Institute. Jaques emphasized the analogy between individual therapy and organizational change. His underlying hypothesis is that many organizational problems are rooted in unconscious motives and their solution opposed by unconscious resistances. The excavation and working through of such material becomes the major means to organizational change, in his view. The basic assumption of the laboratory training method, on the other hand, is that the major problems of human organization are not unconscious and irrational, or at least that they can be successfully attacked at the conscious level and in terms of behavior observable and understandable by the members of the group themselves.

Group Therapy within Organizations

An interesting attempt to produce organizational change through group therapy introduced into the organization itself has been utilized by the Tavistock Institute in England and is reported by Elliot Jaques (1951). . . . The essence of the procedure is to have the organization change itself by means of group processes occurring at every level in the organization. The immediate target in this approach is the improvement of people's understanding of their organizational interrelationships and their own personal motives. The remote target is organizational restructuring by responsible organizational members themselves. The basic philosophy flows from individual therapy. The research team of outsiders is only one change agent; the major agents of change are the organizational members themselves. To quote Jaques, the research team is "to act only in advisory or interpretive capacity. The team is not here to solve problems. . . . They may, however, be able to help with the continuing development of methods of getting a smoother organization."

In accordance with this philosophy, the research team began its program only after gaining acceptance from the [organizational leadership]. Instead of applying the therapeutic approach in literal fashion, the Tavistock researchers focused upon organizational problems. Their preliminary move was a historical investigation of the plant, followed by an organizational study to establish the role structure of the system. This latter study included "an examination . . . of how far the social structure of the factory had proved effective in coping with the forces which affected production and group relations."

After the presentation of these background reports . . . , various sections of the organization began to ask the research team for cooperation on specific problems. The procedure of the research team was to direct the groups with which they worked toward the discovery of underlying causes and the expression of partly unconscious motives. Resistances emerging in group sessions were sometimes interpreted by the research teams; in other instances, the group was left to make its own discoveries. . . .

The Tavistock researchers regard two factors as necessary for successful working-through, and a third is desirable, though not always essential. The first factor is similar to Dewey's old initial condition for problem solving, the existence of a felt difficulty. The group must be hurting; its members must recognize a severe and painful problem. The second factor is group solidarity or cohesiveness. Members must have commitment to the group and its objectives. Otherwise, they will not have the motivation to overcome the additional anxieties involved in problem solution. The third condition is a state of frustration created by the failure of denial and other mechanisms of defense to function in their accustomed manner. Groups tend to avoid facing up to the basic causes of their problems through various devices of avoidance and denial. When group members, through the help of a consultant or by other means, find that running away from the problem gives them no relief, they are ready for more realistic exploration. . . .

Recently there have been promising attempts to adapt small-group approaches, especially sensitivity training and its variants, to [take] account of the organizational context. The work of Schein and Bennis (1965), Argyris (1964), and Blake and Mouton (1964) are outstanding examples. The final pages of the work by Bradford, Gibb, and Benne (1964) speak of the "extended use of T-groups and laboratory methods in nonlaboratory (that is, organizational) settings." The Tavistock work deserves to be recognized, however, as the first purposeful and successful fusion of the therapeutic and organizational approaches.

The Systematic Use of Feedback and Group Discussion: The Approach of Floyd Mann

Most organizations have at least one kind of feedback from the environment to guide their operations and indicate the need for organizational change. This feedback is from the reception of their product accorded by the clientele or market. When an automobile company cannot sell its cars, it must make changes in the nature of its product. But there is another kind of feedback to the organization which derives from its own internal functioning. Two types of such internally generated information are frequently used by organizations. One concerns the technical side of internal functioning and implies an accounting for each production job in the organization. Some factories still follow the Taylor system in this respect, and at the close of every day report forms are passed up the line from each level of the organization describing the number of pieces produced, the utilization of materials, the amount of scrap and waste material, and the number of hours each employee spent on the various aspects of his job.

The second type of internal information concerns the human side of the productive and production-supportive processes of the organization. Typically such feedback reaches the upper echelons only when some problem has become acute. Top management learns that there has been a disastrous slowdown in the foundry or that some key engineers and research people have resigned to take jobs with competing companies [only when] castings are not reaching the assembly line on schedule.

Suggestion systems are sometimes employed both to get ideas about technical improvement and to get feedback on the human problems of organization. Surveys of morale and of employee feelings, attitudes, and beliefs are also conducted by companies to give the latter type of feedback. If there were full and accurate communication up the line, such surveys would not be needed, but the barriers to such upward communication are too numerous and too strong to ignore. Nor are these barriers only to peripheral data about employee attitudes. A sharp distinction between information about technical and human processes is false. The concept of the sociotechnical system of Emery and Trist (1960) rightly gives emphasis to the complex interrelationships of social and technical processes. An adequate morale survey will furnish information both about the feelings of people and the actual operations of the technical or work system.

The great weakness in the use of surveys of employees' ideas and feelings is the inability of management to utilize this type of feedback about the internal functioning of the organization. Sometimes top management feels that it has done the proper thing just by conducting a survey, and proceeds to file the reports in the personnel office; at other times it will pass the findings along to lower echelons with no specific directives about their use. If the results of the survey are read by these subordinates, the natural tendency is to select the items that reinforce their present biases and to discount findings that run contrary to their own ideas.

Employees have two reactions to such unutilized surveys. The first and perhaps the dominant one is satisfaction in having been asked to express their views and in actually ventilating their feelings. The other reaction, which arises particularly when they have been led to expect positive action, is one of frustration in that nothing happens after all their efforts to tell the company what was wrong and what should be done.

To make the survey an effective form of feedback for organizational change, Floyd Mann and his colleagues at the Survey Research Center developed a plan for group discussion of survey results by appropriate "organizational families." ... Mann's use of group discussion by such organizational families is like the Tavistock approach in taking into account the realities of organizational structure. Moreover, the hierarchical character of an enterprise is recognized by starting the feedback process with the top organizational family, for example, the president and the vice-presidents reporting to him. ... The feedback material prepared for each session by the research team is, moreover, of special relevance for the particular organizational family into which it is introduced. . . . In general, then, each organizational family is presented feedback about its own problems in detail and comparative information about the company as a whole or the larger part of the company to which it belongs. . . .

The presentation of survey findings to the various organizational families sometimes brought new problems to light. More often it gave an objective and factual basis to problems that had either been brushed aside or dealt with by some opinionated gesture. Not only had vague reports about the perceptions and feelings of employees been reduced to facts and figures, but comparisons could be made among similar groups and the findings could be related to possible causal factors. In this objective atmosphere, questions could be raised about the data, many of which could be answered by further analysis of the same data. And this was the emphasis of the Mann feedback procedure—group discussion of facts and figures in a task-oriented atmosphere where people were seeking to analyze the problem, identify possible causes as objectively as possible, and agree upon possible solutions. The reason for utilizing organizational families and presenting to them the relevant data about their operations thus becomes clear. The members of a specific organizational family [who] have been involved in these very problems already know a good deal about them, and know what questions should be asked to dig deeper into the available data for answers. Moreover, the group members are the immediate agents for implementing any policy changes with respect to problems at their own level. If they understand the causes, have been involved in a discussion of solutions, and perhaps have proposed the new policy, they will be more effective agents for achieving change.

The feedback technique, utilizing group discussion and group involvement, must be used under certain conditions if it is to realize its potential strength. Mention has already been made of the need for a factual, task-oriented atmosphere. A second necessity is the discretion of each organizational family to consider the implications of findings at its own level. Again, an area of freedom is required to utilize group process. General problem areas may be designated at higher echelons, but the detailed answers must be worked out by people closer to the problem. . . .

A third requirement for the effective use of the feedback procedure is a reporting back up the line of the outcome of meetings at the lower organizational level. When a department was satisfied that it had some answers to its problems and some recommendations about them, its head could present these findings at a subsequent branch meeting. He could report to the branch meeting to what extent various difficulties could be met at the departmental level and to what extent they seemed to arise from branch and company policies which would have to be changed at higher levels in the organization. The branch then could discuss all departmental reports and could attempt a summary report to go to the sessions of top management. At any point in the procedure the research team might be asked to bring back further breakdowns of relevant data.

One great advantage in this type of feedback with group discussion is its utilization of existing organizational structure. The executive line is not bypassed in securing information and implementing policy. Effective working relationships between supervisory levels are improved and two-way communication [is] facilitated. Management policy is better understood and more fully put into practice, and the special knowledge and competence of all levels is more fully utilized. Mann (1957) recognizes that improving organizational functioning means dealing with the systemic properties of organizational structure:

Organizations, as systems of hierarchically ordered, interlocking roles with rights and privileges, reciprocal expectations, and shared frames of reference, contain tremendous forces for stability or change in the behavior of individuals or subgroups. Change processes need to be designed to harness these forces for creating and supporting change [page 162].

Mann also points out five other related sets of facts which make for the efficacy of systematic feedback of survey data through organizational families.

—Participation in the interpretation and analysis of research findings leads to the internalization of information and beliefs. When ideas are a person's own, they are much more likely to be translated into meaningful practices than when they are the suggestions of an outside expert.

—The feedback of information [with] discussion by the appropriate organizational family makes it highly relevant to the functioning of the subgroup and its members. Principles taught at a general level of abstraction are more difficult to apply than the discovery of principles from a person's own immediate experience.

—Knowledge of results can in itself motivate people toward improving their performance. Level-of-aspiration studies indicate that individuals tend to raise their sights when they see the outcome of their efforts. If there is continuous feedback on the basis of some objective criterion of behavior, people will be motivated to attain better scores.

—Group support is especially effective where there is continuing membership in a particular group. The members of an industrial organization, during most of their waking hours, are part of one or two organizational families. If the other members of these permanent groupings also change, there is a continuing reinforcement for individual change. More remote and fleeting group memberships are occasionally significant, but one cannot escape the constant pressures of the here and now.

—Finally, a hierarchical ordering of roles with respect to authority is characteristic of most organizations, or at least of their executive systems. Hence, the introduction of feedback starting at the top of the structure not only gives organizational legitimacy to the process but [also] ensures that, for every individual in the organization, there will be expectations from his immediate superior about his behavior. The changes will have been worked out in part by lower levels in the organization, but, in their final implementation, [they] will have the authority of the organizational line of command. . . .

The procedure of feedback to organizational families as developed by Floyd Mann is similar in many ways to the group therapy approach of the Tavistock Institute. It has the same objective of clarification and improvement of organizational functioning through an objective assessment of problems by the organizational members themselves. It differs in four respects:

Mann had the considerable advantage of providing objective feedback on organizational functioning through detailed data furnished by his comprehensive survey. This made possible a task-oriented atmosphere where facts and figures were the guiding criteria. It also made possible the setting of performance norms, and ensured a representation of the views of all employees in the consideration of problems by the various levels of management.

Mann's technique covered the entire organizational structure in systematic fashion. The Tavistock research team entered only those sections and groups of the organization to which they were specifically invited, and tended to spend more time with top management than with the lower echelons.

The Tavistock investigators were more active participants in the change process than were Mann and his colleagues. . . . This meant that the focus in the [Tavistock] study was more upon irrational sources of difficulty and [Mann's focus was] more upon reducing areas of ignorance through the acquisition of facts and modifying vague opinions with documented beliefs. . . .

Both methods by choice avoid identifying in advance desired changes in organizational structure and functioning. The objective is to induce the organization to change itself. This has a tremendous advantage in removing from the researcher the onus of deciding what needs to be changed. It has the possible disadvantage of making an organization more vigorous in its present mode of operation even when there may be basic defects in its operating philosophy. For example, a nonunion factory, if subjected to the Tavistock group therapy, might emerge with a management clearer in its conception and more ingenious in its pursuit of ways to prevent union organization. In general, the organizational change attained by either the therapy or the feedback technique is likely to be in the direction of more efficient functioning but not in the direction of basic structural change. The oligarchy will still remain an oligarchy; the autocracy, still an autocracy. These methods represent the philosophy of mild and bland reform, not radical change.

To state it more precisely, the primary target of the feedback technique employed by Mann is improvement of both personal and role relationships within the organizational family. The objective is not to introduce a systemic change but to improve the relationships among the members of each organizational family and between organizational families, through their discussion of their common problems. . . .

This approach thus raises the question of the effective limits of change which is not system-wide in its character. Lippitt, Watson, and Westley (1958), in their incisive analysis of planned change, point out the problems raised by interdependence among the subparts of a system with respect to change processes. Change in one subpart can generate forces in other parts to produce related modifications, but interdependence can also mean that more sources of resistance are mobilized against any alteration of established procedures. Hence, these authors emphasize the need for defining the unit in the organization appropriate to the change attempted. . . .

Systemic Change: Changing Organizational Variables (the Morse-Reimer Experiment)

Most of the experimental attempts to produce change in organizations have been directed at individuals and not at the organization itself. This is true of the typical psychological approach with its emphasis upon individual training programs and of the group dynamics movement with its concentration on the small group irrespective of its organizational dependence. The group therapy approach of the Tavistock team recognized the organizational structure, but made no direct attempt to change it. Similarly, the feedback procedure of Mann recognized the interlocking organizational families, but left all change to these families themselves. In everyday life, however, attempts are made to change an organization as a social system, that is, to deal directly with organizational characteristics as properties of the organization rather than as the outcome of group and individual properties. Such an attempt involves the legitimation of changes in the role relationships making up the system. It is sometimes done by executive order, as when two companies merge and large sectors are reorganized or even eliminated. It can come about from revolution from within, as when young reformers capture a state or local political organization, oust the old guard from control, and reorganize the functioning of the political party. Systemic change can come about from pressures from without, as when the government orders the reorganization of an industrial empire which has achieved something of a monopolistic position in a given field of enterprise. Or the outside pressure can be the power of a labor union, which moves in on some of the old management functions of employee discipline, layoff, and dismissal. . . .

One major experiment in which there was a direct and deliberate attempt to change an organizational variable was conducted by Morse and Reimer (1956) in one department of a large business enterprise. The organizational variable selected for modification involved the authority structure of the system, or, more specifically, the degree of organizational decision making at various levels in the company. The experimenters, following the theorizing of F. H. Allport, conceptualized this variable as the degree of *axiality,* since organizations can be described as having an *axis* of control and regulation of their processes extending from the person or persons in the highest authority position down to the rank-and-file members of the organization. In the words of Morse and Reimer (1955):

The hierarchical location of the regulation and control processes on this axis is the degree of *axiality* of the organization. A description of the degree of axiality of an organization as a whole can be obtained by examining, for each hierarchical level in turn, the degree to which the organization is controlled and regulated by people at higher levels in the organization compared to the degree to which it is controlled and regulated by individuals at a given level or lower in the hierarchy [page 1].

In this experiment the objective was to change the role structure with respect to decision making and its accompanying activities so that the lower hierarchical levels in the structure would have more power and responsibility for carrying on the work of the organization. The essential idea was that all the advantages of small group democracy are lost in an organization in which the group has virtually no power to make decisions of any importance. Unless a given person or group in the legitimized authority structure is assigned responsibility for decision making, all the training of individuals or of small groups to utilize group process and group decision are likely to be transitory or even abortive in their outcome.

We do not change organizations by occasional demonstrations of the value of the democratic process. The ongoing forces are structurally fixed in the system and the legitimate authority will not be affected to any appreciable degree without a direct attack upon its permanent structure. Hence, the experimenters worked with the top echelons in the company to attain a legitimized change in organizational structure, so that the rank-and-file employees would be given the authority and responsibility for carrying out not only their own previous assignment but also the previous functions of the first-line supervisors. . . .

In other words, axiality, or the degree of control and regulation of the activities of the organization, cannot be changed at one level without affecting the whole organization. In fact, this is characteristic of any systemic property. If we are really dealing with an organizational or system variable, its manipulation will involve the entire organization. To achieve organizational change, we have to deal with these systemic variables. Individual or group change applies only to specific points in organizational space, [which] is more likely to be vitiated by the enduring systemic properties than to [be altered by] them.

Change of organizational characteristics is regarded as inherently difficult to bring off because it means changing so much, and, of course, this is correct. What is overlooked, however, is that modification of major organizational processes by working with less relevant variables is infinitely more difficult to attain, even though working with such variables may entail less effort on the part of the change agent. For example, it is relatively easy to persuade many individuals to sign petitions renouncing war as a way of settling disputes between nations. Pacifist pledges of individuals have always been meaningless, however, when the latent war-making structure of the nation becomes its manifest structure in times of crisis. Unless national structures become modified to accept the jurisdiction of a larger international structure like the United Nations, war is inevitable.

The target of experimental change in the Morse and Reimer experiment was the variable of control and regulation of organizational processes. The proposed change was to shift the locus of control downward in the structure. To accomplish this purpose, a variety of procedures was employed.

First in sequence was the persuasion of the executive vice-president and his assistants of the desirability of the change. Part of the persuasion was accomplished through group sessions of his own staff and the research team, part through the presentation of findings from a previous survey in his own company, the implications of which supported downward delegation. The results of the survey showed that the higher-producing sections in the organization were less closely supervised and had more group involvement of their members than the lower-producing sections. . . .

A second procedure was the use of group discussion at various levels in the organization to prepare the employees for the anticipated change. This method of preparation also included the training of supervisors for their new roles.

The third procedure was the official introduction of the change as the new policy of the company, in a presentation by the executive vice-president himself to the employees. In other words, the change was legitimized as new role requirements by the proper authority structure. Finally, group discussion and decision making was the mode of operation by which the rank-and-file employees and first-line supervisors implemented the new program. . . . The program of downward delegation was called the Autonomy Program; the program of tighter control from above, the hierarchically controlled program.

Self-actualization was measured by combining answers to the following five questions into an index score. (1) Is your job a real challenge to what you think you can do? (2) How much chance does your job give you to learn things you are interested in? (3) Are the things you are learning in your job helping to train you for a better job in the company? (4) How much chance do you have to try out your ideas on the job? (5) How much does your job give you a chance to do the things you are best at? Significant differences were found in the predicted direction, with an increase in self-actualization in the autonomy program and a decrease in the hierarchically controlled program.

The programs also had differential effects on attitudes toward supervision. Relations with the assistant manager and the division manager improved significantly in the autonomy program and deteriorated in the hierarchically controlled program. Similarly, attraction to the company increased in the [autonomy] program and decreased in the [hierarchically controlled] program. The results on intrinsic job satisfaction were less clear-cut. As predicted, there was a significant decrease in the hierarchically controlled program, but, contrary to prediction, there was no significant change in the autonomy program, though there was some slight improvement. . . .

There were marked differences between the two experimental groups in their liking for the programs to which they had been assigned. . . . For example, whereas 24 percent of the autonomy group reported more cooperation and 18 percent more friendliness among the girls than had existed prior to the program, not a single employee in the hierarchically controlled program gave such a positive response.

Unfortunately there were no good overall measures of productivity, or total costs to the company in relation to amount produced by the two programs. Both experimental groups showed significant increases in productivity on the basis of company figures for the costs of clerk time to get the job done, whereas the original predictions called for an increase in the autonomy program and a decrease in the hierarchically controlled program. As a matter of fact, the increase in the hierarchical program was greater than that in the autonomy program on the clerk-time measure of productivity.

On the other hand, the costs in terms of clerk time do not cover the costs of turnover. Of the fifty-four girls who left the company from the four divisions during the course of the experiment, twenty-three made unfavorable comments in their exit interviews with members of the personnel department about pressure and too rigorous work standards. Of these twenty-three, nineteen were from the hierarchically controlled program. . . .

Two other factors in extrapolating the results of this experiment to other situations should be kept in mind. The first of these is the character of the employees. The overwhelming majority of clerks were girls recently graduated from high school who intended to stay only a few years with the company before getting married. They had little commitment to their jobs as a permanent occupation. Hence, they were probably less responsive to either experimental treatment than men with more involvement in their occupation. Though they disliked the hierarchically controlled program, these young, unorganized girls were not as likely to quit, go on strike, or rebel in an overt manner as more involved people might do. Management in the hierarchical program was able to increase productivity by tightening the screws. In other situations, management may not be able to overpower its workers in this fashion because of the presence of unions, or the presence of outside job opportunities for skilled workers, or the active resentment of a more occupation-conscious worker.

The second limiting factor in this experiment was the constant rate of work flow to all sections. This meant that the cooperative group spirit engendered in the autonomy program could not be fully expressed in increased productivity without disrupting the group. . . . Increased productivity actually came about in the autonomy program when the girls decided not to replace a member who was leaving to get married or to have a baby. But they could hardly be expected to dismember their group if no one was willing to leave, and they showed no inclination to do so. If the girls themselves could have determined their quotas of work, there would have been more opportunity for increases in productivity, as in the Bavelas experiment, in which workers raised their sights about what was an acceptable, fair day's work. Under these circumstances, the autonomy program might well have showed larger gains in productivity. Alternatively, as Likert (1956) suggests, the continuation of the experiment might have produced continued gains in the productivity of the autonomy program and reversal of gains in the hierarchical program. However plausible these possibilities, they are only that, and await confirmation or rejection in future research. Meanwhile, the increases in productivity in the hierarchical program constitute a clear disconfirmation of the original prediction, and a reminder of the effective power of hierarchy under conditions favorable to it.

. . . The great difficulty with the therapy and feedback approach is that, in the first place, we do not know if any significant organizational change will occur and, in the second place, if change does take place, what precisely has occurred. What is necessary . . . is a wide net of measures continued over time to discover the central change and its impact. Any organizational change which experimenters want to bring about to increase knowledge in this field must, of course, gain acceptance from the authority structure of the organization, and this itself imposes great limitations on scientific manipulations. Nonetheless, on many occasions organizations are open to modification, and organizational leaders contemplate change programs themselves. Within this framework, researchers can introduce the controls and measurements, and sometimes stipulate the means or sequence of change to yield more documented knowledge about social systems than we now possess.

The Target of Change as the Fit Between the
Technical and Social Subsystems

Organizational structure as the direct target for change includes all types of patterned relationships which comprise a system or sub-system. It is useful, however, to consider two dimensions of any production system, the technical system and the accompanying social-psychological system, and the fit between these two interlocking arrangements. Trist and his Tavistock colleagues (1963) have developed the concept of the sociotechnical system to take account of these two related dimensions of the organization of work:

> The concept of a socio-technical system arose from the consideration that any production system requires both a technological organization—equipment and process layout—and a work organization relating to each other those who carry out the necessary tasks. The technological demands place limits on the type of work organization possible, but a work organization has social and psychological properties of its own that are independent of technology. . . . [Rice, 1958, page 4].

Some technical systems may make imperative a particular type of social arrangement; for others there may be alternative social-psychological systems possible within the technical requirements of the machines and tools for getting the task done. And yet one social-psychological system may be far superior to another, both with respect to member satisfaction and organizational productivity. The target for Trist and his research group has been to find the best fit between the technical and social systems, and to introduce into a given industry the reforms needed to attain that fit. Priority is accorded the technical requirements of task accomplishment, but this does not mean that any so-called technical improvement imported from another industry is accepted uncritically as an appropriate modification of an existing work structure.

The assumptions of this approach as presented by Rice (1958) start with the following proposition:

> The performance of the primary task is supported by powerful social and psychological forces which ensure that a considerable capacity for cooperation is evoked among the members of the organization created to perform it [page 33].

The sources of gratification in getting the job done are: (1) closure or a sense of completion in finishing a meaningful unit of work, (2) some control over their own activities by those engaged in a task, and (3) satisfactory relationships with those performing related tasks. . . .

To achieve better work organization Rice makes the following additional assumptions:

Group stability is more easily maintained when the range of skills required of group members is such that all members of the group can comprehend all the skills and, without having, or wanting to have them, could aspire to their acquisition [pages 37-38].

In other words the greater the differences in skill the more difficult it is for members to communicate and the harder it is to develop group cohesiveness. Similarly,

The fewer the differences there are in prestige and status within a group, the more likely is the internal structure of a group to be stable and the more likely are its members to accept internal leadership [page 38].

And, finally,

When members of small work groups become disaffected to the extent that they can no longer fit into their own work group, those disaffected should be able to move to other small work groups engaged in similar tasks [page 39].

These assumptions describe the conditions under which a social-psychological system can operate to further organizational goals and to increase member satisfaction. An ideal arrangement for a socio-technical system would be one in which the technical aspects of the work could be organized in such a manner that the immediate work group would have a meaningful unit of activity, some degree of responsibility for its task, and a satisfactory set of interpersonal relationships. And the greater the differences in skills, prestige, and status among members of the work group, the more difficult it will be to establish and maintain satisfactory interpersonal relationships.

The Trist Studies of British Coal Mines

The relationship between the technical and the social systems in British coal mines has been studied by Trist and Bamforth (1951) and other Tavistock researchers, with respect to problems of technological change in the industry. The production side of coal mining includes three different types of operations: (1) the winning of the coal by hand or machine from the coal face, (2) the loading and transportation of the coal from the face, and (3) the supportive and preparatory activities of advancing the roof supports and of bringing up the conveyor system as the mining cuts deeper into the coal face. The early organization of these technical operations in many British mines was a simple system of small, self-contained units working independently. . . . Each work group enforced its own standards of production and had considerable autonomy in its task. This simple system of working had advantages in mines in which irregularities of coal seams put a premium upon the adaptability of work groups. Each team could set its own work pace as the conditions required, and each worker as a complete miner could adapt to the changing situation. Moreover, there were many psychological advantages in the system. Workers gained satisfaction from being engaged in meaningful cycles of activity, in having considerable autonomy and variety of work, and in being part of a group of their own choosing.

This traditional system of single-place working was replaced in Britain by the longwall method of mining, partly because of the introduction of the face conveyor. . . . These technical changes in the coal mining process were accompanied by a reorganization of jobs and of work relationships. . . . Division of labor in which each worker was limited to a single task replaced the integrated task and complete miner of single-place working. . . . Though the longwall technology clearly required some modification of the older social system of single-place working, the kind of job fractionation introduced and the neglect of the motivational forces of the primary work group were mistakes of the first order. . . . The conventional longwall system, because it failed to develop a work system appropriate to the utilization of common experience and ability, depressed the productive performance of the miners, . . . failed to maintain the natural or spontaneous coordination of the work cycle which had existed prior to its introduction, . . . [increased] the psychological separation between work groups . . . by distinctions of status, . . . and, finally, the miners found the fractionation of their jobs distasteful. . . .

A Comparison of Two Different Social Systems for Dealing with the Same Technical Problems of Production: The Conventional Longwall versus the Composite Longwall System

The Tavistock researchers found that not all pits had moved to the conventional longwall method with its job specialization and machine theory applications. Especially in pits in which coal was found in short faces, the traditions of the single-place system had sometimes been carried over into the new technological system, with its new face conveyors and its new cutters. A systematic comparison was therefore possible between two pits, one of which had taken over the conventional longwall method and the other of which had adapted the composite method of the older system to the new technology. . . . The major difference between the composite system in the single working place and in longwall mining was that in the former system there was complete rotation of tasks, while in the latter not all men were necessarily rotated through all the specialized tasks required by the new machines. There was still, however, variety in the work in that all men were rotated through a number of different jobs.

The composite work method applied to longwall mining thus restored the continuity of task effort so lacking in the conventional system. In the composite system little external coordination of activity is required because the men move naturally from one task to the next as part of the requirements of their overall role. There is no lag between phases and no group conflict over the difficulties created by one group for the succeeding group.

The cohesiveness of the composite group stems from several sources. The group selects its own members, . . . assumes responsibility both for the overall task and for the allocation of members to the various jobs, . . . [and] the method of payment recognizes and increases the interdependence of the group members because monetary rewards are tied directly to . . . performance. . . .

The observations of the Tavistock researchers on the functioning of the two longwall systems and their theoretical analysis of the superiority of the composite system were put to test by a factual comparison of the two systems in operation. . . . One measure of the effectiveness of group functioning is the rate of absenteeism, both voluntary and involuntary. Absence rates usually are not sensitive measures, because the total rate of absenteeism under normal industrial conditions tends to be very low. Yet the differences between the conventional and the composite systems are striking; total absence rates in the conventional panel are two and a half times as great as in composite panels, and voluntary absence is ten times as great. . . .

The productivity measures also implied clearly the superiority of the composite to the conventional method. Production was much more regular in the composite system. . . .

Rice's Studies of Indian Textile Mills

The impact of a behavioral science approach, with its emphasis upon adequate theory and hardheaded experimental findings, should not be discounted. An inroad was made in the British mining industry, and the follow-up studies of Rice (1958), another Tavistock researcher, in the calico mills of India attest to the validity of their conceptualization of a productive organization as a sociotechnical system in which the subsystems must be articulated for effective group performance. Rice's action research was conducted in a single company with two textile mills in Ahmedabad, employing some eight thousand workers. . . . The general objective of the project was to help in the solution of social and psychological problems arising from changes in methods of work and managerial practice.

The first major problem of the research team had to do with the failure of the introduction of automatic looms to improve productivity. Though the morale of workers appeared good, and the supervisors and workers seemed to get along well, neither the quantity nor the quality of cloth was higher than that woven on the old nonautomatic looms. Observation of the work process revealed that twelve different occupational roles had been assigned individual workers to assure continuous operation of the looms. Workers had been assigned to these different specialized operations in accordance with American and British standards for machine production. . . .

With the exception of the jobbers and assistant jobbers who did comprise a group, the twenty-nine workers constituted an aggregate of individuals with a confused pattern of interrelationships. Though the three smash hands served the eight weavers, the priorities of the eight weavers for their services had not been clearly established. Similar ambiguities in relationships existed among the other types of workers. Moreover, the task demands varied in that the thickness of the yarn for the different types of cloth changed the work load differentially for the various types of workers. . . . No rigid specifications could therefore be set down for the timing of the interdependent activities of the workers; nor did the technical system with its job fractionation and individual role responsibility encourage any internal group structure making for cooperation. Moreover, there was no psychological reward in the accomplishment of a whole task, either by the individual alone or by his participation in the group.

If productivity was to be raised to take advantage of the new automatic looms, management faced two alternative courses of action. One was to retain the present technical system and to police it with more supervisors. The other was to reorganize the sociotechnical system to provide internal group structure related to task accomplishment. The first alternative would add to personnel costs and would risk resistance by the workers to more external controls. "The workers would not only continue to experience the discomfort of their unstructured confusion but would feel further coerced and policed."

The researchers, therefore, proposed to management, after further study of the problem, a reorganization by which a group of workers would be responsible for a group of looms, with some sharing of the previously fractioned job assignments and with an overall group leader. Management accepted the proposal and planned to introduce it in one section of the weaving shed through a series of group meetings and discussions with successive levels of supervision and, finally, with workers. There was such spontaneous acceptance of the plan, however, that the supervisors and workers immediately took over the scheme and proceeded to implement it. Through a process of mutual choice, the workers formed four groups of seven men each, four in the weaving subgroup and three in the gating and maintenance subgroup. Moreover, they agreed to take over the ancillary services previously allocated to workers performing only a particular service.

By and large the history of the effects of the experimental plan is an amazing success story. This does not mean that all problems were automatically solved, that quantity and quality of production continuously soared, and that no new problems confronted management or workers. . . . The ups and downs in quantity and quality indicate that difficulties did arise in the new system and that they were resolved successfully by an alert management working with employees motivated to maintain the new system. . . .

The success of the experimental program led to its extension to the entire weaving shed, a change which the workers under the old system themselves pressed for. The motivational lift of the new system was palpable to any observer in its initial stages. . . . In spite of the great difference in culture between India and Western societies, the same psychological findings in worker motivation are apparent. When people have a meaningful task and have membership in a satisfactory primary work group organized meaningfully for task accomplishment, they work harder and are more satisfied with their work. . . .

Change and Stability

Though organizations are always in some degree of flux and rarely, if ever, attain a perfect state of equilibrium, major changes are the exception rather than the rule. They can be attributed to two sources: (1) changed inputs from the environment including the organizational supersystem, and (2) internal system strain or imbalance.

Changed Inputs

Changes in information or energic input into the organization are of two types. The first, new or modified production imports, has to do with modifications of quantity or quality in the inflow of materials and messages. These changes may be due directly to environmental changes, such as the discovery of new resources and the depletion of old ones, or to changes in the transactional process through which the organizational output provides energic return and reinforcement. The saturation of a market with a given type of product is a case in point; it demands a search for new markets, a change in product, or a revival of demand. Changes in input may also come from the supersystem which legitimizes various aspects of organizational functioning, as when new laws are enacted affecting taxes, labor relations, or restrictive trade agreements.

A second type of change has to do with maintenance inputs, which represent the values and motivations of the organizational members. In general, this type of change is evolutionary. For example, in the United States the growth in intensity and extensity of the democratic ethic has slowly affected the character and expectations of the American people. When they assume their organizational roles today in industry, in government, or in school, they expect, and, if necessary, demand, more democratic rights and privileges than most people asked or aspired to a hundred years ago. Such changes in maintenance inputs can be facilitated by outside systems, as labor unions have facilitated democratic developments within industry. Slower, more evolutionary changes in norms and values may go unnoticed until they accumulate at some critical point or threshold area and are consolidated around some precipitating event.

Internal Strain and Imbalance

Organizations function by means of adjustments and compromises among competitive and even conflicting elements in their structure and membership. These diverse elements produce system strain of two kinds: (1) the competition between different functional subsystems, or horizontal strain, and (2) vertical strain, the conflict between various levels in the hierarchy of power, privilege, and reward. . . . Thus, the research and development people, with the task of innovation and adaptation, may want to move the entire organization in a different direction than seems reasonable to people in the production subsystems. Or two divisions of a single subsystem—two departments in a university, for example—may be in competition for the same resources. Each represents to the dean the greater importance of its particular program.

In addition to conflicts engendered by differences in function, subsystems may be in conflict because of their differential rates of growth. One subsystem may for a variety of reasons show a very rapid rate of growth. It becomes a leading subsystem and other subsystems move to adjust to it, either by following its pattern or attempting to check its development. The interdependence of all units in producing a stable overall system means that no one subsystem can move very far out of line without evoking strain. Other subsystems catch up by acquiring more momentum, or the leading subsystem is checked in its expansion, or the entire organization undergoes some degree of restructuring to find a new equilibrium.

For example, suppose that the professional and technical schools of a university accept large increases in enrollment while the liberal arts college attempts to hold constant the number of new students accepted. The liberal arts college now finds its stable position threatened by the demands of the other schools of the university for more space and more resources. Moreover, service teaching of the college for other schools increases relative to its use of resources for its own students, since it must admit to its classes all qualified students in the larger university of which it is a part.

Hierarchical or Vertical Conflict. Every organization requires some communality of goals which transcends the differential loyalties of subunits and binds the organization together. Such communality is difficult to achieve, particularly when there are large differentials in rewards and power between hierarchical ranks. The conflict evoked by such distinctions is made sharper if the different levels in the organization are defined more in terms of ascribed than achieved status. If the worker on the floor of the factory can never move up the rungs of the hierarchical ladder because of his limited education, he and his fellow workers have a common set of interests not identical with those occupying the officer positions or those eligible for them. This source of strain takes on greater significance in a democracy than a tradition-oriented society since the values of the democratic society emphasize equality of opportunity.

It is our thesis, however, that these sources of internal strain are not the most potent causes of organizational change. The set of conditions which we have called changed inputs from without are the critical factors in the significant modification of organizations. Often the changes from without interact with internal strains to promote organizational revolution. The Marxian theory that change arises from basic internal contradictions that become aggravated as the system develops seems to us disproved by the facts of history. Systems develop many mechanisms for handling internal conflict. Though they change in this process, the change is slow and generally does not alter the basic character of the system. The highly developed capitalistic countries in which internal contradictions were to have led to revolution, according to Marx, have been able to compromise their internal conflicts and maintain their essential systemic character. On the other hand, the countries which have experienced revolutions are those which suffered changed inputs. The blows of World War I destroyed the social structure of czarist Russia and only then were the revolutionists able to come to power. Similarly the Chinese regime of Chiang Kai-shek was weakened by years of assault from without before it was overcome by internal revolution. The overthrow of the ancient Manchu dynasty in the earlier years of this century illustrates the same pattern of decisive external defeat as the predecessor of internal revolution.

The basic hypothesis is that organizations and other social structures are open systems which attain stability through their authority structures, reward mechanisms, and value systems, and which are changed primarily from without by means of some significant change in input. Some organizations, less open than most, may resist new inputs indefinitely and may perish rather than change. We would predict, however, that, in the absence of external changes, organizations are likely to be reformed from within in limited ways. More drastic or revolutionary changes are initiated or made possible by external forces.

A large-scale business organization set up along hierarchical lines and pursuing a policy of profit maximization will not become a producers' cooperative or some other kind of democratic collectivity unless it collides with important environmental obstacles and is subjected to new inputs. A trade union with protective policies for its own members, including discriminatory hiring practices and restrictive apprentice training, becomes more open and democratic primarily as it meets obstacles to its way of operating in the larger society. A university is transformed from a teaching institution into a research-teaching complex primarily because outside funds are made available for the research function.

Two qualifications to our emphasis on external events remain to be made. First, we recognize that every organization, as a unit in a supersystem, not only is influenced by events in that supersystem but also contributes to those events. We have, for example, spoken of the ways in which American industry has been influenced by the spread of democratic doctrine and values in the larger culture. It is no less true that life within the organization feeds into that culture as members of the organization move back and forth across the organizational boundary. The contribution of any single organization may be impossible to trace, but the relation of the organization to the outside world is nevertheless a two-way transaction.

The second qualification has to do with the cumulative effects of small internal changes. Until we have evidence from longitudinal studies of a more ambitious kind than have yet been attempted, the profundity of such cumulative changes in organizations remains a subject of speculation. It seems a logical possibility that a succession of such internally generated changes might in time produce organizational transformations of great depth without the advent of external forces. Our reading of organizational history nevertheless argues the primary role of external forces in major organizational change.

Summary

The study and the accomplishment of organizational change has been handicapped by the tendency to disregard systemic properties of organizations and to confuse individual change with change in organizational variables. More specifically, scientists and practitioners have assumed too often that an individual change will produce a corresponding organizational change. This assumption seems to us indefensible. To clarify the issue, this chapter [has analyzed] seven approaches to organizational change and [considered] their characteristic strengths and weaknesses.

Information—The supplying of additional cognitive input has real but limited value as a way of creating organizational change. It can support other methods, give the rationale for proposed changes, and explain what will be expected of individuals. It is not, however, a source of motivation; other methods are required to provide the necessary motive force to change. Moreover, the target of information is necessarily the individual and not the organization.

Individual counseling and therapy—These methods represent attempts, in part successful, to avoid the limitations of mere information giving and to bring about individual change at a deeper level. It is true that the production of new insight can lead to deeper and more enduring changes in attitudes, and therefore to tendencies toward altered behavior. The target of such attempts is still the individual, however, and the translation of his new insights to organizational change is left wholly to him.

Influence of the peer group—A third, and in many ways a more potent, approach to organizational change is through the influence of the peer group. It is based on the undeniable fact that peers do constitute strong influences on individual behavior, and that a process of change successfully initiated in a peer group may become self-energizing and self-reinforcing. A dilemma is encountered, however, in trying to maximize the relevance of the peer group approach to organizational change. If the peer group consists of strangers without a common organizational affiliation, they face the same problems of transferring their insights and individual changes that we have already noted for individual approaches. If, on the other hand, the peer group is taken intact from the organization, it is likely to be inhibited in its change efforts by the role and authority structure which characterize it in the organizational setting.

Sensitivity training—This technique is essentially an ingenious extension of the peer-group approach to individual and organizational change. The primary target of change remains the individual, although recent variations of this training technique deal specifically with the problem of adapting individual change to the organizational context.

Group therapy in organizations—This approach is best illustrated by the work of Jaques, and some of his colleagues in the Tavistock Institute. It has shown significant results and represents an original and important fusion of individual therapy and the social psychology of organizations. Its most serious limitation is the assumption that organizational conflicts are primarily the expression of individual characteristics and neuroses, for the most part unrecognized by the individual.

Feedback—This approach to organizational change developed out of the attempt to make survey research results more usable by management. It has evolved into a well-defined procedure which relies on discussion of relevant findings by organizational families, each consisting of a supervisor and his immediate subordinates. The organization-wide use of feedback begins with the president and his executive vice-presidents, and works through the hierarchy of organizational families in order. The targets of this demonstrably effective technique are personal and role relations within the organizational family.

Systemic change—In our view this is the most powerful approach to changing human organizations. It requires the direct manipulation of organizational variables. One example of this approach is the work of Morse and Reimer, in which the target of change was the hierarchical distribution of decision-making power in a large clerical organization. Other examples are provided in the work of Trist and Rice, in mining and textile industries, respectively. The target of change in their work is the goodness of fit between the social and the technical systems which comprise the organization.

The concluding sections of this chapter dealt with the broad issue of change and stability in organizations, and considered the relative significance of inputs from the environment and internal strains as sources of organizational change. The argument is made that changed inputs of various kinds are the most important sources of organizational change.

References

Allport, G. W. (1945). "Catharsis and the Reduction of Prejudice." *Journal of Social Issues*, 1:1-8.

―――(1954). *The Nature of Prejudice*. Cambridge, Mass.: Addison-Wesley.

Argyris, C. (1964). *Integrating the Individual and the Organization*. New York: Wiley.

Blake, R. R., and Mouton, Jane S. (1964). *The Managerial Grid*. Houston, Texas: Gulf.

Bradford, L., Gibb, J., and Benne, K., eds. (1964). *T-group Theory and Laboratory Method: Innovation in Re-education*. New York: Wiley.

Emery, F. E., and Trist, E. L. (1960). "Socio-technical Systems," in *Management Sciences Models and Techniques*, Volume II. London: Pergamon Press.

Hoffman, L. R., Harburg, E., and Maier, N. R. F. (1962). "Differences and Disagreements as Factors in Creative Group Problem-solving." *Journal of Abnormal and Social Psychology*, 64:206-214.

Jaques, E. (1951). *The Changing Culture of a Factory*. London: Tavistock Publications.

Kahn, R. L., and Boulding, Elise, eds. (1964). *Power and Conflict in Organizations*. New York: Basic Books.

Katz, D., Sarnoff, I., and McClintock, C. (1956). "Ego-defense and Attitude Change." *Human Relations*, 9:27-45.

Levine, J., and Butler, J. (1952). "Lecture vs. Group Decision in Changing Behavior." *Journal of Applied Psychology*, 36:29-33.

Lewin, K. (1947). "Frontiers in Group Dynamics." *Human Relations*, 1:5-41.

―――(1952). "Group Decision and Social Change," in G. E. Swanson, T. M. Newcomb, and E. L. Hartley, eds., *Readings in Social Psychology*, rev. ed. New York: Holt, pp. 459-473.

Likert, R. (1956). *Developing Patterns of Management*, Volume II. General Management Series, No. 182. New York: American Management Association, pp. 3-29.

Lippitt, R., Watson, J., and Westley, B. (1958). *The Dynamics of Planned Change*. New York: Harcourt, Brace.

Maier, N. R. F. (1950). "The Quality of Group Decisions as Influenced by the Discussion Leader." *Human Relations,* 3:155-174.

——— (1952). *Principles of Human Relations.* New York: Wiley.

——— (1953). "An Experimental Test of the Effect of Training on Discussion Leadership." *Human Relations,* 6:161-173.

———, and Hoffman, L. R. (1961). "Overcoming Superior-Subordinate Communication Problems in Management," in N. R. F. Maier, L. R. Hoffman, J. G. Hooven, and W. H. Read, eds., *Supervisor-Subordinate Communication in Management.* Research Study, No. 52. New York: American Management Association.

Mann, F. C. (1957). "Studying and Creating Change: A Means to Understanding Social Organization," in *Research in Industrial Human Relations.* Industrial Relations Research Association, No. 17. Madison, Wisc.: the association, pp. 146-167.

Mayo, E. (1933). *The Human Problems of an Industrial Civilization.* New York: Macmillan.

Morse, Nancy, and Reimer, E. (1955). Mimeographed report on organizational change, Survey Research Center, University of Michigan.

———, and Reimer, E. (1956). "The Experimental Change of a Major Organizational Variable." *Journal of Abnormal and Social Psychology,* 52:120-129.

Pelz, D. C. (1956). "Some Social Factors Related to Performance in a Research Organization." *Administrative Science Quarterly,* 1:310-325.

Rice, A. K. (1958). *Productivity and Social Organization: The Ahmedabad Experiment.* London: Tavistock Publications.

Schein, E. H., and Bennis, W. G. (1965). *Personal and Organizational Change through Group Methods.* New York: Wiley.

Seashore, S. E. (1954). *Group Cohesiveness in the Industrial Work Group.* Ann Arbor, Mich.: Institute for Social Research.

Trist, E. L., and Bamforth, K. W. (1951). "Some Social and Psychological Consequences of the Long-wall Method of Coal-getting." *Human Relations,* 4:3-38.

———, Higgin, G. W., Murray, H., and Pollock, A. B. (1963). *Organizational Choice.* London: Tavistock Publications.

Goals and Sagas

3 Organizational Influences on Innovative Roles

Sam D. Sieber

The paucity of research in the field of education diffusion and innovation renders anything we might say on the subject highly speculative. It is true that a large literature on diffusion exists in scientific and technical fields, such as agriculture, medicine, the behavioral sciences, and industry (Paisley, 1965; Rogers, 1962). But the findings of these fields have limited application to education, for reasons that we shall presently discuss. Further, the studies conducted under the inspiration of Mort at Teachers College (Ross, 1958), comprising the bulk of diffusion research on education, tell us little about specific processes of innovation and hindrances to change. And there are indications that even the findings about diffusion rates that were produced by this tradition have been outdated by recent acceleration in the production and distribution of educational ideas. Such factors as the Cold War and the National Defense Education Act, the explosion of knowledge and expansion of the knowledge industry, community pressures for greater efficiency in education fostered by the baby boom, building shortages and higher tax rates, and changing occupational patterns have created great ferment in education (Miller, 1967). These trends have pressed for faster adoption of new ideas

Reprinted from *Knowledge Production and Utilization in Educational Administration*, edited by Terry L. Eidell and Joanne M. Kitchel (Eugene, Ore.: University Council for Educational Administration and Center for the Advanced Study of Educational Administration, University of Oregon, 1968), pp. 120-142.

and practices, and the new R&D structures have provided facilitative mechanisms (Sieber, 1967). Under the circumstances, it seems likely that the historical lag between invention and adoption has been substantially reduced.

Several authorities have even claimed that a new problem has emerged in many schools—the problem of too hasty adoption. Grobman, a participant in the Biological Sciences Curriculum Study, has stated:

> ... some of the curriculum ideas have had more of an impact than I would have liked to see, since I think there has been over-hasty adoption in a "bandwagon" or desperation attitude of many curriculum innovations, in contrast to the generation it has taken to bring about change in the past. At the moment, it seems to me quite clear that innovation is having an impact, and the pressing problem is how do we direct the impact and how do we assess it? [Wiles, 1965, page 2].

The chaotic character of educational change today has been abetted by crisis-oriented legislation at local and federal levels. Despite the fact that most professional educators, owing to their own crisis orientation, warmly endorse this trend, the outcome is a myriad of educational fads whose sole virtue is often political. The best ideas and practices are easily lost in the stampede.

And yet, who is carrying out research on the causes and effects of overdiffusion and of uncritical adoption, or on the best means of "directing the impact" on a national scale? Or, for that matter, who is even attempting to describe the national network of diffusion in a systematic, empirical fashion? The strategy and findings of Mort's research seem oddly irrelevant in our new era of educational change. One would prefer to ask the professors who recommended the "best practices" that were included in Mort's Adaptability Scale how they arrived at their judgments, rather than to appraise the up-to-dateness of an educational program by the number of such innovations claimed by the school. In these times, the latter strategy might be better suited to appraising the amount of faddism in many schools.

Inasmuch as the research on educational diffusion and development has fallen behind the times, the best that can be done at this stage is to offer a set of perspectives based on heuristic assumptions of fact in the pious hope of stimulating research.

Distinctive Features of the Educational System as Starting Points for Research

There are four aspects of our public educational system that ought to be given more attention in seeking to understand processes and outcomes of change and which, when taken together, distinguish education from the social systems of medical practice, industry, and agriculture.[1] Because of these distinctions, the applicability of diffusion research in these fields to educational structures is severely limited. These aspects are the following: vulnerability to the social environment; the professional self-image and associated values of educational personnel; the diffuseness of educational goals; and the need for coordination and control of the primary clientele as well as of the employees of the system. We view education, then, as a *vulnerable formal organization with diffuse goals, whose functionnaries are quasi professionals, and which is devoted to processing people within its boundaries.* The implications of these features for diffusion and innovation are tremendous, but seem to be scarcely recognized by either researchers or practitioners.

In the discussion that follows, I will first indicate how these aspects of the system affect innovation, then note the inadequacy of current strategies of change which overlook these features. Finally, I will briefly suggest how these same aspects might be exploited by means of an alternative strategy.

Vulnerability

The vulnerability of an organization refers to the extent to which the organization is subject to powerful influences stemming from its environment irrespective of the goals and resources of the organization. A formal definition of vulnerability, therefore, might be: *the probability of being subjected to pressures that are incompatible with one's goals without the capacity to resist.* If external pressures were wholly compatible with the goals of the system and resources were adequate to attain these goals, the system would be in perfect harmony with its environment. Vulnerability, in the sense of exposure to untoward influence, would not be an issue. A high degree of vulnerability, therefore, can be detected in three characteristics of the organization: (1) subjugation to the environment, (2) discrepancy between the demands of the environment and the goals of the organization, and (3) inadequate resources for achievement of organizational goals. Since "subjugation to the environment" is obvious in

---

1. We owe a greater debt to three writers on this subject than can be signified in specific references in footnotes. They are: Bidwell (1965), Miles (1965), and Wayland (1964, 1967). We are also indebted to the participants in the UCEA Seminar, in a faculty seminar on educational systems, Columbia University, and in a graduate training seminar, Columbia University, for helpful comments on an earlier version of the paper.

the case of American educational organizations, at least with regard to nominal-legal control, we will pay more attention here to the other two conditions of vulnerability.

Owing to periodic maladjustments between external demands and organizational outcomes, most organizations are occasionally subject to environmental pressures that conflict with organizational goals. The educational system, however, is especially prone to such maladjustments. This tendency arises from trying to fulfill the distinctive functions of education in a rapidly changing social order—the functions of socializing and training recruits in fundamental ways, and of allocating them to adult roles. The socialization-training function is made problematic by the accelerated expansion of knowledge and skills required by the society and by major shifts in value systems, which trends produce a recurring lag between the output of the educational enterprise and the potential, available inputs (new knowledge, skills, and values). The fulfillment of the allocation function is frustrated by changes in occupational patterns, and by increasing urbanization and leisure time. For these reasons, transformations in both the structure of adult roles, and in the knowledge and skills required to fill both old and new roles, place great strain on the educational system. It is small wonder, then, that education is frequently accused of "falling behind the times."

Evidence of goal conflict between school and community is afforded by a recent study conducted by the Bureau of Applied Social Research. This study shows that most parents do not share the educational goals of their children's teachers. In a study of mothers from all types of backgrounds and communities, it was found that 56 percent espoused a goal for the local school that was different from the goal expressed by the teacher of their children.[2]

The ability of an organization to mobilize resources for the attainment of its goals also affects vulnerability. For without the needed resources, the organization loses the initiative for directed change in conformity with its objectives, and must rely more heavily upon conditional handouts from the environment. (Earmarked funds from the federal government typify what we have in mind when we refer to a conditional handout.) We therefore need to examine the resource level of the system in assessing its vulnerability.

The increasing democratization of education, reflected in desegregation, emphasis on comprehensive schools, and reduction in the high school dropout rate, means that the system is obliged to deal

---

2. From a . . . project report by David E. Wilder *et al.*

with a growing percentage of the school age population from increasingly diversified backgrounds. Between 1947 and 1964, the proportion of sixteen and seventeen year olds who were enrolled in public schools jumped from 68 percent to 88 percent (U.S. Dept. of HEW, 1965). Add to this trend the large-scale shifts in population and the continued reliance upon an outmoded financial structure (Conant, 1967), and it becomes apparent that the educational system is suffering from internal problems of mobilizing resources at the same time that it is confronted with urgent new demands from society at large. Moreover, because education is both highly bureaucratized and decentralized, it is difficult to adjust the machinery to new demands fast enough to satisfy their proponents. Education of the disadvantaged has been a national theme for several years, for example, but there are still virtually no teacher-training institutions with special programs for teachers who plan to work in lower-class neighborhoods.

The consequences of vulnerability to local pressures should not be overstated because school personnel are sometimes adept in manipulating public opinion and in evading scrutiny and the parents' anticipation of being "cooled out" may often discourage them from complaining. But local publics are not the only sources of pressure and influence. Wayland (1964) has stressed the existence of a national system of agencies concerned with education, or ancillary structures, that frequently dominate decisions at the local level. Teacher-training institutions, professional associations, accreditation associations, examination systems, textbook publishers, federal and state agencies, and, by no means least, colleges and technical schools which set requirements are all members of a national network of communication and power, and their influence reaches into every local district. In most communities this national system reduces local formal control of education to a mere shadow of its ideological intent.

In sum, the gap between social demands and the activities and outputs of the system is substantial, and it has been enlarged in recent years due to several factors. Consequently, the goals and accomplishments of the educational system have failed to gibe with the expectations held by powerful sectors of the environment, and these sectors have therefore redoubled their efforts to dictate school practices, or at the very least to press the schools to display tokens of progress. The end result is that schools have found it increasingly difficult to seize the initiative for innovation.

The vulnerability of school systems holds several specific implications for innovation. First, changes in practice that run the risk of disturbing the local community are eschewed. This response is quite evident in the instance of school board members. Gallup (1966) asked a national sample of school board trustees to estimate how much difficulty would be entailed in introducing thirteen selected practices into their schools. The four practices most often regarded as "very difficult" were innovations that threatened the values or life styles of the community: (1) the use of pass or fail grades to reduce classroom competition, a practice which would run counter to the ideology of competition as a mainspring of effort, would make it difficult for graduates to get into college, and would fail to inform parents of their children's progress; (2) the reduction of summer vacation to four weeks, which would interfere with the vacationing habits of parents; (3) a nationally standardized high school test for seniors, which would raise the specter of formal, national control over local standards and practices; and (4) an extension of the school day by one hour, which would be costly and would reduce the amount of time available for extracurricular activities, especially athletics. The wisdom of imputing fear of community reactions to the board members is borne out by the fact that these four innovations were precisely those most often considered "a poor idea" by the parents in the same communities as the board members in Gallup's survey.

A second consequence of vulnerability is that innovations are adopted which are promoted by local publics. Indeed, political feasibility often carries greater weight than does educational value in determining the adoption of certain innovations. The new practices imported into schools tend to be nondisruptive, or watered down versions of major innovations, or outright services to the community.[3] The strategy of adopting such practices has the effect of neutralizing elements in the community that favor radical change by offering tokens of progress.

Further, innovations that are persuasively publicized across the nation become candidates for adoption, regardless of their educational significance. Wiles (1965) cites the example of new mathematics programs:

3. Evidence of the differential response to a practice that *threatens* the community versus a practice that *serves* the community is afforded by Allen. Comparison of the diffusion rates of driver training (a service) with the idea of pupils studying the community (a threat) showed that driver training was adopted by 90 percent of the schools in eighteen years, while community study required sixty years to reach this level of adoption (Allen, 1956; cited in Rogers, 1962, p. 41).

The power of the mass media in this respect was illustrated last year (1963) by the demand placed on school boards and school personnel for new mathematics programs after *Look* magazine had carried a feature story on the new mathematics.

The phenomenal increase in enrollment in new mathematics courses after Sputnik (an increase of 595 percent between 1948-49 and 1962-63) was widely sustained by public opinion.

Although we might be inclined to applaud the adoption of the new mathematics, the same pressures apply to a range of more controversial practices, and, in the climate of educational criticism that prevails today, it is not uncommon for practices to be urged upon the school irrespective of the needs of the district. Illustrative of irrelevant pressures for innovation are the results of a content analysis of the published platforms of ten candidates for a school board in a relatively well-educated suburban district (Kerr, 1964). Out of a total of fifteen specific education practices recommended by the candidates (omitting financial matters), twelve were already in operation in the system. Moreover, the candidates failed to mention a host of innovations that the schools had not adopted. These omissions, and the irrelevance of the stated recommendations, suggest that the candidates' ideas were gleaned randomly from popular literature. The irrelevance of the candidates' recommendations was by no means apparent to the voting public, who seemed to be only a little worse informed about the schools than the candidates.

When publicity for an innovation is translated into legislation, questionable practices may be locked into school systems for several years with little hope for honest assessment. Thus, Cronbach (1966) has pointed out:

There is no evidence to justify . . . the California legislation that requires instruction in foreign language in grades six to eight; the assumptions used to justify the requirements are untested and, with the law now a fait accompli, no one is about to test them. The energies of the people who might be giving thoughtful attention to language instruction are diverted into a crash program to write curriculum materials and train teachers [page 7].

The vulnerability of the system might also affect internal relationships in a fashion that reduces serious educational experimentation. An organization that is subject to control by a local constituency, and whose activities are potentially visible (by virtue of the fact that its clientele moves in and out of the system every day), requires a high degree of consensus on goals and procedures in order to present a united front. Lacking such consensus, the organization's leaders must insist on a certain measure of secrecy. These conditions might promote dominative relationships between administrators and teachers, and also strong informal control among teachers, that might tend to countervail the exercise of professional discretion. Thus, radical departures from typical classroom practices are subtly discouraged lest parents make invidious comparisons with other staff members. The same kind of restraint probably acts upon principals and, perhaps, even upon higher administrative personnel.[4] In short, caution may be generated within the school apart from anticipation of either support or condemnation by the community. Efforts that are exerted beyond the call of duty by an individual practitioner might be viewed with apprehension because they threaten to raise community expectations for other staff members. Restriction of productivity on the part of industrial workers due to vulnerability to shifting standards of performance has been an object of study for almost 40 years. Presumably the assumption that teaching is a "profession" has prevented us from examining teachers in the same light.

Vulnerability to national ancillary structures also has its consequences for innovative roles. As serious as the problem of resistance to certain new practices undoubtedly is, from the standpoint of many schools an equally serious problem is excessive diffusion. Hearing as much as we do about the urgent need for dissemination of new ideas and practices, one would think that there were no professional journals, mass periodicals, newsletters, syllabi, in-service courses, consultants, accreditation teams, textbooks, curriculum committees, publishers' representatives, conferences, summer course work, or new teachers entering the system fresh from education courses. Many of our schools that are swamped with innovative ideas might consequently find it difficult to discriminate among them. Considerable disagreement among staff members regarding the allocation of resources to different innovations might be a further consequence. In many schools, excessive diffusion might produce a constant dither over the best means of keeping up to date, leading to the tryout of one fad after another. Finally, it would be interesting to know whether this climate of competing interests and information sources produces a debilitating ambivalence, or even cynicism, as is sometimes claimed; and, further, whether these circumstances reinforce the importance of local political feasibility as an adoption criterion.

---

4. It seems clear, for example, that the resistance of school superintendents to national testing programs stems from apprehension over the public's penchant for invidious comparison among districts.

The research on these questions remains to be done, but it is clear that the vulnerability of educational organizations is a factor that needs to be taken into account in planning for innovation.

Quasi Professionalism

A second major aspect of educational systems is the self-image of professionalism held by school personnel. Members of occupations that are commonly regarded as "professions" are characterized by three features: (1) they perform a personal service that is regarded as indispensable in modern society; (2) they possess a high degree of technical competence; and (3) they enjoy considerable autonomy in their work. It cannot be denied that teachers are performing an indispensable personal service, but there is substantial doubt that they exhibit the remaining features of professionalism. With respect to autonomy, Brickell (1961) has described working conditions as follows:

> ... the teacher is not an independent professional, not a private entrepreneur free to alter his working situation when he chooses—not free to decide what he will teach to whom at what time and at what price. He is instead a member of the staff of a stable institution [page 19].

There are also certain attributes of the teaching force that distinguish the occupation from recognized professional groups. The overwhelming proportion are women; they are heavily recruited from the middle and lower-middle classes; the lower half of the ability continuum falls far below the average for other professions; only about half of secondary school teachers and one-quarter of elementary teachers have any training beyond college; salaries have failed to compete favorably with salary ranges in occupations requiring equivalent levels of preparation; teaching stands at the bottom of the professions in prestige; and occupational commitment is extremely low, as revealed by the fact that most teachers do not expect to remain in teaching until retirement, and only a small proportion of those who receive teacher training remain in the occupation longer than ten years (Jessup, 1967). For all these reasons, teaching is not a profession in the sense that we understand law and medicine to be professions. It appears, nevertheless, that teachers adopt the full-fledged professions as their reference groups. (This might be due to their identification with college professors and the upward mobility aspirations of lower middle class members.) The institutionalized gap between occupational reality and the aspirations of teachers is characteristic of "quasi professions."[5]

In the first place, the quasi-professional status of teaching induces apprehension toward actions that are designed to improve performance because it is feared that such actions will increase the discrepancy between real status and level of aspiration. In effect, quasi-professionalism produces status-insecurity. Thus, innovations that are proposed by the administration are often resisted by teachers because they imply further restrictions on "professional" autonomy. Even expert consultants from outside the district are sometimes rejected because they threaten the teacher's insecure self-image as an "expert" in his own domain. Teachers, who are anxious to preserve the modicum of authority, expertise, and social standing that they possess, might reject administrative efforts despite the possibility of their better serving educational needs.

Similar treatment might be accorded the innovative ideas of laymen. The situation regarding laymen might be more stressful for teachers than for other quasi professionals because of the vulnerability of the organization. Thus, because parents have legitimate control over the organization they do not hesitate to propose changes in the school. No doubt teachers have developed a repertoire of "cooling out" techniques for dealing with laymen; by such means, worthwhile ideas for improving the instructional program might be rejected by teachers simply because they issue from laymen.

Status insecurity in organizations has also been observed to cause "ritualism" or overcompliance with means to the neglect of ends. The teacher who dismisses his class for independent study, . . . withholds a grade until a slow student has had a chance to master the material, or deviates widely from an approved lesson plan is risking a reprimand that he can ill afford in his insecure position. So teachers tend to overcomply with regulations, even when innovative behavior is nominally condoned or when the educational goal is clearly better served by "irregular" behavior. Ritualism might undermine the purpose of a new, demonstrably worthwhile innovation since it is always possible to comply too rigidly with even the best procedures. If discretion is never exercised, it is doubtful that any classroom innovation will work effectively.

5. We prefer this term to the more common usage of "semiprofession" because the latter suggests an exact quantitative measurement, when in fact quasi professions vary considerably in their approximation to full-fledged professions. Also, the adjective "quasi" contains a subjective element, in the sense of "resemblance" to full-fledged professions, that is missing in the prefix "semi."

The insecure professional self-image of teachers might also account for a notable tendency among teachers to avoid informal communication on matters of teaching and learning. My own observation of faculty rooms over a period of a year suggests that informal discussion of classroom practices is minimal. Further evidence comes from a survey in which teachers were asked to nominate practices they knew about that might contribute to the mental health condition of pupils (Lippitt, 1965). Out of a total of 330 practices that were mentioned, only 30 were indicative of knowledge of what other teachers were doing—the overwhelming majority were practices that the teachers themselves were following. The researcher concluded, "People usually do not know what other people are doing within their school buildings." Concealment by quasi-professionals of an inadequate base of knowledge and a limited set of skills might be necessary to permit them to preserve their professional identity. Such behavior might be especially appropriate when it becomes a matter of revealing classroom difficulties to other teachers. Advice might be least often sought, therefore, on precisely those problems that are most critical.

Still another possible consequence of status insecurity is that energies which might be devoted to educational experimentation are channeled into status enhancement activities, especially through participation in the local teachers' association or union. Corwin (1965) has shown that the more professionally oriented teachers are more likely to exhibit militancy. My own field observations of the behavior of teachers during a period of incipient unionization demonstrates that instructional responsibilities are readily displaced by involvement in organizational protest.

The rejection of bureaucratic incentives for greater effort is another consequence of quasi professionalism that bears on innovative roles. Professional self-esteem rests upon two bases: unstinting service to the individual needs of clients (which depends upon a large measure of privatized discretion), and recognition among colleagues. But formal incentive systems related to performance rest upon observable behavior, and such incentive systems shift control from colleagues to administrators. In other words, incentive systems violate two of the core values of professionalism. Thus, local merit plans are opposed as at once undermining collegial authority and violating the privileged nature of the professional-client relationship.

A final consequence of quasi professionalism requires examination. Because the claim to professional status rests most securely on the service-orientation of teaching, this aspect of the teaching role might receive disproportionate emphasis, either because of selective recruitment of people-oriented individuals to the occupation, or because of compensation by those already in the occupation. Research tends to indicate that the teacher-pupil relationship is the most important source of occupational gratification for most teachers. Neither expertise (teaching skills and knowledge of subject-matter) nor independence from supervision can compete with service to clients as a source of satisfaction. One effect might be that teachers are "captured" by their clientele, especially through contacts in extracurricular activities. Gordon (1957) has shown, for example, that contacts in extracurricular activities make it easier for students to manipulate the classroom behavior of teachers with respect to grading.

Further, since students are involuntary participants in the organization, emphasis on the affective-particularistic aspect of the relationship with students affords an alternative to technical expertise as a means of controlling and motivating students. And this emphasis also serves to legitimate the demand for greater discretion and autonomy. Because it is presumed that many students are unique and must be dealt with on their own terms, and that every classroom is different from every other classroom, it becomes bootless to suggest innovations that were developed for other students in other classrooms. In effect, the intimacy of the teacher-student relationship spurns the advice of outsiders. This state of affairs might explain the situation observed by Lippitt (1965):

We find in teachers a resistance or an inhibition to adopting another teacher's inventions. This is quite different, we find, from the active scouting for the newest in some of the other fields. Our interviews seem to suggest, for example, that the idea of adopting somebody else's practice somehow is a notion of imitation and that as such it is bad [page 13].

Goal-diffuseness

A great deal has been said about the difficulty of specifying the multiple, terminal goals of education and of measuring their attainment, especially the long-range socialization goals. Goal-diffuseness refers to this lack of clarity and focus among the goals of educational organizations. It arises from the wide array of constituencies that our comprehensive, compulsory system is obliged to serve.

The diffuseness of terminal goals reinforces the effects of vulnerability and of status insecurity on the emergence of innovative roles. First, with regard to vulnerability—because it is difficult to adduce evidence for the effectiveness of an educational practice, it is often hard to oppose the naive demands of laymen, or to sell to the public innovations that are thought by educators to be of special value. Given the national norms of the profession with respect to innovation, and because problems of evaluation make it difficult to sort out the chaff from the grain, practitioners are vulnerable to the blandishments of educational hucksters. As a result, the problems of overdiffusion and uncritical adoption arise. Finally, the diffuseness of goals facilitates the illusion of consensus between school personnel and the public, which permits conflict to develop over the instrumental goals of the school and community. This point needs further clarification.

Instrumental goals, as contrasted with terminal goals, arise from a multitude of adjustments to problems that are confronted by the schools. Since the problems confronted by school personnel and those confronted by the public differ, their instrumental goals will tend to differ. For example, as mentioned earlier, many teachers find it expedient to emphasize the nurturant aspect of their relationship with students in order to preserve their professional identity, to motivate students individually, and to avoid a hardening of the anti-scholastic student subculture. According to a recent study of preferred teaching styles (which reflect instrumental goals), 62 percent of the teachers described themselves as pursuing a permissive, discovery-oriented style, and 90 percent of the principals stated that they preferred this style (Sieber and Wilder, 1967). Note that this style may well involve a nurturant, affective relationship between teachers and students, thereby reflecting the instrumental goals of educators. But parents are evidently more concerned with the substantive and the authoritarian aspects of instruction. Only 30 percent of the mothers preferred the permissive, discovery-oriented style. A large minority of the working-class mothers (especially in the city) were concerned about classroom control, and large proportions of both working- and middle-class mothers were concerned about adequate coverage of subject matter and with regular testing of progress. These emphases reflect the instrumental goals of parents who are interested in instilling discipline and in preparing their children for college or for employment. Stated in terms of consensus between teachers and parents, it was found that children of more than two-thirds of the mothers had a teacher whose self-description was not in accord with the mothers' preferences for teaching styles.

Earlier we mentioned that 56 percent of the mothers disagreed with the terminal goals of the teacher. It seems, then, that there is a higher degree of consensus regarding terminal goals than instrumental goals. This might be a consequence of the lack of clarity in terminal goals, which permits verbal agreement despite fundamental differences in day-to-day outlook. Further, disagreement on terminal goals is less disturbing to parents than disagreement on instrumental goals. The mothers in our study were much more likely to be dissatisfied if they felt that the teacher was not complying with their expectations of classroom teaching styles (instrumental goals) than if they felt that the school did not share their long-run, educational goals (terminal goals).

If the terminal goals of education were more clear-cut, parents and educators could probably come to a better understanding of what is expected in the classroom. Under present circumstances of goal-diffuseness, however, potential conflict may build up over instrumental goals, and, as mentioned earlier, goal conflict between an organization and its dominant environment is one of the distinguishing characteristics of vulnerability.

Ritualistic adherence to certain instructional procedures and school regulations might be reinforced by goal-diffuseness, also. Lack of consensus on goals, owing to their multiplicity and vagueness, might encourage overcompliance with the methods of education. In fact, the "retreat to methods" in teacher preparation might need reexamination in the light of educational goal-diffuseness.

Goal-diffuseness also contributes to professional insecurity. Despite an emphasis on instructional skills rather than on terminal goals, clarity of terminal goals is probably an important condition for the development of technical competence. Unable to reach agreement on the efficacy of particular skills, owing partly to the vagueness of goals and to the problem of measuring attainment of goals, teachers lack *expertise* as a basis of authority, which relegates them to a quasi-professional status. We have already suggested several consequences for innovativeness that flow from quasi professionalism.

Incidentally, it also seems likely that the difficulty of measuring outcomes would tend to demoralize those teachers who do not possess considerable personal self-confidence. The effect might be to lessen motivation to try out new practices, especially those that involve considerable inconvenience in the initial stages. In other words, a sort of fatalistic attitude may set in because of the difficulty of attaining objective certainty about a particular practice.

Formal Coordination and Control

Thus far we have virtually ignored the impact of the formal organizational context on the emergence of innovative roles. School systems contain elaborate means for rationalizing the flow of recruits through the system—through sequential and horizontal organization of the curriculum, through counseling, and through quality control mechanisms that determine promotability and placement within academic strata. And there are also mechanisms for governing and rewarding the staff and for allocating resources throughout a large number of subdivisions. Further, because participation by the clients of schools is nonvoluntary and because the clients are located within the organization, student control becomes an important organizational concern. Finally, owing to the commonweal function of education, accountability to parents and taxpayers is required, which necessitates further bureaucratic provisions. Because of all these management problems, school systems assume a bureaucratic structure with a hierarchy of offices, a division of labor with specially trained incumbents, a proliferation of rules, an elaborate record-keeping system, and so on.[6]

We have already alluded to the effects of the managerial structure of education on innovative behavior in our discussion of quasi professionalism, since it is partly due to organizational requirements that teachers are unable to achieve full-fledged professional status. Thus, they are required to use specific textbooks on certain subjects and allotted a specific period of time to deal with the client (which reduces discretion); they are held accountable to administrators (which reduces collegial authority); and they are required to control the client by means of formal sanctions (which lessens the importance of expertise as a basis of authority over clients, and may conflict with the service orientation of teachers).[7] In short, the bureaucratic setting of education creates strain for the professional role, which in turn produces some of the effects of quasi professionalism already mentioned.

But organizational requirements influence the adoption and implementation of new practices in more direct ways, also. Many educational innovations are designed to meet the varied needs of students— or, as educators say, to "individualize instruction." This objective is one of the core values of professionalism. But when pursued within the typical organizational structure of education, which is largely devoted to coordination and control, the objective is exceedingly difficult to realize. Carlson (1965) provides us with a good example. He found that teachers who were supervising programmed instruc-

6. There may also be a historical reason for the emphasis of our schools on bureaucratic efficiency, as persuasively argued by Callahan (1962).

7. See Blau and Scott (1962, pp. 241-247) for further discussion of the dilemmas arising from the confrontation of bureaucratic discipline and professionalism.

tion "... were actually restricting the output of the students who were proceeding at the fastest rates."

The logic of restricting output of rapid learners is tidy and makes good sense from at least one viewpoint. Explaining the same troublesome point to five students who are encountering it concurrently is less time consuming than explaining it to the same five students as they encounter it at different times. For the teacher who complains that there is never enough time, this appears to make good sense. In fact, insistence that all students move at the same rate, which is attempted in many classrooms, can be supported by the same logic [page 77].

The more rapid advancement of certain students conflicts with the principle of organizational efficiency that dictates the processing of cohorts instead of individuals. Perhaps one reason that medical practice has low productivity is due to the difficulty of treating groups, which arises from the urgency of the individual client's need. Students are not usually perceived as "emergency cases," however, and must therefore await "treatment" along with their cohorts. Organizational efficiency is therefore allowed to become prepotent.

Fundamental changes in organizational structure, such as nongraded schools, might be required to reap the benefits of programmed instruction. And the nongraded pattern probably requires further modifications, such as the creation of teams of instructors so that information about individual pupils can be shared more rapidly. But this means that even slight departures from traditional methods of coordination and control might necessitate further organizational adjustments, thereby disrupting normal operations throughout a large sector of the school system.

Perhaps it is more common for these adjustments to be altogether avoided, which produces negative feedback on the original innovation, as in the case of the teachers observed by Carlson. The hesitation to make further adjustments in the organization, then, may account partly for the "watering down" of innovations that is so frequently observed. And, because the school can nevertheless point with pride to its core curriculum, its team teaching, or its programmed instruction when confronting either the public or other educators, there is little pressure for bringing the innovation to full fruition.

To be sure, there exist relatively nondisruptive innovations, such as technological devices that chiefly supplement routine instruction; and there are even innovations that reduce organizational friction. Hayes (1966) claims that the creation of special classes for the slow-learning, [the] neurologically impaired, and [the] emotionally disturbed can often be traced to the desire to remove irritants from the classrooms. Obviously, the organizational context may determine the adoption as well as the nonadoption of innovations. What this suggests is that a comprehensive taxonomy of innovations should make allowance for organizational consequences. But considerable research is needed before specific features of innovations can be related to organizational response.

The Combination of System Attributes

Although we have tended to stress the consequences for innovative roles of each of the four organizational attributes taken separately, we have occasionally referred to problems that emerge from combinations of attributes. No doubt a thoroughgoing analysis growing out of empirical work would give greater attention to the interaction of these attributes. Possibly some of the most critical problems facing change agents can be delineated only by consideration of these interaction effects. For example, the combination of the need for coordination and control, on the one hand, and professionalism, on the other, produces the problem of "structural looseness" (Bidwell, 1965). The structured isolation of teachers (in classrooms) makes coordination and control in the service of innovation quite difficult (Wayland, 1967). And because "remote control" mechanisms are necessitated (syllabi, student accounting, and others), structural looseness creates problems of clerical overload for teachers, which aggravates their already insecure status. In addition, it permits teachers to preserve their illusion of autonomy while inroads continue to be made on their professional sovereignty.

Figure 3-1 summarizes our discussion to this point in the form of a flowchart. The diagram is not intended to represent an elegant theoretical system. Presentation in graphic form, however, might help clarify the linkages that require research.

Existing and Needed Strategies

It seems to me that there are three classical strategies for inducing change in education.[8] Each strategy rests upon a major assumption about the motivations of practitioners. What might be called the "rational man" strategy is founded upon the assumption that practitioners are impelled by rational decision making to formulate clear-cut objectives regarding the efficient allocation of resources. The rational man considers ignorance to be the chief barrier to innova-

8. The following comments are distilled from an earlier paper (Sieber, 1967).

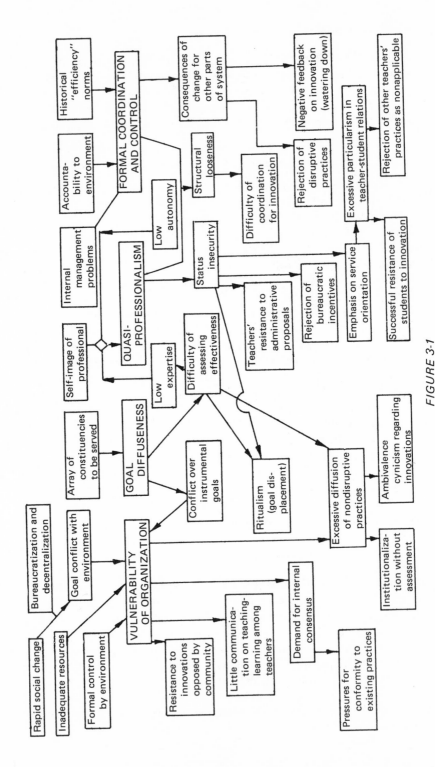

FIGURE 3-1

Structural properties affecting innovation

tion. The channels of influence employed in this strategy include didactic teacher preparation, research reports, and conferences—in short, all forms of one-way communication between the change agent and the practitioner. One-way communication is sufficient in terms of this strategy because the major need of the practitioner is information.

There is comparatively little entailed in pursuing the rational man strategy, and the coverage is comparatively wide; hence, this strategy has much to recommend it. Unfortunately, the yield leaves much to be desired. What the approach overlooks is the necessity of learning about the practitioner's values and organizational circumstances by means of two-way communication, achieved either by face-to-face contacts or by detailed knowledge of the typical values and circumstances of the "target system." It also assumes that goals are few and clear-cut, when in fact they are diffuse. Essentially, the strategy of the rational man neglects consideration of the four attributes of the educational system that were discussed earlier.

An alternative strategy involves the participation of members of the system and rests on the assumption that practitioners are willing and able to cooperate in new ventures. The strategy might therefore be termed the "cooperator" strategy. Two-way communication is the hallmark of the strategy, and its proponents include school consultants, on-site evaluation experts, human relations experts, and demonstrators. The effort required by the cooperator strategy is greater than the effort required by the rational man strategy. And, barring the development of a widespread system of "extension agents," the coverage is probably limited. What is lost in extensiveness may be compensated for somewhat by gains in intensiveness, however. Nevertheless, the yield of the cooperator strategy in terms of the total educational system is probably as limited as that of the rational man approach. One reason is that the strategy overemphasizes the personalistic aspects of the practitioner's lot, and therefore requires intensive treatment of individual personalities. And, what is more important, insufficient attention is paid to the status insecurity generated by quasi professionalism and to the formal organizational attributes of vulnerability, goal-diffuseness, and coordination and control. Thus, there is a tendency to view resistance to change in schools as a matter of personal insecurity, habit formation, or sheer lethargy, rather than as a matter of status insecurity, peer group pressures, or bureaucratic hindrances.

A third strategy is derived from the notion that practitioners are powerless to innovate. Even assuming that they have complete information and the ability to overcome their resistances, they would still be unable to make major modifications in the structure of education. This approach might be called the strategy of the "powerless participant." Influence is provided through legal and bureaucratic channels with directives flowing downward and evidence of compliance flowing upward. The change agents operating under this strategy represent the three branches of government at local, state, and federal levels, as well as the various pressure groups at each level.

The effort entailed in the powerless participant strategy is great, but the coverage is quite wide because national or state action can reach into a large number of systems in a relatively short time. On first consideration, it would appear that the yield of the strategy is also great because many innovations in schools are supported by legal or bureaucratic regulations. However, these regulations are often applied to preexisting patterns of behavior and norms; that is, they often serve mainly to legitimate and to standardize a particular normative pattern. It is, therefore, difficult to know if it was a new directive that wrought a particular change, or if the change resulted from gradual diffusion facilitated by legal action. Further, there are many reasons to suspect that administrative directives within schools are averted, sabotaged, watered down, and even rescinded in the face of opposition from students, teachers, administrators, or the community. The effects of quasi professionalism and of vulnerability are often responsible for the subversion of formal directives. Also, the necessity of controlling and motivating students by nonformal means, mentioned earlier, exerts a corrosive influence on formal regulations. In short, practitioners are by no means powerless to shape their organizational setting, although the power they exercise may not be exerted in behalf of rational innovation.

The three strategies fail because men are not wholly rational, cooperative, nor powerless. But in certain instances, they exhibit elements peculiar to each of the three patterns of behavior. What is needed, therefore, is a strategy that takes into account the conditions under which practitioners will respond to the tactics comprised in each of the three classical strategies. The needed strategy, in short, should possess the resources of all three strategies and should include guidelines for their employment under particular conditions. I call the needed approach the strategy of the "status-occupant."

In presenting the image of practitioners as status-occupants, it is assumed that they are imbedded in an intricate network of role relationships that holds its shape as a consequence of shared values, shared solutions to status problems, and shared sanctions for deviance and conformity. Efforts to change one component of this structure without consideration of the other components will ordinarily result in failure. Because much more thought needs to be given to the implications of our theory for innovative roles, I can here only suggest a few implications for strategy.

In light of the preceding theoretical discussion, it would appear that overhauling is needed at both the local and national levels. Locally, the organization of schools should be revamped to permit teachers to behave in accordance with their professional self-image. For example, a teacher who wishes to become a local expert on some new development might be allowed to apply to the school board for special authority to try out the development. If approved, the teacher would be provided with special funds, released from routine teaching duties, and authorized to modify regulations, reallocate resources, reassign students, and dole out rewards and penalties for those under his jurisdiction for a specified period, say, four months. The role of local administrators vis-à-vis these teachers would be restricted to one of facilitation and consultation. Other teachers would probably agree to this bestowal of power on one of their peers because of their desire to have the same opportunity at some later time, their resentment of administrative domination, and their respect for the change agent's position in the informal structure of peer relations. The change agent, therefore, might have considerable assurance that his ideas would be given a fair trial.

Some such arrangement would increase professional autonomy, serve as an incentive for innovative proposals, and enhance the expertise of teachers. In effect, the change agent would simulate the role and authority of the teacher-principal of a small school whose effectiveness stems from his status of *prima inter pares.*

Outside the local setting it might be necessary to organize agencies that represent several national ancillary structures and that are intended to have national impact. Agencies such as these might be required to avert the problems arising from local and regional vulnerability, and to exploit national vulnerability to better advantage. A national base of operations is necessary to draw upon structures that are themselves nationwide in scope and, also, to attract the best talent from all over the country. These agencies should not add to the profusion of staff organizations related to education, however, but should function as coordinating bodies. Thus, each agency would draw upon the resources of federal and state offices, publishing houses, accreditation agencies, universities, and the mass media—in brief, those powerful ancillary structures to which schools are already so highly vulnerable.

Each national coordinating body might focus its attention on a single innovation at a time so that resources and commitments are not spread too thin and duplication of effort is avoided. The tactics of the different change agents comprised in the three classical strategies mentioned earlier would be combined. Their efforts would entail new regulations or legislation, consultation and demonstration, summarizations of research evidence, development of new educational products, and mass communication among communities and schools. When a campaign centering on a particular innovation has been set into motion by lower-level staff, the top planners at each agency could reconvene to consider their next innovative thrust.

It should be borne in mind that our two proposals for reorganization are simply by way of illustrating a strategy that combines the tactics of the three classical strategies, and at the same time overcomes their distinctive difficulties. These difficulties arise from the dominant organizational properties of education. Hence, in the final analysis, it is the organizational properties that need to be taken into account in the formulation of innovative strategies.

References

Allen, Harley E. (1956). "An Analysis of the Results of the 'Time-Scale' Application to Metropolitan School Study Council Schools." Unpublished doctoral project, Teachers College, Columbia University.

Bidwell, Charles E. (1965). "The School as a Formal Organization," in James G. March, ed., *Handbook of Organizations*. Chicago: Rand McNally.

Blau, Peter M., and Scott, Richard .W. (1962). *Formal Organizations: A Comparative Approach*. San Francisco: Chandler.

Brickell, Henry M. (1961). *Organizing New York State for Educational Change*. Albany: New York State Education Department.

Callahan, Raymond (1962). *Education and the Cult of Efficiency*. Chicago: University of Chicago Press.

Carlson, Richard O. (1965). *Adoption of Educational Innovations*. Eugene, Ore.: Center for the Advanced Study of Educational Administration.

Conant, James B. (1967). *The Comprehensive High School*. New York: McGraw-Hill.

Corwin, Ronald G. (1954). "Militant Professionalism, Initiative and Compliance in Public Education." *Sociology of Education*, 38(Summer):310-331.

Cronbach, Lee J. (1966). "The Role of the University in the Improvement of Education," in *Expanding Horizons of Knowledge about Man*. Yeshiva University Symposium.

Gallup International, Inc. (1966). *School Board Members' Reactions to Educational Innovations*. Princeton, N.J.

Gordon, C. W. (1957). *The Social System of the High School*. Glencoe, Ill.: Free Press.

Hayes, Paul C. (1966). "On the Local School," in *Planning for Educational Change*, a special issue of *Theory into Practice*, 5(February):46-50.

Jessup, Dorothy (1967). "Problems in Education and Resistance to Change in U.S. Public Schools." Department of Sociology, Columbia University, mimeo.

Kerr, Norman D. (1964). "The School Board as an Agency of Legitimation." *Sociology of Education*, 38(Fall):34-59.

Lippitt, Ronald (1965). "Roles and Processes in Curriculum Development and Change," in *Strategy for Curriculum Change*. Washington, D.C.: Association for Supervision and Curriculum Development.

Miles, Matthew (1965). "Some Properties of Schools as Social Systems." Horace Mann-Lincoln Institute of School Experimentation, Teachers College, Columbia University, mimeo.

Miller, Richard I. (1967). "An Overview of Educational Change," in Richard I. Miller, ed., *Perspectives on Educational Change*. New York: Appleton-Century-Crofts, pp. 1-20.

Paisley, William J. (1965). *The Flow of (Behavioral) Science Information, A Review of the Research Literature*. Stanford, Calif.: Institute for Communication Research, Stanford University.

Sieber, Sam D. (1967). "Institutional Setting," in *The Role of Educational Research in Educational Change*. Bloomington, Ind.: National Institute for the Study of Educational Change.

_____ (in press). "Images of the Practitioner and Strategies for Inducing Educational Change." *Teachers College Record*.

_____ and Wilder, David E. (in press). "Teaching Styles: Parental Preferences and Professional Role Definitions." *Sociology of Education*.

Wayland, Sloan R. (1964). "Structural Features of American Education as Basic Factors in Innovation," in Matthew Miles, ed., *Innovation in Education*. New York: Teachers College, Columbia University.

_____ (1967). *The Context of Innovation: Some Organizational Attributes of Schools*. New York: Teachers College, Columbia University.

Wiles, Kimball (1965). "Contrasts in Strategies of Change," in *Strategy for Curriculum Change*. Washington, D.C.: Association for Supervision and Curriculum Development.

4 The Organizational Saga in Higher Education

Burton R. Clark

Saga, originally referring to a medieval Icelandic or Norse account of achievements and events in the history of a person or group, has come to mean a narrative of heroic exploits, of a unique development that has deeply stirred the emotions of participants and descendants. Thus, a saga is not simply a story but a story that at some time has had a particular base of believers. The term often refers also to the actual history itself, thereby including a stream of events, the participants, and the written or spoken interpretation. The element of belief is crucial, for, without the credible story, the events and persons become history; with the development of belief, a particular bit of history becomes a definition full of pride and identity for the group.

Introduction

An organizational saga is a collective understanding of unique accomplishment in a formally established group. The group's definition

Reprinted from *Administrative Science Quarterly*, 17.2(June 1972):178-184. *Author's note:* Revised version of paper presented at the 65th Annual Meeting of the American Sociological Association, September 1970, Washington, D.C. I wish to thank Wendell Bell, Maren L. Carden, Kai Erikson, and Stanley Udy for discussion and comment. Parts of an early draft of this paper have been used to connect organizational belief to problems of governance in colleges and universities (Clark, 1971).

of the accomplishment, intrinsically historical but embellished through retelling and rewriting, links stages of organizational development. The participants have added affect, an emotional loading, which places their conception between the coolness of rational purpose and the warmth of sentiment found in religion and magic. An organizational saga presents some rational explanation of how certain means led to certain ends, but it also includes affect that turns a formal place into a beloved institution, to which participants may be passionately devoted. Encountering such devotion, the observer may become unsure of his own analytical detachment as he tests the overtones of the institutional spirit or spirit of place.

The study of organizational sagas highlights nonstructural and nonrational dimensions of organizational life and achievement. Macro-organizational theory has concentrated on the role of structure and technology in organizational effectiveness (Gross, 1964; Litterer, 1965; March, 1965; Thompson, 1967; Price, 1968; Perrow, 1970). A needed corrective is more research on the cultural and expressive aspects of organizations, particularly on the role of belief and sentiment at broad levels of organization. The human relations approach in organizational analysis, centered largely on group interaction, showed some awareness of the role of organization symbols (Whyte, 1948, chapter 23), but this conceptual lead has not been taken as a serious basis for research. Also, in the literature on organizations and purposive communities, "ideology" refers to unified and shared belief (Selznick, 1949; Bendix, 1956; Price, 1968, pages 104-110; Carden, 1969); but the concept of ideology has lost denotative power, having been stretched by varying uses. For the phenomenon discussed in this paper, "saga" seems to provide the appropriate denotation. With a general emphasis on normative bonds, organizational saga refers to a unified set of publicly expressed beliefs about the formal group that (a) is rooted in history, (b) claims unique accomplishment, and (c) is held with sentiment by the group.

To develop the concept in this paper, extreme cases and exaggerations of the ideal type are used, but the concept will be close to reality and widely applicable when the phenomenon is examined in weak as well as strong expression. In many organizations, even some highly utilitarian ones, some segment of their personnel probably develops in time at least a weak saga. Those who have persisted together for some years in one place will have had, at minimum, a thin stream of shared experience, which they elaborate into a plausible account of group uniqueness. Whether developed primarily by management or by employees, the story helps rationalize for the individual his commitment of time and energy for years, perhaps for a lifetime, to a particular enterprise. Even when weak, the belief can compensate in part for the loss of meaning in much modern work, giving some drama and some cultural identity to one's otherwise entirely instrumental efforts. At the other end of the continuum, a saga engages one so intensely as to make his immediate place overwhelmingly valuable. It can even produce a striking distortion, with the organization becoming the only reality, the outside world becoming illusion. Generally the almost complete capture of affect and perception is associated with only a few utopian communities, fanatical political factions, and religious sects. But some formal rationalized organizations, as, for example, [in] business and education, can also become utopian, fanatical, or sectarian.

Organizational sagas vary in durability. They can arise quickly in relatively unstructured social settings, as in professional sports organizations that operate in the volatile context of contact with large spectator audiences through the mass media. A professional baseball or football team may create a rags-to-riches legend in a few months' time that excites millions of people. But such a saga is also very fragile as an ongoing definition of the organization. The story can be removed quickly from the collective understanding of the present and future, for successful performance is often unstable, and the events that set the direction of belief can be readily reversed, with the great winners quickly becoming habitual losers. In such cases, there seems to be an unstable structural connection between the organization and the base of believers. The base of belief is not anchored within the organization nor in personal ties between insiders and outsiders, but is mediated by mass media, away from the control of the organization. Such sagas continue only as the organization keeps repeating its earlier success and also keeps the detached followers from straying to other sources of excitement and identification.

In contrast, organizational sagas show high durability when built slowly in structured social contexts, for example, the educational system—specifically, for the purposes of this paper, three liberal arts colleges in the United States. In the many small private colleges, the story of special performance emerges not in a few months but over a decade or two. When the saga is firmly developed, it is embodied in many components of the organization, affecting the definition and performance of the organization and finding protection in the webbing of the institutional parts. It is not volatile and can be relegated to the past only by years of attenuation or organizational decline.

Since the concept of organizational saga was developed from research on Reed, Antioch, and Swarthmore, three distinctive and highly regarded colleges (Clark, 1970), material and categories from their developmental histories are used to illustrate the development of a saga, and its positive effects on organizational participation and effectiveness are then considered.[1]

Development of Saga

Two stages can be distinguished in the development of an organizational saga, initiation and fulfillment. Initiation takes place under varying conditions and occurs within a relatively short period of time; fulfillment is related to features of the organization that are enduring and more predictable.

Initiation

Strong sagas do not develop in passive organizations tuned to adaptive servicing of demand or to the fulfilling of roles dictated by higher authorities (Clark, 1956, 1960). The saga is initially a strong purpose, conceived and enunciated by a single man or a small cadre (Selznick, 1957) whose first task is to find a setting that is open, or can be opened, to a special effort. The most obvious setting is the autonomous new organization, where there is no established structure, no rigid custom, especially if a deliberate effort has been made to establish initial autonomy and bordering outsiders are preoccupied. There a leader may also have the advantage of building from the top down, appointing lieutenants and picking up recruits in accord with his ideas.

Reed College is strongly characterized by a saga, and its story of hard-won excellence and nonconformity began as strong purpose in a new organization. Its first president, William T. Foster, a thirty-year-old, high-minded reformer, from the sophisticated East of Harvard and Bowdoin went to the untutored Northwest, to an unbuilt campus in suburban Portland in 1910, precisely because he did not want to be limited by established institutions, all of which were, to his mind, corrupt in practice. The projected college in Oregon was clear ground, intellectually as well as physically, and he could there assemble the people and devise the practices that would finally give

1. For some discussion of the risks and tensions associated with organizational sagas, particularly that of success in one period leading to later rigidity and stagnation, see Clark (1970, pp. 258-261). Hale (1970) gives an illuminating discussion of various effects of a persistent saga in a theological seminary.

the United States an academically pure college, a Balliol for America.

The second setting for initiation is the established organization in a crisis of decay. Those in charge, after years of attempting incremental adjustments (Lindblom, 1959), realize finally that they must either give up established ways or have the organization fail. Preferring that it survive, they may relinquish the leadership to one proposing a plan that promises revival and later strength, or they may even accept a man of utopian intent. Deep crisis in the established organization thus creates some of the conditions of a new organization. It suspends past practice, forces some bordering groups to stand back or even to turn their backs on failure of the organization, and it tends to catch the attention of the reformer looking for an opportunity.

Antioch College is a dramatic example of such a setting. Started in the 1860's, its first sixty years were characterized by little money, weak staff, few students, and obscurity. Conditions worsened in the 1910's under the inflation and other strains of World War I. In 1919 a charismatic utopian reformer, Arthur E. Morgan, decided it was more advantageous to take over an old college with buildings and a charter than to start a new one. First as trustee and then as president, he began in the early 1920's an institutional renovation that overturned everything. As president he found it easy to push aside old, weak organizational structures and usages. He elaborated a plan of general education involving an unusual combination of work, study, and community participation, and he set about to devise the implementing tool. Crisis and charisma made possible a radical transformation out of which came a second Antioch, a college soon characterized by a sense of exciting history, unique practice, and exceptional performance.

The third context for initiation is the established organization that is not in crisis, not collapsing from long decline, yet ready for evolutionary change. This is the most difficult situation to predict, having to do with degree of rigidity. In both ideology and structure, institutionalized colleges vary in openness to change. In those under church control, for example, the colleges of the more liberal Protestant denominations have been more hospitable than Catholic colleges, at least until recently, to educational experimentation. A college with a tradition of presidential power is more open to change than one where the trustees and the professors exert control over the president. Particularly promising is the college with a self-defined need for educational leadership. This is the opening for which some reformers watch, the sound place that has some ambition to increase its academic stature, as, for example, Swarthmore College.

Swarthmore began in the 1860's, and had become, by 1920, a secure and stable college, prudently managed by Quaker trustees and administrators and solidly based on traditional support from nearby Quaker families in Pennsylvania, New Jersey, and Maryland. Such an organization would not usually be thought promising for reform, but Frank Aydelotte, who became its president in 1920, judged it ready for change. Magnetic in personality, highly placed within the elite circle of former Rhodes scholars, personally liked by important foundation officials, and recommended as a scholarly leader, he was offered other college presidencies, but he chose Swarthmore as a place open to change through a combination of financial health, liberal Quaker ethos, and some institutional ambition. His judgment proved correct, although the tolerance for his changes in the 1920's and 1930's was narrow at times. He began the gradual introduction of a modified Oxford honors program and related changes, which resulted in noteworthy achievements that supporters were to identify later as "the Swarthmore saga" (Swarthmore College Faculty, 1941).

Fulfillment

Although the conditions of initiation of a saga vary, the means of fulfillment are more predictable. There are many ways in which a unified sense of a special history is expressed; for example, even a patch of sidewalk or a coffee room may evoke emotion among the believers, but one can delimit the components at the center of the development of a saga. These may center, in colleges, on the personnel, the program, the external social base, the student subculture, and the imagery of the saga.

Personnel. In a college, the key group of believers is the senior faculty. When they are hostile to a new idea, its attenuation is likely; when they are passive, its success is weak; and when they are devoted to it, a saga is probable. A single leader, a college president, can initiate the change, but the organizational idea will not be expanded over the years and expressed in performance unless ranking and powerful members of the faculty become committed to it and remain committed even after the initiator is gone. In committing themselves deeply, taking some credit for the change and seeking to ensure its perpetuation, they routinize the charisma of the leader in collegial authority. The faculty cadre of believers helps to effect the legend, then to protect it against later leaders and other new participants who, less pure in belief, might turn the organization in some other direction.

Such faculty cadres were well developed at Reed by 1925, after the time of its first two presidents; at Antioch, by the early 1930's, after Morgan, disappointed with his followers, left for the board of directors of the new TVA; and at Swarthmore, by the 1930's, and particularly by 1940, after Aydelotte's twenty years of persistent effort. In all three colleges, after the departure of the change agent(s), the senior faculty with the succeeding president, a man appropriate for consolidation, undertook the full working out of the experiment. The faculty believers also replaced themselves through socialization and selective recruitment and retention in the 1940's and 1950's. Meanwhile, new potential innovators had sometimes to be stopped. In such instances, the faculty was able to exert influence to shield the distinctive effort from erosion or deflection. At Reed, for example, major clashes between president and faculty in the late 1930's and the early 1950's were precipitated by a new change-oriented president, coming in from the outside, disagreeing with a faculty proud of what had been done, attached deeply to what the college had become, and determined to maintain what was for them the distinctive Reed style. From the standpoint of constructing a regional and national model of purity and severity in undergraduate education, the Reed faculty did on those occasions act to create while acting to conserve.

Program. For a college to transform purpose into a credible story of unique accomplishment, there must be visible practices with which claims of distinctiveness can be supported; that is, unusual courses, noteworthy requirements, or special methods of teaching. On the basis of seemingly unique practices, the program becomes a set of communal symbols and rituals, invested with meaning. Not reporting grades to the students becomes a symbol, as at Reed, that the college cares about learning for learning's sake; thus mere technique becomes part of a saga.

In all the three colleges, the program was seen as distinctive by both insiders and outsiders. At Swarthmore it was the special seminars and other practices of the honors program, capped by written and oral examination by teams of visiting outsiders in the last days of the senior year. At Antioch it was the work-study cycle, the special set of general education requirements, community government, and community involvement. At Reed it was the required freshman lecture-and-seminar courses, the junior qualifying examination, and the thesis in the senior year. Such practices became central to a belief that things had been done so differently, and so much against the mainstream, and often against imposing odds, that the group had generated a saga.

Social base. The saga also becomes fixed in the minds of outside believers devoted to the organization, usually the alumni. The alumni are the best located to hold beliefs enduringly pure, since they can be as strongly identified with a special organizational history as the older faculty and administrators and yet do not have to face directly the new problems generated by a changing environment or students. Their thoughts can remain centered on the past, rooted in the days when, as students, they participated intimately in the unique ways and accomplishments of the campus.

Liberal alumni, as those of Reed, Antioch, and Swarthmore here, seek to conserve what they believe to be a unique liberal institution and to protect it from the conservative forces of society that might change it—that is, to make it like other colleges. At Reed, for example, dropouts as well as graduates were struck by the intellectual excellence of their small college, convinced that college life there had been unlike college life anywhere else, and they were ready to conserve the practices that seemed to sustain that excellence. Here, too, conserving acts can be seen for a time as contributing to an innovation, protecting the full working out of a distinctive effort.

Student subculture. The student body is the third group of believers, not overwhelmingly important but still a necessary support for the saga. To become and remain a saga, a change must be supported by the student subculture over decades, and the ideology of the subculture must integrate with the central ideas of the believing administrators and faculty. When the students define themselves as personally responsible for upholding the image of the college, then a design or plan has become an organizational saga.

At Antioch, Reed, and Swarthmore, the student subcultures were powerful mechanisms for carrying a developing saga from one generation to another. Reed students, almost from the beginning and extending at least to the early 1960's, were great believers in the uniqueness of their college, constantly on the alert for any action that would alter it, ever fearful that administration or faculty might succumb to pressures that would make Reed just like other colleges. Students at Antioch and Swarthmore also offered unstinting support for the ideology of their institution. All three student bodies steadily and dependably transferred the ideology from one generation to another. Often socializing deeply, they helped to produce the graduate who never quite rid himself of the wish to go back to the campus.

Imagery of saga. Upheld by faculty, alumni, and students, expressed in teaching practices, the saga is even more widely expressed as a generalized tradition in statues and ceremonies, written histories and current catalogues, even in an "air about the place" felt by

participants and some outsiders. The more unique the history and
the more forceful the claim to a place in history, the more intensely
cultivated the ways of sharing memory and symbolizing the institution. The saga is a strong self-fulfilling belief; working through institutional self-image and public image, it is indeed a switchman (Weber, 1946), helping to determine the tracks along which action is
pushed by men's self-defined interests. The early belief of one stage
brings about the actions that warrant a stronger version of the same
belief in a later period. As the account develops, believers come to
sense its many constituent symbols as inextricably bound together,
and the part takes its meaning from the whole. For example, at
Antioch a deep attachment developed in the 1930's and 1940's to
Morgan's philosophy of the whole man and to its expression in a
unique combination of work, study, community participation, and
many practices thought to embody freedom and nonconformity.
Some of the faculty of those years who remained in the 1940's and
1950's had many memories and impressions that seemed to form a
symbolic whole: personnel counselors, folk dancing in Red Square,
Morgan's towering physique, the battles of community government,
the pacifism of the late 1930's, the frequent dash of students to
off-campus jobs, the dedicated deans who personified central values.
Public image also grew strong and sharp, directing liberals and radi-
cals to the college and conservatives to other places. The symbolic
expressions themselves were a strong perpetuating force.

Conclusion

An organizational saga is a powerful means of unity in the formal
place. It makes links across internal divisions and organizational
boundaries as internal and external groups share their common belief. With deep emotional commitment, believers define themselves
by their organizational affiliation, and, in their bond to other believers, they share an intense sense of the unique. In an organization
defined by a strong saga, there is a feeling that there is the small
world of the lucky few and the large routine one of the rest of the
world. Such an emotional bond turns the membership into a community, even a cult.

An organizational saga is thus a valuable resource, created over a
number of years out of the social components of the formal enterprise. As participants become ideologues, their common definition
becomes a foundation for trust and for extreme loyalty. Such bonds
give the organization a competitive edge in recruiting and maintain-

ing personnel and help it to avoid the vicious circle in which some actual or anticipated erosion of organizational strength leads to the loss of some personnel, which leads to further decline and loss. Loyalty causes individuals to stay with a system, to save and improve it rather than to leave to serve their self-interest elsewhere (Hirschman, 1970). The genesis and persistence of loyalty is a key organizational and analytical problem. Enduring loyalty follows from a collective belief of participants that their organization is distinctive. Such a belief comes from a credible story of uncommon effort, achievement, and form.

Pride in the organized group and pride in one's identity as taken from the group are personal returns that are uncommon in modern social involvement. The development of sagas is one way in which men in organizations increase such returns, reducing their sense of isolation and increasing their personal pride and pleasure in organizational life. Studying the evocative narratives and devotional ties of formal systems leads to a better understanding of the fundamental capacities of organizations to enhance or diminish the lives of participants. The organization possessing a saga is a place in which participants, for a time at least, happily accept their bond.

References

Bendix, R. (1956). *Work and Authority in Industry*. New York: John Wiley.

Carden, M. L. (1969). *Oneida: Utopian Community to Modern Corporation*. Baltimore, Md.: Johns Hopkins Press.

Clark, B. R. (1956). *Adult Education in Transition: A Study of Institutional Insecurity*. Berkeley: University of California Press.

———(1960). *The Open Door College. A Case Study*. New York: McGraw-Hill.

———(1970). *The Distinctive College: Antioch, Reed, and Swarthmore*. Chicago: Aldine.

———(1971). "Belief and Loyalty in College Organization." *Journal of Higher Education*, 42.6:499-515.

Gross, B. M. (1964). *The Managing of Organizations*, 2 vols. New York: Free Press.

Hale, J. R. (1970). "The Making and Testing of an Organizational Saga: A Case-Study of the Lutheran Theological Seminary at Gettysburg, Pennsylvania, with Special Reference to the Problem of Merger, 1959-1969." Unpublished dissertation, Columbia University.

Hirschman, A. O. (1970). *Exit, Voice, and Loyalty*. Cambridge, Mass.: Harvard University Press.

Lindblom, C. E. (1959). "The Science of 'Muddling Through.' " *Public Administration Review*, 19:79-88.

Litterer, J. A. (1965). *The Analysis of Organizations.* New York: John Wiley.

March, J. G., ed. (1965). *Handbook of Organizations.* Chicago: Rand McNally.

Perrow, C. (1970). *Organizational Analysis.* Belmont, Calif.: Wadsworth.

Price, J. L. (1968). *Organizational Effectiveness: An Inventory of Propositions.* Homewood, Ill.: Richard D. Irwin.

Selznick, P. (1949). *TVA and the Grass Roots.* Berkeley: University of California Press.

———(1957). *Leadership in Administration.* New York: Harper & Row.

Swarthmore College Faculty (1941). *An Adventure in Education: Swarthmore College under Frank Aydelotte.* New York: Macmillan.

Thompson, J. D. (1967). *Organizations in Action.* New York: McGraw-Hill.

Weber, M. (1946). *From Max Weber: Essays in Sociology,* tr. and ed. by H. H. Gerth and C. Wright Mills. New York: Oxford University Press.

Whyte, W. F. (1948). *Human Relations in the Restaurant Industry.* New York: McGraw-Hill.

Technology

5 Organizational Influences on Educational Innovation

Terrence E. Deal
John W. Meyer
W. Richard Scott

School superintendents, principals, and teachers do not have to be reminded of the general public pressure for educational reform. Nor do they have to be told that they are becoming more accountable for making changes in instruction that result in better reading and math achievement. In fact, they are immersed in a climate that favors innovation and change. What they want to know is how schools can swiftly incorporate new instructional materials and teaching techniques and make the adjustments in social relationships and work arrangements that are necessary to support the new patterns of work. They need knowledge that will enable schools to adopt and support new and highly complex instructional and organizational innovations.

Early studies of innovation reaffirmed the difficulties involved in making instructional or organizational changes in social institutions like schools. As an example, Mort's (1941) early work predicted that fifteen years would be required before a promising educational innovation would be adopted by 3 percent of the nation's schools, while fifty years would pass before the diffusion was complete. Other studies of educational change were heavily influenced by innovation diffusion work in other fields, such as agriculture, where innovations

Adapted from "Organizational Support for Innovative Instructional Programs: District and School Levels," presented at the annual meeting of the American Educational Research Association, Chicago, April 1974. This research was conducted at the Stanford Center for Research and Development in Teaching pursuant to contract NE-C-00-3-0062 with the National Institute of Education, Department of Health, Education, and Welfare.

were adopted and implemented by individuals rather than by organizations. But there are important differences in the educational setting, where complex organizations are involved, that limit the value of this work for educators.

Some scholars have emphasized the relationship between the characteristics of school district structure or environment and the adoption of innovation. These studies find that the school districts more likely to adopt innovations are those that are wealthy (Havelock, 1973; Ross, 1958); large (Baldridge and Burnham, 1973; Havelock, 1973), and have change-oriented superintendents enmeshed in a network of other innovative superintendents (Carlson, 1965). Others have found organizational autonomy, decentralized authority, staff professionalism, and features of organizational climate such as openness, trust, and free communication to be correlates of innovative behavior (Pincus, 1974).

Studies of innovation adoption which do not include a consideration of the problems generated by recent instructional or staffing changes in education will probably be of no practical assistance to schools. It is generally agreed that the mortality rate of such innovations is extraordinarily high, and only some of this turnover can be attributed to weaknesses in the innovations. It seems that one important reason why educational innovations fail to survive lies in the absence of organizational support for such changes, both at the individual school and the district levels.

This chapter is a preliminary report on the first wave of a longitudinal study relating organizational characteristics of school districts and schools to the support and maintenance of innovations, virtually all of which increase the complexity of instruction and work. Many of the newer instructional or staffing developments create the need for higher levels of organizational coordination, differentiation, specialization, and problem-solving capacity in districts and schools, capacities frequently underdeveloped in traditional patterns of school organization. As a result, when schools adopt new instructional techniques or staffing patterns, they must modify their organization; either that or a rapid turnover of innovations or a return to traditional teaching patterns can be predicted. In other words, the longitudinal design focuses attention on the organizational features necessary to support and maintain complex instructional innovations rather than on the characteristics associated with the act of adoption.

This chapter can only report on the data at a single point in time—data collected during the first wave of the longitudinal study. This means that when district and school organizational characteristics are related to innovative classroom practice, there is no way to distinguish between innovations that will survive and those that will not. Some schools in the sample reporting innovative practices may be unable to maintain these changes in the second wave. Thus, the design of the first wave of the study is not different from previous studies on innovation. What is somewhat unique is the approach to the conception and measurement of innovation.

Two types of innovation are identified: instructional and organizational. The concept of instructional innovation is influenced by the sociological view of technology (Perrow, 1965; Thompson, 1967), which produces a focus on instructional differentiation as a key variable. The technology of schools is instruction. Instructional systems which differentiate students on the basis of their abilities, learning styles, or other relevant characteristics and attempt to match different students with differing instructional techniques and materials are viewed as more technologically complex systems. Similarly, the concept of organizational innovation places great emphasis on organizational differentiation—the use of teachers or other staff specialists whose specialization renders them more interdependent as organizational members. Any departures from the traditional arrangement in which one teacher, isolated from colleagues or other sources of help, plans and teaches a single class of students using a common set of materials for all, either in instructional methods and materials or in collaborative arrangements among teachers and other staff members, are considered innovative here. In short, any changes in instructional approaches or organizational arrangements that increase the complexity of the classroom are considered innovative.

This is reflected in the methods used to obtain information. Rather than presenting superintendents and principals with a list of contemporary innovations, we asked them to describe their current instructional patterns and classroom organization. We also asked principals to typify their school's use of teacher groups and their instructional program in reading in grades one through three instead of providing them with a list of instructional innovations possibly adopted. The focus was on reading because developmental efforts in reading have been more vigorous than in other areas.

Research Questions, Sample, and Procedures

The present analysis relates organizational characteristics at both the district and school levels to two educational innovations: the differentiation of reading instruction, and the organization of teachers into small work groups to teach reading.

The relationship of district and school structural characteristics to innovation in instruction and teacher work arrangements was explored using two basic research questions:

—What organizational features of schools or school districts are associated with instructional differentiation in reading?

—What organizational features at the school district or school level predict the organization of teachers into collaborative work groups?

The data reported are taken from a stratified random sample of schools in the six-county San Francisco Bay Area. There are data on 188 elementary schools located in thirty-four school districts. The size of the districts ranged from districts with one school to districts with 133 schools. The sample included thirty-five districts in urban, suburban, and rural areas; only one district refused to participate. Within districts, the number of schools selected varied according to the size of the district. Of the principals originally selected, 90 percent participated by completing a questionnaire and being interviewed by a member of the research staff. At the district level, the superintendent, his associate, or the top line officer for elementary schools completed a questionnaire and was interviewed.

We expected initially that patterns of educational innovation would be either sensitive to, or explained by, organizational concepts such as level of resources, size, formalization, and complexity. We expected also that these concepts and other organizational characteristics would permit the construction of two alternate models that could be compared with the conventional structure of schools by looking at the incidence of complex developments in the organization of classroom instruction and work in each. One of the two alternate models would have been a variation of the hierarchical or centralized model, with a more highly developed staff structure at the district level. The other would have been a professional model, with district patterns more decentralized and, therefore, the principal and teachers in the individual schools systematically making decisions about the adoption of more complex instructional and work patterns. In the cross-sectional analysis we expected to find relatively more complex instruction and teacher work arrangements in either of the alternate models than existed in the more traditional districts. This expectation was based on the hypothesis underlying our longitudinal study in that we expected the staff-line or professional model to offer stronger support for differentiated and interdependent classroom instruction.

The pattern of the findings was not, however, consistent with the expectations generated by the models. Rather, the story we have to tell is in some ways simpler and in some ways more complex than we had anticipated. In any event, only a few variables, some at the school and some at the district level, survived our initial screening, and these measures must be described before we report our specific findings and interpretations.

Independent Variables

At the district level, characteristics associated with innovation include per student expenditure, external funding, special administrative ratio, and size. Per student expenditure is the total amount of district money spent on instruction standardized by the districts' average daily attendance. External funding is the total amount of special state and federal assistance a district school receives for reading programs for grades one to three. Examples of this aid are Miller-Unruh and Title I funds. Special administrative ratio is the proportion of special administrators to the total district administrative staff, and it includes administrators responsible for special areas like guidance, special education, and coordination of personnel in special subject areas. District size is measured by the total number of schools in the district.

At the local school level, the variables that survived as correlates of innovation included three structural characteristics: principal leadership, the school's evaluation structure, and school size. Also, open space (a measure of the school's architectural openness) and community climate (an indicator of the community's attitude toward education) emerge as significantly related to innovation.

The indicator of principal leadership is an index based on a principal's report of his relative influence in several key decision areas and his perception of the amount of time he spends stimulating change in his school. The school's evaluation structure is also measured by an index built from the principal's report of how frequently he evaluates reading teachers in grades one to three and how frequently the school's reading program is evaluated. The open-space variable is based on the total number of open-space pods or instructional spaces in a school where two or more teachers regularly work at the same time. School size is the number of students enrolled in the school. For the index of community climate, the principal was asked to choose one of three possible categories as characterizing the school's adult community: innovative, traditional, or mixed.

Dependent Variables—Innovation in Instruction and Work Arrangements

We are interested in explaining two kinds of educational innovation: instructional innovation and innovation in the way teachers are organized for work. The term *innovation* is used because it is widely accepted among both field educators and educational researchers. What we mean by the term is complexity. From field work with educators, it seems that this conception fits.

In order to measure the complexity of classroom instruction, we constructed an index of the differentiation of reading instruction in the first three grades from the number of distinct sets of reading materials the principal reports in use in more than half the classrooms of the first three grades, the principal's response to three items typifying patterns of instruction, and objective ratings of the curricular materials currently in use in the early grades. How the first component was arrived at is self-explanatory. The second component was determined by the principal's report on materials grouping, that is, the extent to which all students used the same or different materials; student pacing, that is, the extent to which students worked at the same or different paces; and teacher choice, that is, the amount of choice a teacher had in selecting materials for assignments. For the third component—the objective ratings of reading sets—experts were employed to score materials reported on several dimensions, such as the inclusion of phonetic concentration and accommodation to varying ability levels. Ratings were dichotomized as "high" and "low"; the index used the number of reading sets scoring "high" on these two dimensions. Each of the principal responses and the two objective ratings were dichotomized, and a combined differentiation score was obtained by totaling the six items.

The corresponding measure of organizational complexity was an index of teacher collaboration—the percentage of teachers (grades one to three) in the school grouped into teams for reading. The principal was asked to identify collaborative teacher work groups in his school. He was then asked to indicate the number of teachers in each and to choose one of five criteria that most closely described how the teachers in that group worked together. (See Appendixes) In order to qualify as a team, the principal reported that teachers either planned together, taught together, or had collective responsibility for students. The index of teacher collaboration was obtained by dividing the number of teachers in groups meeting one of three criteria by the total number of teachers (grades one to three) in the school. The independent and dependent variables in our analysis are summarized in Table 5-1.

TABLE 5-1. Summary of district and school organizational characteristics and two measures of innovation—instructional differentiation and teaming for reading instruction[a]

Independent variables	*Dependent variables*
District level	Reading instruction differentiation
Per student expenditure	An index combining principal's typifica-
Based on average daily attendance.	tion of the extent to which reading in-
External funds	struction in the school is differentiated
Amount of special state and federal	and the differentiation rating given the
funds received by the district.	reading materials used by teachers in the
Special administrator ratio	school.
Proportion of total district adminis-	
trative staff in special administrative	
positions.	
District size	
Total number of schools in district.	
School level	Teaming for reading instruction
Principal leadership	The proportion of teachers in the school
An index based on principal's report	reported by the principals as planning to-
of the number of issues over which	gether, teaching together, or having joint
he has strong influence compared to	responsibility for students in reading.
teachers or district administrators	
and the amount of time he spends	
stimulating educational change.	
School evaluation structure	
An index based on principal's report	
of the frequency with which reading	
teachers are evaluated and the fre-	
quency with which the reading pro-	
gram is evaluated.	
Open space	
Principal's report of the number of	
architecturally open instructional	
spaces in the school.	
School community climate	
Principal's report of community atti-	
tudes toward school—innovative, tra-	
ditional, or mixed.	
School size	
Number of students enrolled in the	
school.	

[a]For purposes of regression analysis, all variables with extreme values were recorded to reduce the effect of skewed distributions.

Results of the Analysis

Viewed descriptively, the results of our cross-sectional analysis show schools to be involved in a wide range of innovation in organization and instruction. Clearly, elementary schools in the San Francisco Bay Area have moved away from a pattern of self-contained classrooms where a single teacher, isolated from colleagues, teaches a group of thirty students the same lesson. Even the common modification of whole-class instruction into three ability groups appears to be changing (see Table 5-2).

These results are not surprising. Carlson (1956), Miles (1964), Havelock (1973), and others find schools adopting a large volume and wide variety of instructional or organizational innovations. The educational climate both in school systems and in the general educational community appears to have moved from a preservation of the status quo to a commitment to change or innovation that makes the classroom and instruction more complex.

When a principal reports the adoption of an innovation, we find that the change is not necessarily significant. As an example, 73 percent of the principals in our sample report having teacher teams in their schools. However, when we inquire further into the way such teams function, we find that 70 percent of those reported function at a very low level of interdependence. Only 30 percent actually teach together or have joint responsibility for a single group of students.

Although simple measures of innovation suggest radical changes in the schools of this area, our more detailed inquiry reveals that few schools are truly reconstituted in more complex ways. The detailed character of our measures reveals lower levels of innovation than other studies using checklists of innovations adopted at the district level.

The two dependent measures selected as representing complex changes in instruction and classroom organization tap two important aspects of the total educational innovation reported by schools in the sample. In order to examine the relationship of these two measures of innovation—instructional differentiation and teaming—to district- and school-level organizational factors, we used multiple regression as the mode of analysis. Multiple regression allows us to enter several organizational factors simultaneously into an equation with either teaming or instructional differentiation and to look at the independent effects of each organizational factor when all others in the equation are held constant.

As we look at the results in Table 5-3, we see that significant district-level predictors of differentiated reading instruction are per student expenditure, external funding, special administration

TABLE 5-2. Percentage of principals reporting instructional, organizational, and architectural innovations in 188 Bay Area schools

Instructional	Principals reporting	Organizational	Principals reporting	Architectural	Principals reporting
Four or more groups of students in a typical classroom use different materials	43.1	Some teachers organized in teams	73.4	One or more open-space instructional pods in school	50.0
Reading program integrated with other subjects	24.6	At least one team of teachers in which each teaches a different grade level	30.0		
Major changes in reading program in the last two years	49.5	One or more multi-graded or ungraded classrooms	43.7		
One or more classrooms where students have high autonomy	26.6	More than two special classroom teachers	86.6		
One or more classes where students work independently	61.6	Two or more paid classroom aides	67.8		
		Two or more adult volunteers	87.5		
		One or more specialists based at school	49.5		
		One or more specialists operating from the district	87.0		

TABLE 5-3. Regression analysis: Normalized regression coefficients (Beta) showing the relationship of district and school organizational characteristics to reading instruction differentiation and teachers in teams for reading

	District level				School level					Total variance expenditure (R^2)
Measures of innovation	Per student expenditure	External funding	Special administration ratio	District size	Principal leadership	Evaluation structure	Open space	School size	Community climate	
Differentiation of reading instruction	.27[a]	.22[a]	.17[a]	-.36[a]	.18[a]	.12[a]	.29[a]	-.19[a]	.02	.23
Teachers in teams for reading instruction	.21[a]	-.07	.26[a]	.03	.15[a]	-.01	.30[a]	-.02	.15[a]	.23

[a]Significance level = p $<$ .01.

ratio,[1] and district size. The first three characteristics affect instructional differentiation positively. Of these, per student expenditure shows the strongest effect. The special administration ratio is significantly weaker. District size, on the other hand, negatively affects instructional differentiation and is the strongest predictor variable in the equation. When, in a separate analysis, we look at the correlates of size, size is related both to a district's urban location (.60) and its minority population (.47), but even when we control for these two factors (not shown in Table 5-3), size has a significant negative relationship to differentiation. This is discussed again later.

At the school level, open space has the strongest independent effect on reading differentiation. Principal leadership and evaluation structure relate significantly to differentiation; the relationship of school size to differentiation is consistent with that of district size. At the school level, however, the relationship is not as substantial. The relationship of community climate to reading differentiation is not significant.

The pattern of relationships for teaming is different. The district-level characteristic per pupil expenditure shows a strong relationship to the principal's report of the proportion of teachers in his school grouped for reading. However, the relationship is weaker for teaming than it was for differentiation. In contrast, special administrative ratio is now somewhat stronger than it was for differentiation. External funding does not show a significant relationship to teaming; nor does district size.

At the school level, open space and principal leadership predict teaming in about the same way as they predicted reading differentiation. However, school evaluation structure and school size are no longer significant predictors, for neither is related to teaming. Community climate, now that we look at the percentage of teachers in teams for reading, becomes a significant predictor.

In summary, size of both schools and school districts appears to be a characteristic that constrains curricular innovation. On the other hand, district wealth, and external funding, both of which are characteristics of districts in large, urban areas (simple correlations of .27 and .22, respectively), appear as facilitating forces. A strong principal and a vigorous evaluation structure, both of which permit frequent evaluation of teachers and programs, are organizational features of a school that relate to instructional differentiation, but, as we note

1. This is the only case in Table 5-3 where the introduction of additional variables has a substantial effect. When we include minority population and urban location in the equation, special administration ratio becomes insignificant.

later, the causal direction seems less clear than it does for the district-level variables. Open-space schools, a phenomenon of suburban areas (correlation, .29), are likely to have reading programs that are differentiated.

Open-space schools with strong principals in an innovative community climate are likely to have teachers organized in teams for reading. District wealth and special administrators also tend to have positive effects on the development of teacher work groups.

Some Problems of Interpretation

The analysis of the district- and school-level factors that relate to our two measures of educational innovation presents a picture that is misleadingly clear, for the results are inconsistent. The pattern of relationships for the district and school organizational factors are different for teaming and for differentiation. Also, other organizational characteristics that do not work at either the school or district level raise many questions about the ones that do. The following discussion comments on some of these problems, leaving aside school size because of its questionable validity.[2] The results are graphically displayed in Figure 5-1. Looking at this visual representation of the data from an organizational perspective is somewhat troubling.

District-level organizational characteristics related to innovation are special administrative ratio, per pupil expenditure, and external funding. Money and special administrators affect both measures; external funding affects only instructional differentiation.

The special administrative ratio relates more strongly to teaming than it does to instructional differentiation.[3] But what is the process through which special administrators at the district level affect either instructional differentiation or teaming? One obvious possibility is that these specialists create programs that create new patterns of instruction or work arrangements. If this were true, we would expect that specialists from the district based in the schools or school-based specialists would have the same effect. They do not. The lack of a

2. We suspect that the relationship between school size and differentiation is artifactual since in large schools the principal, our only source of information, might be further from the classroom and therefore underestimate the number of materials used in a typical classroom. The differentiation index could be unduly sensitive to this bias.

3. As we noted above, some of our analyses suggest that this variable does not have a significant impact on differentiation, although Table 5-3 presents an analysis in which this aspect occurs.

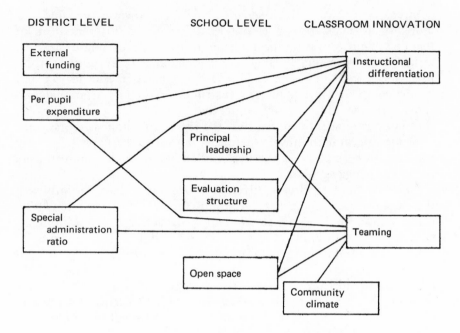

FIGURE 5-1
Significant positive relationships between district-
and school-level characteristics and classroom innovation

similar positive relationship of the specialists to either differentiation
or teaming dampens the possibility that special administrators work
through specialists stationed at the school. The possibility appears to
be eliminated when we look at the relationship between two other
specialist roles and the special administrative ratio. The correlations
are −.16 and .06, respectively. Another explanation is that special
administrators influence instructional differentiation or teacher work
arrangements through the principal. But such a relationship is ruled
out by the correlation between principal leadership and special administrators (−.12). A better link is between the evaluation structure
and special administrators. But here the correlation is .08. Evaluation
is not related to teaming, while special administrators are. It is not
likely, therefore, that special administrators have an impact on instruction or teaming through evaluation.

A final attempt to locate the formal mechanism through which
special administrators might work was to explore the possibility that,
through a network of policies and rules, administrators increase the

complexity of work. In a separate analysis, however, we find our index of formalization does not relate to either differentiation or teaming. Our general interpretation is that special administrators, rather than operating through regular channels of authority, infuse their ideas into the general innovative climate in the district and influence the adoption of new instructional or organizational patterns through simple communication about new possibilities or through personal influence. Thus, the effect of administrators seems idiosyncratic, not the result of formal authority. Perhaps this is why the literature emphasizes the personal ability of such administrators to act as change agents.

External funding affects differentiation, but it does not influence the organization of teachers in groups for reading instruction.[4] Because many funds external to school districts have conditions attached and because, in the case of Title I and Title II funds, specifically, these conditions generally support diagnostic, prescriptive, and individualized instruction, it makes sense that external funds would increase our measure of instructional differentiation. If the process through which these funds worked were of a clear-cut, bureaucratic kind, we would expect that our measures of external funds obtained from the principal at the school level would also affect differentiation. This, however, is not the case, as our measures of external funding at the school level are not related to the differentiation of reading instruction. It is not at all clear how the presence of external funds at the district level affects reading instruction at the school level. In many cases, school-based specialists are funded externally, but, as we have seen, these specialists in a school do not, by themselves, seem to increase instructional differentiation. We are left with a question as to precisely how external funding influences differentiation.

The relationship of money to both differentiation and teaming is simplest to explain. High expenditure of dollars per pupil will buy materials. This would affect the differentiation index since it is based largely on instructional materials. It also seems plausible that a high per pupil expenditure would increase the likelihood of using teachers in groups for reading instruction because money will buy released time, in-service training, and other resources required by the increased coordination needs of more interdependent work structures.

4. External funding correlates closely with district size (.78), urban location (.54), and the district's minority population (.60). With these strong intercorrelations, the effects of external funding may be inflated.

But the expenditure of money for innovation itself does not appear to be a highly organized process. There are no organizational linkages that would suggest how money systematically affects innovation.

At the school level, the relationship between organizational characteristics and innovation seems somewhat more clear-cut although it still leaves many organizational questions unanswered. Principal leadership, his influence and the amount of time he reports spending on stimulating change, relates to both curricular differentiation and teaming. This relationship seems perfectly logical, although it should be noted that its effect, compared to other variables, is not great. Except for the weak relationship with community climate, it is strange that we do not find variables that might account for variation in principal leadership. The leadership factor itself seems weakly structured.

The school's evaluation structure is related to instructional differentiation, but not to teaming. This index is related to that of principal leadership (.20), a relationship we would expect, given the role of the principal as formal evaluator. We are not, however, overwhelmed by the relative strength of this variable; nor are we certain of its causal direction. It seems as likely that highly differentiated instructional programs encourage more frequent evaluations as it does that well-developed evaluation structures make teachers more accessible and therefore lead to differentiation.

The school level variable that consistently and significantly accounts for both types of educational innovation is open space. Because of our previous study of the impact of open space on teachers' perceptions of their work, we are persuaded that, through various means, open space has a significant effect on the reconstitution of teacher work arrangements. We are also convinced that, because of the greater student autonomy that open space seems to encourage, these more flexible architectual arrangements would stimulate instructional differentiation. The factors that account for the construction of open-space classrooms are, however, historical and circumstantial, and there is no evidence of school districts systematically adopting open-space schools to promote curricular innovation.

Open-space schools are a phenomenon of the suburban area (r = .29) where schools have been constructed within the last five years to keep up with rapidly expanding populations. The primary rationale for constructing open-space schools is that such structures are cheaper and more flexible. In fact, we find a negative correlation ($-.24$) between district money and open space.

The effects of open space on instructional differentiation and teaming, while they are highly significant, stem more from history and demographic factors than from a systematic organizational attempt on the part of school districts to alter the fabric of instruction or work relationships among teachers.

One final note on district size. Its significantly negative relationship to instructional differentiation in our analysis is highly inconsistent with previous studies of innovation (Baldridge and Burnham, 1973; Havelock, 1973). We will not attempt to reconcile the apparent inconsistency here except to point out that these other studies asked for lists of innovations at the district level, a methodological approach that may favor size. Because we measure innovation at the school level, we have considerable confidence in the relationship of size to innovation in this study.

Discussion

We set out initially to examine the relationship between two levels of school organization and innovations in instruction and the organization of work at the classroom level. But, an examination of the relationships among these three levels fails to establish that the linkage is essentially organizational in character. Rather, there is a disconnected pattern of district and school influences on innovation at the classroom level. These linkages are not what we would expect, given a formally coordinated organization. Also, some of the variables showing the strongest relationship to the two measures of educational innovation are not organizational but historical and contextual.

There is some evidence of central control and coordination at the district level. The district secures and stimulates the flow of money from local sources and from outside the district and hires special administrators who seem to encourage innovation at the classroom level. At the local school level we find that a principal's strength and leadership stimulate differentiated instruction and the organization of teachers into small work groups; there is also some evidence of community influence. The classroom is affected somewhat by the higher levels or by sources of authority outside the bureaucratic structure, but it remains largely independent of the characteristics of school or school district.

The structural image emerging from our preliminary analysis is one of a series of loosely connected autonomous units. In adopting new patterns of work or new instructional materials and techniques, the higher organizational levels do not control or coordinate the responses of the lower ones. Innovations do not appear to enter the school through formal organizational channels. On this basis, it appears that school organizations are doubly segmented: schools within the district; classrooms within the schools. Each segment or level reacts to a highly innovative educational climate, selecting from this environment new and more complex organizational and instructional forms without centralized coordination and control to make selection systematic.

What are the consequences of this doubly segmented character of school organization? In the prevailing educational climate where change and innovation are at a premium, there are enormous changes in classroom organization and instruction, but these are not highly organized or structured at the district or even the school level. Higher levels appear to contribute ideas and alternatives and to expand the educational horizons of those at another level by contributing to an already innovative climate. While this structure may increase the volume of innovative practices adopted at the classroom level, we have some questions about the extent to which the innovations will be supported or maintained without formal and systematic linkages with other levels.

We know, from Cohen and Bredo's (1974) analysis, that there is a significant relationship between organizational structure and instruction at the classroom level. They have suggested that certain structures within teacher teams are related to aspects of instructional differentiation. When we look at our larger sample of elementary schools, however, we find that the correlation between instruction and teaming is .19. This suggests that the two innovations are not being adopted simultaneously although their relationship, as indicated by the Cohen-Bredo work, suggests that one may require the other.

Philosophical and cultural developments have contributed to a prevailing climate in education where innovation and change are highly encouraged by both the educational research community and the general lay public. But the adoption of innovation has been largely unsystematic and uncoordinated, with the result that innovations adopted may not have the organizational support necessary to move them toward implementation and installation. When an innovation is in trouble, the prevailing response is to select another from the vast array available.

We do not mean to assign the major responsibility for this state of affairs to schools or to those who administer them. It is a responsibility that the educational research community shares. We have concentrated on developing new knowledge and products rather than on developing the organizational conditions necessary to implement and support those available now or in the future.

At the end of our longitudinal study we hope to be able to see more clearly the causal linkages between school organization and the maintenance of innovation. If the speculations based on preliminary analysis are accurate, we would expect to find a difference between structural factors predictive of educational change in the first wave and characteristics necessary to support, maintain, and successfully modify the newly adopted practices as measured in the second wave.

One explanation for the high turnover of innovations is that necessary structural conditions either do not exist or they have been discouraged partially by emphasis on change for the sake of change. There appears to be lack of authority to manage or coordinate complex instructional or organizational innovations at a higher level. This no doubt reflects another feature of the climate of innovation in which coordination or control carry negative connotations. But we argue that some organizational coordination and control may be necessary to support more complex and sophisticated modifications in instruction or the organization of work at the classroom level encouraged by the climate of innovation.

The implications of this line of argument for schools runs somewhat counter to the recent emphasis on the creation of teacher centers or other structural modifications that encourage the dissemination of new educational practices. A segmented organization such as we have described is unlikely to provide support for any complex system of instruction or teacher organization. Advocating the creation of linkages in no way implies that school bureaucracies should reinforce the status quo. It does suggest that organizational change comes hard, and that, to survive, alterations in either the instructional or organizational status quo must have appropriate support from various levels in the organization. It is this kind of knowledge about how to organize districts and schools for effective instruction that educators are seeking.

References

Baldridge, J. V., and Burnham, R. (1973). "The Adoption of Innovations: The Effect of Organizational Size, Differentiation, and Environment," Research and Development Memorandum No. 108. Stanford, Calif.: School of Education, Stanford University, May.

Carlson, R. D. (1965). *Adoption of Educational Innovations.* Eugene, Ore.: Center for the Advanced Study of Educational Administration, University of Oregon.

Cohen, E. G., and Bredo, E. (1974). "Organizational Support for Innovative Instructional Programs." Paper presented at the annual meeting of the American Educational Research Association, April.

Havelock, R. G. (1973). *The Change Agent's Guide to Innovation in Education.* Englewood Cliffs, N.J.: Educational Technology Publications.

Marram, G. D., Dornbusch, S. M., and Scott, W. R. (1972). "The Impact of Teaming and the Visibility of Teaching on the Professionalism of Elementary School Teachers," Technical Report No. 33. Stanford, Calif.: Stanford Center for Research and Development in Teaching.

Meyer, J. W., Cohen, E. G., Brunetti, F. A., Molnar, S., and Salmon, E. L. (1971). "The Impact of the Open-Space School upon Teacher Influence and Autonomy: The Effects of an Educational Innovation," Technical Report No. 21. Stanford, Calif.: Stanford Center for Research and Development in Teaching.

Miles, D. R. (1964). *Planned Change in Education.* New York: Bureau of Publications, Teachers College, Columbia University.

Mort, P. R., and Cornell, F. G. (1941). *American Schools in Transition.* New York: Bureau of Publications, Teachers College, Columbia University.

Perrow, C. (1965). "Hospitals: Technology, Structure, and Goals," in J. G. March, ed., *Handbook of Organizations.* Chicago: Rand McNally and Co.

Pincus, J. (1974). "Incentives for Innovation in the Public Schools." *Review of Educational Research,* 44.1:113-144.

Ross, D. H. (1958). *Administration for Adaptability: A Source Book Drawing Together the Results of More than 150 Individual Studies Related to the Question of Why and How Schools Improve.* New York: Metropolitan School Study Council.

Scott, W. R., Dornbusch, S. M., Evashwick, C. J., Magnani, L., and Sagatun, I. (1972). "Task Conceptions and Work Arrangements. Research and Development," Memorandum No. 97. Stanford, Calif.: Stanford Center for Research and Development in Teaching.

Thompson, J. D. (1967). *Organizations in Action.* New York: McGraw-Hill Book Company.

Appendix A. Variables under Consideration

OPERATIONAL MEASURES, DISTRICT LEVEL		
Variable	*Measure*	*Source*
Per student expenditure	Total budget categories 100-800 (less 500)	*California School District Financial Analysis*—agency for research in education
District size	ADA Number of schools	California Public School *Directory*
External funding	Amount schools receive in external reading funds 0 = none 1 = $1-19,999 2 = $20,000-39,999 3 = $40,000-49,999 4 = $50,000-79,999 5 = $80,000-199,999 6 = $200,000-499,999 7 = $500,000-999,999 8 = $1 million +	S.Q.[a]: Are there elementary schools in district which currently receive special state or federal assistance which provides support for reading in grades 1-3 (like Miller-Unruh or Title I)?
Special administrative ratio	Proportion special adm. District staff (all active at district level)	S.Q.: Administrators with responsibilities for special areas like guidance, special education, multicultural education, community relations, or coordination of personnel in special subareas. Does *not* include people who *do not* supervise or evaluate other professional or certified personnel
Formalization	Three point scale: explicit, general, ad hoc	S.I.: If a school wished to adopt a reading program, how explicit are district policies and procedures which a principal would follow in seeking approval?

ENVIRONMENTAL MEASURES, DISTRICT LEVEL		
Variable	*Measure*	*Source*
Urban location	Density of population (San Jose, San Francisco, Oakland, S. San Francisco equal urban)	Consensus: The school districts were dichotomized based on information obtained from census tract data, and consensus was obtained from 10 independent raters knowledgeable of the Bay Area.
Minority population	Percent nonwhite students in district	California State Department of Education, Educational Statistics Department

OPERATIONAL MEASURES, SCHOOL LEVEL		
Variable	*Measure*	*Source*
Open space	Number of open-space pods	P.I.: Does your school have any "open-space pods" or other instructional spaces where two or more teachers regularly work at the same time?
School size	Total number of students in school enrollment	California State Department of Education, Educational Statistics Department, Racial and Ethnic Funding of California Public Schools
School specialists based at school	Number of specialist FTE's evaluated at school level	P.Q.: List certificated persons in your school, excluding regular teachers or teachers with special classes (evaluated and paid by district), based primarily at school
School specialists based at district	Number of specialist FTE's evaluated and paid at district level	P.Q.: List certificated persons in your school, excluding regular teachers or teachers with special classes (evaluated and paid by district), based at district primarily
School evaluation structure	Combination of two variables	P.I.: In general, how frequently do you evaluate how well or poorly teachers are doing on the task of teaching reading? (7-point scale, from very frequently to never) P.I.: How often do you evaluate the success of the reading program in grades 1-3? (4-point scale, yearly to daily)
Principal leadership	Combination of two variables	P.I.: Compared to all the other factors influencing the situation, how influential are you as principal? (5-point scale, not at all to extremely) P.I.: Rate yourself on a scale from one to five on how much time you are able to spend stimulating change within the school. (5-point scale, almost no time to a great deal of time)

[a]The initials preceding the question refer to the instrument in which it was asked; there were four instruments:

S.Q. = Superintendent questionnaire
S.I. = Superintendent interview
P.Q. = Principal questionnaire
P.I. = Principal interview

OPERATIONAL MEASURES OF INNOVATION		
Variable	Measure	Source
Reading instruction differentiation	Compilation of dichotomized variables	P.I.: Number sets high phonetic concentration and number high ability concentration; were obtained from a coding of the materials listed by the principal. The materials were rated by people knowledgeable in the field and consensus was obtained by 10 independent raters also knowledgeable of the materials
		P.I.: During reading instruction in most classes in grades 1-3, how much variation is there in the materials used? (4-point scale, from all use same to each uses different)
		P.I.: Within most classes in grades 1-3, how do students generally work during reading instruction? (4-point scale, from all work at the same pace to each works at his/her own pace)
		P.I.: In your reading program for grades 1-3, how much choice do materials provide the teacher in assigning students work? (3-point scale, few, some, and many)
		P.I.: Number of sets used in half or more of the classrooms obtained by comparing the number of classes listed for a set reported used to the total number of reading classes in grades 1-3 and then totaling for each school those sets used in more than half of the reported classes

TEAMING FOR READING INSTRUCTION		
Variable	Measure	Source
Percent teachers in groups for reading	Number of teachers in groups for reading meeting criteria B, C, and D, grades 1-3	P.I.: Please tell how many groups of teachers in your school, how many in each group, and which of the following criteria they meet:
	Total number reading teachers grades 1-3	B: Meet and/or plan together at least once every other week. C: Jointly teach same lesson to same group of pupils. D: Collectively responsible for group of students.

Appendix B. Basic correlation matrix summarizing district- and school-level organizational variables and dependent measures of innovation

	Reading instruction differentiation	Per student expenditure	External funds	Special administrator ratio	School community climate	District	Principal leadership	School evaluation structure	Open space	School size	Teaming for reading instruction
Reading instruction differentiation	1.0	.17	−.05	.09	.07	−.07	.17	.17	.22	−.20	.19
Per student expenditure		1.00	.02	.08	.16	.36	.11	.10	−.24	−.26	.21
External funds			1.00	.31	.07	.78	−.02	.10	−.05	.20	.02
Special administrator ratio				1.00	.11	.28	−.12	.08	−.06	.23	.24
School community climate					1.00	.13	.17	−.06	−.03	−.08	.23
District size						1.00	.10	.18	−.12	.15	.11
Principal leadership							1.00	.20	−.02	−.00	.16
School evaluation structure								1.00	.04	−.04	.06
Open space									1.00	.15	.22
School size										1.00	.01
Teaming for reading instruction											1.00

Appendix C. Basic Information—All Variables in Regression Equation
on Reading Instruction Differentiation

Variable	Slope	Standard error	F ratio	Beta	Mean	Standard deviation
Per student expenditure	.00093	.00035	7.14	.27	.1027	229.989
Amount of external funds	.08900	.0575	2.39	.22	5.424[a]	1.981
Special administrative ratio	.01057	.00523	4.08	.17	17.5099	13.0302
		DISTRICT SIZE				
Number of schools in district	−.0256	.01084	5.61	−.36	22.154	11.413
Principal leadership in school	.118	.0536	4.86	.18	4.457	1.227
School evaluation structure	.0591	.0397	2.21	.12	7.0000	1.635
Number of open space pods in school	.0852	.0231	13.61	.29	1.436	2.786
Number of students in school	−.00092	.00041	5.03	−.19	489.340	167.713
School community climate	.0195	.10327	0.04	.02	1.825	.625
		DEPENDENT VARIABLE				
Reading instruction differentiation index					1.9943	.803

[a]Note that 5.42 is based on a construct (see Appendix A). This mean refers to slightly more than $199,999.

Appendix D. Basic Information—All Variables in Regression Equation on Teaming

Variable	Slope	Standard error	F ratio	Beta	Mean	Standard deviation
Per student expenditure (average daily attendance)	.00105	.00050	4.32	.21	1027.798	229.989
Amount of external funds	−.0387	.0831	0.22	−.07	5.424[a]	1.982
Special administrative ratio	.0230	.00755	9.26	.26	17.5099	13.0302
DISTRICT SIZE						
Number of schools in district	.00293	.0157	0.04	.03	22.154	11.414
Principal leadership in school	.1406	.0775	3.29	.15	4.457	1.227
School evaluation structure	−.01054	.0574	0.03	−.01	7.0000	1.635
Number of open-space pods in school	.126	.0334	14.43	.30	1.436	2.787
Number of students in school	−.00012	.00059	0.04	−.02	489.3404	167.713
School community climate	.284	.149	3.64	.15	1.825	.626
DEPENDENT VARIABLE						
Percent of schools where teachers team for reading					2.0652	1.162

[a]Note that 5.42 is based on a construct (see Appendix A). This mean refers to slightly more than $199,999.

6 Elementary School Organization and Innovative Instructional Practices

Elizabeth G. Cohen
Eric R. Bredo

In the available literature on educational innovation, the subject is often handled in a diffuse but concrete manner, with emphasis on adoption rather than implementation. Little attention is paid to the way such innovations affect teaching. This study differs in two respects: It identifies particular current instructional and organizational practices as examples of changes in the structure and technology of teaching, thereby making use of sociological literature on the relationship of organizational structure to technology. Secondly, it examines what these current practices mean for teachers in terms of new ways of working together and new ways of teaching. Rather than being content with a superintendent's or principal's report on innovative practices, we asked a sample of teachers just how they work together on teaching teams; we also asked them to report in some detail on grouping practices and on the usage and variety of instructional materials in the classroom.

This relatively abstract approach to innovation can help us to understand the difference between a successful or unsuccessful implementation of a new instructional practice such as individualization. Because many people believe that learning can be more effectively accomplished by individualization, that is, by differentiating the instructional materials and the mode of teaching for different students in the classroom, a variety of complex curricular materials have been developed and used. Data on achievement in individualized

Adapted from "Organizational Support for Innovative Instructional Programs: Staff Level," presented at the annual meeting of the American Educational Research Association, Chicago, April 1974. This research was conducted at the Stanford Center for Research and Development in Teaching pursuant to contract NE-C-00-3-0062 with the National Institute of Education, Department of Health, Education, and Welfare.

classrooms, as contrasted with more traditional ones, have not definitively shown the advantage of the newer approach. The reason is felt to lie not in the incorrectness of the underlying educational idea but in the variety of ways different teachers approach the same curriculum materials and in the difficulties teachers encounter when instructing twenty-five youngsters on a one-to-one basis.

Organizational sociology suggests that certain technological innovations, such as individualization, require changes in the traditional organization of an elementary school. Bidwell (1965) and Lortie (1964) have characterized the traditional elementary school as an organization with a simple division of labor, where teachers work alone on separate tasks, with little coordination of their separate activities. In order to understand what constitutes an effective program of individualization, it is necessary to understand the more general problem of what kinds of division of labor, coordination, and integration represent sufficient conditions for implementing complex technology.

This study is based on questionnaires completed by teachers in sixteen schools in the San Francisco Bay Area. The data represent the first wave of a two-year longitudinal study of the relationship of school organization to instructional technology. The long-range goal of the research program called Environment for Teaching is to achieve some understanding of the organizational conditions required for successful implementation of changes in curriculum and instruction—what we refer to as the technology of teaching.

The first research question concerns whether or not it is possible to make a general characterization of the level of instructional practice of a given teacher on selected dimensions of technology. If there is consistency across disciplines in the level of technology being used, then it is possible to talk about assisting the classroom staff in raising the level of complexity of their instructional practice.

A second research question involved the association between structural and technological variables. We hypothesized that teaming would be associated with more complex instructional practice. Teaming represents more complex organizational structure than the traditional pattern of isolated classroom teachers. Technologically speaking, the introduction of certain instructional practices such as complex grouping and the simultaneous use of multiple instructional materials also represents an increase in complexity. The growing complexity of instructional practice makes new and difficult demands on the isolated teacher. Thus we have arrived at the prediction that we will find teaming (more complex structure) in association with multiple classroom groups and instructional materials (more complex technology).

Another hypothesis derived from organizational literature relates the rigidity of the division of labor among the staff to the complexity of the technology being used. In the educational setting this proposition can be tested by comparing the instruction of teaching teams having a more rigid division of labor and less interdependence with those having a less rigid division of labor and more interdependence. If the instructional activity being used requires repeated decision making and is not amenable to preprogramming (for example, flexible grouping), we would expect to find more interdependent teams with less rigid division of labor than in classrooms using routine or preprogrammed technology. These two research propositions can be diagramed as shown in Figure 6-1.

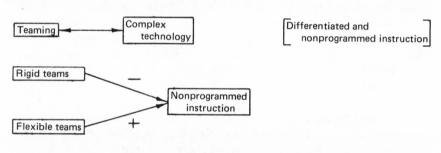

FIGURE 6-1
Diagram of two research propositions

These analyses are only a preliminary step in the research process. They do not include a measure of effects on students. In addition, because of the limits of cross-sectional data, the results cannot show that structural variables are a precondition for levels of technology sustained over time. Nonetheless, this analysis allows us to examine the heuristic value of conceptualizing innovation in terms of structure and technology. If this conceptualization yields improved understanding of instructional practice, future studies can go on to predict consequences for student learning.

Theoretical Background

Teaming: A Structural Innovation

In the random sample survey described by Deal, Meyer, and Scott (see Chapter 5), 73.4 percent of the principals reported that at least some of their teachers were organized into teams. Clearly for the Bay Area (and probably for the United States), the division of labor in elementary school is no longer as simple as that described by Bidwell and Lortie. Particularly in open-space schools, which are common in the Bay Area, teams are a familiar aspect of school organizations.

The Environment for Teaching Program, under the auspices of the Stanford Center for Research and Development in Teaching, has been studying teams for a number of years and has shown that teaming can represent a fundamental change in the interaction and influence structure of teachers. There are, however, important differences in what is called a team. Some teams meet only occasionally to consider curricular development. Others share responsibility for a large group of students and work together frequently in both planning and executing instruction. If teaming is to represent a marked change in the organization of the school, its research definition must imply significant change in the division of labor and the level of interdependence between teachers. For this study, the questionnaire defined collaborative practices as the planning of instruction, student evaluation, joint instruction, and coordination of student discipline. Only teachers who reported one or more of these practices were classified as "team members."

Even with the examination limited to teams, operationally defined in terms of a significant increase in collaboration, there are important variations in the ways such groups organize their work. Labor may be divided according to area of specialization ("turn teaching") or according to the ability group of the students. After a team working in this manner has decided what they are to teach and who they are to teach, interdependence is often limited, and the group meets infrequently. Such team organization reflects a relatively rigid division of labor.

In contrast, other teams appear to work more flexibly, carrying out the joint instruction of a single group of pupils. Assignment of tasks to team members is often varied according to the requirements of particular situations. These teams reflect a relatively flexible division of labor.

Dimensions of Technology

In this conceptualization, only indicators of instructional practice are classified as "technology." In contrast, recent changes in school organization, such as teaming or the introduction of teacher aides, are classified as changes in structure. We use technology in the broadest sense of the word, referring to the educational means utilized to achieve certain student outcomes. It is not restricted to mean simply "educational hardware."

There are at least two dimensions on which educational technologies may vary in complexity. Some practices currently considered innovative represent variation along one dimension; some practices represent variation along the other. The two dimensions are differentiation and nonprogrammed instruction.

Differentiation. This dimension concerns the extent to which a classroom is organized so that teachers treat students differently. At one end of the continuum students are treated uniformly, much like "large-batch" processing in industry. This is the traditional method of instruction. At the other end of the continuum, each student is working at his or her own pace on different materials, which corresponds with the concept of individualization. At midpoint the teacher may vary the number of groups of children and the pacing and variety of materials for such groups. A high level of differentiation might be associated with a heavily preprogrammed "teacher proof" curriculum, or it might be found in a classroom where a teacher allowed students to select from a wide variety of materials as in the "open" classroom. In other words, knowing the level of differentiation in a classroom does not, theoretically, imply anything about the other dimension having to do with the programming of instruction; it only refers to the materials and the number of student groupings.

Nonprogrammed instruction. This dimension, in contrast to differentiation concerns the mode of teacher decision making, and it reflects the manner in which students receive treatment or are given assignments. At one end of the continuum, preprogramming of materials or a traditional method of covering specified areas of curriculum at specified times might make decisions routine. In contrast, children might select their own tasks, or assignment to small instructional groups might be based on continuous assessment of individual progress. In either case teacher decision making is based on continuous feedback during the course of teaching.

Structure and Technology

We propose to test the following proposition concerning the relationship between structure and technology:

Teaming will be associated with more differentiated and nonprogrammed instructional practice.

In addition, we have used the research literature on organizations to derive a second proposition concerning the flexibility of the division of labor on teams and the use of nonprogrammed instruction. For some time sociologists have been suggesting that rigid or tight role prescriptions are more likely to be associated with routine or certain tasks and nonflexible role prescriptions with less routine or uncertain tasks. March and Simon (1958), for instance, argue that relatively certain and stable tasks can be coordinated through programming (for example, rules, schedules, plans), whereas uncertain tasks require more immediate verbal communication to effect coordination. Similarly, Burns and Stalker's (1961) study of organizational innovation suggests that a "mechanistic" form of organization with considerable division of labor is most appropriate under stable conditions, but that an "organic" form with more flexible roles is suitable when there is a high rate of innovation, that is, when tasks change rapidly. Perrow (1970) has also argued that nonroutine tasks will be associated with a less rigid and less tightly prescribed division of labor.

Applying this generalization to the relationship between team organization and variation in the nature of the teaching task, we can infer that:

Teachers on teams in which there is a relatively rigid division of labor are likely to have more programmed instruction than those on teams with a more flexible division of labor.

Examples of programmed instruction would be invariable sequencing of subject matter or permanent assignment of pupils to ability groups.

Sampling and Measurement

Sample Selection

For this study, we administered questionnaires to all the teachers in sixteen elementary schools in the San Francisco Bay Area. As noted before, the schools were part of a much larger stratified random sample of Bay Area elementary schools, where the principals participated in another phase of the study (Deal, Meyer, and Scott, chapter 5). The sixteen schools were selected from the larger sample on the basis of the principal's responses to initial questionnaires in an attempt to maximize variation in teaming, in the use of specialists, and in reported instructional practice. Only schools with a grade range of K-6 were considered. There were forty-six self-proclaimed teaching teams in both self-contained and open-space schools. The sample of teams thus included all of the teams in the sixteen schools. Questionnaires were marked to identify the members of the same team. A total of 232 individual questionnaires were returned by teachers, giving a response rate of about 95 percent.

Concept Measurement

The questionnaire covered a variety of staffing patterns in the elementary school, but in this analysis the focus is on teaming as one structural change from the traditional pattern of staff utilization. All the concepts used in the analysis were measured by items contained in this questionnaire. Many items inquired in detail about the way that teams worked together.

Structure. Teaming is seen as a higher level of organizational complexity than the traditional pattern of teachers who do not work together on any significant instructional tasks. Working together increases structural complexity because the performance of one staff member is now dependent on the performance of a teammate. As noted above, the operational definition of teaming required the teachers to report that they collaborated with other teachers on one or more of the following tasks: planning of instruction, student evaluation, joint instruction, and coordination of student discipline. This definition was, if anything, an overly inclusive measure of a significant increase in interdependence.

To measure the relative degree of rigidity or flexibility in the division of labor employed within the subsample of teachers on teams, indicators indexes involving stability, clarity of role differentiation on the team, and degree of interdependence of team members were chosen. An example of a team organization with a relatively rigid division of labor occurs when teachers divide students by ability or subject matter and use the assignment as the basis of what each team member is supposed to be doing for a specified time period. This instructional practice, referred to as "cross-grouping," is common in team situations. After cross-grouping takes place, scheduling can direct the teachers as to "who does what with whom at what time," and the level of interdependence among team members is relatively low. An item on the questionnaire concerning the frequency of cross-grouping in each subject was used to provide an operational definition of a relatively rigid division of labor.

The practice of "joint teaching" is an example of a relatively flexible division of labor on teaching teams. When teams engage in joint teaching, they can simultaneously teach a common group of students the same subject in the same teaching space; they can rotate among groups or individual students, helping and encouraging as they go, or they can take turns introducing different concepts, even during the course of a single lesson. Teacher roles, in this case, are much less stable and clear. In addition, a much higher level of communication and interdependence is necessary. Just as with the cross-grouping question, teachers were asked how frequently they did joint teaching in each of three subjects: mathematics, reading, and social studies.

Technology. Differentiation and nonprogrammed instruction were each measured by a set of indexes. In the case of differentiation, one index referred to the extent of grouping used in the class. Teachers were asked to rank four patterns of grouping, to show which way they organized their students most frequently. These four patterns were: whole class grouped together; two or three groups; four or more groups; or students working individually. The second index of differentiation measured variation in instructional materials. Teachers were asked to characterize their general practice: all students generally use the same materials; two or three groups, each using different materials; four or more groups, each using different materials; or an individualized program with each student using different materials. The response categories to these two questions were used as a scale ranging from whole-class treatment to individualization.

There were three indexes of nonprogrammed instruction: frequency of group change; the granting of autonomy to pupils; and little importance of sequencing in dictating student tasks. Group change is the frequency with which the membership of instructional groups changes. If student instructional groups are flexible and membership changes frequently, the educational decision making must be nonprogrammed as compared to the case where there is a rigid, caste-like system with stable group membership. Autonomy is defined as the frequency with which students are given a choice of assignment or activity. If students are frequently given autonomy in choosing tasks, we see the instruction as nonprogrammed compared to the case where the students are rarely given choice. Lastly, if the instructional program is not highly sequenced and it is not important for one concept or topic to follow another in a set order, this, too, is considered an index of nonprogrammed instruction in comparison to the class where instruction is highly sequenced.

Teachers were asked to report on these three aspects of their instruction, separately for reading, mathematics, and social studies. They reported on the frequency with which classroom groupings changed membership, the frequency of free student choice of activity, and the importance of presentation of lessons or concepts in a particular order to the instructional program in each subject area.

Results

In reporting results the interrelationship of indexes of differentiation and nonprogrammed instruction across subject areas for a given classroom must first be examined. This examination permits us to see whether we can make an overall characterization of a classroom as to technological level of complexity. Then, the prediction of an association between teaming and increased complexity of instructional practice is tested, and, finally, the proposition comparing teams differing in flexibility of their division of labor.

Patterns of Instructional Practice

The types of instructional practices teachers reported using in each of the three subjects were quite different. Marked differences in grouping practices are shown in Table 6-1.

TABLE 6-1. Percentage of teachers reporting various grouping practices, by subject

	Subject		
Type of grouping	Math (N = 212)	Reading (N = 216)	Social studies (N = 208)
Whole class	26	10	74
Two to three groups	32	35	11
Four or more groups	8	31	5
Individualized	34	24	10
TOTAL	100	100	100

It seems that reading is likely to be conducted in small groups, while whole-class instruction is typical in social studies. Math shows the greatest variation: the most frequent patterns are two to three small groups or whole-class instruction.

Despite differences in the way a subject is taught, Table 6-2 shows that there are moderately high associations between a teacher's report of differentiation and routinization in one subject, and the same teacher's report in another subject. In other words, teachers tend to be consistent across subjects, and there is a general tendency toward differentiation or routinization that is characteristic of a particular teacher and class.

Not only is the relative complexity of instruction consistent across subject areas in a particular teacher's practice, but Table 6-3 shows

TABLE 6-2. Correlations of instructional practices across subjects for three instructional variables

Instructional practices, by subject	Subject		
	Math	Reading	Social studies
Materials variation			
Math	1.00	.41[a]	.20
Reading	—	1.00	.24[a]
Social studies	—	—	1.00
Group change			
Math	1.00	.60[a]	.48[a]
Reading	—	1.00	.31[a]
Social studies	—	—	1.00
Autonomy			
Math	1.00	.55[a]	.41[a]
Reading	—	1.00	.37[a]
Social studies	—	—	1.00

[a] $p < .001$

that all five indicators of instructional practice are correlated with each other. These interrelationships suggest that teachers who are high on one of the indicators of technological complexity tend to be high on others. It is not surprising that the several indicators of nonprogrammed instruction and differentiation are intercorrelated within each of the two dimensions, but we had not predicted that indicators of the two dimensions would be significantly interrelated. In other words, those teachers who differentiate their instruction are also likely to have nonprogrammed instruction. Conversely, those that do not differentiate are likely to use more programmed practices.

TABLE 6-3. Intercorrelations of instructional variables, collapsed across subjects (N = 208)

Instructional variables	Differentiation		Nonprogrammed instruction		
	Grouping	Materials variation	Autonomy	Group change	Sequencing
Differentiation					
Grouping	1.00	.56[a]	.40[a]	.31[a]	.20[b]
Materials variation	—	1.00	.42[a]	.35[a]	.28[c]
Nonprogrammed instruction					
Autonomy	—	—	1.00	.37[a]	.23[a]
Group change	—	—	—	1.00	.21[c]
Sequencing	—	—	—	—	1.00

[a] $p < .001$
[b] $p < .01$
[c] $p < .05$

Summarizing these three tables, there is a positive association between indexes of complexity across subject matter areas in classrooms; teachers who report one innovative instructional practice also tend to report others. These findings hold despite considerable difference in the complexity of typical practice in different subjects. Second, there is a positive intercorrelation between the different indexes we have used for each dimension of complexity of the technology: the degree of programming and differentiation. Finally, it is clear that the two dimensions of technology are associated: differentated and nonprogrammed instruction are positively associated.

Teaming and Technological Complexity

The relationships between teaming and the two dimensions of technology are shown in Table 6-4.

TABLE 6-4. Relationships between teaming and instructional practices

Relation	Degrees of freedom	x^2
Teaming and differentiation		
Team x Grouping	2	9.3[b]
Team x Materials variation	2	13.2[b]
Teaming and nonprogrammed instruction		
Team x Group change	1	1.4
Team x Sequencing	2	9.1[c]
Team x Autonomy	2	15.4[a]

[a] $p < .001$
[b] $p < .01$
[c] $p < .05$

The chi-square values in the table show that there are significant relationships between teaming and both indicators of instructional differentiation. In both cases these relationships are positive: those that are on teams report more differentiated instructional practices than those that are not on teams. Teaming is also related to two of the three indicators of programming, but the relationship is negative: those that team have less programmed instructional practices.

Except for the nonsignificant relationship between the presence of teaming and the frequency of pupil group change, these findings support the prediction of a positive association between increased complexity in school organization and increased complexity in technology. In other words, those teachers in our sample who are team members are more likely than teachers not on teams to report that they have many instructional groups in their classes and that they use a wide variety of instructional materials. They are also less likely to stress the sequencing of subject matter and more likely to allow children to choose tasks frequently.

Team Analysis: Division of Labor and Instructional Programming

In order to test the proposition on team organization and programming of teaching tasks, it was necessary to analyze the data at the team, rather than the individual, level. Scores for teammates were averaged together to obtain aggregate scores. Tables in this section are based solely on information from teachers in the sample classified as team members. There were 46 teams composed of a total of 103 teachers, an effective reduction in sample size from a previous total of more than two hundred. This reduced sample size makes it more difficult to reach high levels of statistical significance.

We distinguished earlier between two different types of teams: those with highly differentiated roles and those with more flexible, undifferentiated role structures. We also suggested that the use of cross-grouping was indicative of stable role differentiation and lowered interdependence. The use of joint teaching resulted in more flexible, undifferentiated roles and increased interdependence. Table 6-5 shows the relationships between these two methods of collaboration and the three indexes of programming.

TABLE 6-5. Correlations of cross-grouping and joint teaching with indicators of instructional routinization

Types of collaboration	Indexes of nonprogrammed instruction		
	Group change	Autonomy	Sequencing unimportant
Cross-grouping	−.23	−.16	.04
Joint teaching	.64[a]	.16	−.11

[a] $p < .01$

In Table 6-5, the predicted association between flexibility in team organization and programming is clearly supported only for the item measuring frequency of instructional group change. Teams using cross-grouping are less likely to make frequent changes in instructional groups than teams that do not cross-group (although the correlation is not quite significant at the .05 level). Also, the report of joint teaching by members of a given team is positively correlated with frequency of membership change (+.64). The relationship for autonomy is in the predicted direction, but it does not reach statistical significance. Team organization does not appear to relate to the importance placed on sequencing.

Because of differences between subject matters, it is advisable to examine the relationship between team organization and instructional programming separately for mathematics, reading, and social studies (Table 6-6). There is a marked positive association between joint teaching and frequent group change for each subject area. The relationship between cross-grouping and group change is negative, as predicted, but considerably weaker when broken down by subject matter. The positive relationship of joint teaching and autonomy is stronger for mathematics than reading or social studies. The negative relationship between cross-grouping and autonomy turns out to be much more characteristic of mathematics and reading than social studies. Sequencing continues to show no significant relationship to team organization. In general, the predicted pattern holds for frequency of group change and for autonomy in Table 6-6.

It is important to examine the independent relations of cross-grouping and joint teaching to routinization because some teams may both cross-group and joint teach (in different subjects), with the result that relationships may partially cancel each other. Table 6-7 shows the results of a multiple regression analysis that allows us to separate the contributions of cross-grouping and joint teaching to explaining variance in two indicators of routinization. (Instructional sequencing was not included; multiple regression analysis results were not significant.)

The Betas, or standardized regression coefficients, in this table show that cross-grouping is still negatively related to group change, and joint teaching is positively related to group change. When we examine the relationship with autonomy, however, it is apparent that, while joint teaching is positively related, cross-grouping is not related at all. Together, cross-grouping and joint teaching account for 63 percent of the variance (R^2) in group change, and 33 percent of the variance in autonomy.

In summary, the relationships between role rigidity and instructional programming are generally as expected—with the exception of sequencing, where the relationships were not significant. It appears that cross-grouping decreases the likelihood of group change although it has no relationship to autonomy. Joint teaching, on the other hand, increases the likelihood of group change as well as the likelihood of student autonomy.

TABLE 6-6. Correlations of cross-grouping and joint teaching with indicators of instructional routinization, by subject

Types of collaboration, by subject	Indexes of nonprogrammed instruction								
	Group change			Autonomy			Sequencing unimportant		
	Mathematics	Reading	Social studies	Mathematics	Reading	Social studies	Mathematics	Reading	Social studies
Cross-grouping									
Mathematics	-.09	—	—	-.29	—	—	-.02	—	—
Reading	—	-.18	—	—	-.38[a]	—	—	-.003	—
Social studies	—	—	-.07	—	—	.04	—	—	-.06
Joint teaching									
Mathematics	.42[a]	—	—	.28[a]	—	—	.01	—	—
Reading	—	.47[a]	—	—	.13	—	—	-.03	—
Social studies	—	—	.28[b]	—	—	.13	—	—	-.25

[a] p < .01
[b] p < .05

TABLE 6-7. Regression of cross-grouping and joint teaching on two indexes of programming: Group change and autonomy

Dependent variable	Independent variables	Beta	R^2
Group change	1. Cross-grouping 2. Joint teaching	-.47[a] .66[a]	.63
Autonomy	1. Cross-grouping 2. Joint teaching	.05 .57[a]	.33

[a] $p < .01$, using the F test.

Discussion and Conclusions

Viewing today's innovative practices in a more abstract manner has resulted in findings with practical potential:

1. There is a positive association between indicators of complexity of instructional practice across subject matters for a given classroom.
2. Teaming is associated with more highly differentiated and less routinized instructional practice.
3. Within the sample of teams, there is a strong positive correlation between joint teaching and the frequency of the change in membership of student groups; independent of this association, there is a strong negative correlation between cross-grouping and the frequency of group change.

This data analysis suggests that classroom instructional practice can be characterized technologically, much as an organizational theorist might classify the technology of an industry, a hospital, or a mental health organization. Teachers were relatively consistent in their reported levels of differentiation and programming across subject areas. In other words, teachers who attempt one complex, innovative instructional practice also attempt others. Likewise, teachers who use traditional methods of grouping and programmed decision making in one subject tend to use these methods in other areas. These data support the prediction of an association between increased complexity in the organization of teachers and increased complexity in the technology of the classroom, especially differentiation of instructional practice.

Why would teaming make complex methods of grouping and materials usage more likely? To begin with, it seems likely that instructional differentiation can create a number of difficulties for the teacher. An increase in the number of students engaged in different lessons or activities can only increase the problems of properly monitoring, guiding, and evaluating student progress—simply because there is more to do all at one time.

Increased differentiation also increases the burden of locating adequate materials to teach each student or group of students. Teaming can help in reducing this burden for it is possible to share the available stock of instructional materials and efforts to acquire or develop new materials can be collective. Teams also help simplify the program if team members specialize by subject area. With more time to prepare and develop activities for a single subject, each teacher's load is lightened, even though the total number of pupils receiving complex instruction increases.

One cannot, however, conclude from these data that the formation of teaching teams causes increased differentiation of instructional practice. Several alternative explanations must be considered. One explanation is that the innovations in instructional practice were introduced first and led to the organization of teams. A second explanation is that both teaming and innovative instructional practice are characteristic of certain schools where everything fashionable in education diffuses across both structure and technology. Neither alternative explanation can be eliminated through the use of cross-sectional data. The second stage of this study should, however, prove helpful in ascertaining likely antecedent variables.

When the analysis moves to the actual working relationships of team members, it is much harder to argue that we are looking at a simple diffusion of fashionable practices, and we feel we have stronger grounds for arguing that some types of teaching technology are not feasible without supporting modes of organization. The data provide good support for the hypothesis that practices such as flexible group instruction are unlikely to occur unless team members work closely together with more flexible role differentiation, as in joint teaching.

These data also offer an explanation as to why the mere presence of teaming was not associated with increased frequency of pupil group change. Many teams cross-group and are thus unlikely to change group membership frequently, while other teams joint teach and are very likely to change group membership frequently. Teaming, by itself, is probably not a sufficient condition for such nonprogrammed techniques as flexible group instruction. If the principal and teachers wish to utilize techniques such as flexible grouping, then the way in which the team works together deserves administrative support and attention. It may be the case that a team which has developed cross-grouping as its only mode of operation has chosen to do so as a solution to problems it would experience in working more closely together. If this team is to fully implement a sophisticated nonprogrammed mode of instruction, its problems of interaction and communication may require some improvement.

Viewing instructional practices in terms of our two dimensions— differentiation and programming—has clarified the relation between work group structure and instruction. At the same time, our findings suggest the need for further clarification of how classrooms function that are high on both dimensions of technology. We did not expect that teachers who were more likely to grant autonomy to children in choice of task would also be likely to report high levels of individualization. This type of classroom should make proper monitoring and evaluation of students extremely difficult, especially for the teacher working alone. If some of these autonomous classrooms are exhibiting weaknesses in diagnosis and evaluation of students, pushing this line of inquiry further seems an important topic for further investigation.

By developing and testing propositions about necessary organizational arrangements for innovations that can be classified according to general technological criteria, we can move toward practical guidance for principals and teachers. Educators frequently want to try a particular innovation, but presently have no way of classifying it as to the demands that will be made on the staff. They also have no way of conceiving how suitable organizational support for the innovation might be developed. Without this improvement in conceptual tools and empirical knowledge, it is difficult to see how schools can anticipate and solve the many new problems generated by innovative practices.

References

Bidwell, C. E. (1965). "The School as a Formal Organization," in J. G. March, ed., *Handbook of Organizations*. Chicago: Rand McNally.

Burns, T., and Stalker, G. (1961). *The Management of Innovation*. London: Tavistock.

Lortie, Dan (1964). "The Teacher and Team Teaching: Suggestions for Long-range Research," in Judson Shaplin and Henry Olds, eds., *Team Teaching*. New York: Harper and Row.

March, J. G., and Simon, H. (1958). *Organizations*. New York: Wiley.

Perrow, Charles (1970). *Organizational Analysis: A Sociological View*. Belmont, Calif.: Wadsworth Publishing Company, Inc.

Environment

7 Organizational Innovation: Individual, Structural, and Environmental Impacts

J. Victor Baldridge

People with widely varying interests—anthropologists, sociologists, organizational theorists, social psychologists—have long been interested in the diffusion processes of technological and social inventions. Studies of innovation cover a broad spectrum of social life: smallpox inoculations (Miller, 1957); educational innovations (Mort and Cornell, 1938; Ross, 1958; Miles, 1964; Carlson, 1967; Knight, 1967; Guba, 1968; Keeley, 1968; Corwin, 1972); agricultural inventions (Lionberger, 1960; Rogers, 1962); child-rearing practices among American mothers (Brim, 1954; Maccoby *et al.,* 1959); medical inventions (Caplow, 1952; Coleman, 1966); the introduction of modern machinery into underdeveloped nations (Goldsen and Ralis, 1957). Without question, then, the diffusion of innovation—the factors promoting it, the barriers holding it back, the patterns of communication surrounding it, and evaluations of success—continues to interest social scientists.

One growing branch of the research deals with organizational innovations, the diffusion of new organizational practices. The research

This chapter was prepared with the assistance of Jeannette Wheeler, project writer. We wish to express our debt to several people who participated in the studies that support it. Kenneth Knight supervised the Bay Area project and William Gorth, Gerald Hamrin, Olan Knight, William Penny, and William Schmick participated as co-workers. The research reported here was conducted at the Stanford Center for Research and Development in Teaching pursuant to contract NE-C-00-3-0062 with the National Institute of Education, Department of Health, Education, and Welfare. This chapter is R&D Memorandum No. 124 of the Center.

question usually is: What characteristics distinguish highly innovative organizations from less innovative ones? The answer most often takes one of three forms:

1. Certain individuals are prone to innovative behavior (for example, younger, more cosmopolitan, better-educated males). Therefore, organizations with a high percentage of such individuals are likely to be more innovative. (See Rogers, 1962, and Rogers and Shoemaker, 1971, for extensive reviews of literature in this tradition.)

2. Great organizational complexity and large size promote innovative behavior because of specialized expertise in subunits and because of critical masses of problems that demand solution. (See Wilson, 1963; Hage and Aiken, 1967; Sapolsky, 1967.)

3. Heterogeneous or changing environments are likely to cause problems for organizations that need innovative organizational solutions. (See Evan, 1965; Terreberry, 1965; Baldridge, 1971.)

Beginning in 1968, the Stanford Center for Research and Development in Teaching, part of the federal education research network, sponsored two studies that examined organizational change and innovation. The goal of these studies was to provide a cohesive, integrated, long-term effort to study change in educational organizations. The major objectives were: to test the three major hypotheses about organizational innovation in the same research effort, to test the hypotheses in large samples since a weakness of organizational innovation studies has been small sample sizes, and to spell out some of the policy implications of our findings for the management of educational organizations.

Research Methodology

In 1968 the first of the Stanford studies examined twenty randomly selected schools in seven districts in the San Francisco Bay Area. Complete information about the districts and schools was collected from interviews with district superintendents and principals of individual schools and from district records. In addition, three groups of individual teachers were interviewed: (1) "opinion leaders"—those nominated by principals and department chairmen as being leaders in change efforts (N = 53, all interviewed); (2) "change participants" (N = 428, 309 interviewed); (3) a 50 percent random sample of all faculty members (N = 861, 775 interviewed).

The second study in the Stanford series focused on 1,227 Illinois school districts during the year 1969-70. Only large school districts were considered since small districts of one or two schools would not normally be considered "complex" organizations. The 264 schools studied were randomly selected from elementary districts with over a thousand students and secondary districts with over five hundred students. The data were collected from three sources: a questionnaire sent to each district superintendent, which resulted in a usable sample of 184 schools (70 percent); punched card records of enrollments and other school district characteristics for each district involved, provided by the division of finance and statistics of the Illinois Office of the Superintendent of Public Instruction; and environmental and demographic data for each district drawn from the *County and City Data Book* and the *Census of Governments, 1962*. Because available demographic and population data were based on counties and some school districts were located in more than one county, the location of the district offices was the deciding factor. Although districts and counties were not entirely coterminous, the procedure gave a reasonably accurate estimate of the population characteristics of the district. The Chicago school district was omitted from the analysis because it was assumed to be atypical.

The Dependent Variable: Innovations

One consistent theme in the innovation literature has been the concentration on limited kinds of technological innovations. For example, in the widely used agricultural diffusion studies, the innovation studied had several characteristics. First, it was highly technical, and its effectiveness had been proved before it was disseminated (for example, new types of seeds). Second, there was a relatively short payoff time in which the person adopting the innovation could tell whether it was working and could judge its continued use (one season's crops could usually convince a farmer to use a new seed). Third, evaluation of the innovation's technical efficiency was readily apparent and results were easily interpreted (the farmer could decide on the productivity of the new grain). Finally, the decision maker adopting the innovation was either an individual or a small group, not a complex organization (the individual farmer could choose a new seed without a complicated organizational decision).

It is important to realize that most major social and educational innovations are not so technically narrow or so easily implemented (see Table 7-1). The technology of social action programs is complicated and depends heavily on professional judgment, creative insight, and practical experience. Nor do the results from social or educational technology often allow a brief period during which an innova-

TABLE 7-1. Comparison of different types of innovations

Types of innovations usually examined by the literature on innovation and diffusion	Most educational innovations and social action programs
Clear technology—The processes and their outcomes are readily understood and applied.	Unclear technology—Processes and their outcomes are not readily understood or easily applied.
Short-range payoff—Results can be seen in a relatively short time.	Long-range payoff—Results will be seen after a long time period has elapsed.
Clear evaluations—It is possible to get a clear reading on whether the innovation is effective.	Organizational adoption—A complex decision is needed on whether to implement or reject innovation.
Individual adopter—Individual decides to accept or reject the innovation.	Unclear evaluations—It is not always possible to set definite guidelines or evaluate effectiveness of innovation.
Examples	Examples
—Drugs —New agricultural products or techniques —Machinery and tools	—Modular scheduling —Team teaching —New research strategies —New advising procedures for students

tion's effectiveness can be evaluated. Instead, it may take months or years to determine whether the innovation has strengthened or improved an organization. Most organizational innovations are also difficult to evaluate. The decision base of a farmer is simpler than that of a teacher, a school, or a social action agency. If the grain grows, the farmer knows his innovation is working. But how does a school know whether students have learned social studies better under a new system? Or how does a social action agency evaluate its success at rehabilitating criminals? Finally, the adopter of most social innovations is often a complex organization—school district, university, city government, county welfare agency. The complexity of the decision process and the multiple chains of command necessary to implement a decision make the diffusion of social innovation entirely different from the simple one-man adoption of a new seed, a new drug, or a new piece of equipment.

Different analytic tools must be developed to understand the complex process of organizational innovation. In order to examine the adoption of seeds by a farmer, for example, political coalitions and organizational decision making are not important. It would be suicide, however, not to understand those dynamics in adopting a new social studies curriculum in a public school. To examine innovations such as welfare reform or school integration, it is critical to analyze the reward structure, the authority lines, and the decision-making processes of large organizations. Although rare, research on this type of complex situation does exist in the studies of community adoptions of fluoridation during the 1950's (Crain, 1962), and the adoption of innovations in complex school districts (Burnham, 1972; and Corwin, 1972).

The Stanford studies were precise in examining organizational innovations and changes with relatively unclear technologies, long-range payoffs, organizational rather than individual adopters, and evaluations that might not be readily apparent. Most major social action and organizational changes fall into this bracket. There were three other conditions:

Extensity—the innovation covered a relatively large number of people or processes within the organization and was not limited to a small subgroup.

Importance—knowledgeable observers believed the innovation had real potential for creating change in a major educational area.

Longevity potential—the innovations were well established and appeared able to continue for a significant time period.

In each study the determination of what innovations met these criteria was specific to the situation. In the Bay Area study, principals, superintendents, and department chairmen specified innovations that met our criteria. Of the innovations nominated, one "curricular" innovation (new reading program) and one "organizational" innovation (new team teaching approach) were selected in each school.

In the Illinois study intensive interviews were held with school superintendents to compile a list of twenty major innovations that met the criteria we had proposed. School districts were then asked to specify the ones they adopted.

With this information we were able to answer two different questions: Do people who participate in organizational changes have special characteristics? Do organizations with high rates of innovation have unique features? Three statements preview the results:

1. Individual characteristics, such as sex, age, and personal attitudes, do not seem to be important determinants of innovative behavior among people in complex organizations. However, administrative positions and roles do seem to have an impact on the involvement of an individual in the innovation process.

2. Structural characteristics of the organization, such as size and complexity, strongly affect the organization's innovative behavior.

3. Environmental input from the community and other organizations is a major determinant of an organization's innovation behavior.

Do Individual Characteristics and Organizational Position Determine Innovative Behavior?

Most research on innovation diffusion has concentrated narrowly on factors causing an individual user to adopt or reject an invention. Usually the dependent variable concerned individual adopters' characteristics: Will mothers adopt birth control pills or will natives substitute a steel ax for traditional stone ones? Sometimes the rate of adoption is the dependent variable: How fast will individuals with X characteristic adopt the innovation as compared to individuals with Y characteristic? The independent factors producing the behavior are typically individualistic: Are the adopters young or old, traditional or modern, rich or poor, opinion leaders or followers, of high social status or low? (See Rogers and Shoemaker, 1971, and Rogers' review, 1962.) Arguments about individual characteristics as determinants of innovative behavior have also been specifically offered for educational organizations (Carlson, 1967).

In spite of the individualistic tradition in the literature, we assumed that individual characteristics would not be particularly significant in predicting leaders in organizational change. The Bay Area project compared three groups: opinion leaders, or prime movers in pushing for new curricula or organizational changes; participants, or those involved in the change as followers rather than leaders; and all faculty, or a random sample of the entire faculty of all the schools. If individual characteristics were actually important for predicting change-oriented behavior, there should be rather sharp differences, with opinion leaders at one extreme and all faculty at the other. The literature had suggested that opinion leaders would likely be males, older, less satisfied with their careers, of higher social origin and education, and of significantly higher cosmopolitanism as measured by travel, scholarly journals read, and work experience outside their district. Our results, however, do not support the assertions in the literature. Table 7-2 shows no important differences between the random sample of the faculty and the participants in change. The opinion leaders are a little older, more often males, and have slightly more education, but the differences are small and not statistically significant. This important finding contradicts years of research on innovation diffusion. Our conclusion that individual demographic

TABLE 7-2. Comparison of individual characteristics for opinion leaders and participants involved in change, as well as those of all faculty

Role	Sex: Proportion male (percent)	Median age	Median career satisfaction[a]	Median social origin score[b]	Median degree attainment[c]	Median units past BA degree	Median education index	Median recent units of education	Median "inside" years	Median "outside" years	Median work experience index	Median other districts worked in[d]	Median conferences attended this year[d]	Median summer institutes attended[d]	Median journals read regularly[d]	Median cosmopolitan index[d]
Opinion leaders (N = 53)	74.1%	39.0	1.4	39.7* s.c. III	3.9	94.0	8.5	6.7	7.7	1.3	6.5	2.2	3.9	1.2	3.4	11.4
Participants (N = 309)	66.6%	37.4	1.5	42.1* s.c. III	3.7	91.7	8.1	5.7	7.5	1.8	6.2	1.9	3.1	1.1	3.3	9.8
All faculty (N = 775)	62.4%	35.5	1.7	39.8	3.6	82.7	7.8	6.8	6.0	1.7	5.7	1.9	2.7	1.1	2.9	8.9

[a]Five-point scale; higher score = less satisfaction.
[b]Lower score = higher social class, Hollingshead; two-factor index of social position, range 11-77.
[c]1 = no formal education, 3 = bachelor's, 5 = doctor's.
[d]Indicator of "cosmopolitanism."

characteristics and attitudes are poor predictors of innovative behavior is supported by Hage and Aiken (1970, pages 122-123), who report:

> The results of our study [of social welfare agencies] clearly suggest that structural properties were much more highly associated with the rate of program change than attitudes toward change. This implies that the structure of an organization may be more crucial for the successful implementation of change than the particular blend of personality types in an organization.

Individual characteristics do not explain much about innovative behavior of people in the organizational context. The explanation seems quite simply that when individuals are the innovation adopters, as most previous studies assumed, then individual characteristics are important. When organizations are innovation adopters, however, then organizational characteristics probably account for differences in innovative behavior.

Factors that bridge the individual level and the organizational level are organizational positions and authority roles, factors that our data *do* show to be important for understanding people's participation in change processes. The Bay Area study found a number of positional characteristics that influenced a change:

1. All participants in the change process—teachers, chairmen, and administrators—nominated department chairmen and administrators as critical initiators of change out of proportion to their number (see Table 7-3).
2. Administrators and department chairmen were nominated as the dominant evaluators, the people who made judgments about the quality of work in the change process (see Table 7-3).
3. Administrators and department chairmen were most often nominated as the people who controlled organization sanctions, such as salaries, working conditions, and class assignments (see Figure 7-1).
4. Department chairmen were seen as particularly important communication links between teachers carrying out changes and administrators supporting those changes with resources (not shown).

From our data it appears that administrative leadership and authority is vital to successful innovation. Three explanations seem plausible. First, administrators and department chairmen are links in the communication process that ties together teachers and resources in the change process. Second, administrators are seen as almost exclusively responsible for the distribution of organizational sanc-

TABLE 7-3. Participants in innovative changes nominated as key leaders or initiators of change and evaluators of work in a change activity

	Initiators of change							
	Teacher		Chairman		Administrator		TOTAL	
Participants	Percent	Number	Percent	Number	Percent	Number	Percent	Number
Teachers	46	128	26	72	28	79	100	279
Department chairmen	8	7	31	27	61	53	100	87
Administrators	41	43	11	12	48	51	100	106
TOTAL	38	178	23	183	39	183	100	472

	Evaluators of work in the change activity							
	Teacher		Chairman		Administrator		TOTAL	
Participants	Percent	Number	Percent	Number	Percent	Number	Percent	Number
Teachers	48	396	20	163	32	260	100	819
Department chairmen	24	77	26	81	50	156	100	314
Administrators	40	121	26	78	34	101	100	300
TOTAL	42	594	22	322	36	517	100	1,433

tions and, as a consequence, their support is seen as critical in the change process. Third, the interviews that accompanied the questionnaires indicated that the administrators were extremely important as "boundary role" people, which means that they served as a link between demands and ideas from the outside and innovations occurring inside.

In sum, it appears that, although individual characteristics are not particularly critical in predicting who will be change leaders, organizational position and role are highly influential. It is only when individual characteristics are coupled with an administrative position that has authority and resources that they become vital to the innovation equation.

Shifting Attention to Organizational Features: Size and Complexity

It is rare to find organizational characteristics treated in the diffusion literature. For example, Rogers' (1962) monumental review of the innovation literature summarized the research conclusions in fifty-two major propositions, but not one referred to a complex organization as the innovation adopter or to organizational features as independent variables affecting the process. In fact, Rogers and Shoemaker, in their revision (1971, page 71) of the innovation overview, explicitly state: "By far the most popular diffusion research topic has been variables related to individual innovativeness." Chapters added to deal with organizational innovation once again investigated individual behavior, but they were located within organizational settings this time.

Inattention to organizational factors persists despite the fact that most major social policy inventions being diffused today are used by complex organizations. Educational inventions, community action projects, new technologies in industry, and new health delivery systems are social inventions primarily adopted by complex organizations, not by individuals. More attention to organizational features in the innovation process is needed because organizations are now the major adopters of social inventions and because organizational factors and organizational dynamics are the major independent variables that seem to influence the amount, the rate, and the permanence of innovation. Two characteristics affecting an organization's innovative capacity are size and administrative complexity. These factors are closely related. Many studies have shown that increases in size are directly related to increases in complexity as measured by hierarchical levels, the number of administrative positions, and the ratio of administrators to other employees (Blau, 1970).

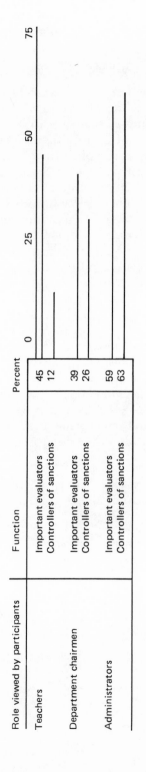

FIGURE 7-1

Participants' view of roles concerned with the evaluation and control of sanctions in the change process

Argument

In most situations increased size and complexity are expected to result in increased innovation. Increased structural complexity (partly caused by large size) requires specialists who see varying problems, handle specialized subtasks, and then initiate search procedures for more efficient techniques to accomplish their goals (see the discussion by March and Simon, 1958). This diversity also tends to produce high levels of conflict where separate but highly interdependent components interact. As problems and solutions multiply, conflicts over resources and goals must be resolved by such integration mechanisms as hierarchical decision making or joint policy making by coordinating committees. Both differentiation, in terms of structural units, and integration, in terms of coordinating mechanisms, help to promote innovation: the former, by creating specialists to seek new solutions; the latter, by providing mechanisms for overcoming conflict (see Lawrence and Lorsch, 1967). Thus, as the number of differentiated subcomponents increases, the quantity of alternatives and solutions also increases in response to perceived unique problems. The diversity of incentive systems and task structures resulting from differentiation is another major reason for increased innovation.

Size, alone, greatly affects innovation. Not only does increased size promote complexity (Blau, 1970), but it also creates problems of coordination, control, and management which, in themselves, demand innovative practices. Moreover, increased size can make spe-

TABLE 7-4. Comparison of size and environmental influence (percentages)

Outside influencing factors	Influence rating		Number of encounters	
	Small schools	Large schools	Small schools	Large schools
State funds	35	52	13	21
Community individuals	46	60	34	48
State law	51	51	29	38
Federal law	37	43	12	21
Federal funds	24	58	10	20
Parent-school organization	40	49	39	51
Local businesses	23	32	17	20
Private foundations	16	13	9	7
Community groups	13	25	11	19
Federal advice	8	20	6	8
State advice	8	18	10	14

cial solutions for certain problems feasible. For example, a small school district is unlikely to have enough handicapped students to initiate special programs, but a large district is apt to have enough such students that special programs are required. Finally, increased size expands the possibilities for interacting with the environment of the school district since additional clients multiply the number of interested outsiders making their special demands, as Table 7-4 from the Bay Area project clearly shows.

Results

Empirical results clearly support the theoretical argument, at least in the two studies supported by Stanford, for increased size and complexity were positively related to innovation. The analysis of innovations in Bay Area schools and districts showed a perfect rank order between increasing district size and increased adoption of innovations. In the individual schools more than three times as many major innovations were listed for the ten largest as for the ten smallest schools. In the Illinois study superintendents identified the major innovations their district had adopted and continued to use for at least two years. From a variety of analyses it is apparent that increasing size and complexity are associated with increased innovation. Table 7-5 shows that, when districts are separated into high adopters and low adopters, the high adopters are larger and structurally more complex than the low ones. There are nearly twice as many students, 50 percent more administrative positions, twice as many full-time administrators, and about 25 percent more conflict-preventing policy systems. Table 7-6, the basic correlation matrix showing the relationship among all variables, substantiates the same relationships: the rate of innovation is correlated with size at .46, the number of administrative components at .45, job specialization at .48, and conflict prevention committees at .24.

Interpretation

The data strongly support the argument that size and complexity are associated with increased educational innovation. This has important policy implications, for although we have no hard data on this judgmental issue, our analysis of hundreds of schools and districts has led us to conclude that schools and school districts, as an organizational subtype, are underorganized. In comparison with most complex organizations, schools and school districts have less role differentiation, fewer problem-solving experts, and a smaller number of support services. It seems reasonable to consider that organizations adopting innovations will sustain those innovations to the extent that a complex organizational system is built to support them.

To translate these ideas into administrative changes, it is first suggested that more role specialization, the creation of specialized positions and administrative roles, will support innovation. The more organizations develop hierarchical differentiation, the more they will be able to handle innovation. In schools, for example, when there are mid-level managers between teachers and district administrators the system can give more support to teachers in their specialized roles. Mid-level positions could include a variety of curriculum experts, skilled technology directors (audiovisual materials, instructional computers), and "change agents" hired to foster and disseminate innovation.

It is also suggested that innovations are likely to be spread widely in an organization that has centralized coordination of responsibility for developing and supporting innovation. In some cases centralized decision making acts as a catalyst for the diffusion of innovation. Decentralization may promote innovation, as many people have argued, but, once initiated, innovation spreads and is sustained by a centralized and administratively complex management. This runs counter to many beliefs and myths surrounding school innovation—that it is supported by decentralization and simple organization. It appears, instead, that schools need more organization and more administrative support if the innovation, once introduced, is to succeed.

It can finally be argued that innovations can achieve long-term support and demonstrate their effectiveness only if they are systematically evaluated. Little serious evaluation is being done in most social organizations where new programs have been implemented. Evaluation units should be an integral part of any social action program. The progress of changes should constantly be monitored, and the feedback should continuously influence the decision-making process. One way to provide creative complexity in organizations is to build evaluation units into the mid-level management structure. In the enriched organizational structure that results more difficult innovations could be undertaken because the individuals directly involved would have backup support, staff help, and specialized resources at their disposal. Increased mid-level management and centralization in social action programs helps spread innovations; the barriers that often alienate individuals are missing. Increased complexity also provides organizational members with a career ladder that encourages innovative behavior appropriate to different levels within the system. A major hindrance to innovation, for example, is the essentially "flat" teacher career line. When advancement is usually reserved for administrators, there is little structural incentive to change.

Environmental Factors and the Innovation Process

Although structural complexity and size are critical elements for promoting change, environmental factors may have an even greater influence. Organization theorists have given increasing attention to the environment in which an organization functions. Organizations obtain input from the environment, process that input, and feed back finished products to the external world. The surroundings place many demands on organizations, however. School districts, in particular, have permeable boundaries susceptible to the influence of their various clients (see Bidwell, 1965; Sieber, 1968). Community interest and influence, always powerful factors in schools, now affect social programs—community mental health and economic opportunity—through "community control" movements.

Environmental variability is a powerful stimulus to the organization. In a rapidly changing environment expectations increase faster than the services offered, and demands for services outrun the ability to pay for them. A more heterogeneous environment demands diverse services, a varied clientele, and a greater competition for scarce resources from the more fragmented socioeconomic and demographic forces. Increased diversity and uncertainty call for remedial action from an organization, thereby encouraging innovative responses. Corwin (1972, page 442) suggests that an organization is more open to change when "it is located in a changing, modern, urbanized setting where it is in close cooperation with a coalition of other cosmopolitan organizations that can supplement its skills and resources." The character of the client population served determines the demand for services, the scope of activities, and the human resources to be utilized by an organization. Similarly, since many inputs in the exchange relationship may be resolved financially, the community's wealth is a major environmental variable.

Both the Illinois and the Bay Area studies used demographic data as indicators of a school environment's variability. In particular, it was assumed that heterogeneous, changing environments would pose unique problems for school districts, causing them to implement many innovations. Therefore, census-type data indicative of environ-

TABLE 7-5. List of variables, indicators, definitions, and sources

Variable	Indicators	Definition	Source	Innovation districts	
				High Adopted 34 percent or more	Low Adopted less than 34 percent
Innovations adopted (dependent)	Percentage of innovations adopted	Of those innovations possible for a district, what percentage had it adopted?	Superintendent's questionnaire		
Size and complexity factor	Number of students	District average daily attendance for 1968-69	State education department	5,335	2,561
	Organizational components	Number of programs and positions formally organized in each district	Superintendent's questionnaire	12.26	8.20
	Specialization	Number of full-time equivalent administrators assigned to the programs reported for organizational components	''	25.10	13.89
	Conflict prevention devices	Sum total of district's use of (a) policy defining the jurisdiction and responsibilities for each major department, (b) rules governing interdepartmental arrangements, (c) job descriptions for administrative positions, or (d) an organizational chart	''	2.88	2.10
Environmental heterogeneity	Population density	Density of population per square mile within each county (greater density = higher heterogeneity)	Census Bureau	2,134	1,135
	Percent urbanization	Percentage of the county population classified as urban by U.S. Census Bureau (more urban = higher heterogeneity)	Census Bureau	73.95	58.24
	Percent nonwhite	Percentage of nonwhites in each county (more nonwhites = higher heterogeneity)	Census Bureau	7.79	4.76
	Local taxing agencies	Number of public taxing agencies within the county in competition with school districts for tax dollars (more agencies = higher heterogeneity)	City and county data book	209.40	136.44

TABLE 7-5 (continued)

| | | | | Innovation districts | |
Variable	Indicators	Definition	Source	High	Low
Environmental heterogeneity (continued)	Percentage of government expenses to noneducation uses	Ratio of total educational expenditures to total direct general expenditures for local government. Inversely related to environmental variability, since a county in which education is the largest public endeavor would have a high educational expenditure ratio, but few other activities (lower ratio = higher heterogeneity)	City and county data book	51.6	47.2
	Percentage not owning home	Percentage of nonowner-occupied housing in a county was assumed to be a measure of transiency in the environment (less ownership = higher heterogeneity)	Census Bureau	38.7	34.7
Environmental change	Change in funds	Percentage of change in operating expenses, 1964-1969 (AV)	State education department	69.39	44.90
	Growth of county	Percentage of change in district daily attendance from 1964-1969	State education department	17.52	16.54
	Migration	Percentage of population moving in or out, 1964-1969	Census Bureau	5.59	-1.18
	Change in wealth	Percentage of change in the assessed valuation of the district, 1964-1969 (AV/ADA)	State education department	1.86	1.72
	Change in racial composition	Percentage of change in percent nonwhite in each district, 1964-1969	Census Bureau	3.28	3.10
	Wealth	Assessed valuation of district	State education department	$32,470	$31,905

mental variability and heterogeneity, including population density, urbanization, the nonwhite percentage in the district, the amount of homeownership, and the number of other governmental agencies competing for resources, were selected.

Empirical Results

The primary environmental data came from the Illinois study, where the variables were categorized as either environmental *heterogeneity* or *change*. Results were different for the two types of environment.

Environmental heterogeneity seems to have a strong impact on organizational innovation. Table 7-5 shows that all six indicators of environmental heterogeneity have the predicted relationship to innovation. Four of the six are fairly strong, with highly innovative districts having much higher population density, about 50 percent higher urbanization, about 75 percent higher rates of nonwhites, and not quite twice as many other governmental agencies in their environment. The differences on expenditure rates and homeownership are not as strong, but they are in the predicted direction. The correlation matrix in Table 7-6 offers additional support for our hypothesis. The relationships between indicators of environmental heterogeneity and innovation range from a low of .25 (between nonwhite and innovation) and a high of .37 (between urban and innovation).

The second cluster of environmental variables dealt with environmental change: amount of money, cost of operating, population growth, migration, and racial composition. Changes in these factors seemed to create new demands that caused districts to innovate.

The results, however, do not justify the seemingly plausible hypothesis. Table 7-5 shows that high-innovation districts differ only slightly from low-innovation districts. Although all the differences are in the predicted direction, only two—changes in funds and migration—seem large enough to be interesting. In Table 7-6 the correlations between these change measures and innovation are extremely low. In short, the various data analyses indicate that environmental change, at least as measured with these indicators, does not influence the innovative behavior of school districts to any significant degree.

Policy Implications: Enhancing Environmental Relations
to Promote Innovation

The multiple demands of environmental heterogeneity cause problems and stimulate innovative behavior in an attempt to solve them.

TABLE 7-6. Basic correlation matrix of percentage of innovations adopted

	Size	Complexity	Specialization	Conflict prevention	Population density	Urbanization (percent)	Nonwhite (percent)	Local Taxing Agencies (number)	Government expenses to education (percent)	Homeownership (percent)	Change in funds (AV)	Growth of county	In-out migration	Change in wealth (AV-ADA)	Change in racial composition	District wealth
COMPLEXITY																
Size	1.00															
Complexity	.68	1.00														
Specialization	.91	.80	1.00													
Conflict prevention	.14	.18	.19	1.00												
ENVIRONMENTAL HETEROGENEITY																
Population density	.12	.09	.09	.16	1.00											
Urban (percent)	.35	.27	.30	.20	.76	1.00										
Nonwhite (percent)	.12	.12	.10	.14	.89	.67	1.00									
Local taxing agencies (number)	.14	.12	.11	.17	.99	.80	.88	1.00								
Government expenses to education (percent)	-.15	-.13	-.11	-.15	-.88	-.72	-.79	-.86	1.00							
Homeownership (percent)	-.13	-.13	-.09	-.12	-.88	-.59	-.84	-.86	.80	1.00						
ENVIRONMENTAL CHANGE																
Change in funds (AV)	.16	.08	.13	-.02	.20	.24	.15	.20	-.16	-.07	1.00					
Growth of county	.12	.07	.08	.10	.17	.29	.13	.21	-.09	-.07	.64	1.00				
In-out migration	-.04	-.06	-.03	.10	-.34	-.09	-.38	-.29	.44	.64	.12	.25	1.00			
Change in wealth (AV-ADA)	-.16	-.08	-.13	-.05	-.06	-.10	-.02	-.07	.04	.06	.27	.30	.05	1.00		
Change in racial composition	.17	.11	.20	.14	.22	.30	.23	.24	-.18	-.19	-.09	.07	-.05	.00	1.00	
District wealth	-.13	.05	-.12	.02	.18	.12	.13	.20	-.10	-.18	-.10	-.06	-.11	-.03	.05	1.00

Organizations that wish to be innovative, to maintain long-range adaptive behavior, and to be responsive to their external constituencies must build viable links with the environment. Constructing and maintaining bridges is difficult, but the following suggestions seem reasonable.

Organizations must continually strive to develop mechanisms that link them with their environment. Many school districts, poverty programs, and a few city governments have begun programs of community involvement through policy councils and advisory committees. This strategy can stimulate innovative practices, but these limited forms of community input must be enriched by additional imaginative approaches.

Another linking mechanism should be a continuing program of needs assessment. Few social organizations have systematically analyzed demographic data to chart and anticipate changes in their community's social structure. Unemployment statistics, wage rates, and the economic and job structure of the community are often ignored in social planning. Cooperative efforts of social agencies could set up regional data centers to process and share demographic information.

An organization could also respond to outside influences through the establishment of technical advisory boards. Community groups have been used by some social organizations, but rarely does long-range technical advice come from a panel of outside experts. Rather than risking an innovative procedure without adequate technical knowledge, a continuing source for technical advice would raise the level of expertise and exposure to the innovation. Such advisory boards have been effectively used in government agencies and in research and development centers, and a skillfully constructed program could give systematic technical help to organizations without becoming a one-shot consulting job for outsiders.

Environmental relationships again further innovation when social action programs cooperate with each other to develop strong interorganizational relations. It has been recognized that innovations are more difficult to promote in structurally simple organizations because such organizations lack resources or specialized manpower. Small school systems with inadequate facilities could, by sharing resources on a regional basis, build innovative programs beyond their individual capacities. Even where political fragmentation and local jealousies make mutual cooperation difficult, mutual sharing of resources still has merit as a strategy to advance innovative behavior.

It is just as important that organizations be stimulated by reaching out to unlike organizations for help and technical knowledge. Facilities readily available to many school districts, for example, are the faculty, libraries, computer facilities, and laboratories of local colleges or universities. Other virtually untapped resources are local industries and governmental agencies that could be strong adjuncts to any social action program. Only lack of imagination, resources, and trained personnel seems to stand between an organization's link with other organizations.

Part of an environmental outreach program should include special intermediary positions between an organization and its community—the development of strong boundary roles. Top administrators of any organization always fill a boundary role, but other links are needed to expand openings to the environment. For example, if advisory councils and technical advisory boards were established, coordinators would be necessary to act in a liaison capacity. If needs assessment became an ongoing process within an organization, people with technical skills and connections with outside organizations would be needed to gather and process information. If interorganizational relations are to exist with colleges, school districts, or industries, qualified personnel are essential to fill boundary roles. In short, if a social system is to interact effectively with its environment, structural complexity and role differentiation must be built in. These boundary roles would function as influential avenues for disseminating innovative procedures as well as channels to provide feedback from the environment.

Summary and Conclusions

This article has argued that traditional research on innovation and organizational change has too often focused on the wrong clusters of variables. In particular, orientation toward the early phases of the innovation cycle, concentration on small-scale technical innovations, and individualistic biases have hindered our understanding of major organizational innovation. In contrast, a more productive analysis of the change process should concentrate on complex technologies with unclear evaluations, shift focus from individualistic variables to roles and organizational structure, and examine environmental factors closely.

The second half of the article presented an overview of results from two research projects on organizational change. The results in both cases support the premise that a large, complex organization with a changing, heterogeneous environment is likely to be more innovative than a small, simple organization with a relatively stable, homogeneous environment. The basic logic concerns a "demand structure": Size makes a series of demands about coordination, control, and complexity to which an organization must respond. Differentiation and structural complexity produce specialists searching for new solutions to task demands within their specialized realms. And, a heterogeneous and changing environment surrounding an organization makes numerous demands for responsive behavior.

These structural characteristics of organizations go far toward explaining innovative behavior. They certainly cannot replace other interpretations such as the personality characteristics of administrators or the unique character of the innovations. When coupled with the alternative explanations, however, the structural variables account for much innovative behavior.

These findings have a number of serious policy implications for people who wish to make changes in educational or other types of organizations. The findings support the argument that size affects innovation and that masses of organizational participants generate a "demand structure" to facilitate innovation. School administrators throughout the country have been arguing for years that consolidating small districts would result in efficiencies and economic benefits. In addition, the results suggest that consolidation would promote innovative practices.

The findings also suggest that differentiation and structural complexity are critical for innovation. For example, relatively undifferentiated smaller school systems do not have enough problem-solving capacity nor enough specialized experts to promote innovative behavior. Deliberate attempts at differentiation can be made, such as employing "change agents" to disseminate emerging innovations and technologies. Other strategies to foster organizational innovation are to establish cooperative agencies to gather data and process information and to set up interorganizational committees on innovation.

The concern for structural factors that promote innovation also suggests that we must more carefully study structural factors that will sustain innovation. Unless innovations are structurally, financially, and politically supported within the organization, they are likely to fail, as those who have tried to change organizations can sadly testify. In short, we need research to answer such questions about the actual implementation phases as: What kinds of reward structures are necessary to support the innovation? What kinds of political coalitions are needed to give the innovation viability? What kind of authority structure will support the innovation rather than undermine it? How should the new program be financed? How can the innovation be evaluated as to its effectiveness?

Finally, our data suggest that environmental variability is a critical factor in promoting innovation. In the past, serious innovation in education occurred when community control advocates gained enough power to bring significant input into their district. In effect, we are arguing that any social organization seeking innovation must make itself vulnerable by opening channels of communication and influence to its environment.

This final shift in perspective concerns the overall orientation of organizations toward the problem of innovation and change. Terminology alone pulls us in the wrong direction, for the "adoption of innovations" induces thoughts of a commercial distribution of products from manufacturer to potential buyer. With that perspective, the research and development community may be tempted to become hucksters of particular products, and, in their need to sell, they may overlook the need to build problem-solving capacity into the organizations they are serving. Researchers, developers, administrators, and educators have seldom created an innovative environment where alternatives could be considered and options explored.

In a penetrating comment, Donald Campbell (in Weiss, 1972, page 189) suggests that the tradition of social innovation that ties itself to particular products and techniques has led to social waste and has forced the defense of innovations that did not deserve defending. Campbell argues instead for a risk-taking approach to solving social problems, exploring a variety of innovations and techniques:

If the political and administrative system has committed itself in advance to the correctness and efficacy of its reforms, it cannot tolerate learning of failure. To be truly scientific we must be able to experiment. We must be able to advocate without that excess of commitment that blinds us to reality testing . . . .

One simple shift in political posture which would reduce the problem is the shift from the advocacy of a specific reform to the advocacy of the seriousness of the problem, and hence to the advocacy of persistence in alternative reform efforts should the first one fail. The political stance would become: "This is a serious problem. We propose to initiate Policy A on an experimental basis. If after five years there has been no significant improvement, we will shift to Policy B." By making explicit that a given problem solution was only one of several that the administrator or party could in good conscience advocate, and by having ready a plausible alternative, the administrator could afford honest evaluation of outcomes. Negative results, a failure of the first program, would not jeopardize his job, for his job would be to keep after the problem until something was found that worked.

We must not be in the business of disseminating a particular, exciting new product; we must be in the business of creating organizations with built-in capacities for assessing their needs and creating viable alternatives. The adoption of any specific innovation is a sideline activity that must not consume our energies. Our continuing enterprise should be the building of flexible organizations responsive to their environments, organizations with reserves of expertise and resources to sustain long-range problem solving.

References

Baldridge, J. Victor (1971). *Power and Conflict in the University*. New York: John Wiley and Sons.

Bidwell, Charles E. (1965). "The Schools as a Formal Organization," in James G. March, ed., *Handbook of Organizations*. Chicago: Rand McNally, pp. 972-1022.

Blau, Peter M. (1970). "A Formal Theory of Differentiation in Organizations." *American Sociological Review*, 35.2:201-218.

Brim, Orville (1954). "The Acceptance of New Behavior in Child-Rearing." *Human Relations*, 7:473-492.

Burnham, Robert (1972). "Environmental and Structural Determinants of Innovation in School Districts." Unpublished dissertation, Stanford University.

Caplow, Theodore (1952). "Market Attitudes: A Research Report from the Medical Field." *Harvard Business Review*, 30:105-112.

Carlson, R. O. (1967). *Adoption of Educational Innovations*. Eugene, Ore.: University of Oregon Press.

Coleman, James Samuel, Katz, Elihu, and Menzel, Herbert (1966). *Medical Innovation: A Diffusion Study*. Indianapolis, Ind.: Bobbs-Merrill.

Corwin, Ronald G. (1972). "Strategies for Organizational Innovation: An Empirical Comparison." *American Sociological Review*, 37:441-452.

Crain, Robert L. (1962). "Inter-city Influence in the Diffusion of Fluoridation." Unpublished dissertation, Department of Sociology, University of Chicago.

Dal Santo, John (1968). "School Administrators' Perception of Critical Factors of Planned Change in Selected Illinois School Districts." Unpublished dissertation, Illinois State University.

Evan, William (1965). "Superior-Subordinate Conflict in Research Organizations." *Administrative Science Quarterly*, 10:52-64.

Goldsen, Rose K., and Ralis, Max (1957). "Factors Related to Acceptance of Innovations in Bang Chan, Thailand." Southeast Asia Program Data Paper 25. Ithaca, N.Y.: Cornell University.

Guba, Egon G. (1968). "Diffusion of Innovations." *Educational Leadership*, 25:292-295.

Hage, Jerald, and Aiken, Michael (1967). "Program Change and Organizational Properties: A Comparative Analysis." *American Journal of Sociology*, 72:503-519.

————, and Aiken, Michael (1970). *Social Change in Complex Organizations*. New York: Random House.

Hamrin, Gerald W. (1970). "An Analysis of Factors Influencing Educational Change." Unpublished dissertation, Stanford University.

Keeley, Jean A. (1968). "Criteria for Innovations." *Educational Leadership*, 25:304-307.

Knight, K. E. (1967). "A Descriptive Model of the Intra-Firm Innovation Process." *Journal of Business*, 40:478-496.

Knight, Olan L. (1970). "Characteristics of Educators Involved in the Change Process." Unpublished dissertation, Stanford University.

Lawrence, Paul R., and Lorsch, Jay W. (1967). *Organization and Environment: Managing Differentiation and Integration.* Boston, Mass.: Graduate School of Business Administration, Harvard University.

Lionberger, Herbert F. (1960). *Adoption of New Ideas and Practices: A Summary of the Research Dealing with the Acceptance of Technological Change in Agriculture with Implications for Action in Facilitating Social Change.* Ames, Iowa: Iowa State University Press.

Maccoby, N., *et al.* (1959). " 'Critical Periods' in Seeking and Accepting Information." Paper presented at the American Psychological Association meeting.

March, James G., and Simon, Herbert (1958). *Organizations.* New York: John Wiley and Sons.

Miles, M. B., ed. (1964). *Innovation in Education.* New York: Bureau of Publications, Teachers College, Columbia University.

Miller, Genevieve (1957). *The Adoption of Inoculation for Small Pox in England and France.* Philadelphia: University of Pennsylvania Press.

Mort, Paul R., and Cornell, Francis G. (1938). *Adaptability of Public School Systems.* New York: Bureau of Publications, Teachers College, Columbia University, Metropolitan School Study Council.

Penny, William A. (1970). "Characteristics of Educators Involved in the Change Process." Unpublished dissertation, Stanford University.

Rogers, Everett M. (1962). *Diffusion of Innovations.* New York: Free Press.

————, and F. Floyd Shoemaker (1971). *Communication of Innovations.* New York: Free Press.

Ross, Donald H. (1958). *Administration for Adaptability: A Source Book Drawing Together the Results of More than 150 Individual Studies Related to the Question of Why and How Schools Improve.* New York: Metropolitan School Study Council.

Sapolsky, Harvey M. (1967). "Organizational Structure and Innovation." *Journal of Business*, 40:497-510.

Schmick, William A. (1970). "The Influence of Organizational Positions on Change Implementation in High Schools with Elected and Appointed Department Heads." Unpublished dissertation, Stanford University.

Sieber, Sam D. (1968). "Organizational Influences on Innovative Roles," in Terry L. Eidell and Joanne M. Kitchel, eds., *Knowledge Production and Utilization in Educational Administration.* Eugene, Ore.: Center for Advanced Study of Educational Administration, pp. 120-142.

Terreberry, Shirley (1965). "The Evolution of Administrative Environments." *Administrative Science Quarterly*, 12:590-613.

Weiss, Carol H. (1972). *Evaluating Action Programs: Readings in Social Action and Education.* Boston: Allyn and Bacon.

Wilson, James O. (1963). "Innovation in Organization: Notes toward a Theory," in J. D. Thompson, ed., *Approaches to Organizational Design.* Pittsburgh: University of Pittsburgh Press, pp. 193-218.

8 The School as Social System: Indicators for Change

Max G. Abbott

A systems approach to organizational analysis is one in which the functioning of the organization is considered in terms of a continuous series of transactions between that organization and its supporting environment. Central to this approach are the concepts of suprasystem and subsystem. Except at some abstract hypothetical level, at which a system may be considered to be totally inclusive and comprehensive, all social systems are viewed as being subsystems of some broader suprasystem. Thus, a given organization, in this case the school organization, is conceptualized as a functionally differentiated subsystem of the broader social system in which it is embedded. This implies that the school is differentiated from other subsystems of the broader social system in terms of the particular functions that it is expected to perform to contribute to the effective functioning of the broader system. To perform its functions, and thus to maintain a steady state with its environment, the school organization (1) receives from its environment inputs in the form of personnel and material resources, (2) it utilizes those inputs as sources of energy, to (3) produce for its environment an output in the form of a "certain type of 'trained capacity' on the part of the students who have been subjected to its influence" (Parsons, 1956, page 65).

As is the case with other organizations, the school does not exist in a static world. Its environment is in a constant state of flux, a

Reprinted from *Socio-Economic Planning Services*, 2(1969):167-174.

condition that necessitates a continuous redefinition of the organization's relationship to its environment. Thus, adaptation is essential if the school organization is to maintain a viable relationship with the broader social system. Adaptation may take one of two forms: first, it may occur through attempts to control the environment; second, it may occur through internal changes within the organization.

Numerous attempts have been made by the schools to achieve environmental control. Special legislation has been enacted to ensure the necessary financial resources for continued operation. Autonomous agencies have been established to insulate the school organization from the influence of other political agencies. Public relations efforts have been engaged in to convince the general public that the schools were performing their functions adequately.

Regardless of an organization's success in attempting to control its environment, however, those attempts are insufficient to ensure organizational viability. New social movements, shifting economic conditions, altered political arrangements, and technological inventions and applications all have social implications; either singly or in combination they create social forces that are only partly amenable to manipulation and control. These forces impact upon the subsystems of any social order in such a way as to produce demands for internal adjustments. Thus, innovation and change represent another major mechanism employed by the school organization to adapt to its environment.

Internal adjustments may occur as adventitious and haphazard responses to environmental pressures which are intuitively sensed but only vaguely understood, or they may occur as deliberate and planned actions resulting from a conscious assessment of the exigencies associated with changing social conditions. Although it is undoubtedly the case that even the most deliberately self-conscious organizations adapt somewhat adventitiously and haphazardly, the more successful an organization is in assessing the shifting forces in its environment, and in making appropriate adjustments to those forces, the more successful will that organization be in resisting temporary pressures to accommodate to transitory social movements.

In achieving and maintaining a steady state with its environment while preserving its own corporate and functional identity, therefore, the problem for the school organization is that of assessing accurately changing social forces, of reacting minimally to those that are peripheral or transitory, and of adjusting intelligently to those that are basic and enduring. This can be accomplished only through deliberate planning and foresight and through conscious attempts to direct the shifting forces through which the organization interacts with its environment. The remainder of this paper, therefore, represents in outline form the beginning of an attempt to determine those properties or attributes of the school organization that will increase the probabilities of bringing about deliberate and planned change.

In attempting this type of analysis, we are immediately confronted with two major problems that have not yet been adequately resolved. The first of these is a definitional problem: What is an appropriate definition for the term innovation? For the present, innovation shall be defined as a qualitative change that results in a restructuring of relationships or events. Thus, for example, the addition of a teacher to a faculty would not by itself represent an innovation. On the other hand, a redefinition of the teacher's role vis-à-vis students, administrators, or other teachers would be an innovation.

Within this framework, innovations may be introduced into the schools in respect to: (1) subject matter content and organization, (2) instructional procedures and technologies, (3) methods of organizing students for learning, (4) methods of organizing teachers and students for instruction, and (5) methods of organizing schools for administrative and supervisory purposes.

The second major problem is that of deciding on the basic unit for analysis. It is tempting to concentrate on the individual and to attempt analyses in psychological terms. Such an approach is unsatisfactory, however, since it represents an overly simplified view of the nature of the role relationships that constitute a social system. Since most organizational change involves changing roles, and the structure that defines them, it appears to be essential to utilize an identifiable social group as the unit of analysis. For the present, I propose to look at a given school as the basic unit of analysis and to consider such other phenomena as relationships between the school and the central office or subgroupings within the school as variables to be investigated. In this analysis, variables must be defined in terms of group norms or patterns of characteristics rather than in terms of individual needs and characteristics.

In analyzing the process by which innovations are introduced into a school, and in relating that process to organizational attributes or properties, it would appear to be useful to break the process into three conceptually distinct phases. The first of these is an awareness phase during which dissatisfaction with the status quo arises and through which a search for alternatives is generated. The major issue here is to identify and specify those organizational attributes that are likely to lead to dissatisfaction and to produce search behavior.

The second phase may be termed a search phase, in which search activities proceed and through which new procedures or new arrangements are identified and proposed as possible solutions to the problems that gave rise to the initial dissatisfactions. The essential issue here is to identify and specify those organizational attributes that influence the direction the search will take and the kinds of solutions that will be proposed.

The third phase may be viewed as an implementation phase, during which organizational energies are devoted to implementing those new procedures or arrangements that have been agreed upon. Two issues of concern regarding the implementation phase are: (1) the identification and specification of those organizational attributes that are associated with the acceptance or rejection of various types of innovations, and (2) the identification and specification of those organizational attributes that tend toward the meaningful implementation of the substance of innovations in contrast to the superficial adoption of innovations in form only.

Awareness Phase

Awareness of the need for innovation occurs when practices and procedures which have been considered to be satisfactory no longer appear to be so. The process through which such awareness occurs may be considered in terms of a satisfaction-dissatisfaction balance. To quote March and Simon (1958):

> ... organizations give preferred treatment to alternatives that represent continuation of present programs over those that represent change. But this preference is not derived by calculating explicitly the costs of innovation or weighing those costs. Instead, persistence comes about primarily because the ... organization does not search for or consider alternatives to the present course of action unless that present course is in some sense "unsatisfactory."
> The amount of *search* decreases as *satisfaction* increases. Where search for new alternatives is suppressed, program continuity is facilitated [pages 173-174].

Although this general proposition helps us to understand why change does not occur, it is not very helpful in explaining the conditions under which innovation will occur. To understand the occasions for innovation, or to explain the sources of dissatisfaction, it is necessary to employ the notion of "levels of aspiration." In general terms, dissatisfaction with existing procedures or arrangements will occur when there exists a perceived disparity between performance and aspirations. Two major problems in analyzing the occasions for innovation, then, are: (1) determining the bases for establishing levels of aspiration, and (2) identifying the conditions under which a disparity between performance and aspirations will be perceived.

The first and perhaps most important source of levels of aspiration is past performance. When other factors are held constant, organizations tend over time to adjust their aspirations for performance to coincide closely with past performance. A second major source of levels of aspiration resides in the comparisons that organizations make with other similar organizations. In general, organizations tend to adjust their levels of aspiration to coincide with the performance achieved by other organizations with which they compare themselves. From these generalizations, a number of more specific propositions and hypotheses might be derived regarding the relationships between organizational attributes and the initiation of search behavior.

Proposition 1. *In the absence of objective criteria against which performance might be assessed, dissatisfaction with past performance will be most likely to occur when stress is imposed from sources that are external to organization itself.* When objective criteria for assessing performance are not available, aspirations are left vague, and schools encounter difficulty in determining whether or not performance is satisfactory. In such a situation, aspirations tend to be defined in terms of current and past performance. Under these conditions, dissatisfaction and accompanying search activities are not likely to occur unless external demands and criticism reach such a point as to threaten to destroy the relationship that exists between the school and its environment. The criticism that followed the launching of Sputnik I, and the ensuing flurry of innovative activity in the schools, is a case in point. It might be noted parenthetically that the dissatisfaction with the schools that was expressed by the general public following Sputnik I had a comparative base; that is, it grew out of comparisons that were made between American and Russian schools.

Proposition 2. *The extent to which objective criteria for performance will lead to search behavior and innovative activity varies with both the source and nature of the criteria.* It would appear to be obvious that objective criteria alone will not lead automatically to a search for new organizational arrangements and procedures. In the first place, objective criteria may either enhance or inhibit innovation, depending upon the outcomes toward which they are directed. In the second place if criteria are to influence behavior they must be accepted and internalized by those members of the organization whose behaviors they are intended to affect. From these generalizations, two hypotheses might be derived.

Hypothesis 2-A. *Objective criteria for performance will increase search behavior within a given school only if those criteria are stated, at least in part, in terms of the need for innovative activities.*

Hypothesis 2-B. *Objective performance criteria that are imposed upon a school organization from external sources will bear little or no relationship to the amount of search behavior engaged in by members of that organization. When a relationship does exist, it will tend to be negative.*

Proposition 3. *In the absence of objective criteria against which performance might be assessed, search for new organizational arrangements and procedures that is initiated from within an organization will result from comparisons that are made with relevant others.* Although it was indicated in Proposition 1 that dissatisfaction with past performance will most likely occur when stress is imposed from external sources, dissatisfaction may also result when individuals or groups perceive their own performance as comparing unfavorably with that of other relevant individuals or groups, even though no objective criteria for performance are available. From this proposition, the following hypotheses are suggested.

Hypothesis 3-A. *Within a school or school district, the amount of search behavior engaged in by individuals will be related directly to the extent to which the work structure provides opportunities for those individuals to observe the performance of others engaged in similar work or to be aware of the outcomes of that performance.*

Hypothesis 3-B. *The amount of search behavior engaged in by a school faculty as a work group will be related directly to the opportunities that the members of that faculty have to be aware of the performance of other similar schools.*

Based upon Hypothesis 3-B, it would be expected that search behavior will occur most frequently in suburban schools and school districts, that it will occur somewhat less frequently in schools in large urban centers, and that it will occur least frequently in isolated rural schools.

Proposition 4. *In general, internally initiated search behavior will most likely occur as a continuous process in those organizations in which the task structure requires collaborative planning and in which explicit provisions are made for such planning.* This proposition is similar to March and Simon's (1958, pages 186-187) "Gresham's Law" of planning, which states that "if all the resources of an organization are busily employed in carrying on existing programs, the process of initiating new programs will be slow and halting at best." In addition to the need for planning that is implied in "Gresham's Law," however, this proposition suggests that the time freed for planning will be more likely to lead to search for improved practices as a continuing activity if a number of individuals, whose work is interrelated, plan together. Thus, this proposition reflects the importance of opportunities for individuals to observe, and to compare themselves with, relevant others.

Because factors other than time are important in determining the outcome of group planning, however, the two following hypotheses are suggested:

Hypothesis 4-A. *The extent to which collaborative planning will lead to search behavior depends in part upon the professional orientations of those involved in planning. When the norms of the planning group are "cosmopolitan," search behavior will be more likely to ensue than when the norms of the group are "local."*

Hypothesis 4-B. *The extent to which collaborative planning will lead to search behavior depends in part upon the sources from which members of the planning group seek satisfaction. When members of the group emphasize "task accomplishment" as a source of satisfaction, search behavior will be more likely to ensue than when they emphasize "social interaction" as a source of satisfaction.*

Search Phase

Once an awareness of the need for new organizational arrangements and procedures has been created and search activities have been generated, numerous proposals are possible as solutions to the problems that led to the initial dissatisfaction. To understand innovation thoroughly, it is necessary to identify and specify the organizational attributes that are likely to influence the direction the search will take and that will determine the types of solutions that will be proposed.

Proposition 5. *Perhaps the most general statement that can be made regarding this phase of innovation is that those proposals that are perceived by members of the organization as being threatening to their status will tend to be rejected as possible alternatives.* It is not necessary that a proposal for change have been demonstrated to decrease status; it is only necessary that such a possibility be perceived. From this proposition, two hypotheses suggest themselves for testing.

Hypothesis 5-A. *Innovative practices that appear to decrease the direct control that teachers exercise over children will tend to be rejected during the search phase of innovation.*

Hypothesis 5-B. *Innovative practices whose consequences cannot be predicted with reasonable accuracy in advance of their adoption will tend to be rejected because of their potential threat to status.*

Proposition 6. *The type of innovation considered and proposed for adoption will be determined in large part by the nature of the conditions that contributed to the generation of search activities.*

Hypothesis 6-A. *Search behavior that is generated by stress imposed from external sources will tend to be superficial and will emphasize those types of innovations that have high public relations and image enhancement value but that disturb minimally routine operations in the schools.*

Hypothesis 6-B. *Search behavior that is generated through administrative action will tend to take precedence over other search activities, but solutions will be sought which have a minimum impact upon the way teachers function in their classrooms.*

Hypothesis 6-C. *Search behavior that is generated as a result of shared perceptions among teachers regarding particular problems will occur less frequently than will search generated from other sources, but the search that occurs will tend to be more thorough and a wider range of possible alternatives will be considered.*

Proposition 7. *The type of innovation considered and proposed for adoption will be determined in large part by the climate that exists in the organization.* Although organizational climate may be defined in various ways, included as factors for consideration here are at least the dimensions identified by Halpin and Croft (1963).

The following hypotheses related to this proposition are suggested for testing.

Hypothesis 7-A. *Search activities in schools with an "open climate" will tend to be more extensive with a wider range of alternatives being considered than will search in schools with a "closed climate."*

Hypothesis 7-B. *Search activities in schools with an "open climate" will tend to focus on innovations that are related to improved instructional practices and arrangements with less concern regarding their impact on the social relationships of teachers and administrators, while search activities in schools with a closed "climate" will tend to focus on innovations that are related to improved social relationships with less concern for instructional practices and arrangements.*

Hypothesis 7-C. *Schools that are characterized by a heavy emphasis upon "control ideology" will tend to restrict their search activities and will reject any proposal that would appear to diminish the disciplinary control that teachers have over their students.*

Implementation Phase

As was indicated earlier, the issues of concern regarding the implementation phase of innovation are: (1) the identification and specification of those organizational attributes that are associated with the acceptance or rejection of various types of innovations, and (2) the identification and specification of those organizational attributes that tend toward the meaningful implementation of the substance of innovations in contrast to the superficial adoption of innovations in form only.

Proposition 8. *In general, there will be a positive relationship between the degree of faculty participation in searching for and proposing courses of action and the adoption of innovations.*

Hypothesis 8-A. *Schools in which faculty members participate in the search for courses of action will have a higher rate of adoption of those innovations proposed than will schools in which faculty members do not participate or in which their participation is minimal.*

Hypothesis 8-B. *Innovations adopted will be more thoroughly understood and implemented with greater meaning in schools in which faculty members participate in the search than they will in schools in which such participation does not occur.*

Proposition 9. *The type of innovation adopted and the extent to which the innovations are implemented in substance will be influenced by the climate that exists in the organization.*

Hypothesis 9-A. *Schools with an "open climate" will be more likely to adopt innovations related to the organization of teachers and students for instructional purposes than will schools with a "closed climate."*

Hypothesis 9-B. *Schools with an "open climate" will be more likely to adopt innovations that alter the administrative and supervisory structure of the organization than will schools with a "closed climate."*

Hypothesis 9-C. *Innovations adopted will be more thoroughly understood and will be implemented with greater attention to their substance in schools with an "open climate" than in schools with a "closed climate."*

Proposition 10. *The type of innovation adopted will be determined in large part by the types of rules that exist and by the extent to which the norms of the group support rule observance.*

Hypothesis 10-A. *Schools with a highly elaborated set of rules and regulations will adopt fewer proposals for innovation than will schools with less highly elaborated rules and regulations, and the innovations in such schools will receive more superficial attention.*

Hypothesis 10-B. *Schools in which rules tend to emphasize hierarchical lines of authority for decision making and conflict resolution will tend to adopt innovations that affect classroom practices but will tend not to adopt innovations that alter the relationship between teachers and supervisors or between teachers and administrators. In such cases innovations will be adopted largely in form with little concern for substance.*

The current state of knowledge regarding the schools and organizational change is such that the propositions and hypotheses suggested here are more speculative than definitive. Nevertheless, they are based on current organizational theory, supported in part by empirical research conducted in nonschool organizations. Empirical research in school organizations, based upon these propositions, should lead to their refinement and thus to a more definitive set of propositions regarding organizational attributes and innovation.

References

Halpin, A. W., and Croft, D. B. (1963). *The Organizational Climate of Schools.* Chicago: Midwest Administration Center, University of Chicago.

March, J. G., and Simon, H. A. (1958). *Organizations.* New York: Wiley.

Parsons, T. (1956). "Suggestions for a Sociological Approach to the Theory of Organizations." *Administrative Science Quarterly,* 1:63-85.

9 Environmental Constraints and Organizational Consequences: The Public School and Its Clients

Richard O. Carlson

Propositions are needed in administrative science about the impact of environmental factors upon organizations. We need to know the ways in which organizational structure and behavior are constrained and facilitated by forces in the environment of an organization. There are a great many factors in what can be called the environment of an organization. Some are quite obvious, such as financial ties, material dependencies, recruitment limitations; others are less obvious, such as prestige. The area of organization-environment relations, however, is one of the least-developed areas in the study of organization. This is true in the case of public school systems,[1] as well as in that of other kinds of organizations.

So that we begin with some common understanding of what is meant by the constraining or facilitating influence of environmental factors upon an organization, let us consider an example. Anyone familiar with school systems in California and Pennsylvania will know that, in the former, citizen committees are extensively used in connection with the building of new schools and rarely used in the latter. Even though the literature about citizen committees emphasizes the notion that to use citizen committees is to be "democratic,"

Reprinted from *Behavioral Science and Educational Administration,* edited by Daniel E. Griffiths. 63rd Yearbook of the National Society for the Study of Education, Part II (Chicago: University of Chicago Press, 1964), pp. 262-276.

1. For selective summaries of the literature in this area, see Campbell (1957) and Cunningham (1960).

it does not seem reasonable to attempt to explain the extensive use in California and the rare use in Pennsylvania by suggesting that school administrators and board members are more "democratic" in the one state than in the other. What seems to be a reasonable explanation, however, is that, in respect to the building of new schools, the school systems in the two states are confronted with different relevant environmental factors. For one thing, California school systems must gain the approval of the voters in order to float bonds to secure money for new buildings. Pennsylvania school systems do not need to secure voter approval; they are free to create a building authority to arrange for the necessary funds. Thus, it can be argued that California school systems have a factor in their environment which constrains them in such a way that they find the strategy of the use of citizen committees to be effective. Lacking this factor (and perhaps others) in their environment, the Pennsylvania school systems do not find the citizen committee to be of strategic use in acquiring new school buildings.

As stated in the opening paragraph, the relationship between an organization and its environment has received little systematic attention in the study of organizations. It has, however, not been totally neglected. Some good studies have been made in connection with public schools, and should be mentioned to provide further illustrations. For example, McDowell (1954) has documented the observation that, as an aspect of the school's environment changes, the job of the principal also changes. He has shown that, when the environment contains largely lower-social-class children, principals encourage parent participation in school affairs, and when the environment contains mostly upper-middle-class children, principals attempt to suppress parent participation in school affairs. And Clark (1956) has indicated how a service character in which professionals are dominated by clients has emerged in adult education in Los Angeles because of the environmental factors of open-ended goals, organizational marginality, and what he calls an enrollment economy.

What is proposed in this chapter is to focus on a single factor in the environment of the public school system and to suggest, by way of propositions, some of the ways in which this factor influences the structure of the school and the behavior of its members. The environmental factor is the nature of the relationship between the organization and the clients.[2]

2. The organizational relevance of this environmental factor has been demonstrated by Burton R. Clark (1956, 1960).

In order to do this, it is necessary to suggest a way of conceptualizing the relationship of clients to an organization. That is, it is necessary to point out what appear to be important variables in the relationship and some extreme values of the variables and to develop a typology of organizations within these variables and values. After doing this, we can go on and raise questions about the impact of the client-organization relationship on organizational structure and behavior.

Domesticated Organizations

Attention will be restricted to service as opposed to production organizations. In the former, but not the latter, a social relation is established with the "objects" of work, and motivation is frequently an important concern.

One way of looking at the relationship of a client to a service organization is to bring into focus the extent to which the relationship contains the element of selectivity on the part of the members of the relationship: the organization and the clients. From this perspective, it is clear that some service organizations select their clients and some do not, and that in some service organization-client relationships, clients must (in the legal sense) participate in the organization and in others they can refuse to participate.[3]

If we put the variables of selectivity on the part of the organization and on the part of the client together, we get the possibility of four types of service organization-client relationships as seen in Figure 9-1.

Most of the service organizations we know in the United States are probably Type I organizations: organizations which, either by formal or informal means, select the clients they wish to deal with and are participated in by clients on a voluntary basis. The private university is a good example. Hospitals and doctors' offices also are of this type. In addition, many of the public welfare service units belong to this type. They apply stringent criteria in the selection of clients, and the potential client is not compelled to accept the service.

3. Blau has demonstrated the relevance of another typology of client-organization relationships which involves power of the client as a variable. He has shown in one social work agency that those clients with power as opposed to those without power were rendered more attention from the professional case workers, were provided with more stable relationship with the case workers, and were served by more case workers with culturally preferred ethnic characteristics. (See Blau and Scott, 1962, pp. 77-79.)

Client control over own
participation in organization
Yes   No

		Yes	Type I	Type III
Organizational control over admission		No	Type II	Type IV

FIGURE 9-1

Selectivity in client-organization relationship in service organizations

Type II service organizations do not select their clients, and participation in the organization is nonmandatory. The state university whose charter specifies that it accept (but not continue to serve) all high school graduates who are at least seventeen years old and who wish to enroll fits in this type, for it is not mandatory for high school graduates to attend college. In addition, most junior colleges and adult education units fit within this type.

Service organizations of Type III are seemingly very rare or nonexistent. This type of organization selects clients and is one in which clients are compelled to participate. An organization which has such a relationship with its members (not clients) is the citizen army, but it is not a service organization. When laws specify that individuals having certain characteristics must embrace a given service, it seems that the service is always provided by an organization that has no control over admission of clients.

There are a number of service organizations of Type IV, such as public schools, state mental hospitals, reform schools, and prisons. The clients of these organizations receive the service on a mandatory basis, and prisons, public schools, and state mental hospitals cannot exercise choice in the matter of clients.

This chapter is concerned with only Type IV organizations and specifically with only one of them, the public school. Something can be gained, however, by attempting to see some of the essential differences between Type I and Type IV organizations (the extreme ideal types of the typology) and thinking about the consequences of the differences.

First, though all service organizations, by general definition, establish a social relationship with their clients and thus face a motivation problem, the typology makes it clear that an equal necessity to motivate clients is not placed on all service organizations. It may perhaps be unnecessary to remark that the problem of inducing clients to participate would seem to be most pronounced in Types III and IV, because these organizations are most likely to be in contact with some clients who have no real desire for their services. This factor undoubtedly has many organizational ramifications. To mention only a few, it would seem to bear upon the attitudes which staff members and clients hold toward each other,[4] personality makeup of staff, prestige of the work, and deployment of organizational resources.

Further, it seems appropriate to call Type IV organizations "domesticated." By this is simply meant that they are not compelled to attend to all of the ordinary and usual needs of an organization. By definition, for example, they do not compete with other organizations for clients; in fact, a steady flow of clients is assured. There is no struggle for survival for this type of organization. Like the domesticated animal, these organizations are fed and cared for. Existence is guaranteed. Though this type of organization does compete in a restricted area for funds, funds are not closely tied to quality of performance. These organizations are domesticated in the sense that they are protected by the society they serve. Society feels some apprehension about domesticated organizations. It sees the support of these organizations as necessary to the maintenance of the social system and creates laws over and above those applying to organized action in general to care for domesticated organizations.

Type I organizations, on the other hand, can be called "wild"; they do struggle for survival. Their existence is not guaranteed, and they do cease to exist. Support for them is closely tied to quality of performance, and a steady flow of clients is not assured. Wild organizations are not protected at vulnerable points as are domesticated organizations.

It is probably obvious in using the words "domesticated" and "wild" that the writer has in mind the extensive research on organisms in domesticated and wild settings. The argument is not that organisms and organizations are alike, but that what is known about organisms under specified conditions and their responses to environments is helpful in making propositions about responses of certain organizations to their environments. Of particular relevance to this discussion is that the research has pointed out the tremendous importance and the occurrence of adaptation by wild organisms to their changing environment.

This suggests the proposition that domesticated organizations,

4. Consider Erving Goffman's (1957) work on "staff-inmate split."

because of their protected state, are slower to change and adapt than are wild organizations. There is some evidence to support this proposition. On the one hand, Mort (1958), a perceptive student of change in public schools, has reported that:

Educational change proceeds very slowly . . . .
After an invention which is destined to spread throughout the school appears, fifteen years typically elapse before it is found in three per cent of the school systems. . . .
After practices have reached the three per cent point of diffusion their rate of spread accelerates. An additional twenty years usually suffices for an almost complete diffusion in an area the size of an average state. There are indications that the rate of spread throughout the nation is not much slower. . . .
School systems do not seem to be geared to the fact that the knowledge of available inventions is necessary if they are to improve and that the individuals operating the schools must master this knowledge [pages 32-33].

On the other hand, consider the example of diffusion of a so-called "miracle" drug among physicians. Recent research indicates that, within seventeen months after its introduction, about 90 percent of the physicians in four communities were using the drug (Katz, 1961).

Organizational and Client Adaptation

Up to this point a system for conceiving the relationship between clients and service organizations has been presented, and out of this the notions of wild and domesticated organizations have been developed. In addition, a proposition dealing with change in domesticated and wild organizations has been posed. With this general background behind us, let us turn to other kinds of consequences of the client-organization relationship in domesticated organizations. Even though the focus will be on the public school system, illustrations will also be offered about other Type IV organizations.

The question which is central in this and the next section of the chapter is this: How do organizations and clients adapt themselves or attempt to control their relationship when neither the client nor the organization enters the relationship voluntarily? This section will give attention to a specific part of the question: What mechanisms are used by public school systems to adapt to an unselected clientele?

Such a question stems from the assumption that Type IV organizations are geared to render what they term adequate service to only some of their clients, and that they are consequently more responsive to clients presenting one set of characteristics than to those presenting another set. Said another way, the question rests on the assumption that Type IV organizations have goals to which they are committed and their achievement is hampered by the presence of the unselected clients, and that in the course of day-to-day operations there emerge within these organizations adaptive mechanisms which tend to minimize the disruptive factors presented by the unselected clients.

It is suggested, as a proposition, that at least two adaptive mechanisms are present in public school systems which can be seen as responses of the organization to the environmental condition of unselected clients.

The first adaptive response of domesticated organizations to the environmental condition of unselected clients is segregation. Segregation takes several forms. "Dumping ground" is a term well known to educators; it signifies that some part of the school program constitutes a place where students are assigned or "dumped" for part of their program, for various reasons, to serve out their remaining school days. Students do not get dumped into the academic areas of the program but, most frequently, into the vocational areas. This practice gives clues as to the type of student the school system is most anxious to serve.

A similar mechanism prevails in mental hospitals; the term "back ward" (as opposed to "front ward") stands for the same meaning as a dumping ground.[5]

Frequently a more extreme form of segregation takes place. In California, in some school systems, there are continuation schools for those students who have proved to be too disruptive for the regular high schools. And New York City has its "600" schools. In a sense, they are the dumping grounds' dumping ground.

[I am] not passing judgment on the practice of segregation; [I am] merely pointing to it as an adaptive response on the part of domesticated organizations to the problem of unselected clients.

Segregation in domesticated organizations frequently may lead to or is accompanied by goal displacement. Goal displacement is a process whereby the original or overriding goal is abandoned (completely or partially) and another goal substituted. In this sense it has frequently been said that government bureaucrats lose sight of the goals of the agency and make the means (rules, regulations, and so forth) the goals. Goal displacement is probably common in most types of organizations, but it is suggested as a proposition that its occurrence

5. Scheff (1961). Also, see McCleery (1961, pp. 266-267) for reference to segregation and administrative segregation in prisons.

in domesticated organizations is often directly related to the problem of unselected clients.

As far as the writer knows, no one has taken a systematic look at the service of public schools with the notion of goal displacement in mind. In tracking down preferential treatment in public schools, however, Hollingshead (1949) pointed out what seems to be a case of goal displacement. After showing that when teachers counsel with parents of lower-class children (children who make up the majority of the students in the general and commercial courses) the emphasis tends to be on discipline problems, and that when they counsel with parents of upper-class children the emphasis is on the pupil's work, he stated:

It is paradoxical that the teachers are so much interested in the work of the children in classes II and III when on the whole these students are the ones who receive the better grades. Lower class children, on the other hand, are given poorer grades, but the teachers consult the parents about discipline far more frequently than they do about the child's work [page 179].

One interpretation of this is that teachers see education as the goal with middle- and upper-class children but substitute discipline as the goal with lower-class children.

There is also some similar evidence that goal displacement occurs with segregation in public mental hospitals in the case of patients in the back wards. Scheff (1961) has stated the case as follows:

The observation that patients are more disciplined than treated on back wards is a common one, and is substantiated by almost all of the observers of mental hospitals. . . . Although there were exceptions [in the hospital reported on here], treatment procedures were converted into controls more often on back wards . . . than on front wards [page 5].

Further, while most modern prison officials suggest that prisons exist to rehabilitate rather than punish, there are, nevertheless, data which indicate that punishment in a number of cases overrides the goal of rehabilitation. Consider the following observations about classifying prisoners.

Our impression is that Custody has a separate and independent system of classifying prisoners which has little, if anything, to do with the recommendations made by the Guidance Center. Each prisoner, who has been classified in the Center on the basis of his case record and a battery of tests is now reclassified in accordance with Custody's estimate of the prisoner as a security risk. The three degrees of security risk—minimum, medium, and maximum—are only remotely related to these earlier findings. They also have little to do with any objective standard which might enable one to distinguish between prisoners of different degrees of security risk. The custodial classification seems to be based rather on the conventional middle-class evaluation of different crimes. Crimes involving violence, sexual or other, are rated as maximum security risks, despite the fact that murderers and sex offenders have the best parole records. Similarly, former escapees from reform schools never get less than a medium security classification presumably on the ground that once an escapee, always an escapee. Yet, the individual case might well warrant less severe treatment.

. . . The custodial classification, in terms of security risk, is therefore unrelated to the program of correction. It is solely dictated by the consideration that those who have received the highest sentences must be the "most dangerous" to society and the most incorrigible—a view which coincides with that of the sensationalist press. They must be the most severely punished, therefore, not only in terms of the longer duration of their sentences, but also by the more severe treatment while they are in prison [Powelson and Bendix, 1951, pages 76-77].

As a second mechanism, preferential treatment may be suggested. There are very substantial data to support the notion that a school system typically does not treat all students alike but engages in the practice of preferential treatment of some students. It has been documented that the preferential treatment involves such matters as grades, withdrawal from school, discipline, punishment, and curricula and that middle- and upper-class children as opposed to lower-class children are treated preferentially.[6] Widespread familiarity with these facts eliminates the need for their detailed documentation here.

Preferential treatment is also practiced in public mental hospitals, as the following remarks (Gallagher, Levinson, and Erlich, 1957) demonstrate:

It is our thesis that, in arriving at a treatment decision, the psychiatrist explicitly or implicitly considers various socio-psychological characteristics of the patient. Specifically, we propose that the patient's age, social class, degree of custodialism, and degree of authoritarianism will influence the psychiatrist's choice of treatment. Although they are not, strictly speaking, a part of the patient's symptomatology or pathology, these characteristics constitute, as it were, a paradiagnostic basis for psychiatric treatment [page 366].

. . . Psychotherapy is the "treatment of preference" in this hospital [page 374].

. . . [The] facts suggest that the psychiatrists choose mainly for psychotherapy the patients who most strongly resemble themselves. In other words, the psychiatrists to some extent follow a pattern of homophilic preference in selecting patients for psychotherapy [page 375].

What this indicates is simply that domesticated organizations give preferential treatment to some of their charges. The basis of the

6. The main, but by no means the only, source of documentation of preferential treatment in public schools is Hollingshead (1949).

preferential treatment may differ with the species of domesticated organizations, but nevertheless it exists. The argument here is not why the basis for preferential treatment may differ from domesticated organization to domesticated organization, nor about the value problem of preferential treatment, but merely that domesticated organizations exhibit preferential treatment and seemingly do so as an adaptive mechanism to the environmental condition of unselected clients.

The mechanisms of segregation and preferential treatment in Type IV organizations seem to make the organization-client relationship more tolerable from the point of view of the organization. Through these mechanisms the organization is able to exercise a form of subtle internal selection and sorting of clients as it goes about rendering its service. It is the argument that these mechanisms are adaptive, that they enable the protection of the valued resources of the organization and, therefore, are functional in goal achievement. In the case of the public school, this means that segregating certain students protects teaching time by removing from the mainstream the disruptive elements of unselected clients. And, giving partial treatment to some students protects teaching time in the sense that it channels teaching time and professional attention in general to those students for which the school is geared to supply the most adequate service. Together, these mechanisms facilitate the fulfillment of the goals to which the school commits itself.

In order for adaptive mechanisms such as indicated above to exist, some members of the organization must support the mechanisms. They do not emerge and function in a vacuum. Support of preferential treatment and segregation in the public school system would seem to flow from one set of pressures, and lack of support or sympathy for these adaptive mechanisms would seem to flow from another set of pressures. The question raised, then, is this: Is support of these adaptive mechanisms randomly distributed throughout the public school system, or are some categories of school people more supportive than others? It would seem reasonable to suggest that those most concerned about protecting teaching time, the largest resource of the school system, and instructional goals would be most supportive of these adaptive mechanisms. Drawing on an elementary distinction from organization theory, this directs us to the proposition that those designated as "line" personnel—teachers, principals, and a few central office people who are in charge of instructional time and goals—will support preferential treatment and segregation as responses to unselected clients. And, on the other hand, those designated as "staff" personnel—supervisors, curriculum consultants, and guidance counselors—will be nonsupportive and unsympathetic in respect to these adaptive mechanisms.

Now take a look at the other side of the coin. Instead of looking at how the Type IV organization adapts to its unselected clients, let us examine how the clients adapt to the mandatory service of the domesticated organization. Here the question is: In adjusting to the mandatory service of the public school, what forms of adaptation do students develop?

The adaptation of those students for whom the mandatory relationship is not problematical for either the students or the school can be called a receptive adaptation. The other extreme of the adaptation continuum can be called the dropout adaptation. (Here the client totally withdraws his participation even though it is unlawful to do so or necessitates the invoking of special arrangements.) Between these extremes there are other forms of adaptation which are somewhat problematic for either the student or the school, or both. Students exhibiting these "in-between" forms of adaptation are neither enthusiastic about receiving an education at the hands of the schools nor do they completely reject the arrangement. Such students are mainly concentrated in junior and senior high schools, and their number, no doubt, varies greatly from school to school. It is the "in-between" forms of adaptation of these students, who partially reject the school, on which the following comments center.

Central to these forms of adaptation, between the extremes of receptive and dropout, is that the adaptation rests on a redefinition of the school by the student. That is, a basic part of the adaptation is that the student defines the school in a way other than the school or the general society would define it.

One form of adaptation can be called situational retirement. With this adaptation, the student is physically present but not mentally present. He goes to school because to do otherwise is to be shamed, but he takes no part in what is going on around him. He defines the school as a warm, quiet place where no one will bother him. He goes to school in a manner similar to the way elderly men go to a library and unemployed men go to the movies. No one can say this type of adaptation causes the school any trouble. Attendance is good; so are citizenship and general deportment. On the behavioral side, he is a model student; on the academic side, much is to be desired. In the learning setting, this student occupies himself with inconspicuous activities. Frequently teachers come to rely on him to run errands and to perform other acts necessary in schools but which are not part of the curriculum. In a sense, this type of adaptation rejects what the school has to offer but does not reject the school. Chances are this type of student will not drop out of school.

Another form of adaptation quite unlike situational retirement is rebellious adjustment, because taking the rebellious line is a highly conspicuous form of adaptation. The rebellious adaptation involves some rejection of both the school and what the school has to offer. The student making the rebellious adaptation constantly tests the limits of the situation to see the extent to which he can depart from that which is expected of a student. This is an adaptation which is disruptive to and problematic for the school, and the chances of maintaining this form of adaptation over a long period of time are slim. The rebellious adaptation would seem to be a way station short of dropping out of school. The perspective taken by the student is one of seeing the whole situation as a game of wits, and the object of the game is to see how much one can get away with.

Another form of adaptation between the student and the school is one in which the student sees the school as a place to get side payments which are not usually available elsewhere. There are many fringe benefits in going to school, and when a student continues to attend school because of these fringe benefits rather than because of the central purpose of the school, he has then made a side-payment adaptation. Several forms of this type of adaptation can serve as examples. One form of side-payment adaptation involves the definition of the school as a place where one can engage in competitive team sports. The school frequently recognizes this adaptation by telling the student that, if he is too bad an actor in the areas of primary concern to the school, he will be deprived of what he wants out of school, a chance to play football, basketball, or what have you. Another form of side-payment adaptation derives from the fact that the school is a place where extensive contact can be made with the opposite sex. The purpose of school thus becomes interaction with the opposite sex, and the student taking this adaptation views regular schoolwork as something to put up with so long as the side payment is available. Another form of side-payment adaptation involves the definition of the school as a place to pursue some activity (other than regular learning), such as drama or repairing radios. Here again, the activity gives meaning to the school and is the reason for attendance, and the regular work is tolerated for the sake of the activity.

These "in-between" forms of student adaptation seem to have

relevance for the dropout problem in public schools, a problem which has been labeled as one of vital concern. Their relevance lies in the fact that these forms of adaptation enable the student to gain satisfaction from the school and to remain in school, where otherwise he might not.

Even though the term "holding power" of schools is used in the research literature dealing with dropouts, its implications have not been systematically examined.[7] The term "holding power" implies that characteristics of a school are variables in the dropout problem and that some combination of these variables produces greater holding power than other combinations. But, as has been said, the implications of the term have not been analyzed. The term "dropouts," on the other hand, tends to fix the problem on the characteristics of the students who drop out. It is this perspective which dominates the research literature, and it is a perspective which does not permit the researcher to think about variables within schools.

It would seem that a systematic empirical examination of "in-between" forms of adaptation might reveal some information which might be highly useful in developing recommendations for increasing the holding power of schools. And, on the basis of what has been said above about the side-payment adaptation, we are directed to the following proposition: The more fringe benefits a school makes available to the "reluctant scholar" (which would probably rule out Latin clubs, and the like) and the more it understands the functions of the fringe benefits, the greater will be its holding power.

7. There are exceptions to this statement, but they do not appear to be significant. One exception is that studies have been made of the differences in the holding power of the several states and of the change in holding power over time in the United States. Another exception is [found in] Gaumnitz (1950).

References

Blau, P., and Scott, W. R. (1962). *Formal Organizations*. San Francisco: Chandler Publishing Co.

Campbell, Roald F. (1957). "Situational Factors in Educational Administration," in Roald F. Campbell and Russell T. Gregg, eds., *Administrative Behavior in Education*. New York: Harper and Bros.

Clark, Burton R. (1956). *Adult Education in Transition: A Study of Institutional Insecurity*. Berkeley and Los Angeles: University of California Press.

_____ (1960). *The Open Door College: A Case Study*. New York: McGraw-Hill Book Co.

Cunningham, L. L. (1960) "Research in External Administration—What Do We Know?" in Roald F. Campbell and James M. Lipham, eds., *Administrative Theory as a Guide to Action.* Chicago: Midwest Administration Center, University of Chicago.

Gallagher, Eugene B., Levinson, Daniel J., and Erlich, Iza (1957). "Some Socio-psychological Characteristics of Patients and Their Relevance for Psychiatric Treatment," in M. Greenblatt *et al.*, eds., *The Patient and the Mental Hospital.* Glencoe, Ill.: Free Press.

Gaumnitz, W. H. (1950). *Holding Power and Size of High School.* U.S. Office of Education Circular No. 322. Washington, D.C.: Government Printing Office.

Goffman, Erving (1957). "Characteristics of Total Institutions," in *Symposium on Preventive and Social Psychiatry.* Washington, D.C.: Walter Reed Army Institute of Research.

Hollingshead, A. B. (1949). *Elmtown's Youth.* New York: John Wiley and Sons, Inc., p. 179.

Katz, Elihu (1961). "The Social Itinerary of Technical Change: Two Studies on the Diffusion of Innovation." *Human Organization,* 20(Summer):70-82.

McCleery, R. H. (1961). "Authoritarianism and the Belief System of Incorrigibles," in D. R. Cressey, ed., *The Prison: Studies in Institutional Organization and Change.* New York: Holt, Rinehart and Winston, Inc.

McDowell, Harold D. (1954). "The Principal's Role in a Metropolitan School System." Unpublished dissertation, University of Chicago.

Mort, Paul R. (1958). "Educational Adaptability," in Donald H. Ross, ed., *Administration for Adaptability.* New York: Metropolitan School Study Council, pp. 32-33.

Powelson, Harvey, and Bendix, Reinhard (1951). "Psychiatry in Prison." *Psychiatry,* 14(February):76-77.

Scheff, Thomas J. (1961). "Differential Displacement of Treatment Goals in a Mental Hospital." Paper read at the American Sociological Association meeting.

Structure

10 Some Organizational Characteristics of Multiunit Schools

Roland J. Pellegrin

The program of the Center for the Advanced Study of Educational Administration at the University of Oregon deals with the relationships between educational organization and instruction. Of particular relevance to the Center's mission is the study of the organization of schools in which significant innovations have occurred. For this reason, we were pleased to have the opportunity to study the organization and functioning of the multiunit school.

Our investigation is based on intensive case studies of eight schools. Four of these were multiunit schools; the other four were control schools selected by the Wisconsin R&D Center for Cognitive Learning. . . . We shall report some of our data on three multiunit schools and their controls. The fourth school had not sufficiently implemented the multiunit program to justify its inclusion. In reporting our findings, the schools will not be identified by name.

The three pairs of schools studied are in different school districts.

Reprinted from Roland J. Pellegrin, *Some Organizational Characteristics of Multiunit Schools* (Eugene, Ore.: Center for the Advanced Study of Educational Administration, University of Oregon, 1970). The research reported herein was conducted as part of the research and development program of the Center for the Advanced Study of Educational Administration, a national research and development center which is supported in part by funds from the United States Office of Education, Department of Health, Education, and Welfare (Bureau No. 5-0217, Project No. 2003, Contract No. 4-10-163, Funding Authority—Cooperative Research Act).

In each district we distributed questionnaires to all available professional personnel in the two schools and to central-office personnel whose work relates closely to the program of the elementary schools. These questionnaires were extremely detailed and extensive, covering a variety of matters pertaining to the characteristics of the schools and to the attitudes and goals of the respondents themselves. On the average, the questionnaires took 1½ hours to complete. In addition to gathering data by means of these questionnaires, we also interviewed a majority of the persons to whom the questionnaires were administered. The principal, the unit leaders, half of the teachers, and two nonprofessionals were interviewed in each multiunit school. While the questionnaires did not mention multiunit schools, the interviews dealt mainly with matters pertaining to the multiunit program.

. . . [This] report is preliminary for two reasons: first, we have not yet completed an exhaustive analysis of all our data; second, the scope of our work is too broad to be summarized briefly. We shall undertake two tasks in this presentation. The first will be to summarize certain data dealing with the schools studied, and the second one will be to raise a few questions about the organizational problems that may arise in multiunit schools.

An Organizational Profile of Multiunit Schools

In presenting a summary of organizational characteristics of multiunit schools, we shall focus attention on a few major topics. First, we shall summarize materials dealing with interaction patterns in multiunit and control schools. This will be followed by a discussion of the division of labor, with emphasis on specialization in the unit and on the role of the unit leader. Next is an analysis of decision-making processes and influence hierarchies in multiunit and control schools. Finally, we present a brief discussion of the goals and attitudes of teachers, with special attention to operation objectives and job satisfaction.

Interdependence Relationships in Multiunit and Control Schools

Regardless of its field of activity, an organization is structured in such a manner that it facilitates or encourages the interaction of certain members while it impedes or hinders the interaction of others. Studies of interaction patterns or networks in organizations show [that] high rates of interaction occur under certain organizational conditions and low rates occur under other circumstances. In this research we are concerned only with certain types of interaction patterns among adults in multiunit and control schools. Instead of studying friendship choices or frequency of interaction, as is often done in sociometric analyses, we chose instead to examine what we call "interdependence relationships." This term refers to work-related patterns of interaction between people; it directs attention to those relationships between individuals that affect their ability to get their jobs done.

To identify interdependence relationships, we asked each respondent in the multiunit and control schools to complete the following items in a questionnaire:

1. "List the names of those persons both within and outside your school (other than students) upon whom you depend *most heavily* in order to perform your job effectively;"
2. "Who are the persons listed above, if any, whose job is so closely related to *yours* that you believe the two jobs *must* be performed collaboratively in order for either of you to perform his work effectively?"

Responses to these two questions by teachers and unit leaders provide the data for the sociometric charts in the appendix. These charts give us a view of organizational structure as revealed by a mapping of interdependence relationships.

Let us first note the patterning of interdependence relationships in the school as a whole. Figure 10-1 [see Appendix] diagrams these relationships in one of the multiunit schools in our study. Note that each of the five units of the school constitutes a cluster of interdependent relationships. The members of a unit depend heavily on other members for the successful performance of their work. On the other hand, interaction of the type we are examining is entirely intraunit as far as the relationships of teachers to one another are concerned. It is a striking fact that not a single teacher nominates a teacher (or a unit leader) outside his own unit. We take this to mean that collaborative work effort is confined essentially within the unit.

While the structure of each of the five units is similar, it is not identical. Let us distinguish between what we shall call a "dependence relationship" (a dotted line in the chart indicating nomination in question 1) and an "essential relationship" (indicating nomination also in question 2). Clearly, the units vary in the proportion of essential relationships to dependence relationships.

Unit five has the maximum possible number of essential relationships; each person sees himself as having an essential relationship with every other member of the unit. This represents the highest possible level of interdependence. On the other hand, unit four is the "loosest" collaborative unit, characterized by fewer essential relationships and a lower level of interdependence.

The unit leaders are focal points of interaction in the units and also serve as connecting links between the teacher and the principal. As is the case with teachers, however, no unit leader nominates another unit leader (or a teacher in another unit), indicating an absence of dependence between units of the school. It is worth observing that while this school has an active Instructional Improvement Committee, the absence of interdependence relationships between unit leaders and teachers in different units indicates that collaborative relationships between units is minimal. Otherwise put, the goal of having the Instructional Improvement Committee coordinate the program of the entire school has made little headway if the absence of interdependence relationships is interpreted as evidence of a lack of coordination of the work of units.

The principal receives nominations from most teachers and all of the unit leaders. For three of the five unit leaders, an essential relationship is seen with the principal. Only three teachers, however, view their relationship with the principal as essential.

Figure 10-2 [see Appendix] diagrams the interdependence relationships in a control school. We see at once that the patterning of relationships is quite different from that of the multiunit school. The principal is the obvious focus of nominations, receiving all but two of twenty-five possible nominations, with ten of the twenty-three being essential relationships. There are obviously few interaction clusters among teachers. In every case where self-contained classrooms exist, there are few interdependence relationships. The cluster of relationships at 10 o'clock on the chart is a team teaching situation; that at 6 o'clock involves a special ungraded class to which all three teachers are assigned. With the exception of these special situations, interdependence relationships between teachers are few, rarely essential, and usually related to grade level taught. There is, in fact, only one instance where a nomination is made across grade levels.

Let us at this point make a few generalizations that extend beyond the two schools we have been considering. First, the pattern of relationships in the control school shown in Figure 10-2 is almost identical to that of the other control schools in our sample. Indeed, the pattern is similar to that of other elementary schools we have studied elsewhere in the country. If anything, the control schools show more interdependence relationships than are usually encountered, owing largely to the presence of team teaching and other collaborative undertakings not found in the typical school characterized by the self-contained classroom. The fact is the traditionally organized elementary school in the United States has a primitive division of labor and differentiation of functions in its professional staff. Grade level is the only consistent basis for distinguishing among teachers. Emphasis is on the functions universally performed by teachers, not on the coordination of effort or any form of specialization.

In the other multiunit schools in our sample we find patterns of relationships similar in some respects to the multiunit school shown in Figure 10-1. There are also some variations from one school to the other. As far as similarities are concerned, we find that all multiunit schools have a network of interdependence relationships within each unit.

Consistently, therefore, multiunit schools are successful in encouraging the establishment of some collaborative activity. Interdependence relationships are nonetheless confined to the members of one's own unit. The unit leaders in nearly all cases receive more nominations, especially for essential relationships, than do the teachers. Unit leaders also serve consistently as linkage agents between teachers and the principal.

In other respects we find variations in schools and from one unit to another within a school. The extent and balance of dependence relationships and essential relationships differ from school to school and unit to unit. As Figure 10-3 (see Appendix) shows, it is possible for virtually all relationships to be essential ones in one unit, while another unit in the same school has a pattern containing a mixture of essential and dependence relationships as well as a lack of indicated relationships of either type. Thus, while some collaborative activity is found in all schools, its extent is uneven, reflecting differential success in the development of interdependence relationships.

In no two multiunit schools in our sample is the place of the principal in the interaction network the same. The principal in Figure 10-1 receives more nominations than the principals in the other schools. In one school the principal receives but a few scattered nominations, indicating that he is not the focal point of interaction. This means—recalling the two questions on which the charts are based—that most teachers do not depend heavily on the principal in order to do their work. Instead, each unit operates almost independently, relying heavily on its unit leader for support, advice, and assistance.

The sociometric charts we have discussed map the nominations of teachers and unit leaders. If we examine the responses of principals to the same two questions on which these charts are based, we find differences between multiunit school principals and control school principals. The multiunit school principal reports that his successful job performance depends on a number of people. He lists considerably more names than the control school principal does. The former's list of essential relationships is especially longer than that of his counterpart. Typically, the multiunit principal lists essential relationships with all the unit leaders and his secretary, and occasionally with another person or two.

The control school principal, on the other hand, lists few essential relationships; they are usually limited to his secretary and the custodian. The multiunit school principal is clearly part of an expanded interaction network in which his relations to his faculty have changed considerably from those that prevail in control schools. We will return to the implications of this situation for the job of the principal later in the paper.

In concluding this analysis of interdependence relationships, we should also mention that the interaction network of the unit includes instructional and clerical aides. Nominations of these aides by unit leaders and teachers are frequent, and the relationships are often considered essential. Aides, therefore, are important figures in the network of interdependence relationships within the units of these schools.

Division of Labor in the Multiunit School

Collaborative instruction, planning, and evaluation as called for by the multiunit system can be expected to lead to modifications in the division of labor within the school. In this section of the paper, we ... discuss two important matters bearing on the division of labor. The first is the development of specialization within the unit and the second is the impact of the unit leader position on the positions of the teacher and the principal.

When principals and teachers discuss specialization in the elementary school, they usually conceive of it in terms of subject-matter specialization or departmentalization, both of which are usually regarded in a negative light. Principals especially are likely to take a stand against departmentalization and specialization, contending that the elementary school is an inappropriate setting for making teaching assignments by subject-matter areas. Teachers generally express similar attitudes. Several indicated approvingly during our interviews that all teachers in their school are expected to teach in all areas.

Perhaps because of these biases against specialization, teachers and principals see little of it emerging in the multiunit school. Principals, in fact, gave us no examples of specialization; they are perhaps not close enough to the activities of the unit to be aware of the specialization coming into being. Teachers, interestingly, are similarly unaware of specialization, perhaps because each is aware only of his own role and does not think of the unit in terms of specialization. Even when a teacher reports teaching most of the math in his unit, or says he has taken over all of the work in remedial reading, he discusses the matter in terms of "teaching to one's strengths" rather than conceptualizing the situation as one where specialization is occurring.

In the multiunit school, the unit leader—not the teacher or principal—is concerned with the management and coordination of unit activities. Therefore, it is not surprising to find that interview questions about specialization get quite different responses from unit leaders than from teachers and principals. In general, unit leaders see considerably more specialization than is reported by teachers or principals. A substantial amount of this specialization is conventional in nature—that is, teachers specialize by subject-matter areas. More such specialization exists than is usually perceived by the people involved. If, as is often reported, one teacher in a unit takes over the math instruction and another who is especially good in science takes over most instruction in that subject, it seems clear that the other teachers in the unit, consciously or not, must "specialize" in the other subjects that remain to be taught.

Two other conventional types of specialization are fairly commonplace. In some units, especially in large ones, there remains considerable specialization by grade level, despite the formal abolition of grades as such. There is also specialization in that some teachers work primarily with certain ability groupings or spend much of their time with remedial classes.

Interestingly, however, specialization in the multiunit school is not confined to these conventional forms. Perhaps of more significance for the multiunit school in the long run is the fact that new and often novel kinds of specialization are beginning to emerge in the units. Three main types have come to our attention:

1. Some teachers devote most of their time to working with individual pupils, while others work mainly with small groups or class-sized groups. In two of the schools studied, individualized and small-group instruction are heavily emphasized. In these schools, some teachers reported spending 75 percent of their time working with individual students; others said they devoted the same proportion of

their time to small groups or to class-sized ones. A few teachers took special responsibilities for working with even larger groups than the usual class-sized ones, usually at the beginning or end of study units. There is, then, considerable specialization in some multiunit schools for teaching in an individual, small-group, or large-group setting. In light of the emphasis given to individual and small-group instruction in the multiunit system, the development of such specializations is to be anticipated. There are, however, disparities in the amount of such instruction from one unit to another within a school, and one of the schools studied retained class-sized groups almost exclusively. Individualized instruction in this school consisted almost entirely of routine drill by instructional aides.

2. A second type of evidence of emerging specialization is the fact some teachers are serving as expert advisers to their colleagues. The obvious case where this occurs is when a teacher has had special training in some subject. When such a teacher is in a unit, it is natural for others to rely on his expertise. The availability of this kind of expertise is largely fortuitous, of course, and no unit can expect to obtain expert competence everywhere it is needed through chance circumstances. For this reason, some units have deliberately urged their members to develop specialized competences. Even when specialized training is lacking, a teacher may be asked to take the responsibility for learning about developments pertaining, for example, to certain materials or media and for keeping his fellow teachers informed on the subject. Other teachers in the unit are assigned to other topics. The emergence of this kind of specialization, we believe, is a highly promising development. It permits a type of accumulation and pooling of knowledge not possible under different circumstances.

3. A third type of specialization relates to special assignments. In several units we studied, teachers are given special responsibilities for planning units of instruction. The logic of this procedure is extended in one instance to the entire instructional process; in one unit, the teachers plan the different phases of the instructional units, and each takes responsibility for one or more phases of the total process. When the instructional unit is presented to the students, teachers play special roles in certain phases of the instructional process such as introducing the instructional unit or evaluating it. Such assignments often are temporary and fleeting. This type of division of labor, in fact, is characterized by its variable nature as well as by its temporariness. It offers opportunities to get jobs done that could hardly be obtained in a more permanent and fixed division of labor.

Our second topic bearing on the division of labor in the multiunit school concerns the impact of the position of unit leader on the teacher and the principal. In our interviews with school personnel, we obtained information on how the job of the unit leader contributes to effective work by teachers. In one school our respondents stated that the unit leader facilitates the work of the teacher by doing the following kinds of things: searching for, obtaining, and preparing new materials; scheduling the activities of the unit and arranging for necessary space and facilities; grouping students and making appropriate teaching assignments; handling reporting chores; helping teachers keep up with new developments; discussing instructional problems of individual teachers; advising teachers on their relationships with parents; keeping up teacher morale; and relieving teachers of routine chores. These functions indicate that in this particular school the roles of the unit leader as they relate to the teacher fall both in the realms of instructional leadership and administration.

In the other two schools studied, the roles of the unit leader were less clearly conceptualized. Some people interviewed did conceive of the unit leader's roles in terms of instructional leadership and managerial responsibility. Others, however, saw the unit leader as a minor functionary whose primary duty was to relieve teachers of routine and bothersome chores, or, as a jack-of-all-trades who does whatever is required at a given moment to help out the teachers of the unit.

A considerable amount of attention in our interviews was devoted to the relationships of the unit leader and the principal. We were particularly interested in seeing how the two jobs relate to one another, and we asked questions about tasks unit leaders perform that might be carried out by the principal in the conventionally organized school. All principals and unit leaders agreed that the unit leader has taken over a variety of such tasks. For example, unit leaders were said to handle discipline problems at the level above that of the teacher, to serve as an adviser and morale booster for their teachers, to brief teachers on school and district policies and procedures, to channel information to the teachers from a variety of sources (including the principal), to make arrangements for building use, to obtain consultant help, to arrange field trips, to deal with the central office on a variety of matters, to train new teachers, and to take general responsibility for planning, implementing, and evaluating the curriculum.

One principal told us that in his school "unit leaders do a lot of administrative work. They do the scheduling, run in-service training programs, supervise and evaluate the teachers, group the students, and make basic instructional decisions that I otherwise would have to make."

A second principal indicated that in his school each unit is "a school within a school." Each unit, he explained, is virtually autonomous and independent (this school has no Instructional Improvement Committee). In the third school, the authority and functions of the principal had been transferred to the unit leaders to an even greater extent.

It is clear, therefore, that many of the duties ordinarily performed by principals have been turned over to the unit leader. This situation raises questions about the effectiveness of both sets of roles under prevailing circumstances. We shall mention some of these [later].

Authority, Decision-Making Processes, and Influence

One of the most important aspects of multiunit organization is its effects on authority and decision making. In our research we were concerned with the location of decision-making prerogatives and the extent to which power and influence are concentrated or dispersed in the school. We were particularly interested in discovering the kinds of changes multiunit organization produces in decision-making processes and the status hierarchy.

While we gathered various kinds of data dealing with power and decision making at the school and school district levels, we shall summarize some findings on but two dimensions of the general subject. The first deals with where the authority lies for making certain types of decisions. The second is concerned with the influence hierarchy of the school.

To obtain data on authority structures, we asked each teacher to indicate the role he plays in the decision-making process for various types of classroom-related decisions. The decisions dealt with five activities: the choice of teaching methods used in the classroom, determining the scope and sequence of subject-matter content, the choice of instructional materials other than textbooks, deciding on pupil promotion, and scheduling daily classroom activities.

For each of the five decisions, each respondent was asked to indicate if he had:

a. complete autonomy to make the decision himself,
b. final authority to make the decision after receiving suggestions and recommendations from others,
c. authority to make the decision within certain limits,
d. authority to share the decision with other persons in a group decision-making process, or

e. no voice in making the decision (that is, the decision is made by others).

When the respondent chose any but the first alternative, he was asked to identify the other persons involved in the decision-making process.

To highlight the patterns of responses in the multiunit schools, we first note the situation in the control schools. While there is some variation in responses for the five types of decisions, the general pattern is for the individual teacher to make the decisions, either in consultation with the principal or within certain limits prescribed by him. Decision making affecting each classroom is the prerogative mainly of the two individuals: the teacher, serving as primary decision maker, and the principal, who provides advice or sets the limits within which the teacher has discretion. Few teachers see themselves as involved in group decision making of any kind with regard to any of these items.

The distribution of responses provides a view of the school as being composed of separate, relatively isolated classrooms, with the activities of each classroom being determined primarily by the teacher monitored to a greater or lesser extent by the principal. For the school as a whole, the principal is the central authority figure; he is the only person whose activities extend beyond the individual classroom.

In the multiunit school there is evidence that the decision-making pattern we have just described is being changed significantly. There are some variations in responses for the different types of decisions, and the pattern is somewhat different for each school. Yet there are some important generalizations that emerge. For one thing, fewer teachers see themselves as making decisions individually than is the case in control schools. Substantial numbers of teachers indicate that decisions are shared with others in a group decision-making process. The teachers who indicate they make decisions individually after receiving suggestions and recommendations from others include fellow teachers among these "others." Otherwise stated, there is a notable shift away from reliance on the principal for advice and assistance to a situation in which colleagues serve such a function. In general, decision making is moving from the level of the individual classroom to that of the unit. Decisions are being made by the unit leader and teachers, usually in a collaborative situation.

When the teacher seeks advice from a single figure of authority in the multiunit school, it is likely that he will turn to the unit leader rather than to the principal. Usually the principal is not directly involved in the decision-making processes of the unit. Whether or not he has an indirect impact depends on his ability to work effectively with unit leaders in a building committee or an instructional improvement committee.

What happened in actual practice varied among the schools in our sample. In one school, the Instructional Improvement Committee functioned fairly effectively; decisions of school-wide importance made collaboratively by the principal and the unit leaders affected what went on in the units. In a second school there was no Instructional Improvement Committee, but the principal retained some influence because of his personal relations with individual teachers. The third school presented yet a different case: decisions in the Instructional Improvement Committee rarely dealt with instructional problems of concern to the units. As a result, the principal's influence on decisions made in the unit was slight. Unit affairs were decided by the unit leader and the teachers.

Just as there have been changes in authority and decision making in the multiunit school, there have been modifications in the "influence structure" or "power structure." We asked our respondents to complete the following questionnaire item:

If you wanted to receive approval from the faculty of your school for an idea you were proposing, it would sometimes be helpful to enlist the support of certain other individuals in your school. Please list below, by name and position, the individuals whose support for your ideas would help most in obtaining faculty approval.

Tabulations of the frequency with which individuals were named gave us a picture of the influence hierarchy in each school.

In the control schools, the influence hierarchy is dominated by the principal. Typically, the principal receives three to four times as many nominations as any other individual. Usually only two or three teachers get as many as one-third to one-fourth the number of nominations received by the principal. Nearly all teachers in the school are mentioned once or twice, indicating a lack of consensus about who are the influential teachers. This is, of course, a highly centralized influence structure that revolves around one dominant figure, the principal.

It is to be anticipated that multiunit organization changes this situation. Only one generalization, however, stands for all schools— namely, the unit leaders in all instances emerge as significant persons in the influence hierarchy. In other respects, the changes that occur vary from school to school. The principal in one school received twenty-two nominations, while his three unit leaders received sixteen, fourteen, and eleven, respectively. No one else in the school received over three nominations. In a second school the principal had twenty nominations. Three unit leaders received nine, one received eight, and one received five. No one else received over two nominations.

In both of these schools the principal's influence is obviously shared with the unit leaders. The unit leaders are seen as influential not only by members of their own units, but by some persons in other units as well. Evidence drawn from these two schools reveals that the creation of a new formal position, that of unit leader, has changed the influence structures so that influence is shared by a larger number of persons. At the same time, the principal remains the single most influential person in these schools.

The situation in the third school, however, is quite different. Here one unit leader and the librarian in the Instructional Materials Center each get six nominations; the other two unit leaders, a teacher, and the principal each get five; and two other teachers receive four and three, respectively. This is an example of dispersed influence where the traditional dominance of the principal has evaporated.

To generalize, then, we can see that multiunit organization seemingly insures the development of a more decentralized influence hierarchy than is found in the control schools. The exact form of this decentralized structure, however, varies from school to school. We suspect that in the long run the functioning of the school's Instructional Improvement Committee will be an important determinant of the form of the influence hierarchy.

Operational Goals of Teachers

Given the objectives of the Wisconsin R&D Center in developing the multiunit school model, it is important to ask whether or not it has been possible to make any appreciable changes in the operational work goals which teachers set for themselves. In our questionnaire we listed the following operational goals:

encouraging creativity among students;
maintaining an orderly and quiet classroom;
enriching the course of study or curriculum of the classroom;
giving individual attention to students;
experimenting with new teaching techniques;
diagnosing learning problems of students;
coordinating classroom activities with other parts of the school program;

ensuring that students learn basic skills;

solving personal problems of individual students;

developing student ability in analytical reasoning and problem solving;

developing the aesthetic potential of students.

We asked each teacher to indicate which three of these he considers most vital or important in his work as a teacher.

In the multiunit schools, "giving individual attention to students" and "diagnosing learning problems of students" ranked first and second in importance. In contrast, teachers in the control schools ranked "ensuring that students learn basic skills" first, followed by "developing student ability in analytical reasoning and problem solving." As teachers state their objectives, therefore, we find that individually guided education and diagnosis of learning problems are seen as the primary goals to be pursued by teachers in the multiunit school.

We discovered that from the point of view of the teachers, the "climate of expectations" regarding objectives is seen as different in multiunit and control schools. Evidence of this is provided by data obtained when we asked teachers which of the previously listed items they believe their principal would consider most important in the work of the teacher. Teachers in the multiunit schools listed "experimenting with new teaching techniques" and "giving individual attention to students" as objectives their principals would consider most important. On the other hand, teachers in control schools thought their principals would give first rank to "ensuring that students learn basic skills." Tied for second place were "developing student ability in analytical reasoning and problem solving" and "enriching the course of study or curriculum in the classroom."

Teachers were asked to indicate which objectives they could best achieve given the existing conditions in their school. Multiunit school teachers ranked "experimenting with new teaching techniques" first and "enriching the course of study or curriculum of the classroom" second. Teachers in the control schools ranked "ensuring that children learn basic skills" first and "encouraging creativity among students" second.

Job Satisfaction and Environmental Climate

In our research we also examined some of the social-psychological dimensions of organization analysis. One objective was to measure the attitudes of school personnel toward their work and their work environment. In one part of the study, teachers responded to a ten-

item, job satisfaction scale. For three items, the proportions reporting that they were "highly satisfied" were only slightly greater in the
multiunit than in the control schools. A comparison of the other
seven items reveals considerable differences, all in favor of the multiunit school.

The seven items, together with the proportions responding "highly
satisfied" in multiunit and control schools, are as follows:

satisfaction with progress toward one's personal goals in present
  position, 26 percent and 15 percent;

satisfaction with personal relationships with administrators and
  supervisors, 61 percent and 39 percent;

opportunity to accept responsibility for one's own work or the
  work of others, 61 percent and 43 percent;

seeing positive results from one's efforts, 36 percent and 15 percent;

personal relationships with fellow teachers, 73 percent and 55
  percent;

satisfaction with present job in light of one's career expectations,
  56 percent and 39 percent;

the availability of pertinent instructional materials and aids, 60
  percent and 27 percent.

In another part of the study, teachers responded to items that
were designed to reveal their perceptions of the extent of freedom
and rigidity in school policies. More teachers in multiunit schools
than in control schools (68 percent and 42 percent) believed that it is
highly accurate to say that school policies encourage freedom in the
selection of instructional materials. The statement that "school policies encourage freedom in student use of the library or other learning
resources" was regarded as "highly accurate" by 64 percent of the
teachers in the multiunit schools and 35 percent of those in the
control schools. That school policies encourage freedom in experimenting with new teaching techniques was seen as a highly accurate
statement by 93 percent of the multiunit teachers as compared to 60
percent of the control school teachers. On the other hand, the statement "school policies encourage close adherence to official course
outlines and/or curriculum guides" was seen as highly accurate by
only 6 percent of the teachers in multiunit schools, but by 32 percent in the control schools. Responses to these items provide some
evidence that teachers in multiunit schools perceive their environment to be more free, less rigid, and more open to experimentation
than do the teachers in control schools.

Some Basic Questions about Multiunit School Organization

Many of our conclusions to this point should be heartening to the designers and proponents of the multiunit school. It seems safe to say that the multiunit system holds high promise of ameliorating some of the endemic problems encountered in elementary schools. Nonetheless, in the course of analyzing data on the attributes of the multiunit school, it has become clear that operating schools of this type presents a variety of problems that must be solved if the schools are to function at a high level of effectiveness. It is our conclusion that no single "form" or "model" of multiunit organization has been implemented in the schools we studied. There is, as a matter of fact, considerable variation in structure, policies, and practices. This variation in itself, of course, does not necessarily produce problems.

What does lead to problems is the fact that there has not yet been enough experimentation and systematic study to determine which structural forms and operational policies work best in the multiunit school. Nor is it yet known precisely which roles are effective for which positions in this new context. Particularly important here are questions about the roles associated with the positions of unit leader and principal.

In concluding, we should like to raise a few questions about the structure of the school and the roles of personnel.

1. Our first question deals with the relationship between unit size and unit effectiveness. In raising this question, we make the assumption that a high level of interdependence relationships is required if a unit is to function effectively. That is, we assume that to plan, teach, and evaluate collaboratively, a high level of interdependence among unit members is necessary. This being the case, it becomes appropriate to ask what the organizational conditions are that make it likely that a high level of interdependence will develop.

We should like to call your attention once again to Figure 10-3 in the Appendix. The networks of interdependence relationships obviously are different in the two units shown in this chart. In the smaller unit, the unit leader and the teachers are bound together in reciprocal ties that are, with only one exception, seen as essential relationships by unit members. The larger unit, in contrast, shows a considerably lower level of interdependence. In fact, interdependence relationships between some members of the unit are entirely lacking. Even ties with the unit leader are not always seen as essential relationships. Rather than forming a single network of interdependence relationships, the unit is segmented into subgroupings or subnetworks based largely on what is, in effect, grade level taught. This is a reversion to a pattern of relationships that sometimes develops in the traditional elementary school, as is illustrated in Figure 10-4 [see Appendix].

These differences between small and large units are found consistently in the schools we studied. There is a higher level of interdependence in the smaller units than in the larger ones. Segmentation by grade level frequently appears in the larger units. It is for these reasons that the question of optimal size of units arises as an important practical issue in designing the multiunit school. The pertinent question is this: How many teachers can collaborate effectively with one another, the unit leader, and nonprofessionals in the unit setting?

Social science knowledge about the nature of interaction in human groups tells us that interaction can be close and intense only in relatively small groups. The optimum size of groups is further reduced when group interaction is instrumental in nature—that is, it is not an end in itself. In units of the multiunit school, where instruction is the main objective of the group and improving interaction patterns is but a means to that end, there are certainly limits to the number of people to which an individual can be tied in an effective interdependence network. What the optimum size range is in units is a matter, we believe, that merits serious discussion and study.

2. Questions also arise with regard to the functions of the instructional improvement committee. Two of the three schools studied had [such a] committee. In our interviews we found considerable vagueness in people's minds concerning the functions of the committee. In one school, the committee seemed to serve primarily as a vehicle for channeling news to teachers. To put it in another way, the agenda of meetings of the Instructional Improvement Committee was similar to that of general faculty meetings in a conventional school. The Instructional Improvement Committee in the other school spent more time in discussions related to instruction, but here also understandings were lacking concerning the exact functions of this committee. While it seemed to be generally agreed [that] "the Instructional Improvement Committee should coordinate the curriculum of the entire school," what this coordination should consist of and how it should be accomplished were unclear.

Another problem concerned conflicting authority in relations between the Instructional Improvement Committee and individual units. Which decisions are to be the exclusive prerogative of unit members and which decisions are to be made for the entire school by the Instructional Improvement Committee? We found no clear answers to these questions.

We obtained little evidence in either school that the Instructional Improvement Committee functioned as an important decision-making group. Indeed, there is some evidence to the contrary. For example, if the Instructional Improvement Committee were a closely knit body, interdependence relationships would develop among unit leaders and the principal. As things stand, unit leaders and the principal do not form an interdependence network. In Figure 10-1, for example, we notice that the unit leaders do not nominate each other. Rather, they are tied to their unit members and to the principal individually.

3. A third set of questions deals with specialization among members of the unit. We shall not elaborate extensively on this matter because we have discussed specialization at some length earlier. There is a question as to the extent to which specialization should be encouraged systematically within the unit, and also a question concerning the types of specialization that will contribute most to the effective functioning of units. As noted earlier, considerable bias exists against specialization because it is equated with departmentalization. On the other hand, specializations have emerged in the units that are both natural and creative, as we have shown. Again, this is a matter that should be investigated carefully.

4. Questions also arise concerning the relative emphasis on different roles in the position of unit leader. There is no general agreement concerning the roles that should be emphasized in this position. The position, however, calls for three main sets of roles—instructional leader, administrator, and teacher—and it seems that all three must be performed capably if the unit is to function effectively. An appropriate balance of the three sets of roles is, however, hard to establish and maintain. There probably will be pressure to make continual additions to the administrative responsibilities of unit leaders. If this occurs, we can expect effective performance of the other two sets of roles to suffer, particularly that of instructional leader.

5. Finally, several questions should be posed about the principalship in the multiunit school. The multiunit model, as developed by the Wisconsin R&D Center, envisages an important place for the principal in instructional leadership. Yet it is apparent that the principal's role as an instructional leader must be different from that which he plays in a conventional school. The multiunit school is so organized that many of the usual duties of the principal are shifted to the unit leader. In the multiunit school the teacher naturally turns

first to the unit leader for such assistance, as we showed earlier when we presented data on ways in which the unit leader helps make the teacher's job more effective. The closely knit nature of the unit, together with the almost constant availability of the unit leader for consultation, makes it almost certain that the teacher will turn to the unit leader rather than to the principal for instructional leadership. Even the insecure teacher, who might fear revealing his inadequacies to the principal in the conventional school, cannot hide these deficiencies behind the door of a self-contained classroom in the multiunit school. The teacher in the multiunit school teaches in public, and the pressures of the situation logically lead to consultation with the unit leader when problems occur.

Given the work situation that prevails, then, the unit leader is the natural instructional leader for the unit. The instructional leadership of the principal will not be enhanced if he seeks to usurp the functions of the unit leader. Instead, the potentialities for instructional leadership for the principal lie elsewhere. One appropriate role is for the principal to insure that each unit is properly organized for instruction, that the unit leader and teachers develop the interdependence relationships necessary to make relevant decisions and to carry out their instructional tasks.

On the other hand, the principal can operate effectively as the chairman of the Instructional Improvement Committee. As the coordinator and adviser of the unit leaders, he could make important contributions to the instructional program of the school as a whole. In any case, the role of the principal as an instructional leader merits further attention and clarification.

Appendix. Sociometric Charts

Data on which the following charts are based consist of responses by teachers and unit leaders to the following questions:
1. List the names of those persons . . . on whom you depend *most heavily* in order to perform your job effectively.
2. Who are the persons listed above, if any, whose job is so closely related to *yours* that you believe the two jobs *must* be performed collaboratively in order for either of you to perform his work effectively?

Legend:

X- - - - -➤Y : X named Y in Q. 1.
X◄- - - - ➤Y : X and Y named each other in Q. 1.
X————➤Y : X named Y in Q. 2.
X◄———➤Y : X and Y named each other in Q. 2.
X◄- - ——➤Y : X named Y in Q. 2., Y named X in Q. 1.

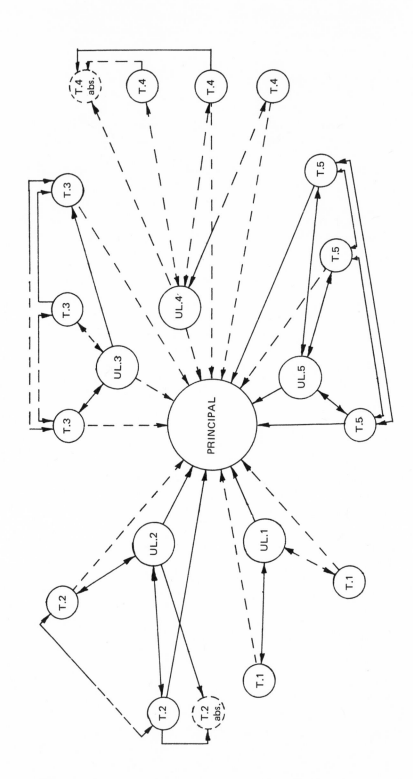

FIGURE 10-1
Interdependence relationships in a multiunit school

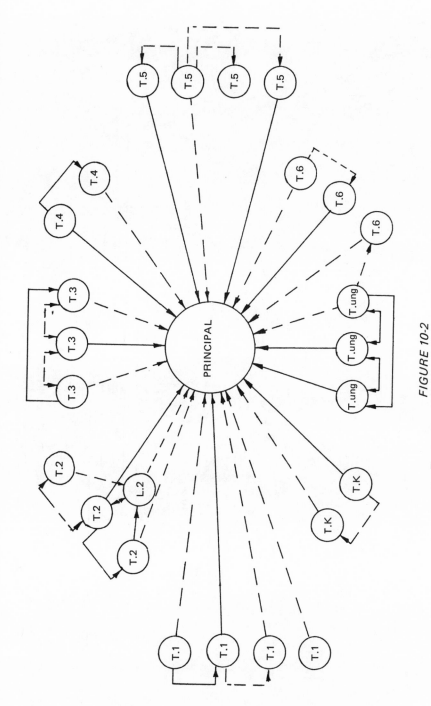

FIGURE 10-2

Interdependence relationships in a control school

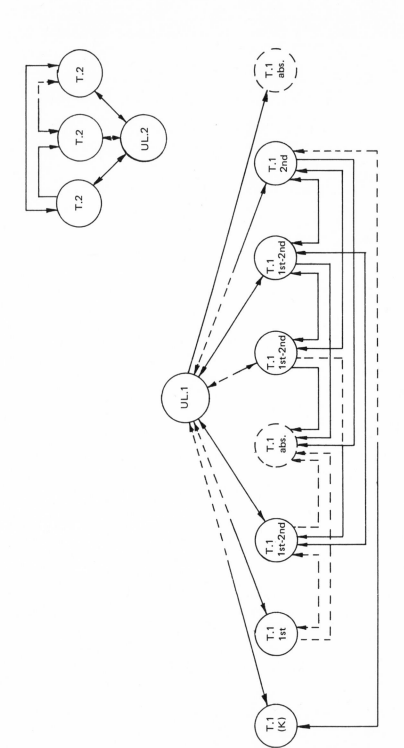

FIGURE 10-3

Comparison of interdependence relationships in a large
unit and a small unit in a multiunit school

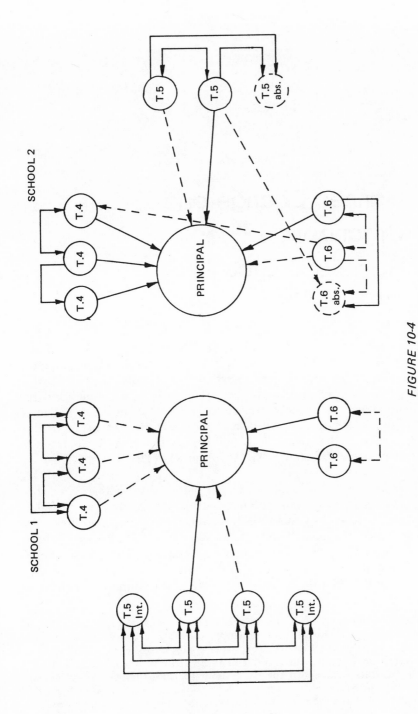

FIGURE 10-4

Development of interdependence relationships in
selected grade levels in two control schools

11 Planned Change and Organizational Health: Figure and Ground

Matthew B. Miles

Any observer of the applied behavioral sciences today would have to note a remarkable interest in the entire problem of planned change. Scientists and practitioners alike are concerned with the stages of planned change in groups, organizations, and communities; with the question of how change processes can be managed in a meaningful sense of that word; and with the characteristics of the "change agent," that miraculous middleman between "What Science Has Proved" and "What We Are Up Against." The very existence of this seminar is a case in point.

There is a growing literature, in journals as diverse as *Applied Anthropology* and *Petroleum Refiner*; there have already been thoughtful attempts to collect this literature, and to conceptualize the problems involved (Lippitt, Watson, and Westley, 1958; Bennis, Benne, and Chinn, 1961). All this is gratifying to beleaguered school administrators—and to everyone who, following Kurt Lewin's most frequently quoted dictum, believes that "there is nothing so practical as a good theory."

Reprinted from *Change Processes in the Public Schools* (Eugene, Ore.: Center for the Advanced Study of Educational Administration, University of Oregon, 1965), pp. 11-34. *Author's note:* This paper comes out of preliminary work in the Project on Organization Development in Schools, at the Horace Mann-Lincoln Institute of School Experimentation, Teachers College, Columbia University. My colleagues on the project, Paula Holzman, Harvey Hornstein, and Dale Lake stimulated many of the ideas recorded here, and gave critical reading to the manuscript.

Yet it seems to me that there is an important, but often overlooked, aspect of what is being said and done about planned change: the notion that any particular planned change effort is deeply conditioned by the state of the system in which it takes place. For example, properties of the organization, such as communication adequacy and the distribution of influence, have a powerful effect on the speed and durability of adoption of any particular innovation, from English 2600 to data processing of teacher marks. To use an image from Gestalt psychology, specific planned change attempts have most typically been "in figure," occupying the focus of attention, while the organization itself has remained the "ground."

I believe this emphasis is both practically and theoretically unfortunate. It is time for us to recognize that successful efforts at planned change must take as a primary target the improvement of organization health—the school system's ability not only to function effectively, but to develop and grow into a more fully functioning system.

Perhaps I can illustrate my assertion that organization properties have often been treated peripherally, or left to sit as background phenomena. If you have examined the literature on the diffusion of innovations, perhaps with the aid of Everett Rogers' excellent compendium (1962) you will notice that a good deal of attention is paid to the individual innovator, to when he adopts the innovation, and why. But the literature remains nearly silent on the organizational setting in which innovation takes place. I suspect this has several antecedents.

For one thing, the typical adopter in most rural sociological studies is an individual farmer rather than a collectivity such as an organization. The farmer's role in the community setting turns out to be important, but, aside from studies on "traditional" versus "modern" community norms, the influence of the larger setting tends to be underplayed.

Paul Mort did, on the other hand, make extensive studies of innovation by organizations—school districts (see Ross, 1958). But Mort, far from being even an amateur sociologist, appeared almost aggressively ignorant of available knowledge about the functioning of organizations and communities. His "common sense" categories and demographic indexes give us no inkling of what was really going on in the districts [that] supplied him with data.

Even Dick Carlson's (1964) study of the adoption of modern math by school superintendents suffers a bit, I think, from a kind of "great man" tendency; the internal dynamics of the school system are seen as less important than characteristics of the local superintendent, such as his position in the reference group of administrators in the region. His data are compelling, but I suspect they would have been even more powerful had he gone into more depth on the dynamics of the local setting.

From the anthropological side, I think it fair to say that there has been an overemphasis on the properties of a particular innovation itself, its diffusion across systems, and its integration within systems —without a corresponding degree of interest in the dynamics and functioning of the receiving organization as such. Art Gallaher (1963) has thoughtfully discussed power structure in innovation-receiving systems, the actual prestige of advocates of the innovation, and other matters influencing how (or if) an innovation will be integrated into the local organization. But even here, I think the analysis is overfocused on the "thinginess" of the particular innovation, taking the local system itself as a kind of unmodifiable ground against which the innovation shows up in stark figure.

[To take] one more example, the currently widespread emphasis on the importance of "dissemination of research findings," and even the recent effort of the U.S. Office [of Education] to provide development and demonstration centers, likewise avoid the problem. They share the popular view that the content or demonstrated efficacy of a particular educational innovation, as such, is the crucial thing in determining whether or not it will be adopted and used effectively. As you can gather, I am taking a decidedly processual view here: organization dynamics are the focus of attention.

I hope I have not misrepresented the views of my colleagues. It would please me to be corrected, in fact. What I do want to counter in this paper is a set of assumptions (by scientists or practitioners) that organization properties—from decision-making methods to interpersonal climate—are simply "there," that they are relatively invariant, and cannot (or should not) themselves be made the subject of planned change efforts.

More generally, the position being taken is this. It seems likely that the state of health of an educational organization can tell us more than anything else about the probable success of any particular change effort. Economy of effort would suggest that we should look at the state of an organization's health as such, and try to improve it—in preference to struggling with a series of more or less inspired short-run change efforts as ends in themselves.

To analogize with persons for a minute: the neurotic who struggles through one unavailing search for "something new" after another will never be genuinely productive until he faces and works through fundamental problems of his own functioning. Genuine productiveness—in organizations as in persons—rests on a clear sense of identity, on adequate connection with reality, on a lively problem-solving stance, and on many other things, to which I would like to turn in a moment. Here I only wish to leave you with the root notion that attention to organization health ought to be priority one for any administrator seriously concerned with innovativeness in today's educational environment.

... I should like, first, to deal with some problems in the very concept of health, both generally and as applied to organizations. The next section reviews the conception of "organization" employed in the rest of the [chapter] and outlines some dimensions of organization health as I see them. All this is rather general, and I should then like to turn to some discussion of the special properties of educational organizations, as such, and what their particular ways of departing from optimum organization health seem to be. Lastly, as an applied behavioral scientist, I would be remiss if I did not discuss some representative technologies for inducing organization health and suggest some principles underlying them.

Most of this paper is frankly speculative, though it is informed by a good deal of current work in the applied behavioral sciences—and even, now and then, by some contact with phenomena such as superintendents, principals, teachers, and children. All of the notions in the paper need vigorous discussion and testing.

Some Problems in the Concept of "Health"

The historical, commonsense notion of health is that it represents absence of illness, disease, suffering, wrongness in an organism. If not arrested, a serious "sickness" may lead to irreversible changes, such as organ impairment, atrophy, or death. But beginning (to my knowledge) with the interesting British work in preventive medicine dubbed the "Peckham Experiment," there has been more and more medical concern with the notion of positive well-being or optimal functioning. That is, disease-freeness, in and of itself, does not guarantee that an organism will, in fact, be coping with life's adventures with a sense of élan and growing while it does so.

This conception of positive health—in many ways a sneaky, vague notion—has also been receiving more and more attention in the mental health literature (see Jahoda, 1958). And there is increasing interest in the fields of psychotherapy and human relations training with the notion of "self-actualization." Both "positive health" and "self-actualization" imply a considerable gap between sheer disease-free-ness, and something that might be called the fully functioning human being. This is an attractive idea; it is consistent with much of our commonsense experience, and it caters to the American notion of the (nearly) infinitely improvable man.

But even if something like "positive health" or "self-actualization" can be said to exist—and Maslow's (1950) case studies are instructive and plausible in this respect—there are some traps and difficulties in applying such concepts to organization functioning. One, of course, is the tendency to go "over-organismic," reifying the organization into some kind of gigantic person, or least organism. This, of course, leads into the hoary disputation about whether systems larger than that of the individual person are "real" (see, for example, Warriner, 1956), a totally unprofitable byway which I do not propose to enter at the moment.

Another danger is that the notion of health implies "sickness"; school administrators are having enough difficulty as it is without being accused of being at the helm of pathological vessels on the stormy seas of innovation. The very image of "sickness" itself diverts attention away from the notion of positive growth and development, implying that only correction of some negative or painful state is required.

Finally, there are the risks involved in any discussion involving "ideal types"—distortion of reality, or blindness to large portions of it, and a prevalence of normative, preachment-type statement making about any particular organization (or, more usually, *all* organizations).

All these objections have some validity; I do not propose to eradi-cate them here, only to bring them to awareness, so they do not hamper the subsequent discussion unduly. In brief, the intellectual risks of an "organization health" approach seem to me far out-weighed by the advantages. A reasonably clear conception of organi-zation health would seem to be an important prerequisite to a wide range of activities involving organizations: research of any meaning-ful sort; attempts to improve the organization as a place to live, work, and learn; and, not least, the day-to-day operations of any par-ticular organization, such as your own school system.[1]

Organizations: Their Nature

Formal definitions show that the author of the paper has paid his debt to "the literature"; they may sometimes even help in delimiting

1. For additional comments on the importance of the concept of organiza-tion health, see Bennis (1962).

the sphere of discussion. *Organization* is here treated as a special case of the more general concept *system,* more particularly *open system.* The latter is defined as:

A bounded collection of interdependent parts, devoted to the accomplishment of some goal or goals, with the parts maintained in a steady state in relation to each other and the environment by means of (1) standard modes of operation, and (2) feedback from the environment about the consequences of system actions [Miles, 1964a, page 13].

Argyris (1964, page 120) poses a broadly similar definition: "(1) a plurality of parts, [which] (2) maintaining themselves through their interrelatedness and, (3) achieving specific objective(s), (4) while accomplishing (2) and (3) adapt to the external environment thereby (5) maintaining their interrelated state of parts."

Either of these definitions would apply to a system such as a candle flame, an air-conditioning unit, or a school district. For our purposes, it is perhaps sufficient to say that the above definitions, in the special case of the "organization," are expected to apply to social systems larger than a face-to-face group, and with a reasonable degree of goal specification (this latter to exclude larger systems, such as communities and nations).

Somewhat more specifically, reference to Figure 11-1 will indicate the notion "educational organization" used as a backdrop [here]. Notice that the usual hierarchical arrangement is absent, since the "parts" are not seen as persons or work groups, but as social-psychological components of the system which crosscut persons and groups. The figure indicates that the organization exists in an environment from which it receives inputs (money, personnel, and children) and to which it releases outputs in terms of goal achievement and morale and learning motivation of the clients in the organization (children). Between the input and the output, to paraphrase T. S. Eliot, falls the shadow of a number of other components. The inhabitants of an educational organization must have reasonably clear perceptions of the goal or goals to which the system is devoted; these in turn affect role specifications and performance for the inhabitants. Systems of reward and penalty regulate role performance, as do the norms governing the style of interpersonal transactions in the system. The arrows in the diagram are intended to indicate directions of influence between parts of the system, as well as to suggest that a variety of feedback loops exist which serve to maintain the system in a reasonably steady state.

If all goes well, desired system outputs are achieved. But this is not

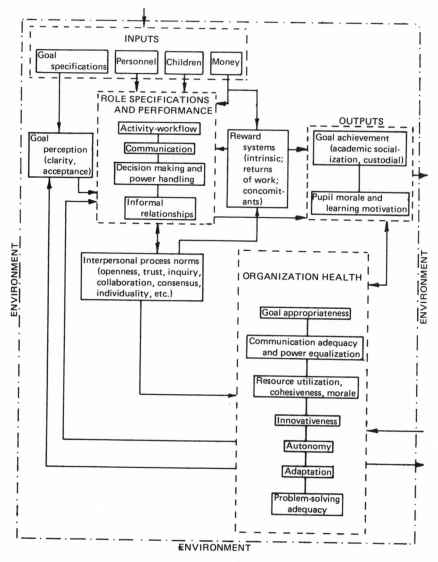

FIGURE 11-1
Schematic model of organization functioning and change environment

all: above and beyond the network of parts and their functioning, we can conceive of a set of system "health" characteristics, which have to do with the continued adequacy and viability of the organization's coping. More of this below. Here it is perhaps sufficient to sketch out the schematic model, and point out that it assumes nothing about the specific kinds of structures—planful or emergent—appearing in any particular system. The model will presumably fit a classical pyramidal scheme, as well as a number of more or less radical variants from this (for example, those suggested by Argyris, 1964).

Organization Health

Our present thinking about organization health is that it can be seen as a set of fairly durable second-order system properties, which tend to transcend short-run effectiveness. A healthy organization in this sense not only survives in its environment, but continues to cope adequately over the long haul, and continuously develops and extends its surviving and coping abilities. Short-run operations on any particular day may be effective or ineffective, but continued survival, adequate coping, and growth are taking place.

A steadily ineffective organization would presumably not be healthy; on balance, "health" implies a summation of effective short-run coping. But notice that an organization *may* cope effectively in the short run (as, for example, by a speedup or a harsh cost-cutting drive), but at the cost of longer-run variables, such as those noted below. The classic example, of course, is an efficiency drive which cuts short-run costs and results in long-run labor dissatisfaction and high turnover.

To illustrate in more detail what is meant by "second-order property," here is a list of ten dimensions of organization health that seem plausible to me. Many of them are drawn by heuristic analogy from the behavior of persons or small groups; this does not mean, of course, that organizations necessarily are precisely homologous to persons or groups—only that thinking in this way may get us somewhere on what, it must be admitted, is a very complex problem indeed. Here then are ten dimensions. They are not, of course, mutually exclusivy, and [they] interact with each other vigorously within any particular organization. Both Jahoda (1958) and Argyris (1964) have commented on the importance of a multiple-criterion approach to the assessment of health, given the present state of our knowledge and the fact that, as a college roommate of mine once remarked with blinding insight, "You know, everything is really connected to everything else."

The first three dimensions are relatively "tasky," in that they deal with organizational goals, the transmission of messages, and the way in which decisions are made.

1. *Goal focus.* In a healthy organization the goal (or more usually goals) of the system would be reasonably clear to the system members and reasonably well accepted by them.[2] This clarity and acceptance, however, should be seen as a necessary but insufficient condition for organization health. The goals must also be achievable with existing or available resources, and be appropriate—more or less congruent with the demands of the environment. The last feature may be most critical. Switching back to the person level for a moment, consider the obsessive patient who sets the clear, accepted, achievable goal for himself of washing his hands 250 times a day. The question remains: Is this an appropriate goal in light of what else there is to do in life?

2. *Communication adequacy.* Since organizations are not simultaneous face-to-face systems like small groups, the movement of information within them becomes crucial. This dimension of organization health implies that there is relatively distortion-free communication "vertically," "horizontally," and across the boundary of the system to and from the surrounding environment. That is, information travels reasonably well—just as the healthy person "knows himself" with a minimum level of repression, distortion, etc. In the healthy organization there is good and prompt sensing of internal strains; there are enough data about problems of the system to ensure that a good diagnosis of system difficulties can be made. People have the information they need, and [they] have gotten it without exerting undue efforts, such as those involved in moseying up to the superintendent's secretary, reading the local newspaper, or calling excessive numbers of special meetings.

3. *Optimal power equalization.* In a healthy organization the distribution of influence is relatively equitable. Subordinates (if there is a formal authority chart) can influence upward, and even more

2. Note that the question of actual goal achievement, as such, is here conceived of as separate, analytically speaking, from the question of organization health. Argyris has suggested that organization effectiveness, a concept resembling the health notion, resides in the organization's ability to (1) achieve goals, (2) maintain itself internally, (3) engage in adaptation processes with the environment—and to accomplish these three "core activities" at a constant or increasing level of effectiveness, given the same or decreasing increments in energy input (Argyris, 1964, p. 123). This three-way scheme is also used in the present discussion.

important—as Likert (1961) has demonstrated—they perceive that their boss can do likewise with *his* boss. In such an organization, intergroup struggles for power would not be bitter, though intergroup conflict, (as in every human system known to man) would undoubtedly be present. The basic stance of persons in such an organization, as they look up, sideways, and down, is that of collaboration rather than explicit or implicit coercion. The units of the organization (persons in roles, work groups, and so forth) would stand in an interdependent relationship to each other, with rather less emphasis on the ability of a "master" part to control the entire operation. The exertion of influence in a healthy organization would presumably rest on the competence of the influencer vis-à-vis the issue at hand, his stake in the outcome, and the amount of knowledge or data he has—rather than on his organizational position, personal charisma, or other factors with little direct relevance to the problem at hand.

These then are three "task-centered" dimensions of organization health. A second group of three dimensions deals essentially with the internal state of the system, and its inhabitants' "maintenance" needs. These are resource utilization, cohesiveness, and morale.

4. *Resource utilization.* We say of a healthy person, such as a second-grader, that he is "working up to his potential." To put this another way, the classroom system is evoking a contribution from him at an appropriate and goal-directed level of tension. At the organization level, "health" would imply that the system's inputs, particularly the personnel, are used effectively. The overall coordination is such that people are neither overloaded nor idling. There is a minimal sense of strain, generally speaking (in the sense that trying to do something with a weak or inappropriate structure puts strain on that structure). In the healthy organization, people may be working very hard indeed, but they feel that they are not working against themselves, or against the organization. The fit between people's own dispositions and the role demands of the system is good. Beyond this, people feel reasonably "self-actualized"; they not only "feel good" in their jobs, but they have a genuine sense of learning, growing, and developing as persons in the process of making their organizational contribution.

5. *Cohesiveness.* We think of a healthy person as one who has a clear sense of identity; he knows who he is, underneath all the specific goals he sets for himself. Beyond this, he likes himself; his stance toward life does not require self-derogation, even when there are aspects of his behavior which are unlovely or ineffective. By

analogy, at the organization level system health would imply that the organization knows "who it is." Its members feel attracted to membership in the organization. They want to stay with it, be influenced by it, and exert their own influence in the collaborative style suggested above.

6. *Morale.* The history of this concept in the social-psychological literature is so appalling that I hesitate to introduce it at all. The implied notion is one of well-being or satisfaction. Satisfaction is not enough for health, of course; a person may report feelings of well-being and satisfaction in his life, while successfully denying deeplying hostilities, anxieties, and conflicts. Yet it still seems useful to evoke, at the organization level, the idea of morale: a summated set of individual sentiments, centering around feelings of well-being, satisfaction, and pleasure, as opposed to feelings of discomfort, unwished-for strain and dissatisfaction. In an unhealthy system, life might be perceived rosily as "good," or as unabashedly bad; in a healthy organization it is hard to entertain the idea that the dominant personal response of organization members would be anything else than one of well-being.

Finally, there are four more dimensions of organization health, which deal with growth and changefulness: the notions of innovativeness, autonomy, adaptation vis-à-vis the environment, and problem-solving adequacy.

7. *Innovativeness.* A healthy system would tend to invent new procedures, move toward new goals, produce new kinds of products, diversify itself, and become more rather than less differentiated over time. In a sense, such a system could be said to grow, develop, and change, rather than remaining routinized and standard. The analogue here is to the self-renewing properties of a Picasso, or to Schachtel's (1959) "activity" orientation (curious, exploring) as contrasted with "embeddedness" orientation (tension-reducing, protective) in persons.[3]

8. *Autonomy.* The healthy person acts "from his own center outward." Seen in a training or therapy group, for example, such a person appears nearly free of the need to submit dependently to authority figures, and [of] the need to rebel and destroy symbolic fathers of any kind. A healthy organization, similarly, would not respond

3. Clark (1962) has suggested that organization health resides primarily in the continuous possibility of both kinds of orientation: toward change and development, and for stability and maintenance. This dual possibility should be realized, he suggests, at the personal, group, intergroup, and total organizational levels.

passively to demands from the outside, feeling itself the tool of the environment, and it would not respond destructively or rebelliously to perceived demands either. It would tend to have a kind of independence from the environment, in the same sense that the healthy person, while he has transactions with others, does not treat their responses as determinative of his own behavior.

9. *Adaptation.* The notions of autonomy and innovativeness are both connected with the idea that a healthy person, group, or organization is in realistic, effective contact with the surroundings. When environmental demands and organization resources do not match, a problem-solving, restructuring approach evolves in which both the environment and the organization become different in some respect. More adequate, continued coping of the organization, as a result of changes in the local system, the relevant portions of the environment, or more usually both, occurs. And such a system has sufficient stability and stress tolerance to manage the difficulties which occur during the adaptation process. Perhaps inherent in this notion is that the system's ability to bring about corrective change in itself is faster than the change cycle in the surrounding environment. Explanations for the disappearance of dinosaurs vary, but it is quite clear that in some way this criterion was not met.

10. *Problem-solving adequacy.* Finally, any healthy organism— even one as theoretically impervious to fallibility as a computer— always has problems, strains, difficulties, and instances of ineffective coping. The issue is not the presence or absence of problems, therefore, but the manner in which the person, group, or organization copes with problems. Argyris (1964) has suggested that, in an effective system, problems are solved with minimal energy; they stay solved; and the problem-solving mechanisms used are not weakened, but maintained or strengthened. An adequate organization, then, has well-developed structures and procedures for sensing the existence of problems, for inventing possible solutions, for deciding on the solutions, for implementing them, and for evaluating their effectiveness. Such an organization would conceive of its own operations (whether directed outward to goal achievement, inward to maintenance, or inward-outward to problems of adaptation) as being controllable. We would see active coping with problems, rather than passive withdrawing, compulsive responses, scapegoating, or denial.

Here, then, are ten dimensions of a healthy organization,[4] stated

4. Little has been said here about the actual form of the organization which is most likely to meet these criteria of organizational health at some optimal

abstractly, even vaguely in many instances. They must, of course, be operationalized into meaningful indicators of organization functioning; the staff of our project is currently into this with more than a little trepidation, but with keen interest to see whether these ways of viewing the health of a system prove to have a reasonable amount of empirical steam behind them.

The Special Case of Educational Organizations

These dimensions can presumably be applied to any type of organization. Much of the theory and empirical data on which they are based was generated in industrial organizations in which "organization improvement" programs have become more and more widespread in the last few years. (See, for example, Bennis, 1963, 1964.) We need, however, to determine the special properties of educational systems (if any) which predispose them to particular types of ill health. It is also necessary to examine whether the technologies of organization improvement which have proved successful industrially need adaption in certain directions before they are likely to be efficacious in schools. If this is not done, we might well expect a recrudescence of the unfortunate enthusiasm of schoolmen for Taylorism and "scientific management" which occurred in the first decades of this century. (See the excellent treatment of this appalling subject in Callahan & Button, 1964.)

In our own time, it has taken a good deal of agitation by people like Dan Griffiths to get school administrators and professors of education to accept the possibility that the school is in fact an organization, and as such shares certain properties with all other organizations, and that administrative theory, if well developed in any field

---

level. Some applied work in organization change (Argyris, 1964; Bennis, 1962) suggests that strongly pyramidal organizations designed around strict division of labor, accountability, limited span of control, etc., are uniquely ill-fitted to the demands of survival in today's world. Argyris (1964) has suggested a number of alternatives to the pyramidal model (such as the use of temporary "product teams" with power base on functional contribution rather than position) which he feels are not only more likely to lead in the direction of organization health but respect the "essential properties" of organizations as open systems. Empirical data on this question are not numerous; however, work with communication nets in small simulated organizations has suggested that relatively loose, power-equalized, full-communication models of organization are much more effective than traditional models when the environment is shifting and changing. This finding also appeared in a study of Scottish electronic firms by Burns and Stalker (1961). See also Likert (1961).

of human endeavor, could apply to the school business. This is quite correct. However, emphasis on the commonality of all types of organizations has tended to obscure the fact that educational systems have special properties which condition the propositions of organization theory in reasonably predictable ways. What, then, are some of these properties?

1. *Goal ambiguity.* For many different reasons, it has seemed difficult to specify the output of educational organizations very precisely. Some of this is realistic: change in human beings is going on, with presumably cumulative effects over a long period of time. But part of this output measurement difficulty also seems to be a form of organization defense or protection against criticism from the surrounding environment (see below).

Whatever the reasons, supposed "unmeasurability" of organizational output (hence, of the effectiveness of particular role occupants) seems a fairly durable feature of educational organizations as we know them today.

In addition, certain goals of the school (such as "academic learning") are often given primacy in public pronouncements while others (for example, the socialization of achievement motivation and appropriate *Gesellschaftlich* behavior for the incoming denizens of an industrial society) are treated as background phenomena. Still others (such as keeping the kids off the streets and out of Mother's way— call it custodial care) are usually taboo as legitimate goal statements.[5]

It is possible, of course, that school system goals are not all that unmeasurable and ambiguous. In some exploratory interviewing we have been doing in two suburban school systems, teachers and principals, almost without exception, denied that "it is difficult to know when you are doing a good job"[6] and denied that "disagreement over the goals of the school" was present. We intend to pursue this further, because our hunch is that such protestations of agreement reflect defensive solutions to the actual problems of goal ambiguity and goal disagreement, which do, in fact, exist.

I believe that this ambiguity and pseudo-consensus around school

5. If you doubt for a minute that custodial care is an important goal of the American public school, try this "Gedanken-experiment." Which would be the most effective form of teacher strike: (a) for teachers to stay home; (b) for teachers to come to school, but teach the children nothing?

6. This is a remarkable assertion, in light of the encyclopedic (and to me gloomily inconclusive) research findings on teacher effectiveness (see Gage, 1963b).

output measurement encourages the institutionalization and ossification of teaching procedures. If it cannot really be determined whether one course of action leads to more output than another, then why stop lecturing? There is a further consequence (stemming particularly from the unacknowledged but powerful custodial function of the school): highly rigid time and personnel allocations in most American schools. Hall passes, the forty-seven-minute period, and the difficulty some teachers have in finding time to go to the toilet are all examples. It is interesting that the increasing use of computers for class scheduling has not, to my knowledge, exploited the enormous potential of information-processing machines for making a *more* rather than less flexible learning environment. In any event, I wish only to make the point that goal ambiguity and procedural rigidity may very well turn out to be closely connected.

2. *Input variability.* Another, possibly unique, property of educational organizations is a very wide variation in input from the environment, particularly in relation to children and personnel. Since the school is defined in America as publicly responsible, it must accept children of a very wide range of ability and motivation to carry out its activities (this holds true, of course, for custodial and socialization goals as well as academic learning goals). The current stress on programs for the "culturally deprived" only serves to divert attention from the fact that the American schools seem never to have been able to cope effectively with children from lower socioeconomic levels.[7]

This is no place to review in any detail the problem of variability in teacher performance, but here again it is important to note that the range of intellectual ability, interpersonal skill and knowledge of subject matter among teachers is probably at least as great as that among pupils. This variability causes considerable stress in educational organizations, and develops the need to provide teaching personnel with methods and procedures which are, in effect, teacher-proof. Wayland (1964) has reviewed this problem as a function of the enormous historical expansion of the scope of American education; he suggests that the teacher's role is now essentially that of a bureaucratic functionary, all protestations of "professionalism" to the contrary.

3. *Role performance invisibility.* Classrooms are in effect the production departments of the educational enterprise; in them teachers

---

7. See, for example, the really staggering data on reading retardation and advancement as a function of social class in Barton and Wilder (1964).

teach. Yet, this role performance is relatively invisible to status equals or superiors. Children can observe, usually very acutely, the quality of a teacher's execution of her role, but they are not allowed to comment on this, and have few (if any) sanctions to bring to bear. Thus, rewards in the teaching profession seem relatively detached from others' estimates of one's performance; the average teacher, as Lortie (1961) has pointed out, gains most satisfaction from intrinsic properties of the role behavior involved. Teaching thus becomes a craft-like occupation, rather than a profession, and substitute criteria for teaching effectiveness, such as "how interested the kids are" begin to appear and are used vigorously. Perhaps this is what our teachers meant when they said it was not difficult to know when they were doing a good job.

4. *Low interdependence.* A further characteristic of educational organizations, when compared with thing-producing systems, seems to be a relatively low interdependence of parts. Teacher A's failure to teach anything to her minions affects the job-relevant behavior of teacher B very little—except in a rather diffuse, blaming sense, as when junior high school teachers devoutly declare their belief that basic skills are not present in newly arrived seventh graders.

This low interdependence has several consequences. First, it tends to reinforce the pyramidal "man-to-man" style of supervision which Likert (1961) and others have shown to be inimical to organization effectiveness. In the case of teachers of young children, it tends to promote a kind of infantilism and boredom; in many teachers, as suggested by a recent study (Peterson, 1964), the peak of productive contribution tends to be in the twenties, with distancing from students and potential routinization starting in the mid-thirties. The reported stresses and strains in most accounts of team teaching—an attempt to increase interdependence in educational organizations— are mute testimony to the strength with which "separatist" norms have become institutionalized in the American public schools.[8]

High interdependence is not without its difficulties, of course. As Golembiewski (1964) has pointed out, the classical division of industrial organizations into specialized departments tends to promote

8. Lortie's (1961) comments on a three-part norm system are relevant here: He comments on the teacher as subscribing to the following beliefs: a) the teacher should be free of interference in his teaching; b) other teachers should be considered and treated as equals (in spite of the fact that they obviously differ in interests and skill); c) teachers should act in a friendly manner toward one another in informal contacts. Note that these norms reinforce each other in such a way as to inhibit effective, interdependent work.

hostility, competitiveness, and disjunction between the authority system and other aspects of the organization such as communication patterns, friendship relationships, and work flow. He suggests an alternative organization model involving the existence of "product divisions," each of which contains in it all the specialties necessary to undertake an operation such as buying materials for, producing, and marketing a washing machine. Schools are organized in a product division manner, in effect. But Golembiewski's analysis—this is crucial—depends on the existence of simple, rapidly available output measures, so that the performance of a product division can be monitored. As we have seen, the absence of such measures—and more fundamentally, the belief that they can never be produced—is a serious barrier to the effectiveness of educational organizations.

5. *Vulnerability.* The American public school, even more than other public organizations, is subject to control, criticism, and a wide variety of "legitimate" demands from the surrounding environment: everyone is a stockholder. Any public organization tends to generate this type of relationship with systems and persons outside its boundary. But a people-processing organization such as the school is dealing with extremely valuable property—children—who return to their parents each night with more or less accurate news of how they have been treated. Thus, in the special kind of organization termed a school, almost any role occupant—board member, superintendent, principal, staff specialist, or teacher—can be criticized by parents or citizens at large. To the system inhabitants, the organization skin seems extremely thin. Many kinds of ingenious defenses are adopted to solve this problem—policies about visiting the classroom, brainwashing of new board members by the superintendent and the old members (cf. Sieber, in press), buffer devices such as the PTA, and so on. Yet, the fact remains that a consumer who does not like the octane rating of his gasoline cannot go to the refinery and criticize the operation of a catcracker, but a parent who feels conflicted about her child's reading ability can be pretty violent with the first-grade teacher. (I might comment that this vulnerability seems most sharp when viewed from the inside. Many parents apparently feel that the school is impregnable, and that they must not raise complaints, rock the boat, and so forth.)

In any event, this state of affairs represents, I believe, a serious failure of adaptation skills of schools as organizations and tends to reduce school system autonomy sharply. In recent years I have met only one school superintendent who told me he was going ahead actively (and successfully) with curriculum and organization changes to which a majority of his community were opposed. As it turned out, he was an old private-school man.

6. *Lay-professional control problems.* Public schools are governed by laymen, most of whom have not been inside a school for twenty years prior to their succession to the board. As a result, they often agree tacitly or explicitly on a division of labor with the superintendent and his staff (the policy—procedure distinction developed by Brickell and Davies is one such example). But even where the board is "well trained" and leaves the execution of policy to the superintendent, notice that the question of educational policy determination still remains a moot one.

And there are internal lay-professional problems as well. In many respects, the principal of an elementary or high school, in terms of expert knowledge, may find himself far behind the capabilities of particular teachers on his staff—and is in this sense a layman as well. The problems of organizations with high proportions of professionals have been studied vigorously (for example, hospitals, and research organizations); I only wish to indicate here that the fruits of such study so far have found little application in schools.[9]

7. *Low technological investment.* Lastly, it seems very clear that the amount of technology per worker in schools is relatively low. From 60 percent to 75 percent of a local school system's budget ordinarily goes to salary, with a fraction for equipment and materials. Even if we count buildings as "technological investment," the picture is rather different from that in most industries. This has consequences: social transactions, rather than sociotechnical transactions, come to be the major mode of organization production. Because of this, it is possible that education, as James Finn has suggested, has never made it out of the folk culture stage. And we are back once again to goal ambiguity and its problems.

These, then, strike me as special strains, ways in [which] educational organizations as such and the public school in particular depart from the generalized model of organization health outlined earlier. In sum, I would suggest that, in terms of the dimensions above, the major difficulties to be expected in most public schools would center around goal focus (as a consequence of goal ambiguity); difficulties

9. It is interesting to note that the greatest inroads of applied behavioral science seem to have been in research-based organizations, in areas such as aerospace, electronics, and petroleum refining. Why this has not happened in schools (and universities) is an interesting question. It may very well be that a knowledge-spreading organization (such as a school) operates rather differently from a knowledge-making one (such as a research group).

in communication adequacy and power equalization stemming from low interdependence; and, perhaps most centrally, failures in innovativeness, autonomy, adaptation, and problem-solving adequacy, because of vulnerability and lay-professional conflict.

Interestingly enough, I do not see any clear reason for believing that internal "maintenance problems" (such as those involved in effective resource utilization, cohesiveness, and morale) are sharp points of strain in most school systems; it may very well be that low interdependence, plus orientation to a professional reference group, carry with them a willingness to "settle for less" than the optimum in these areas.

The Induction of Organization Health

The particular degree of health of any local school system, given a multiple-criterion approach such as that suggested here, undoubtedly varies from time to time. A question of considerable interest is: what can be done to induce a greater degree of organization health in any particular system? By now a fair amount of experience exists, drawn from the interesting blend of consultation and research in which an increasing number of behavioral scientists now find themselves involved, primarily with industrial organizations. These methods can perhaps most usefully be considered as interventions in the ongoing life of a system; this term implies an action which interferes with or reorients processes—either pathological or normal—ordinarily occurring in the system. A teacher's intervention in a child's problem solving serves to reorient his thinking; perhaps more importantly, it can aid the child to mobilize his own energies more effectively. Thus the usual aim of an intervention is to start internal change processes going in the system at hand, rather than only causing an immediate change.

Below are described six interventions aimed at improving organization health.[10] In some cases, plausible statements can be made about which dimensions of health are most typically influenced by a particular intervention. For the most part, however, we do not really know; it is exactly the function of our research project to discover how these are likely to work in educational organizations. In conclusion, some common principles underlying the six interventions are discussed.

10. See Bennis (1963, 1964) for a thorough review of alternative approaches being used.

1. *Team training.* In this approach, the members of an intact work group (for example, the superintendent and his central office personnel) meet for a period of several days away from their offices, with consultant help. They examine their own effectiveness as a problem-solving team, the role of each member in the group and how it affects the group and the person himself, and the operations of the group in relation to its organizational environment. This problem solving may be based on fairly careful prior data collection from individuals as to their views on the current problems of the system; these data are summarized and form the beginning of the group's agenda. Occasionally, exercises and theoretical material on group and organization functioning may be supplied by the outside consultant.

Under these circumstances, the members of the group usually improve in their abilities to express feelings directly, and to listen to— and understand—each other. Communication adequacy is thus considerably increased. The members also deal with internal conflicts in the team and learn to solve problems more effectively as a unit, thus presumably increasing their ability to meet the demands placed upon them by other parts of the system. Over a period of time, beginning with the top decision-making group of the system, this intervention may be repeated with other groups as well. Industrial programs of this sort have been described by Argyris (1962) and Blake, Blansfield, and Mouton (1962).

2. *Survey feedback.* In this approach, data bearing on attitudes, opinions, and beliefs of members of a system are collected via questionnaire. An external researcher summarizes the data for the organization as a whole, and for each of a number of relevant work groups. Each work group, under the guidance of its own superior, and perhaps with consultant help, examines its own summarized data, in comparison with those for the organization as a whole. The group makes plans for change stemming from these discussions and carries them out. The focus of this intervention is on many or all of the work groups within a total setting. The aim is to free up communication, leading to goal clarification and problem-solving work. The relative objectification involved in looking at data helps to reduce feelings of being misunderstood and isolated and makes problems more susceptible to solution, rather than retaining them as a focus for blaming, scapegoating, griping, and so on. For an account of survey feedback procedure, see Mann (1961); Gage (1963a) has tried a similar approach effectively with student-to-teacher feedback, and [he] is now studying teacher-to-principal feedback.

3. *Role workshop.* Sometimes called the "horizontal slice" meet-

ing, this intervention involves all the people in a particular role (for example, elementary principal). They fill out research instruments dealing with role expectations which various others hold for them, the fit between their own wishes and these expectations, their actual role performance, and so forth. These data are summarized, and form the vehicle for a series of activities (discussion, role practice, decision-making exercises, problem solving, and so on) at a workshop attended by all the people in the role. The main focus here is on role clarity, effectiveness, and improved fit between the person and the role. By sharing common role problems, people occupying the role may develop alternative solutions which result in better performance of that role and more "self-actualized" operation in general.

4. *"Target setting" and supporting activities.* In this approach, periodic meetings are held between a superior and each of his subordinates, separately. In a school system, this might involve the superintendent and his staff members, or a principal and his teachers. The work of each subordinate is reviewed in relation to organizational and personal goals, and the superior and subordinate agree collaboratively on new targets for the subordinate's work and personal development. These "targets" are in turn reviewed after some work time (usually six months or so) has elapsed. During that period, other activities such as role meetings, consultation, self-operated data collection, academic courses, and workshops, may be engaged in by the subordinate to develop needed skills and understandings as he works toward the collaboratively set goals. The focus of attention here is the working relationship between superior and subordinate, and the degree to which they are together able to help the subordinate grow and develop on the job. Improved trust, feelings of support, better and more satisfying role performance, and more open communication usually result. Zander (1963) has reviewed thoroughly the problems and values of performance appraisal, including commentary on the target-setting approach.

5. *Organizational diagnosis and problem-solving.* This intervention involves a residential meeting of members of an intact work group, usually at the top of the organization (or in small organizations, up to size forty-fifty, the entire work force). They meet for several days to identify problems facing the system, and the reasons for the existence of these; to invent possible solutions; to decide on needed system changes; and to plan implementation of these through regular channels and newly constructed ones. It differs from team training as described above in that relatively less attention is given to team relationships and interpersonal effectiveness as such, and more to system

problems in the large. The main focus of attention is on the organization and its current functioning. The improvement of problem-solving activity and communication adequacy are typical results. For an account of two such meetings conducted with an industrial organization, see Zand, Miles, and Lytle (forthcoming).

6. *Organizational experiment.* In this approach, a major organizational variable of interest is changed directly,[11] by agreement of the responsible administrators and needed implementation efforts. One such approach is described vividly by Morse and Reimer (1956): in several divisions of a large organization, the level of decision making was moved radically downward, thus giving more autonomy to subordinates; in several other divisions the level of decision making was moved up; and in several divisions no change was made. Such an approach requires the careful collection of pre-post data, and the use of control groups in order to test the consequences of the change. The halo of "experiment" is an aid to acceptance since the arrangement is seen as not only temporary but scientific and responsibly managed. Such an approach ordinarily includes a feedback stage, in which the results are examined carefully and implications for the continuing functioning of the organization [are] drawn.

These, then, are six possible approaches to the induction of organization health. Certain common threads appear to flow through all of them.

1. *Self-study.* These approaches reject the "technocratic" change model involving the recommendations of a detached expert and actively involve the system itself in what might be called organizational introspection. The same holds true for approaches involving group self-study for various teams in the organization and personal introspection and reexamination by role occupants.

In common with the action research movement in education, these approaches also carry the assumption that an operant stance on the part of the organization is both theoretically and practically preferable to the problems involved in dependence on outsiders for system change.

2. *Relational emphasis.* These approaches do not conceive of the organization as a collection of jobs with isolated persons in them, but as a network of groups and role relationships; it is the functioning of these groups and relationships, as such, which requires examination

11. I am reminded of Hollis Caswell's classic remark when asked in 1943 how the newly-formed Horace Mann-Lincoln Institute would proceed in its program of school experimentation: "We'll change the curriculum by changing it."

and self-operated, experimental alteration. The aim is not to ferret out and change the "attitude" of old-fogey Principal A, but to focus on the relationships and group settings in which Principal A's attitudes are evoked.

3. *Increased data flow.* These approaches all involve the heightening or intensification of communication, especially vertically, but also diagonally and horizontally. New feedback loops are often built into the existing system. The use of status-equalizing devices such as intensive residential meetings also encourages fuller and freer flow of information through channels which may have been blocked or have always carried distorted messages.

4. *Norms as a change target.* By focusing on groups and relationships, and increasing data flow, these approaches have the effect of altering existing norms which regulate interpersonal transactions in the organization. If, for example, a work group where the norms are "play it close to the vest, and don't disagree with the boss" engages in a team-training session, it is quite likely—since all group members have participated in the experience—that norms such as "be open about your feelings whether or not they tally with the boss's wishes" will develop. These approaches thus have a strong culture-changing component, based on intensive, data-based interaction with others.[12]

5. *Temporary system approach.* But norm changing is by definition very difficult under the usual pressures of day-to-day operation in the organization. "Business as usual" has to prevail. Most of the interventions described involve the use of residential meetings, which constitute a detached, "cultural island" approach to organizational introspection and self-correction. They are, in effect, temporary systems,[13] where new norms can develop, and where, given the suspension of the usual pressures, meaningful changes can be made in he structure and functioning of the permanent system.

6. *Expert facilitation.* All of these interventions also include the presence of a semidetached consultant figure, whose main functions are to facilitate, provoke, and support the efforts of the system to understand itself, free up communication, and engage in more ade-

12. In retrospect, the crucial role of norms in the maintenance of organizational health has probably been underplayed in this paper. In our research, we are planning to collect data on norms such as those regulating interpersonal authenticity and awareness, trust, objectivity, collaboration, altruistic concern, consensual decision making, innovativeness, and creativity. Most of these are directly coordinated to the dimensions of organizational health reviewed above.

13. See Miles (1964) for an analysis of the special properties of temporary systems for change-inducing purposes.

quate problem-solving behavior. The outsider role, however, is seen as impermanent; it is only associated with the system during the actual period of the intervention itself. If the intervention is successful, the organization itself continues the self-corrective processes which have been begun by the intervention.

Whether or not these interventions, drawn from work with thing-producing organizations, can be used plausibly with people-processing organizations such as schools is an interesting question, to which my colleagues and I are beginning to gather some answers. Our impulse at the moment is to believe that the answer will be affirmative. With the assistance of two or three school systems, we expect to have some empirical data on intervention results in about two years, an eventuality to which we look forward with a good deal of pleasure.

In Conclusion

It might be useful to point out in conclusion that the position taken in this paper is not that an organization must necessarily be brought to a state of perfect health before it can engage in any meaningful short-run innovative projects at all. Rather, we feel it is quite likely that the very act of carrying out small-scale projects in planned change can undoubtedly strengthen the health of an educational organization—but only if direct attention is paid concurrently to the state of the organization. The basic innovative project, we believe, must be one of organization development itself.

References

Argyris, C. (1962). *Interpersonal Competence and Organizational Effectiveness.* Homewood, Ill.: Dorsey Press.

_____ (1964). *Integrating the Individual and the Organization.* New York: Wiley.

Barton, A. H., and Wilder, D. E. (1964). "Research and Practice in the Teaching of Reading: A Progress Report," in M. B. Miles, ed., *Innovation in Education.* New York: Bureau of Publications, Teachers College, Columbia University, pp. 361-398.

Bennis, W. G. (1962). "Towards a 'Truly' Scientific Management: The Concept of Organization Health," in A. Rapaport, ed., *General Systems.* Yearbook of the Society for the Advancement of General Systems Theory. Ann Arbor, Mich.: the Society.

_____ (1963). "A New Role for the Behavioral Sciences: Effecting Organizational Change." *Administrative Science Quarterly*, 8.2:125-165.

_____ (1964). "Theory and Method in Applying Behavioral Science to Planned

Organizational Change." Cambridge, Mass.: Alfred P. Sloan School of Management, M.I.T., mimeo.

———, Benne, K. D., and Chin, R. (1961). *The Planning of Change: Readings in the Applied Behavioral Sciences.* New York: Holt, Rinehart and Winston.

Blake, R. R., Blansfield, M. G., and Mouton, J. S. (1962). "How Executive Team Training Can Help You." *Journal of the American Society of Training Directors,* 16.1:3-11.

Burns, T., and Stalker, G. M. (1961). *The Management of Innovation.* London: Tavistock Publications.

Callahan, R. E., and Button, H. W. (1964). "Historical Change of the Role of the Man in the Organization, 1865-1950," in D. E. Griffiths, ed., *Behavioral Science and Educational Administration.* 63rd Yearbook of the National Society for the Study of Education, Part II. Chicago: University of Chicago Press.

Carlson, R. O. (1964). "School Superintendents and the Adoption of Modern Math: A Social Structure Profile," in M. B. Miles, ed., *Innovation in Education.* New York: Bureau of Publications, Teachers College, Columbia University, pp. 329-342.

Clark, J. V. (1962). *A Healthy Organization.* Los Angeles: Institute of Industrial Relations, University of California.

Gage, N. L. (1963a). "A Method for 'Improving' Teacher Behavior." *Journal of Teacher Education,* 14.3:261-266.

———, ed. (1963b). *Handbook of Research on Teaching.* Chicago: Rand McNally.

Gallaher, A. (1963). "The Role of the Advocate and Directed Change." Paper presented at the Symposium on Identifying Techniques and Principles for Gaining Acceptance of Research Results of Use of Mass Media in Education, Lincoln, Nebraska, November 24-27.

Golembiewski, R. (1964). "Authority as a Problem in Overlays." *Administrative Science Quarterly,* 1.1:23-49.

Jahoda, M. (1958). *Current Concepts of Positive Mental Health.* New York: Basic Books.

Likert, R. (1961). *New Patterns of Management.* New York: McGraw-Hill.

Lippitt, R., Watson, J., and Westley, B. (1958). *The Dynamics of Planned Change.* New York: Harcourt, Brace.

Lortie, D. C. (1961). "Craftsmen and Colleagueship, A Frame for the Investigation of Work Values among Public School Teachers." Paper read at American Sociological Association meeting.

Mann, F. C. (1961). "Studying and Creating Change," in W. G. Bennis, K. D. Benne, and R. Chin, *The Planning of Change: Readings in the Applied Behavioral Sciences.* New York: Holt, Rinehart and Winston, pp. 605-615.

Maslow, A. (1950). "Self-actualizing People: A Study of Psychological Health," in W. Wolff, ed., *Personality Symposium.* New York: Grune and Stratton, pp. 11-34.

Miles, M. B. (1964a). *Innovation in Education.* New York: Bureau of Publications, Teachers College, Columbia University.

———— (1964b). "On Temporary Systems," in M. B. Miles, ed., *Innovation in Education*. New York: Bureau of Publications, Teachers College, Columbia University, pp. 437-492.

Morse, N., and Reimer, E. (1956). "The Experimental Change of a Major Organizational Variable." *Journal of Abnormal and Social Psychology*, 52:120-129.

Peterson, W. A. (1964). "Age, Teacher's Role, and the Institutional Setting," in B. J. Biddle and W. J. Ellena, eds., *Contemporary Research on Teacher Effectiveness*. New York: Holt, Rinehart and Winston, pp. 264-315.

Rogers, E. M. (1962). *Diffusion of Innovations*. New York: Free Press.

Ross, D. H., ed. (1958). *Administration for Adaptability*. New York: Metropolitan School Study Council.

Schachtel, E. G. (1959). *Metamorphosis*. New York: Basic Books.

Sieber, S. D. (in press). "The School Board as an Agency of Legitimation," in *Sociology of Education*. Bureau of Applied Social Research Reprint No. A-404, Columbia University.

Warriner, C. J. (1956). "Groups Are Real: A Reaffirmation." *American Sociological Review*, 21:549-554.

Zand, D., Miles, M. B., and Lytle, W. O., Jr. (forthcoming). "Organizational Improvement through Use of a Temporary Problem-Solving System," in D. E. Zand and P. C. Buhanan, eds., *Organization Development: Theory and Practice*.

Zander, A., ed. (1963). *Performance Appraisals: Effects on Employees and Their Performance*. Ann Arbor, Mich.: Foundation for Research on Human Behavior.

12 The Teacher and Team Teaching: Suggestions for Long-range Research
Daniel C. Lortie

Americans who govern complicated organizations today have little choice—they are forced, more and more, to commit themselves to rationally designed and closely controlled programs of innovation. Schoolmen, where the public demands quality in education, cannot claim exemption from this trend; excellence is not found in schools which bog down in unreflective conservatism or in those which vacillate from fad to fad. But large-scale development guided by research is very difficult, and we find no surplus of able administrators eager to initiate and lead it. We must supplement our scarce resources of imaginative administration with persons interested in the application of social science; we must develop an effective division of labor which combines the commitment, persuasive talents, and capacity for shrewd, immediate decision found in the competent administrator with the detachment, conceptual skill, and ability to suspend judgment that mark the capable social researcher.

This chapter relates the work of the sociologist to that of creative administrators currently wrestling with an important large-scale innovation, team teaching. How can the sociologist, carefully trained to

Abridged version of J. S. Shaplin and Henry Olds, Jr. (eds.), *Team Teaching* (New York: Harper and Row, 1964), ch. 9. The author's most recent conclusions can be found in *Schoolteacher: A Sociological Study* (Chicago: University of Chicago Press, forthcoming).

avoid commitments to specific social solutions, assist those who are forming specific solutions to educational problems? I believe he can be of real assistance if his role is properly understood and provided he is willing to commit himself to using social science in furthering the general goal of rational adaptation among educational institutions. We can find similar roles in our society where persons with a general commitment assist others whose commitments are specific. The certified public accountant, for example, holds a general commitment to the rules of modern business, but he is not bound by the specific decisions of clients. His controlling function is, in fact, jeopardized if serious doubt is cast on the dispassionate quality of his analysis or the impartiality and thoroughness of his reports.

The sociologist can, in my opinion, serve best in a somewhat analogous way. Without prior commitment to a given solution (such as team teaching), he can show his interest in rational planning and rational assessment by assisting in the formulation of research plans for observing a given innovation. Such plans can be made without a priori evaluation and gain both scientific validity and professional repute where the fewest assumptions are made on the desirability or undesirability of a specific program of action. Research plans should incorporate the prior thinking which enables study of the change as it occurs and thus provide those who will make assessments with explicit evidence. For without careful thought before the event, much of import will happen which will go unobserved and unrecorded; without a frame of reference to guide their observations, the most sensitive men can focus on phenomena which later prove unimportant. Team teaching is a major innovation, and the principal assumption here is that it would be most serious if, ten years from now, we lacked the data to know why it did or did not succeed.

. . . We shall focus on how team teaching might influence the teacher at work, and shall use the method (we can call it "functional extrapolation") of comparing what we know about schools today with how they might change under team teaching. This will be done under three major headings: (1) The Teacher and the Authority System, (2) The Teacher and the Reward System, and (3) The Teacher and the Career System. In each instance a description and analysis of the conventional situation will be followed by a tentative prediction of the likely effects of team teaching. The purpose . . . is not to assess team teaching now but to point toward those research questions which will permit the gathering of data that will have value in making a final assessment. Nor is the purpose to delineate final hypotheses since . . . hypotheses change with increased understanding of the phenomena under scrutiny. But if we start to raise questions now, it is likely that our later hypotheses will be truly relevant and that we shall build a useful record of how empirical study has refined our thinking.

A word is necessary on the method of "functional extrapolation." . . . We seek first to understand the consequences of a given pattern of behavior in the public schools (Merton, 1949, ch. 1) . . . based on the unearthing of as many interconnections as we can find—it does not end with the formal or stated purposes attributed to a given behavior pattern. Noting the differences between the proposed innovation and our understanding of the current reality, we can postulate, one at a time, likely effects from the differences. We may continue by asking whether the proposed innovation has other features which might offset the initially expected effects. The process of thought is obviously speculative and selective and suffers from the many gaps in our knowledge of the present situation. It does, however, show certain virtues: it generates hypotheses and guides for research observation, it relates to current sociological theory and research, and it builds a record which can be reviewed and compared with the unfolding reality. Through time it connects theory and research with action and acts to strengthen both.

The Teacher and the Authority System

Every formal organization must find a way to distribute socially approved power (authority) within its ranks if it is to accomplish its purposes effectively, but the specifics of such authority distribution are more complex than is frequently perceived. Our knowledge of the situation in public schools, for example, is still scant. Although there are numerous statements on how authority should be handled in such organizations, we have few studies which describe and analyze what actually occurs. . . . Our lack of knowledge of existing conditions hampers planning for change.

The American public schools can be described as partially bureaucratic in the technical sense of that term (Blau, 1956). Public accountability is attained through lay, policy-making boards, coupled with a hierarchy of administrative offices occupied by personnel selected on technical grounds and trained for their functions. Legal authority is vested in the lay board and its chief administrative official, the superintendent. Theoretically, all other authority is delegated by those at the apex of the system, and subordinates possess no separate legal authority for their activities. In the formal sense, teachers are employees of the school board and superintendent; the law does not recognize them as "independent professionals."

The bureaucratic model, in emphasizing the formal distribution of authority, does not prepare us for many of the events that actually occur in public schools. Teachers, for example, lay claim to and get, informally, certain types of authority despite lack of formal support for it in either law or school system constitutions. We can see the outcropping of these claims in the emphasis on "democratic administration" taught in schools of education and in the adaptations made to faculty opinion by administrators. School officials will assert that no principal can survive long in a school where the faculty is determined to see his resignation. Wise administrators urge that curricula be developed by faculty groups rather than handed down in line decisions. Schoolmen make a sharp distinction between the formal curriculum and what teachers actually do in classrooms and thus implicitly assert the likelihood that the two are different. Several policies favored by administrators have not been implemented because of teacher opposition—one thinks of resistance to administrative discretion in salary payment (merit pay) and to attempts to introduce more hierarchy within faculties. The bureaucratic map of public schools, then, leaves out certain parts of the territory, notably those which point to powers held by teachers (and, of course, students) which are nowhere given formal sanction. . . .

Teachers possess few of the power resources found in other professions. Lieberman (1956) points out the passivity of their occupational associations. They also lack the economic sanctions found in fee professions; their career circuits are relatively undeveloped, and, as we have noted, their formal and legal status within school systems is weak. How do teachers get the authority which observers state they possess? What mechanisms grant them some ability to act in ways consistent with their work values? It is our hypothesis that the authority teachers possess stems from the spatial work arrangements found in most schools and from informal rules that are connected with those arrangements. The self-contained classroom, in this view, is more than a physical reality, for it refers as well to a social system, a set of recurrent and more or less permanent social relationships. Under this arrangement the teacher is separated from immediate supervision, and intrusion into his private domain is prevented by a set of understandings subscribed to by administrative officers and teacher colleagues. A set of norms exists which acts to buttress the ecological separation: (1) the teacher should be free from the interference of other adults while teaching, (2) teachers should be considered and treated as equals, and (3) teachers should act in a nonintervening but friendly manner toward one another. Since these rules apparently reinforce one another, they can be considered a pattern—a pattern which we call "the autonomy-equality pattern." This pattern, it must be emphasized, is not a formally accepted one and probably breaks down in crisis situations involving a teacher and the public. In the usual course of events, however, it seems to summarize how teachers strive to relate to each other and to administrative officials.

If the preceding line of analysis is correct, the type of authority which teachers hold is not the kind we associate with the prestige term *professional,* for it is not the possession of the teacher by right but emerges in an informally supported, ecologically enhanced set of work arrangements. It is authority based on isolation since, unlike professional authority, it is not generally given effective support by a guild or an association. The lack of strong occupational associations, in fact, suggests that teachers are protected against each other as well as against administrators and members of the community. It must be emphasized that this type of authority is fragile, and, confronted with the full formal authority of a school board or an agitated community, it is likely to crumble. There will be variations, as well, in the amount and type of authority teachers possess in different kinds of systems. Small systems continue a pattern which Solomon terms "paternalistic," while in the largest city systems the trend seems to be to a type of unionism which seeks in a variety of ways to create collective authority for classroom teachers (Solomon, 1961). But the general situation appears to be one where teachers get whatever work authority they possess through the informal pattern of autonomy-equality.

The work of the public school teacher is almost inseparable from the arrangements . . . described, and we have no appreciable experience with teaching under alternative structural arrangements. Consequently, we face analytic difficulties in discerning what aspects of teaching stem specifically from these structural arrangements. In advancing hypotheses as to what might happen with team teaching, we can only estimate what the likely effects will be since the influence of the authority factor is not open to precise measurement. But we can begin the necessary if imprecise task we have set ourselves by identifying some of the apparent consequences of the autonomy-equality pattern.

Although the autonomy-equality pattern contradicts the concept of special rewards for special effort, it does allow teachers to differ in their level of effort. Administrators who complain that some teachers try to get away with the least possible effort will give credit to some whose dedication is unlimited. There is, of course, a minimal level of effort built into the school schedule, and there are other controls which decree what effort is minimally acceptable from a public school teacher. But the absence of close observation in conventional self-contained classroom arrangements means that teachers can differ in how hard they work both in the classroom and without. There are, presumably, norms among faculties that define a reasonable week's work, but autonomy-equality makes it very difficult for those who seek to enforce such norms. It is possible for teachers who take their work seriously to put in many extra hours outside the classroom without making a point of it to their colleagues, and, although reliable data are unsurprisingly scarce, our own researches suggest that there are some teachers who work extremely long hours. There is a somewhat boundless quality about teaching which can carry the conscientious teacher into a heavy work schedule. After all, at what point can such a teacher feel that his classes cannot be improved by more preparation or that extra time with students would not teach them more? External controls, then, work to ensure minimal effort and fail to inhibit maximum effort under autonomy-equality. A leveling off can occur only where teachers internalize a common standard of what constitutes appropriate work levels. Some teachers, feeling that additional effort on their part would be self-exploitation, probably hold back. Others, apparently, continue to work extremely hard despite the less vigorous exertions of their colleagues.

Variations in teaching style and content are also favored by the autonomy-equality pattern; for teachers, solving teaching problems in isolation from each other, are likely to select different solutions. The teacher's style—his or her particular way of solving problems— will, over time, reflect unique personality configurations. For some will find that discussion works best for them while others will prefer to use lectures and demonstrations. The content of any curriculum never exhausts the possibilities for treating the materials, and teachers exercise considerable editorial judgment in applying even the most carefully delineated curriculum plans. Differences in teacher values will find expression in the various ways in which they exercise this judgment. Such possibilities for variation have important consequences for the teacher role and who can occupy it. Since considerable variation is possible, a broad range of personality types and a broad range of personal values can be expressed in the role. This means that teaching as an occupation can and probably does recruit persons who are quite diverse in personal makeup and conviction.

Autonomy-equality is associated with variation in the definition of what constitutes good or bad teaching. There is considerable evidence that no clear consensus exists among public school personnel as to what criteria should be applied to evaluate teaching performance. Where clear criteria are lacking, it seems reasonable to expect that people will answer the question of adequacy of performance in ways which satisfy them personally, and indications are that teachers do differ in how they answer these questions for themselves. Autonomy-equality is permissive in this regard, for the teacher who works alone can develop his own answers. He is free, on the other hand, to join associations (such as the once highly influential Progressive Education Association) and to seek to persuade colleagues that his answers are worth general acceptance. Autonomy-equality, then, is associated either with laissez-faire or persuasion, but in general it weakens attempts to impose any single definition of "good teaching" and thus enhances variety. Criteria for good teaching being variable, different conceptions of desirable educational goals can exist simultaneously in a school or school system.

The fourth area where autonomy-equality can be examined is in its consequences for the teacher-class relationship. The frequently heard statement that teaching is an art implies that the decisions made by teachers cannot always be made explicit or formulated in terms of general rules. Supporting evidence for this position is found in those instances where everyone agrees that a given teacher is outstanding, yet all find it difficult to verbalize the reasons for his achievement. The work of the teacher involves a level of intuitive judgment where artistry can be effective without being communicable. Autonomy-equality, inasmuch as it leaves the teacher free to work spontaneously, encourages expression at this intuitive level. Not forced to justify his decisions, the teacher feels free to play his hunches. Such hunches may be based on accurate assessments of student needs, but to make these assessments explicit may be beyond the analytic capacity of the teacher.

A very elusive aspect of the teacher-class relationship, class rapport, seems to be related to the autonomy-equality pattern. Teachers associate effective teaching with a subtle quality of rapport with students, and analysis of their descriptions of high rapport reveals mechanisms studied in a field sociologists call "collective behavior." The tone which teachers ascribe to such moments of high rapport is reminiscent of certain types of controlled crowd situations: there is the same focusing of attention on a common object, the same quick mutual reactions, and the same loss of personal awareness (Blumer, 1957). What we do not yet know is whether such states of high rapport can arise where more than one adult is teaching in a single classroom. Under autonomy-equality the teacher unself-consciously relates directly to the class and need not concern himself with the possibly different reactions emanating from other adults. Can adults work together in a way which permits them the same freewheeling emotional freedom and which results in an equally intense relationship?

There is another question which arises when we ask how autonomy-equality relates to the teacher-class relationship. To what degree is that condition known as satisfactory discipline a function of control by one rather than several adults? Discipline involves many quick judgments and quick actions, and, as any parent knows, such judgments are difficult to make and act on where two parents have not worked out a common stance. Under autonomy-equality, the individual teacher selects the level of discipline he desires. Students cannot, where one teacher is clearly in charge, employ the tactics of *divide et impera*.

In summary, then, we hypothesize that the pattern of autonomy-equality is associated with teaching in several ways. It enhances variation among teachers in the amount of effort they put into their work, the styles they employ, what they teach, and their definitions of what constitutes good teaching and desirable outcomes. We have noted that teaching as an unverbalized art, in teacher-class rapport and in order-maintenance, is adapted to autonomy-equality. If these observations are valid, the autonomy-equality pattern acts to enhance variation among teachers which might otherwise be asserted as prerogatives of the individual professional. There are indications that the teaching craft, as we have developed it, depends upon an isolated work pattern. In short, autonomy-equality supplies teachers with the personal and spontaneous choice which they would have if they possessed the privileges granted those in high-prestige, fee-taking professions. In sociological parlance, autonomy-equality based on isolation is the functional equivalent of the clearly delineated privileges of the doctor, architect, or successful artist. It acts to limit the influence of the formal and bureaucratic order which, on paper, is the structure of the American public school system.

Before we speculate on how team teaching might influence the teaching craft by changing the authority structure, we must consider the alternative forms that authority might take under team teaching.

The writer believes that two polar possibilities exist. Team teaching might strengthen the formal authority structure so greatly that schools will become essentially vertical-bureaucratic in their authority arrangements. It is also possible that team teaching will diffuse authority into the hands of small colleague groups and take the horizontal-collegial form. Since both alternatives are possible from the essential characteristics of team teaching, emphasis on one set of characteristics rather than another would be the determining factor.

There are two features of most team teaching projects that are of enormous sociological importance. First, team teaching insists that teachers work closely together, and it suggests that teachers will often work simultaneously with the same group of students. Thus, the isolation found under autonomy-equality disappears. Secondly, teaching teams frequently contain a hierarchy of authority positions, formally designated by such titles as team leader, senior teacher, and so forth . . . . Thus, the norm of teacher equality is displaced. Two difficult questions arise. Since team teaching seeks to combine elements which, according to our previous discussion, seem to be unstable in mixture (close working relationships and hierarchical rank), which of the two elements is likely to dominate? And, where one rather than another dominates, what are the likely effects on teaching and learning?

What is certainly clear is that widespread adoption of team teaching will bring about significant changes in the status of the American public school teacher. Individualism, previously supported by the autonomy-equality pattern, will be weakened by pressures either from administrative officials or close colleagues, and teachers who rejoice in their working autonomy must face difficult, important questions in taking their stand on the issue of team teaching. Perhaps the most important query they must answer is whether they can find other sources of autonomy once the isolation of autonomy-equality is gone. It is possible that they might find a more powerful type of protection than the tentative and uncertain power based on informal understandings which they now possess.

Authority: The Vertical-Bureaucratic Outcome

In conventional school situations, administrators find it impossible to supervise teachers closely. The span of control is generally too broad and their tasks too numerous to allow full-time involvement in supervisory duties. Team teaching, however, offers a solution to the problem of control by segmenting faculties into small units. Even the largest school, with teams each under a leader, could be brought under effective administrative control. It is conceivable that under some circumstances this possibility for holding a tight rein on the teacher's activities would be seized and used. The structure of the school could feature a lengthened line of authority stretching from the top administration, through principals and team leaders, to classroom teachers. Where team leaders identify themselves with management, they might see themselves not as spokesmen for a group of teachers but as local administrators responsible for implementing school and school system policies. If there were a system where the team leaders generally did assume this stance, few classroom teachers could escape the minute control found in tight administrative structures.

It is difficult to predict the circumstances under which this extreme type of vertical authority would emerge, for it would call for considerable change in the work values of public school personnel. There are some school boards, one suspects, which would welcome the chance to run the show, but how many superintendents would go along with that ambition? Would administrators emerge who see themselves as strong line officers eager and ready to issue multiple orders over detailed matters? One also notes that the possibilities for gaps in the line of authority are numerous and that these gaps are accompanied by the likelihood of role conflicts at several levels in the hierarchy. (Even where the concept of line authority is strong, as in industry, foremen are men in the middle and must choose between identifying up with management or identifying down with the workers.) One can also visualize several variations from the extreme case of clear-cut line authority, and research must be planned to study these varieties when and if they emerge. It is distinctly possible that teaching and learning will differ according to the dominant mode of authority distribution and organization.

The consequences of this type of authority system are manifold, and discussion of them would take more space than is available here. As far as the classroom teacher is concerned, however, it probably would result in routinization of task and subordination of status, especially where team leaders were closely coordinated throughout the school system. Levels of output could be more closely controlled than under current arrangements since the amount of effort expended by individual teachers would be readily apparent and would influence administrators' attitudes and actions toward them. Teaching style and content could come under the control of a dominant leader since he would possess powerful sanctions. Educational objectives would become more specific and standard throughout the system, whether explicitly stated or not. Team leaders would serve as the focal point in the teacher-class relationship, for it is likely that where vertical authority is paramount, students would recognize the higher status and greater authority of the team leader. The range of choices made by the classroom teacher would contract, and the locus of professional decision would be concentrated above him in a formal structure. The possibilities for close coordination of system activities make it likely that a greater degree of curriculum specification would be found throughout all grades and schools. The position of the nonleader teacher would call for less personal initiative and require fewer complex decisions because decisions of any difficulty would, presumably, be made at the team leader level or above. The process involved would be one which industrial sociologists call "deskilling" in the working ranks. . . .

The argument that centralization means quicker adoption of innovations can also be tested by comparing the receptivity to change of vertical-bureaucratic systems with that of other authority distributions. The lines of inquiry suggested, then, are several. Observations should begin on the organizational realities that occur with team teaching, and close attention should be paid to the degree to which school boards eager for close control are able to attain it. The role of the classroom teacher should be watched carefully to see whether it comes to require less personal ability and imagination, and the stances taken by team leaders toward their superordinates and subordinates should be the subject of intense research effort. The mechanisms of supervision should be studied closely, and the levels of effort, styles, emphases, and techniques of teachers should be recorded in a variety of situations. Instructional outcomes should be examined and data gathered in terms of a wide range of things learned, from mechanical skills to abstract values. . . .

Authority: The Horizontal-Collegial Outcome

By initiating close working relationships among small groups of teachers, team teaching might result in a form of authority now rare in public schools—the "collegium," where equals rule their affairs by internal democratic procedures (Hughes, 1957). Although such structures are not common in our society, we do find them in some universities, churches, and artistic groups. The sociological theory devoted to this form of authority is less well developed than that dealing with bureaucratic organization. We should expect, however, that where there is a strong emphasis on internal equality and close, harmonious relationships, such groups will tend to resist formal and lasting status differences. The members will have an interest in granting leadership according to the needs of the immediate group. Leadership in a collegial team will reflect the sentiments and norms of the small group. . . . Even the most informal of groups will feature leadership of some kind. However, attempts by outsiders, such as bureaucratic superiors, to impose a rigid hierarchy are likely to encounter resistance.

Small groups having stability through time tend to develop common ways and common expectations which bind members into a miniature society (Homans, 1950). The group, in short, develops a culture which may encompass a wide variety of concerns. In work groups it may define the nature of high performance, the amount of effort involved in a fair day's work, and the appropriate relationships that should obtain among members and between members and outsiders.

Our analysis of the conventional school situation suggests that teachers in teams will confront many problems requiring solution in the group context. Who will handle discipline when several teachers observe an infraction? How will teachers cope with students who show deference to one team member and none to another? Will team members display disagreements over facts or interpretations in front of their students, or will they stoutly maintain a united front? These questions can, of course, be answered in several ways. But we cannot predict a priori how a given team will answer the questions or whether a group of teams will select similar answers. Our knowledge of small groups and the processes whereby they build cultures permits us to say only that they will come up with collective answers to many of these questions. We cannot say which will be dealt with by the group and which will be left to individual choice, and we cannot predict the specific solutions which will be selected in those areas where collective rules are developed. It seems likely, however, that teams will develop norms to cover both the appropriate level of effort and the style and content of member teaching, and that teacher-student relationships will be a critical area for team concern. . . .

Should the team come to play a central part in the teacher's work orientation, problems of integration would assuredly arise within schools and school systems. Perhaps one development would be competition between teams, and, if this occurred, researchers would have to watch, most specifically, what rules were used to judge winning or losing in such rivalries. Where winning is defined in ways consistent with system objectives, such competition could enhance the achievement of organizational goals. Where the rules are selected for institutionally irrelevant purposes (for example, ease of measuring output and victory), such competition could, however, retard achievement of the system's aims.

One possible outcome from collegial teams could have important repercussions for the "art of teaching." Under autonomy-equality, individual teachers can work at their own teaching and develop highly effective techniques which are not communicated to others. Under vertical-bureaucratic structures, teaching is likely to become formalized into organizational procedures, and, where lay control is heavy, the craft may tend to be ignored or lost if the distinction between teachers and nonteachers is weakened. Collegial teams call for close cooperation, and this may, initially, inhibit the spontaneous improvisation of the isolated teacher and require "scripts" for the teachers. In time, however, this could move teaching into a more recorded form, and improvements might accumulate in a context of conscious choice and refinement. This could lead to a greater emphasis on scientific values (communicability, accumulative experience) coupled with clinical practice, and such an outcome could do much to advance the state of the art.

The hypotheses put forth point to a variety of research possibilities and suggest a variety of techniques: ... detailed observational reports which cover the subtle interactions involved in the development of team cultures; close watch ... on how each team defines its norms and how individual members react to those norms; [and] records of conferences ... supplemented by observations of classroom behavior and running accounts of the attitudes of teachers as individuals. Not to begin early would be serious since turnover among teams may be highly significant. It may represent, for example, the screening out of particular personality types and the selection of others. Such researches can profit from the experience of social scientists in a variety of settings, particularly the studies of industrial work groups. It is clear that research cannot be of the hit-and-run variety, but that research personnel will have to be in steady, regular contact with teams as this new organization of teaching develops.

The Teacher and the Reward System

Organizations are more than systems of authority; they can also be viewed as systems of inducements or rewards for participation in the activities of the organization and adherence to its objectives.... Here [we] inquire briefly into the current situation and ... raise questions on how team teaching might change the system of rewards for teachers. We shall classify rewards into two groups for purposes of this discussion. (1) *Extrinsic* rewards ... attached to a given role ... are, in the main, transferable from one occupant to another: money income, power, and prestige. (2) *Intrinsic* rewards, or gratifi-cations, ... available to persons occupying a given role, ... differ de-pending on what occupants value in that situation. ... Most discus-sions of the teacher's role center almost entirely on extrinsic rewards, but this discussion will deal largely with intrinsic ones. ...

Perhaps the most interesting feature of the system of extrinsic rewards facing American public school teachers is the absence of sharp differentiation. A teacher may spend a lifetime in the field without more than doubling annual income. As Benson (1961) points out, the teacher can be replaced, on retirement, by a junior beginning teacher. Power and prestige differentials among teachers are relatively insignificant under the rules of autonomy-equality. Pro-motion is very limited and usually involves increased administrative responsibility even where the higher status roles are primarily instruc-tional in nature (for example, department head, supervisor). What-ever informal differentiation a principal may choose to make in allo-cating students or rooms or schedules must not arouse the ire of teachers who are quick to spot favoritism and to cry "foul." This lack of differentiation reinforces the concept of equality at the ex-pense of quality, for the outstanding and mediocre, by any defini-tion, receive approximately equal extrinsic rewards.

We should expect that intrinsic rewards differ among teachers according to their personalities and their view of their work, but preliminary research suggests that some intrinsic rewards occur fre-quently even among persons who otherwise seem different. One of the most interesting is craft pride—the satisfaction that comes when a teacher sees definite results from his work. The specific results sought for and obtained differ, of course (one teacher might refer to test scores where another will cite a student whose self-confidence blooms), but indications that one's efforts made a difference are extremely important to teachers working, as they do, in an intangible and indeterminate craft. Even with autonomy-equality and the self-contained classroom, teachers do not find it easy to identify the specific contribution they have made to an individual student or group of students (in fact, we suspect that teachers sometimes define the desirable outcomes of their work in ways which simplify self-assessment and make it possible to enjoy the gratification of getting results). Under autonomy-equality a teacher is relatively free to emphasize a given facet of his role (for example, counselor of troubled students or raiser of perplexing questions) and to spend additional time and effort on it. Thus can intrinsic rewards be magnified and the total role made more gratifying.

There can be little doubt that affective responses from students are of great importance to classroom teachers, but they differ in how they cope with such responses. Some teachers feel little inhibition in seeking student popularity and consider students excellent judges of teacher ability, while others profess enormous skepticism on the reactions of students until they have left school. With the live-and-let-live arrangements of autonomy-equality, teachers are free to opt which stance they will take. Perhaps of greater importance, however, is that the separation of classes and teachers found in conventional situations limits competition among teachers for student approbation and protects those who receive relatively little. They are spared the shame of direct comparison and may, in fact, perceive themselves to be considerably more popular than they are. Autonomy-equality acts to maximize gratifications that derive from student responses by permitting teachers to choose their modes of relating to it.

Teachers talking about the good things in their work are likely, especially at the elementary level, to mention the sociable intercourse they have with other teachers, and their talk reminds one of the "pure sociability" described by Simmel (1961, page 157), where people enjoy interaction per se. The work of teachers places them under two unusual strains. First, teachers, to be effective, must be able to think and talk at the level of their students. Continued day after day, this can result in a kind of infantilization which teachers seem to fear, for it threatens their hold on adulthood and their self-esteem as mature persons. Furthermore, teaching is a controlled activity where spontaneity in the classroom must be inhibited. Therefore, teachers probably need both adult sociability and relatively relaxed, unguarded interaction with others. Although teachers at leisure often do talk shop, autonomy-equality means that each teacher is talking about his unique experiences. Where his colleagues are equals, he can do so in a comfortable, off-guard way without too much fear of consequence for himself and his career. . . .

There are undoubtedly other gratifications of a recurrent nature in teaching (autonomy per se is one—teachers will tell how they failed to perceive its importance on entering the field, but have come to appreciate working as one's own boss). But the major point is that the sheer institutionalization of teaching in the self-contained classroom has created, over the years, a set of vested intrinsic gratifications. Those who have entered teaching and stayed in it are presumably those who have found intrinsic gratifications sufficient to offset the undoubtedly limited extrinsic rewards in the role. Team teaching will certainly expand our understanding of this area since it makes changes in both extrinsic and intrinsic rewards for public school teachers. Will new rewards arise which will make teaching attractive in completely different ways?

Rewards: The Vertical-Bureaucratic Outcome

Where team teaching takes a vertical emphasis, the position of team leader will provide an important amount of differentiation in extrinsic rewards. Presumably pay, authority, and prestige gains will be greatest for team leaders where hierarchical facets receive the greatest encouragement. Schools, as organizations, will augment their resources of incentives with this position and will have more leeway in rewarding those whose services are found to be most valuable. . . . There is, however, a possible side effect of this new step which is of interest to those who would augment the total extrinsic rewards available to teachers.

It is quite possible that the prestige gains made by team leaders will result in prestige losses for teachers who do not occupy that role. One is tempted, in seeking to label these teachers, to call them ordinary teachers to differentiate them from their senior colleagues. We encounter here a somewhat mysterious property of prestige systems —they are at times quite finite in that deference paid to some results in deference lost to others. Where the status "teacher" is undifferentiated, the status of an individual teacher stems primarily from the status of the group. Where some teachers are accorded special recognition, however, the position of those who do not receive such recognition is weakened, for other teachers may ask, overtly or covertly, why they have not attained the more honored post. Should students consider the difference between leaders and nonleaders important? The authority of nonleaders might well wane, and this could lead to an increase in disciplinary problems. In short, two types of extrinsic rewards—prestige and authority—could show a net decrease when we consider *all* teachers under vertically oriented team teaching. Such an outcome is potentially one of enormous gravity, for few persons today wish to reduce the status of the teaching profession. Research should be conducted to examine such changes and to watch for any countervailing trends such as the possibility that vertical team teaching, by establishing higher standards of performance, could raise public evaluation of teachers generally.

It appears certain that intrinsic rewards will change when team teaching results in a heavy emphasis on vertical-bureaucratic authority. Team leaders, where the extreme vertical form prevails, are not likely to gain much over the teacher working under autonomy-equality today. For if team teaching is used as a vehicle for increasing the rigidity of line authority, team leaders may find themselves unable to exercise free choices. When team leaders exercise authority over their subordinates but are not in turn regulated closely by their superiors, they will, of course, obtain whatever gratifications are associated with leading a group of subordinates.

The majority of classroom teachers, however, will have to shift the loci of their intrinsic rewards. For example, close supervision will make it difficult for a teacher to feel that any given outcome is clearly his own achievement. All achievements, and possibly failures, must be shared with the supervisor. Here again, personality differences must clearly be taken into account, for some teachers, more passive or dependent than others, may feel pleasure in meeting the expectations of an immediate superior. On the other hand, the more independent and aggressive teachers would undoubtedly find their satisfactions decreased. The psychic income obtained from student responses would undergo similar changes in situations where teachers of unequal rank worked with the same students. We would expect that, where ranking is taken seriously by teachers, students will also be expected to respect it (students who failed to support the status distinctions would, after all, create tensions among faculty members adjusted to these distinctions). But developing such mechanisms will not be easy, and some junior teachers may compensate by identifying closely with students and thereby challenging faculty solidarity. This problem of aligning student response with faculty hierarchy may prove too difficult, and it could be a strong pressure countering rank and favoring collegial equality. But even if successful mechanisms can be developed, most teachers will still have to accept a lower level of affective response from students than occurs with autonomy-equality.

Emphasis on rank differences would decrease the pure sociability possible among teachers, at least in the presence of superordinates possessing genuine authority. The tendency for persons in stratified groups to choose equals for social purposes is well known and can be seen in the army's provisions for recreational facilities that are separated according to rank. The net cost of this change, however, may not be high if team relationships are internally cordial or if teachers find close, relaxed associations outside their work. But where ordinary teachers fear their superiors' judgments in class, it is unlikely that they will find it easy to mix with them outside. . . .

It is difficult to foresee the effect of vertical orientation on the opportunities for variety among teachers. Certainly the freedom to follow one's own mood will be lost where group planning replaces individual planning, but the leader's attitude toward specialization is probably more crucial. Leaders favoring regular assignments and specialization may inhibit opportunities for change while those who prefer rotation and generality may enhance it. The team situation opens up, in theory, a larger number of potential roles and activities for the individual teacher.

Despite the lack of data . . . on current teacher gratifications and the speculative nature of this discussion, future research might hypothesize . . . a net decrease in rewards of both types for *most* teachers if team teaching follows the vertical-bureaucratic line of development (the comparatively few teachers who have special status in the teams will, of course, receive increased extrinsic rewards). . . . Researchers [might] discover . . . substitute gratifications have arisen, or . . . that teachers develop ways to guarantee the persistence of prized rewards by developing new and subtle informal arrangements within the changed formal organization.

Rewards: The Horizontal-Collegial Outcome

Predicting the effect of collegially oriented teams on the system of extrinsic rewards (money income, prestige, and authority) available to teachers is almost impossible at the present time. First, the ways in which these rewards are distributed will have enormous effect on their legitimacy and psychological meaning as far as teachers are concerned. They could become empty formalities in the eyes of both those who do and those who do not receive them as currently occurs in some schools where the rank of department head is almost meaningless. Secondly, collegial teams which persist will develop a stake in the extrinsic reward system, for they will want to align rewards with their own norms and judgments in the interests of team cohesiveness. Yet central administration will also care about such distributions of rewards since they mobilize efforts to achieve system-wide goals and interests. One would expect, therefore, that there will be a significant and continuing struggle between teams and the central administration for control over the allocation of meaningful rewards. When teams do not subscribe to the means used by top administrators or the specific decisions they make, they will probably depreciate formal differentiation and supplement it with a prestige and authority system of their own. They may never be able to control money rewards (unless teams are given the right to elect leaders), but they could weaken the significance of money differentials for team members.

One situation which would augment the total extrinsic rewards available for all team teachers would be where there is close agreement between administrative and peer judgments on the proper allocation of differential income, prestige, and authority, for in this instance team leaders would receive increments which do not detract from the rewards of other teachers. Other teachers would probably regard such additional rewards as just payment for valuable services rendered. To bring about this high level of consensus will not be easy, and, where it is lacking, it is doubtful that team teaching will add any appreciable set of extrinsic rewards to the total currently available to public school teachers. Those who see the addition of rewards as a basic feature of team teaching should concern themselves, if this reasoning be accurate, with finding ways to ensure consensus among team members and administrative officers. Research efforts could assist in discovering what situations enhance such consensus and what situations militate against it.

The question of what will happen to intrinsic rewards under collegially oriented team teaching is fascinating. As noted before, the type of craft pride found among teachers working under autonomy-equality is essentially individualistic with delight accompanying recognition of one's personal effectiveness with students. But can this type of craft pride be replaced by one which is collective in form? Can teachers come to feel equal pride in the accomplishment of their teams? Commentators have felt for years that the division of labor found in factories results in the alienation of the worker from his product. Dubin (1956), however, . . . points to the possibility that workers obtain alternative forms of gratification from participation in a complex system of specialization. We know little of this phenomenon and are therefore ill equipped to predict under what conditions team identifications can replace individualistic ones. This issue is central, however, if team teaching is to give its participants a sense of pride and accomplishment linked to work effort. It is here that the personality psychologist's researches will be especially valuable, for it seems most likely that some teachers will find team-centered achievement gratifying while others will not. For team teaching to succeed, it will be necessary to identify such personality differences and to recruit those who obtain personal gratification in small-group settings. Without a predisposition [toward] this type of reward, it seems unlikely that team members will put forth their best energies.

The role of affective response from students is also a crucial question when we anticipate collegial teams working with a common group of students. Differential student response could, after all, threaten the solidarity of the team, and members would eventually have to resolve emotionally complex issues of jealousy and pride. One solution lies in heavy controls on competition (professional ethics) which specify just how the individual practitioner may seek to obtain clients, or, more appropriately in this case, impress them. If teams find it necessary to employ such controls, teachers will be less free to seek popularity with students and to win their cooperation. This could result in less affective response and a consequent deprivation for team teachers generally. However, an alternative source of gratification, which will probably become a prized reward, will be found in the approbation of colleagues. The instructional consequences of this change could be most interesting since it raises age-old issues of pedagogy. Who teaches most and best, the teacher who seeks to win students to his side or the teacher who lays down rigorous demands? Freed from the quest for popularity, will teachers increase the work loads they give students, and will this result in an increase or decrease in total learning? It is possible that team teachers may select other ways of coping with differences in student response and may reinforce team members who manage to receive it. If so, what alternative gratifications will occur for those sterner teachers who are either unable or unwilling to win student approval? The questions here are important ones, and working on them as they arise in team teaching should prove informative to educational knowledge and practice in general.

The gratifications associated with colleague interactions are likely to take a different form in collegial-team situations, for close working relationships, long hours at a time, will probably make spontaneous, nonwork intercourse less frequent. Teammates will find it harder in outside interaction to avoid work content and the inevitable tensions associated with it. For some teachers (notably those with rich social lives outside of school), this will probably be a minimal loss since the dangers of infantilization are reduced where adults work together. But the problem of finding free and uncontrolled interactions will be aggravated for some teachers, and this may prove fateful for those whose nonwork lives are lonely. Perhaps such needs will impel teachers to find associations among members of other teams and will thereby act to reduce competition between teams. But researchers observing team teaching would be wise to consider the total needs of people at work, for we have considerable evidence that work interactions fulfill many general needs for people.

Depending on the specific handling of task assignments, horizontally organized team teaching could increase or decrease possibilities for variety. If some team members are highly motivated and prepare carefully, the remaining members of the team may find the intellectual content of their day more interesting and variegated. If assignments are rotated, the individual teacher's work round may be more varied than where autonomy-equality makes repetitive demands. On the other hand, decisions by teams to move toward separate classes and fixed, specialized assignments could result in less variety for individual teachers. For under autonomy-equality a teacher can make changes from one presentation to the next without worrying much about the reactions of other teachers or about an overall plan. . . .

It seems likely that team teaching with a horizontal-collegial emphasis will introduce considerable change in the intrinsic rewards received by teachers. If this [is] so, the consequences are of great importance, for a change in these selective mechanisms which attract people to, and keep people in, teaching will ultimately produce a change in the composition of the teaching force. And this could easily set off a chain reaction of further changes. If we are to understand what directions such change is likely to take, we shall need a constant inventory on the makeup of teachers as team teaching spreads. Close cooperation is indicated, then, between psychologists interested in personality and sociologists interested in the group phenomena involved in team teaching.

The Teacher and the Career System

One of the major objectives of team teaching is to introduce a career line for public school teachers to increase the attractiveness of the field for able male graduates of better-quality colleges and universities. . . . Positions (such as team leader) . . . combine greater rewards with a broader scope of influence and thereby make more rational use of limited numbers of highly qualified personnel. The research sociologist can assist in this phase of team teaching both by indicating potential and unanticipated consequences which could undermine the objective of higher quality teaching, and by suggesting research approaches to monitor the unfolding of intended and unintended processes. Here research has an infrequent ally—time—for team teaching, even if it spread rapidly, will have its greatest effect on teacher careers several years from now. The self-contained classroom model is what potential recruits to teaching now visualize, and it will be some time before potential teachers think in terms of the team form. It will also take several years for us to learn how teachers react to the career possibilities inherent in team teaching.

We can examine the possible effects of team teaching on teaching careers by isolating three key career points: (1) how team teaching will influence the image of teaching held by young people considering education as a career alternative, (2) how team teaching will affect the trial years of the beginning teacher, and (3) what the likely effect of team teaching is on opportunities for advancement for teachers. We shall consider each of these questions in turn and speculate on how the two polar types of team teaching might differ from current career realities.

The Image of Teaching and Potential Candidates

When today's teachers are questioned about their reasons for going into teaching, they are likely to emphasize that teaching afforded the opportunity to work with children, offered them the chance to express a personal predilection (for example, love of a given subject), and promised a secure if modest future. These specific reasons (oversimplifications of a complex set of career decisions) align neatly with the teacher's role under autonomy-equality. Teachers working under conventional arrangements spend the vast proportion of their working time with children, have relative freedom in stressing their interests, indulge in limited interpersonal competition, and face few risks. Young people who are considering teaching as a career and who have been taught in schools with teaching teams will possess a different image of the role than those entering the profession today. They will note the importance of teacher-teacher relations, the necessity for joint planning (with its consequent reductions in personal choices), and the differences between teachers in extrinsic rewards received. How might this different image held by potential members of the field influence the kinds of persons attracted into teaching?

Where students perceive team teaching as heavily stratified (vertical-bureaucratic), it seems probable that two quite different kinds of persons might be interested. The first would be those who fancy themselves in the role of team leader and have the ambition and confidence to try for it. These young persons will be those for whom external signs of prestige, authority, and income are important. But a second group will also be attracted, those who note the lesser responsibilities of the ordinary teachers of the team and feel that they could achieve the more limited objective. . . . The self-contained classroom, although it does place a ceiling on aspiration, also provides a floor under it. No teacher can avoid the ultimate responsibility for a given group of students. But vertical-bureaucratic team teaching will impress some young people as providing comfortable, low-responsibility niches. If team leaders are firm in their bureaucratic role, some potential teachers will not fail to note the discrepancy in decision-making power and responsibility. We can all too readily forget that not everyone is attracted to positions of authority and responsibility. Armies are staffed primarily by men content to stay in the ranks and, as Hughes (1952) points out, managers who complain about unambitious employees might find things intolerable if all decided to seek greater glory. Inasmuch as this latter group is attracted to teaching and not weeded out in the training process (a possibility where those selecting teachers might be tempted to say that they are all right for ordinary teaching), one would still hear the complaints that too many teachers have a marginal commitment to their work.

Vertical-bureaucratic outcomes, as we have noted, would also attract the ambitious youngster. But again a difficult question arises. Would such persons want to stop at the position of team leader, or might they not be pressed to attain positions which offer greater honorifics, namely high administrative positions? Where hierarchical values are emphasized, such an ambition seems rational in terms of the social system, for to be merely a teacher is to link oneself with those unable or unwilling to climb the ladder of bureaucratic prestige. Thus would vertical-bureaucratic teams tend to undermine the objective of creating attractive posts in teaching, and a possible result would be an aggravation of problems rather than a solution. If teaching posts are staffed by persons low in ambition and self-confidence and by ambitious persons using teaching as a stepping-stone, the role of the classroom teacher is depreciated rather than enhanced.

Collegial-horizontal teams will probably create a different impression on students considering teaching as a career. Young people will note, we trust, that some teams work together harmoniously and critically. Such teams should attract youngsters who enjoy association with equals and who fear neither the limelight nor the possibility of criticism. However, whether or not they will be able to express their personal predilections is a somewhat more complex question. Teams which allow members free rein and tolerate diverse opinions before students should attract new teachers with strong personal interests and convictions, but those teams which handle internal tensions by blandness and a united front will probably repel creative persons.

The role of the team leader will not be dramatic in teams which emphasize collegial relationships, and the status of the nonleader teacher will not suffer by comparison. Prospective teachers, therefore, will be impressed less by rank differences among teachers and more by their equal and close working relationships. Where the image of team teaching is horizontal-collegial, the person considering teaching as a career will face less psychological risk. Under vertical-bureaucratic conditions a new teacher faces an all-or-nothing situation—one either achieves the status [of] team leader or not. But the prospective teacher thinking in terms of horizontal-collegial teams may consider it more worthwhile to plan on becoming an ordinary teacher and to hope for leadership status. Most young persons will probably assess teaching in terms of its minimum and maximum possibilities for them. If the minimum is a desirable objective per se, it seems likely that more persons will express an interest.

The research implications of these comments are clear enough. Those studying the effects of team teaching should observe how it influences students in their attitudes toward teaching as a career for themselves. Such studies should pay special attention to which students are attracted by [each] type of team and should compare them both among themselves and with those attracted to teaching where autonomy-equality prevails.

The Trial Period: The Beginning Years

Although there is no intensive research on the subject, it appears that the initial teaching period is currently one of rather severe testing for the neophyte. No matter how carefully he has been prepared for the teaching role, there is the inevitable moment when he must take over a class, establish leadership, and maintain it over a period of time. Not all make it, and the fact that some would-be teachers are either chased out by rebelling students or find the experience more draining than rewarding has important consequences for schools. Schools screen out, in this somewhat harsh fashion, those who cannot meet the minimum demands of the role. We cannot know whether this result is a desirable outcome . . . without close research on the process and clear indexes of desirability. We can say, however, that the screening procedures of sink or swim are closely related to classroom arrangements which make each teacher responsible for a given group of students. Furthermore, it grants to students and to administrators considerable sway in determining who persists in teaching and who does not. Students, in cooperating or failing to cooperate, have a critical effect on the beginning teacher's career; and administrators, in deciding to rehire or not, or in writing a favorable or lukewarm recommendation, also play a crucial role.

Without foreknowledge of the specific mechanisms that teams will develop to recruit and test new members, it is difficult to make any specific predictions of what will happen to the screening process. It seems likely, however, that the judgments of fellow educators will increase in importance and the role of students [will] decline. It is unlikely that teachers working with a new member of the profession will stand by while classes get out of control or will create other situations calculated to disenchant the neophyte. It is likely, in short, that the rigors of sink or swim will be seriously modified.

Strongly hierarchical (vertical-bureaucratic) teams will probably feature the gradual induction of the new teacher, assignment by assignment, for a strong team leader, invested in maintaining the standing and effectiveness of his team, will be loathe to permit dangerous mistakes by beginners. Intervention by the leader will limit the influence of students. The leader and the principal will, where hierarchy reigns, make the key decisions which encourage or discourage the beginning teacher, and their standards will be critical for the composition of the staff. Such standards might vary from those which reject . . . the slightest signs of weakness . . . to those which require a monumental patience with ineptitude. . . . The corrective mechanism supplied by student judgments would be weakened, and administrative judgment made paramount. Those who argue that students are perceptive judges of good teaching will consider this change a loss while those who disagree will not. But those conducting research would be in a position to provide information by observing differences that occur where students play a large role and where students play a small role in selecting teachers. . . .

Horizontal-collegial teams will feature a different situation. Here other teachers, as a group, will play a large role in the induction or rejection of a new teacher. For where members have a large investment in the overall performance of their team, the capacity of a new member is of vital importance. Teams, like team leaders under vertical-bureaucratic arrangements, could decide to carry a slow beginner, and the limits of their tolerance would be crucial for the beginning teacher. Principals and superintendents might well be loathe to overrule judgments made by team members who could accurately claim greater familiarity with the beginner's performance and capabilities. Teams would, we should expect, struggle to get rid of an undesired new member and fight to retain a valued one. The decision to retain a new teacher would, in short, be a public rather than private matter, and the successful teacher would be one who made a favorable impression on colleagues as well as on students and administrators. This alone would be a great source of strength for teams in their relationships with the central administration, for the ability to accept or reject new members could, under some circumstances, be a weapon in struggles over autonomy or control. A further consequence would be to strengthen the persistence of norms developed within the teams, for inasmuch as they exercise selective power, they will do so using the norms where they judge themselves. The role of those placing new teachers in schools with divergent, collegially oriented teams will become important, for the judgment of what team should receive what applicant will have widespread repercussions.

Promotion and Advancement

There are two ways in which teachers can be upwardly mobile. They can leave teaching and move into administrative posts, or they can move geographically into schools which offer students of higher status and other attractions (Becker, 1951). Under autonomy-equality, the controls on promotion to administration seem to be somewhat ascriptive since men, compared to women, seem to obtain these positions earlier and more frequently than strict probability would decree. Geographical mobility, however, is relatively simple under autonomy-equality since teachers can leave a position and take on a new one without creating organizational problems at either end. But changes are taking place in this system as teaching and administration become more professionalized and as postgraduate work becomes more instrumental in sorting out candidates for promotion.

Schools emphasizing the bureaucratic features of team teaching will, we expect, place the power of appointment to team leader positions in the hands of principals and superintendents. The creation of this post means that for teachers wishing advancement as teachers, relationships with administrators will become crucial. It is also likely that horizontal mobility will decrease among team-teaching schools since many will promote from within. The instructional effects of this shift in power cannot be easily predicted, but will probably vary according to the values of line administrators. Where these officials emphasize school-wide activities (committee work, extra administrative duties, public relations) as the basis for promotion, the classroom work of the teacher may be depreciated. But where these officials are willing to emphasize and assess classroom teaching, promotion may go to those with strong teaching records. Of course, unless sharp advances are made in methods of assessing teacher performance, there will be more problems introduced by these promotions. What, for example, of positions held by men versus women? Will male principals (the ever-increasing trend is toward line officers of the male sex) place women as leaders over men as frequently as the opposite? And will principals be able to disregard completely the habitual criteria of age and seniority in making their decisions? Administrators may find that although the added position of team leader creates a new incentive to advance system obligations, it also creates a series of somewhat costly side effects. When team members have little influence on who leads their teams, one might expect that resentment at a mistake will be greater than under current arrangements. Today, a disappointed teacher is at least free to go back to his room and do his own work his own way. With a bad leader he will face problems in doing what he considers a good job.

Where teams operate with collegial authority, the team leadership position will probably come to be valued by teachers and administrators alike, and it will be valued because of its peculiar demands; the talent necessary to play this mediating role will not be plentiful. Corson describes the crucial role of the department head in a university, and the position of a team leader in collegially organized teams will have much in common with that difficult role (Corson, 1960). One can predict that much time and effort will be spent on how to select a new team leader, for, as we have mentioned, this choice will concern all teachers. Promotion to team leader involves more than the distribution of a scarce and potentially valued reward. It presents a number of teachers with a leader who will either advance or hinder the quality of their work and the outcome of their future careers. Many administrators will want to solve the problem as objectively as possible, and the press for such objectivity may result in new attempts to define and measure teacher effectiveness.

The creation of the team leader position will mean that some teachers will develop an ambition to fill the post yet fail in impressing others with their suitability. The development of such inappropriate ambitions means that a disposal problem is created; schools will have to find ways to deal with persons who believe that they deserve the position but do not get it. To retain such persons in small teams could, where their bitterness is strong, prove highly disruptive to team effectiveness. Law firms can solve the problem in part by finding high-paying positions for men they cannot promote to partner status. High-status universities, the most inclined to reject young academics for tenure positions, assist them in finding positions in lower-status colleges. They can do this because a status order is openly recognized in higher education. But schools, in the main, are not openly graded and have little power to find nonschool employment for the disappointed employee. This problem, unless solved, could be potentially dangerous to team teaching, for if any considerable number of established teachers become disenchanted, the probability that it will succeed is sharply reduced.

One could list other questions about how the introduction of a teaching post of high prestige will influence teacher careers. Will it act to slow down geographical mobility by holding teachers in systems on the expectation of promotion? How will it affect the balance of influence in schools of married versus single women? Will enough married women invest themselves in team efforts to earn promotion, or will single women come to dominate through undivided commitment to their work? Will men stabilize their careers at the team leader position, and, if they do, how will principals and superintendents be recruited? These questions indicate that, in the career area as well as elsewhere, considerable research will be needed to support an informed judgment on how team teaching affects schools, teachers, and students. The research needed, as is obvious, will have to include intensive studies of the selection system, the orientation system, and the promotion system for teachers. But we shall also need extensive studies which follow the careers of teachers through time, from one position or system to another. And, as is generally the case, we shall require inquiries into the conventional situation if we are to understand how team teaching changes the general shape of teaching and administrative careers.

It is obvious that this . . . is not a modest proposal. The logistics implied by the research suggestions are those of large-scale, expensive social inquiry. It cannot be undertaken by making a few observational forays into schools with team teaching, but will require a somewhat elaborate structure of its own. A mechanism must be developed specifically for long-range research and assessment, and such a mechanism must provide both for the independence of the researchers and their complete access to schools. Those developing team teaching (teachers, administrators, applied researchers, and others) will have neither the time nor the energy to address themselves to the broader questions raised [here]. Nor should the effectiveness of these creative persons be reduced by requiring them to divert attention from the manifold and pressing problems they must solve if team teaching is to work at all. It is easy to overlook the fact that the hundreds and thousands of small adjustments made by such persons in our schools actually amounts to the construction of a complex new social organization. The study of this organization and the longer-range research program involved is a job for professional researchers who have neither a stake in nor a responsibility for the solution of the manifold operating problems.

But if our proposal is not modest, neither is team teaching. It is no minor technical change in schools, and we cannot conceal its potential ramifications by such innocuous phrases as "staff utilization" or "personnel policies." . . . Since schools are crucial agencies in the socialization of successive generations, it seems obvious that basic changes in them are potentially basic changes in our way of life. Surely we ought not to make casual assessments of such innovations; our policy makers in education and the community at large should be provided with every shred of evidence we can assemble to ease their task. . . .

References

Becker, Howard S. (1951). "Role and Career Problems of the Chicago Public School Teacher." Unpublished dissertation, University of Chicago.

Benson, Charles (1961). *The Economics of Public Education.* Boston: Houghton Mifflin.

Blau, Peter M. (1956). *Bureaucracy in Modern Society.* New York: Random House.

Blumer, H. (1957). "Collective Behavior," in A. M. Lee, ed., *Principles of Sociology.* New York: Barnes & Noble.

Corson, John Jay (1960). *Governance of Colleges and Universities.* New York: McGraw-Hill.

Dubin, Robert (1956). "Industrial Workers' Worlds: A Study of the 'Central Life Interests' of Industrial Workers." *Social Problems,* 4:131-142.

Homans, George (1950). *The Human Group.* New York: Harcourt, Brace.

Hughes, Everett C. (1952). *Where Peoples Meet.* New York: Free Press.

———(1957). "Institutions," in A. M. Lee, ed., *Principles of Sociology.* New York: Barnes & Noble.

Lieberman, Myron (1956). *Education as a Profession.* Englewood Cliffs, N.J.: Prentice-Hall.

Merton, Robert K. (1949). *Social Theory and Social Structure.* New York: Free Press.

Simmel, Georg (1961). "The Sociology of Sociability," in Talcott Parsons *et al.,* *Theories of Society,* Volume I. New York: Free Press.

Solomon, Benjamin (1961). "A Profession Taken for Granted." *The School Review,* 69(Autumn):286-299.

PART TWO
STRATEGIES

Knowledge of organizational subsystems and how they interrelate is important for understanding organizational change. For scholars who study change, however, knowledge is the ultimate end; for educational administrators, it is only the beginning. Administrators must apply the knowledge and use it to improve educational organizations. For example, it is not enough for administrators to know that a major impetus for educational change comes from the environment. They must be able to assess the environment and either influence the direction of community attitudes toward education or make internal changes that permit the school to adapt to changed conceptions of teaching and learning.

How do administrators stimulate and control innovation and change? They rely on strategy. While perspectives provide a conceptual map to determine the target of changes and to estimate the impact of change on the other subsystems, strategy requires administrative action to bring about the desired change. The appropriate strategy depends on what is changing, what is being changed, and the nature of the situation or context.

Four general categories of strategies have been identified: change agent, leadership, evaluation, and political. These categories do not necessarily incorporate all the strategies available to administrators, and, because the categories are broad, they overlap considerably. They do, however, provide a way to organize several studies of administrative initiative to produce innovation and change. Of the categories, change agent strategies involve administrative action that goes beyond the organization; evaluation and leadership strategies are administrative actions or behaviors that take place within the organization; political strategies are administrative actions that influence either the environment or internal events.

Change Agent. Popular administrative strategy in change and innovation is to import an outside consultant to diagnose problems and recommend or institute change. Usually the outside agent is a university professor, an administrator from a neighboring school district, a private consultant, or a representative from a professional association. An important criteria in selecting the change agent, one that is often overlooked, is his particular perspective on organizational change. Consultants come in all shapes, sizes, varieties, and orientations. Some focus on interpersonal relations; some are political; some emphasize structural and instructional changes; others carry the magical black bag with one remedy good for all organizational ills.

Selecting the appropriate change agents is largely a matter of matching the right perspective with the right problem. The chapters in this section concentrate on the change agent approach. The first of these chapters, by Baldridge, discusses the recommendations of a team of three consultants who focused their talent and attention on the problems of a school of education in a large university. The basic problem of the school was diagnosed as organizational; the proposed solutions involved a major reorganization of the school. The team of consultants had a structural orientation and, as can be seen, their primary recommendation was based on a matrix plan of reorganization. The next chapter, by Schmuck and Runkel, outlines a systemic approach for the consultant interested in promoting organizational change and adaptation. The authors discuss features of organizational training and how such training can be used by a consultant to produce organizational change.

Leadership. In the science and practice of educational administration, leadership is a central process or strategy for stimulating change. Although administrators are often constrained by other organizational forces or environmental pressures, the importance of their role in changing educational practice cannot be underestimated. In this section the administrator's role at two different levels in education—the elementary school and the university—is examined with respect to both the causes and consequences of leadership in educational change processes.

Chesler, Schmuck, and Runkel look at the principal's role in facilitating innovation. Their emphasis is on the principal's own support of new ideas and that which he builds into the school through experimentation and sharing. Warren Bennis looks at the change attempts that were made at the State University of New York (Buffalo) under the leadership of President Martin Meyerson. He shows how Meyerson's leadership efforts met with massive resistance from the environment as well as from within the university and suggests ways to avoid similar outcomes.

Evaluation. The role of evaluation in schools has been amplified by recent pressure for accountability. Evaluation of teaching, evaluation of other administrators, and evaluation of educational programs have become important responsibilities of nearly every educational administrator. We are interested in evaluation as an administrative strategy for producing and controlling innovation. Evaluation can be used to demonstrate the need for change, it can be used to determine whether change has taken place, and it can be used to determine the outcomes of any particular innovation. Earlier, in Chapter 5, Deal, Meyer, and Scott provided evidence that there is more frequent evaluation of teaching when instructional practices are innovative.

In this section there is a study by Charters and Jones, who question the sole emphasis placed on evaluating the outcomes of change and argue that we need first to see whether the intended change has occurred before we attempt to measure outcome differences between experimental and control groups. They examine the impact of differentiated staffing on student achievement, concluding that differentiated staffing showed no "significant differences." In the experimental school where differentiated staffing was supposed to exist, however, it was never implemented. The study, therefore, appraises the effects of a nonevent and essentially compares two control groups. One wonders how many "no significant differences" between experimental and conventional programs could be explained in the same way.

Political. The current educational context requires that administrators have superb political skills. They must be able to successfully wield political strategies both within and outside the school setting. The administrator must persuade, cajole, and bring pressure to bear on the community and must maneuver successfully through the political labyrinth both to stimulate change and to protect innovations until they have been adequately tested. But administrators must also be able to deal with internal politics. Teachers often do not share the perceptions of a change-oriented administrator. For a variety of reasons the altered educational trajectory proposed by an administrator often runs counter to the interests of teachers, associations, or unions.

Hampson argues that there is a general reversion to politics in education and that political strategies have an important place in curriculum change. He illustrates the process of curriculum change at the local district level, identifies the decision points in the process, gives the cast of characters, and looks carefully at the interplay between the actors and the change strategies that emerges when there is interaction around the central decision points of a specific curriculum change. Baldridge argues that administrative proposals for educational change often run headlong into entrenched professionals who are more interested in serving themselves than their clients. For these situations, he borrows from Machiavelli and the social sciences in suggesting some basic political strategies for a Machiavellian approach to educational change.

Change Agents

13 Organizational Change and the
Consultant's Role:
Rules for Effective Action

J. Victor Baldridge

It is now common for organizations to invite consultants to help
with organizational problems. Usually such consultations deal with
rather specific matters—installing a new technological system (computers), implementing new government guidelines (regulation against
discrimination), handling complex legal issues (antitrust suits). The
use of consultants under such issue-specific circumstances is fairly
well understood; it is, in fact, standard operating procedure.

Occasionally, however, organizations invite consultants to examine
the more general problems of management style, interpersonal
dynamics, or departmental structure. Sometimes consultants are
simply charged with the ambiguous task of examining vague feelings
of inefficiency, organizational conflict, or lack of responsiveness to
environmental demands. Under these circumstances the procedures
for effectively using consultants and for jointly solving organizational
difficulties are more problematic, and it was under such circumstances that a large midwestern university (hereafter called Midwest)
requested help from a team of consultants to study some general
problems within its huge College of Education in 1972.

Organizational theorists frequently write about their scholarly research, but they rarely comment on consulting activities, which occupy much of their time. Because there is a dearth of information

J. Myron Atkin and Robert Howsam participated on the consultant team and
helped prepare the final report of the team, upon which this article depends
heavily.

about the consultant's role, in this chapter we reflect on the process and how it might be made more effective. Using the Midwest case as an example, we propose a set of "rules" for effective consultation when the issues are relatively general.

Rule One: Set up the consultant's task to maximize internal and external expertise

In the early stages of this effort the dean and the consultants conferred about some of the problems that faced the Midwest College of Education and about strategies for examining those problems. A strategy was needed that would:

—provide outside expertise on organizational issues;

—marshal talent, knowledge, and expertise from within Midwest;

—provide a joint learning process for the consultants, for the dean and his staff, and for key faculty members;

—offer political support for the proposals; and

—provide manageable procedures for translating the proposals into action.

Insiders versus Outsiders: Strengths and Weaknesses

Several different strategies were examined, focusing primarily on the merits of using an "outside" versus an "inside" group. Either has potential strengths and weaknesses.

The strengths of using an outside consultant group, on the one hand, lie in the fresh perspectives that can be brought to bear, the opportunity to obtain expertise in areas where this is required, the isolation from internal politics that might otherwise color decisions, and the greater objectivity that is possible when there is no ego-investment in the status quo. One-shot consultants can, however, fail to understand the dynamics of the unique local situation, with "objectivity" being little more than ignorance, and they can be used as "patsies" to support the policies of the chief administrator. Channels for implementation are not open to an outside group; nor does any consultant have much ego-investment (or authority) to actualize recommendations. Also, the outside group can easily be used as a scapegoat by either unhappy faculty members or unhappy administrators —"outsiders" can be blamed for many sins after they are conveniently gone.

One strength of an internal task force, on the other hand, is that it possesses insight that an outside team could never have. If composed of strong faculty members, staff, and students, the home front people will grant it more legitimacy and help balance the charge that the consultants are pawns of the administration. Most important, the internal task force has ego-investment in seeing that its recommendations are implemented, not just filed and forgotten. They constitute a committed, interested party that can aid (or challenge) administrative officers during the implementation phase.

The main negative aspect of having an internal task force is that it can create greater conflict around the issue when uncovering political problems within the college by recalling old battles and opening old wounds. It is well to expect this to happen. If such conflict does not occur at the planning stage, this simply means that it will happen later, when the input can less readily shape the decisions. It is probably better to fight these battles in the open and head-on during the decision process, rather than underground at a later time. Another negative aspect is additional cost in terms of money, commitment, faculty time, administrative staff time, and so forth. Further, insiders may be so ego-involved and locked into old ways that they are unable to gain fresh perspectives on problems.

The Strategy at Midwest University

After the relative merits of different strategies were weighed at Midwest, three major groups were included in the evaluation process: the dean and his staff; an internal task force composed of faculty, staff, and students; and a three-man outside team consisting of an organizational theorist and the deans of two large colleges of education similar to that at Midwest, one of whom also had some training in organizational theory.

Deliberations were underway throughout the winter and spring of 1972. The dean and the chairman of the consultant team held one preplanning meeting. The consultant team met four times with the internal task force and four times with the dean's staff. Each meeting lasted at least one whole day, and the first order of business was diagnosing the problems that provoked the study.

Rule Two: Assess needs and problems seriously

It seems somewhat absurd to mention that a careful assessment of needs is required. Is not all change preceded by such analysis? It is unfortunate that a variety of problems can often create a short circuit at this stage of organizational change.

Barriers to Effective Diagnosis of Problems

The "captured" administrator. All too often, administrators are prisoners of their own pat diagnoses of what the organization needs. Often, and with the best of intentions, they apply their own specialized notion of what the organization needs to every problem that arises. People often have axes to grind, and, in addition, administrators usually adopt a preconceived solution that is near to their own center of control. This is not necessarily bad; we all tend to specialize and to concentrate efforts for change in our own sphere of activity. This may, however, result in persistent bias and neglect the needs of the whole organization.

Consultants and their bags of tricks. The process of diagnosis can also be short-circuited by outside consultants with preconceived solutions. Many organizational consultants come with "black bags" filled with special tricks of the trade that are supposed to solve organizational problems. Consultants, after all, are also prisoners of their range of skills and their special interests. For this reason any organization hiring consultants should thoroughly explore the particular biases and procedures they bring to the situation.

The "iceberg" phenomenon. The diagnostic process can again be short-circuited by this phenomenon. That is, an apparent problem may be adequately diagnosed, but it may only be symptomatic—the visible tip of a deeper-seated or more extensive difficulty. The overt symptom may be corrected, but the larger problem may remain. A thoroughgoing diagnosis of organizational problems is needed before any change is undertaken, and experts from the entire organization should be consulted. Diagnosis cannot be limited to the world views of a few people.

Diagnosing the Problems at Midwest University

The first stage of the process at Midwest was devoted to defining as sharply as possible the problems hampering the college. This was a major enterprise, for often the loudest complaints simply indicate deeper issues. In this case the original focus on changing the organization chart was gradually enlarged to include a host of other issues, from which the following problems emerged:

Lack of clarity in the mission. The College of Education was large, with literally hundreds of goals and activities. There was no way for it to have a single goal, for it served many constituencies and provided a variety of services to the educational community. It was generally agreed, however, that efforts needed to be focused and goals clarified, or the college would be unable to concentrate its resources on high-quality operations. Faced with both a budgetary crisis and intense pressure for change from outside groups, the college simply could not continue its previous activities without establishing their worth in the larger context of needs and realities.

Although goals had been discussed and priorities had been set in the past, change had been slow, and shifts in priorities had been marginal, with little impact on the college or its traditional activities. Statements of goals largely reaffirmed existing values and thrusts; change and adaptation were minimal. It was generally felt that the college's goals were too diffuse, ambiguous, and confusing. If the college had limited resources, if it wanted to help solve important social problems, if it needed direction about future programs, and if it was to marshal support for more effective organization, then its goals and missions had to be more sharply defined.

There was a consensus that no new committees and task forces (a procedure used extensively in past years that had produced several sets of priorities) should be appointed because the lack of clarity in goals was due to inaction rather than absence of goals. It was suggested that it would be wise to implement stated goals through a few key decisions, especially in the area of faculty appointments and structural reorganization.

Departmental fragmentation. The college was fractured into a maze of departments that had little logical framework beyond tradition and personal allegiances. It is perhaps not too harsh to say that departments were based on past loyalties, historical accident, and functional arrangements. These had served past needs better than they were serving the critical demands of the present or would serve those of the future. The sheer number of departments was bewildering, and the odd sizes and differences in complexity were striking. In some cases whole divisions, representing huge numbers of faculty, reported to the dean through a single administrator; in others, tiny departments were represented by a seat on the administrative council. Some divisions, such as educational psychology, were based on academic disciplines; others, such as educational administration, were arranged around specialized career goals; still others, such as elementary education, were split by educational level. The dean had an overwhelming number of administrators reporting to him, and they represented quite disparate numbers of faculty.

All this would have been inconsequential had it made no difference in the effectiveness of the college. Logical neatness is the hobgoblin of little minds in organizational structure as it is in other areas of life—if the consequences are not critical. However, in this case the task forces thought the consequences were serious: staffing tended to become so tightly identified with small departments and their parochial concerns that the overall mission of the college was hampered; cross-departmental activities, increasingly demanded by the social crises in the world outside, were difficult to arrange; duplication of effort was widespread (during one discussion a faculty member asserted that if several specific departments were combined, duplicate course offerings could be substantially reduced); line-item budgets were completely tied to departments and were inflexible when new needs arose; the multiplicity of departments hindered effective collegial communication, limited the amount of cross-disciplinary contact, and generally fragmented the faculty.

Faculty staffing. The faculty, of course, was the critical component for translating the college's mission into action. During the course of the discussions a major conclusion gradually surfaced: the departments had such total control over the faculty that there was almost no flexibility to deploy faculty into new missions. Most of the college budget was tied up in faculty salaries; most of the faculty were tenured; almost all appointments were made by the departments, with only pro forma review at higher levels; the departments were extremely reluctant to give up slots when people retired, resigned, or failed to be promoted. All these factors combined to give little flexibility in deploying faculty at a time when quick response to social needs, organizational innovation, and programmatic adaptiveness were essential.

Policy making and operations at the college level. Various administrators, from department heads to the dean, complained of problems concerned with policy making and administrative functions at the college level: there was little or no data base upon which to make most critical decisions; too many people were reporting direct to the dean; various staff members in the dean's office were insufficiently differentiated as to function; the administrative council was probably not well constituted, for it had ambiguous representation and functions and was so overwhelmed by daily duties that it had little time for long-range planning and future-oriented work; the relations between faculty senate committees and the administrative council had not worked out well when setting policy.

Budget restrictions. The College of Education, like other units within the university, had been forced to cut back its operations; the student base was slightly smaller, and the budget had been cut. At such a time it was imperative that the college have maximum flexibility to redeploy staff, shift program emphases, and release funds for new demands, and it was these critical tasks that the college was often unable to accomplish.

Factors To Be Considered in Proposing Solutions

The goal, of course, was to find organizational and programmatic strategies that would help alleviate these problems, which did not occur in a vacuum, and so proposed solutions must take into account the unique characteristics of the college, its clientele, and its history. In addition, not all possible solutions were viable because of political and cost factors. Without going into them at great length, it is still helpful to outline the general criteria for acceptable solutions.

Rule Three: Changes must take into account the organization's unique history, strengths, and weaknesses

Organizations have their roots deep in history; they have traditions and patterns of life that have evolved over a long period. It is important to realize that organizational change is always relative to a specific situation and to the unique circumstances of a given organization. Change simply does not "take" if the history and tradition of the organization are opposed to it. For example, in this period of tightened financial resources the outcry is for more "efficiency" and "scientific management" in educational organizations. All too often these well-intentioned programs are undermined because they are forced on the organization without enough concern for its special conditions and historical procedures. Many potentially valuable changes must be severely modified if they are to blend into the life of the organization. To assess the fit between innovation and the organization's history and tradition is a complex process, and it must be done carefully.

Outside consultants can propose a variety of organizational strategies and theoretical principles that might help, but only longtime insiders can provide insight and perspective about the unique strengths and weaknesses of the organization. Let us put our bias right at the forefront: *Organizations should maximize their critical strengths and strive to shore up or cut out their weaknesses, irrespective of the organizational plans adopted.* There is no easy way to make those tough decisions. Only sophisticated know-how or a practical feel for the unique situation can identify the pockets of power and the pockets of weakness. A major part of a good administrator's job is to identify the incisive, critical minds on the staff, listening to everyone but giving weight to those who think creatively, who know what they are saying, and who interpret and integrate their ideas so that they are translated into effective strategies of action.

At Midwest the consultant team could not offer suggestions about areas to strengthen or to change; the members lacked the necessary insight for such a critical task. The internal task force and the dean's staff, along with other relevant constituencies, had to make these tough decisions. Before the organization could ever be successfully restructured, hard-nosed thinking had to be done about priorities and strengths in the college. Part of that task was to assess the goals of external constituencies.

Rule Four: Take the environment into account when considering organizational changes

Organizational changes are almost never dictated entirely by internal factors. The environment is a major impetus for change, as new environmental demands create new ideas, new procedures, and new activities. Not only does the environment promote change, but internal changes must be supported by environmental connections. A change in disciplinary rules for students in a school district, for example, may be popular with students and teachers, but opposed by the surrounding community. New accounting procedures for business firms may generate enormous hostility among clients because of their complexity. In short, there are two basic questions whose answers are often the key to substantial organizational change: What does the environment *need*? What will the environment *support*?

At Midwest the consultation process explicitly considered the external environment, for everyone realized that the college had to respond to its educational constituencies, to state regulations, and to university guidelines—all factors in any change equation. Several considerations emerged from the evaluation process at Midwest:

1. The college should be more responsive to the needs of the educational community and should not allow internal priorities to lose touch with outside realities.

2. The college should not be timid vis-à-vis state regulations. In many cases the regulations are out of touch with reality, conservative in nature, and vague in form. It is entirely plausible that a college should help shape those regulations by its actions and innovations, not be a passive victim bound by outside rigidities.

3. A vigorous, bold approach to reforming the college and its programs would probably win more support from the university's cen-

tral administration—a major external constituency from the viewpoint of the college—than would an attempt to coexist with constraints. This does not mean that the college should ignore the university's goals and guidelines, but surely the interests of both college and university coincide when the goal is to continue the traditions of a great college.

Rule Five: Serious changes must affect the organizational structure as well as individual attitudes

A prime problem with much of the literature on organizational change is that it often focuses narrowly on individual attitudes. It is important to stress that any important change in individual attitudes must often be supported by corresponding change in the organizational structure. For example, let us assume that it would be good if professors at Midwest were to cooperate more fully in interdisciplinary programs. One strategy would be persuasion—to convince the professors that the change was important. Persuasion can be reinforced, however, by changing organizational features such as the sanction and evaluation processing. If professors were paid more for carrying out the new procedure or if interdisciplinary program directors controlled tenure instead of departments, this would reinforce the change in attitude. Similar support for attitudinal change includes shifts in the authority structure, participation in decision making, and technical support such as new technology and procedures. In short, any change that requires a shift in the attitude of key personnel can be reinforced by changing the organizational structures that support and undergird those attitudes. At Midwest such structural changes were proposed in a new "matrix" plan.

Rule Six: Make changes that are both politically and economically feasible

Although it might be desirable to have a College of Education teach classes in revolution, stressing the role of education in undermining the class system, only the most risk-oriented administrator would propose such a drastic change in, for example, the hostile environment of a politically conservative state. It is important not only to make changes that will survive in the organization's environment, but also to gauge the amount of political opposition that may come from within. Powerful interest groups in an organization may fight proposed changes, and they may have the clout to stop them. A vital part of a shrewd administrator's job is assessing which things will succeed politically and which will fail. Often it is best not to try changes that are doomed. If the change is so basic that it must be done despite political opposition, however, then it is crucial for the planning process to marshal interest groups and coalitions for support. Rational planning often falls completely apart in the face of poor political strategy. At Midwest, for example, the consultation efforts always had to be focused on solutions that would not provoke hostile political reaction from key faculty members.

Politics and cost are almost inseparable. Many plans fail because they are not viable in terms of what the organization can afford. All too often those who planned the changes did not take into account the financial cost to the organization. It is important to do some elementary calculations long before time and money have been expended; such preliminary spadework can save much wasted energy and hard feeling. Usually it means expert advice and help, with a variety of opinions invoked.

It is important to remember that one of the largest costs is personnel time. Before the change is undertaken, available personnel, talent, and expertise must be carefully assessed. It is senseless to plan changes that require unavailable skills; if there is no prospect of obtaining qualified personnel, it is best to forget the proposed innovation. At Midwest many proposed solutions were simply out of the question because resources, including personnel, were scarce.

Rule Seven: Use changes that are effective in solving the problems diagnosed

The most cost-effective plan in the most favorable political environment will still fail if it does not solve the problem. The critical questions are: Will the proposed changes actually solve the problems that were diagnosed? Will they involve costs in terms of money and personnel that make sense to the organization? Will they solve the problem so that it stays solved? Will the changes become part of the organizational structure, or will they prove too dependent on individual personalities for implementation?

Too often proposed changes meet all criteria except the effectiveness one. Changes may be based on a valid diagnosis, be sensitive to both the environment and the organization's history, and be feasible politically and cost wise. Nevertheless, unless they actually solve the problem they are a waste of time. At Midwest some decisions arrived at jointly were meant to meet the effectiveness rule.

Proposals for Reorganization and for Mission Effectiveness

In light of all the problems listed earlier and of the various consider-ations that must enter into the decision process, the series of rec-ommendations offered will be discussed, not because the specific suggestions can be applied everywhere but because some of them might be useful for other institutions, and because knowing the *con-tent* of the consultants' recommendations adds depth to the discus-sion of the consultation *process.*

Recommendation 1: The College of Education should continue to define its mission and goals more sharply, channeling resources and renewal efforts into areas of strength and future promise, while at the same time eliminating or combining weaker areas and those hav-ing little promise or filling few social needs. This overarching recom-mendation colored everything else in the report. The *mission* of the college and its *goals* were the heart of the matter. No amount of tinkering with the organizational structure could take the place of hardheaded assessment of where the college was going and what its future efforts should be. The consultants argued that mission clarifi-cation did not demand new task forces and committees; instead, it required effective action to implement goals already articulated.

Recommendation 2: In order to achieve flexibility in deploying resources the dean should at once implement a policy of "position control" and channel the resources thus captured into areas of mis-sion priority. Position control is a simple concept: all vacancies at the assistant professor level or above were to be automatically placed in the dean's hands to redeploy for the overall benefit of the college. The written policies of the university already gave the dean this power; the operational tendency, however, had been for departments to retain vacancies. Among the pervasive problems was insufficient flexibility in faculty deployment, including line-item budgets that hampered the process of allocating faculty to new areas of concern and departments so narrowly defined that college interests and mis-sions had lower priority than departmental goals. Effective position control could solve some of these problems.

Recommendation 3: With the new resources generated by the position control process, some new personnel should be acquired who have national reputations in the areas of highest priority for the college. We noted earlier that mission definitions needed to be crys-tallized and strongly promoted and that position control could gen-erate new flexible resources which, coupled with some strong new personnel appointments, could effect significant change at the

College of Education. New people, new priorities, some flexible resources could combine to catalyze deep-rooted change.

Recommendation 4: The department structure should be reorganized in a two-stage process. Initially there should be five divisions, with all present departments located within those divisions. Later, departments could be eliminated, and the five divisions would become the home of all faculty. (The details of such a process were to be spelled out later.) In order to provide more flexibility and to eliminate administrative confusion (as well as to address other problems listed earlier under the head of departmental fragmentation), it was suggested that the five divisions be: curriculum and instruction, specialized career programs, vocational-technical education, physical education, and foundation areas. The dean would assign departments to the appropriate division.

Recommendation 5: A "matrix" plan of organization should be adopted as the long-range goal. Under a matrix plan all departments would be collapsed into the five major divisions, and all faculty would have their homes in a division instead of in a department. Specific details of this recommendation follow.

The Matrix Plan of Organization

The recommendations listed above were to be dovetailed with a new pattern of organization called the "Matrix Plan." This section explains in skeletal form the plan and its anticipated consequences.

Basic Elements

Essentially the matrix plan called for two interacting kinds of organizational structure: the traditional *departmental* one and a new mechanism for delivering *programs.* Departments have traditionally been responsible for faculty and student personnel, program determination, and program delivery. The plan separates personnel from program, with the former residing in departments and the latter in projects and programs. Departments may propose programs—anyone may—but not operate them.

The matrix is composed of departments on the horizontal dimension and of programs on the vertical. Examples of proposed departments and programs for Midwest's College of Education appear in Figure 13-1.

EXAMPLES OF PROGRAMS	DEPARTMENTS				
	Curriculum instruction	Specialized careers	Foundation areas	Vocational-technical	Physical education
Administrative training	XXX	XX	XX	X	
Ph.D. program in educational psychology	X	XX	XXXX		
Elementary credential	XXX	XXXX	X		X
Vocational specialist	X	XX	X	XXXX	X
Urban education, etc.	X	XX	XXX	X	X

X = Faculty members assigned jointly to departments and programs.

FIGURE 13-1

Example of a matrix for Midwest's College of Education

Operational Rules for a Matrix Plan

1. Departments include all faculty. All personnel matters such as appointment, promotion, and tenure reside there. The department is the home base from which the faculty member operates.

2. Departments would be organized on one of several possible bases: subject specialization, discipline, careers for which students are prepared, and so forth.

3. Students would be in programs and student personnel matters (admissions, retention, certificates, degrees) would be managed through them.

4. Projects would provide all instruction and do development and research work; they form the delivery system.

5. Both faculty and students would be assigned to projects and programs for their activities.

6. Projects and programs would be organized on principles similar to what is widely known as PPBS (Program Planning Budgeting System) and they would be characterized by:

a. precisely stated objectives,

b. a program to meet the objectives,

c. a definite life span, and

d. resources of faculty and student time, services, and space, with faculty usually assigned from more than one department under

e. a management plan which in each case provides a director,

f. an evaluation plan which includes both formative (systemic, self-regenerating) and summative elements, or

g. accountability for achievement of objectives.

7. An administrative structure at the college level would be based on the needs of a matrix plan. At least three identifiable functions are essential to the matrix plan:

a. deciding on programs and projects and rank-ordering them by priority,

b. allocating resources to new or continuing projects, and

c. evaluation.

These functions could be assigned to associate deans. They might be variously combined or expanded, and councils or committees could be added.

8. In addition to other consultative bodies, the dean would have two major administrative councils:

a. the council of deans, and

b. the committee (or council) of project directors (representative when groups become large).

Arrangements for meeting jointly or for commingling the two might be preferred.

Effects of Matrix Plan

The following is a list of consequences expected to flow from a matrix organization, with some obviously being positive and others having both good and bad aspects:

1. Much more staffing flexibility.

2. Shorter response time to social needs, that is, adaptability.

3. More interdisciplinary capability.

4. More coordinated focus on program goals.

5. Greater ability to discontinue programs and move to other issues.

6. Somewhat less autonomy for individual professors.

7. Stronger program leadership.

8. Shorter time spans of work.

9. More systematic planning, coordination, and evaluation, at greater time cost.

10. More collective and collaborative effort by faculty, with less prima donna behavior.

11. Different evaluation criteria for faculty (weighing contribution to mission-oriented programs as well as traditional scholarly ones).
12. More centralized, coordinated effort from dean's office.
13. Systematic institutional research and data-based self-analysis.

Implementation

If taken seriously, the plans outlined above could have major impact on the Midwest College of Education. Plans, of course, are only the beginning; the real test of reform is implementation. A number of issues need careful attention.

First, the program should be implemented in gradual steps so that ideas can be tested, allowing continuous adjustment. The timetable allows a series of steps over a three-year period, several to be taken in the first year:

1. Restructure the dean's staff.
2. Reduce the division to five, assigning each department to a division.
3. Restructure the administrative council.
4. Gather information about use of the matrix plan in other organizations.
5. Institute position control.
6. Continue mission clarification.
7. Establish searches and budgetary adjustments for new faculty.
8. Establish a few test programs that would utilize the matrix program concept through "shadow budgets."

After a year or so of testing and probing, planning could begin for a full-blown matrix approach.

Second, individuals and their career investments should be protected during implementation. Human considerations and individual careers are, of course, paramount; in the final analysis it is people who make an enterprise work, who set its goals, who translate plans into action. Everyone connected with the evaluation process shared some common assumptions and orientations about academic and scholarly life: the need for personal autonomy, self-direction, control over the academic process by the faculty, and evaluation by competent peers rather than by bureaucratic machinery. It was urged that reforms be implemented humanely and gradually to allow people whose programs and careers would be affected the necessary time and opportunity to adjust to the changing situation. It bears repeating that individual careers and personal investments must be protected; the institution must maintain the confidence of its key personnel while proceeding to change. For this reason we continually stress the need for slow processes, for individual protection, and for backup to those most directly affected.

Summary

The consultant's role is complex when the issues at stake are general problems that do not have straightforward solutions. Organizations can, however, make better use of consultants if they observe a few basic rules when dealing with the change process:

1. Set up the consultant's task to maximize internal and external expertise.
2. Assess needs and problems seriously.
3. Take into account the organization's unique history, strengths, and weaknesses when making changes.
4. Take the environment into account when considering organizational changes.
5. Realize that serious changes alter the organizational structure as well as individual attitudes.
6. Make changes that are both politically and economically feasible.
7. Use effective changes to solve the diagnosed problems.

Some of the concrete recommendations made while considering this actual case of consultation with the College of Education at Midwest University exemplify the approach proposed here.

14 Organizational Training

Richard A. Schmuck
Philip J. Runkel

Few effective strategies have been employed to help school districts improve the group processes in their schools. Apparently many educators believe that productive group dynamics automatically arise out of the skillful actions of top-flight, highly motivated, and well-trained personnel. After all, it is argued, as long as the teachers are capable, the administrators experienced, and the curriculum materials up to date, why spend energy on developing communication skills, group agreements, conflict-management procedures, and team morale? Won't these aspects develop naturally? Available evidence indicates they do not.

What attempts there have been to improve group processes in schools have centered on training individuals to be more competent participants in groups. Two educational strategies have been most emphasized: one stressing cognitive change, the other affective change. Examples of the former are college classes, workshops, and in-service training programs; the most prominent example of the latter is the sensitivity group (T group).

The cognitive change strategy appears to be ineffective for changing school organizations. It is based on the assumption that knowledge about social psychology and administrative science will lead to

Reprinted from Richard A. Schmuck, Philip J. Runkel, Steven L. Saturen, Ronald T. Martell, and C. Brooklyn Derr, *Handbook of Organization Development in Schools* (Palo Alto, Calif.: Mayfield Publishing Company, 1972), ch. 2.

changes in the group behavior of individuals, which in turn will help to improve the functioning of the staff to which they belong. But knowledge alone does not necessarily lead to behavioral changes. The reason is, in part, that educators confronted with discrepancies between their ideal and actual performances often feel anxious and become defensive. Moreover, even if individual behavioral changes do occur, structural changes in the school organization are not likely to result from them. At best, we think, the cognitive change strategy helps educators talk more articulately about how the school ought to be run.

The T group, an affective change strategy, provides an arena where a participant can explore the impact his behavior has on others, experience the forces affecting a group's commitment to a decision, its cohesiveness, level of trust, and openness. He also can experience power, status, influence, and leadership styles firsthand; learn to express and deal with his feelings; try out new behaviors; learn to appreciate and accept human differences; and explore the assumptions and theories he has about human behavior. Our experience has been that T groups can have helpful effects for the participants, who may experience an increased level of trust and openness, high cohesiveness and commitment to the group, dispersion of leadership, and appreciation of the strengths and potential contribution of other members. Research has not shown, however, that the T group in itself will bring about increased efficiency, effectiveness, and team development for organizations.[1]

Organizational training, in contrast, offers a set of action steps by which a school district or some part of it can begin to move toward improved ways of accomplishing tasks.[2] At some point during innovation, a staff must stop talking about change and attempt a new manner of operation. When it makes such a trial effort, it is engaged in training itself in the new way of operating. Organizational training improves the ability of members of a school organization to change themselves. When a condition of deliberate internal changeability has been established, we refer to the district as being in a state of heightened adaptability.[3]

1. Campbell and Dunnette (1968) and Friedlander (1968), among others, have recounted the weak effects of sensitivity training in programs of organizational development. For a trial within the realm of public education, see Lanksy et al. (1969).

2. The technology described here is also delineated in somewhat more detail in Langmeyer, Schmuck, and Runkel (1971).

3. We mean by *adaptable* what Gardner (1963) means by *self-renewing* and what Buckley (1967) calls *morphogenetic.*

In contrast to the cognitive and affective change strategies described above, organizational training—as we have used the term—always contains at least four features: (1) training the organization's subsystems as working groups rather than individuals, (2) training in communication skills, (3) training in group problem solving, and (4) a developmental sequence of experiential training that moves from simulations and exercises performed away from the normal operation of the school to problem solving on real issues in the work setting.

The typical training design teaches, legitimizes, and makes normative a systematic, adaptive, and flexible technique of problem solving in groups. The technique typically begins with clarifying the problem areas and desirable goals, goes on to analyzing the forces that keep problems from moving toward solution, sets priorities on the forces to be increased or decreased, makes plans for action, and finally evaluates the effects of the action taken. To prepare for such problem solving, the training sequence begins with practice in methods of increasing the face-to-face flow of valid information. The skills we have emphasized are paraphrasing (making sure that you understand the other person's message), describing behavior (avoiding inference), describing feelings (not simply venting them), and checking one's perception of another's feelings (describing to another how you think he is feeling, so that he can verify or deny your perception).

The importance of introducing and practicing skills of communication and listening cannot be overstated. Acquiring these skills is the foundation of improving meetings, clarifying supervision, dealing with emotions as problems, giving helpful information about interpersonal relations, and generally extending the amount of shared, accurate information. Educators sometimes assume either that they have already acquired the interpersonal skills needed to carry out their work or that such skills cannot be learned. Organizational training proposes to help educators learn such skills in the context of the actual work groups with which they are dealing. . . .

Organizational training differs from the sort of help offered by a traditional management consulting firm. The traditional consultant generally accepts problems as they are defined by the administrators of the organization. He then gathers information to ascertain the severity of the problem and the conditions that might bear upon it. Finally, he issues a report containing the steps he advises his client take to overcome the problem. But a traditional consultant rarely stays with an organization long enough to help it carry the recommendations into practice. Consultants taking the viewpoint of organizational training, in contrast, explore problems from the perspectives of all parts of the district and include relevant parties within and outside the district in designing and implementing change. Frequent training sessions help school personnel to carry out the practices which they themselves may design.

Although organizational training makes use of the organization as its own laboratory for experiential and inductive learning, laboratory groups are used in very different ways from sensitivity groups or T groups. The targets of organizational training are the membership as a whole and its subgroups. The training seeks to increase the effectiveness of groups as task-oriented entities and leads participants to function more effectively as role takers carrying out specific tasks in the particular job setting. The goal of this sort of training is not to change personalities; it is to change the functioning of work groups and the ways roles are carried out. We make no demand on the individual that he change his nature or behave differently with persons off the job. Naturally, deep feelings often arise from task-oriented activities. To the extent that such feelings inhibit a group from accomplishing its organizational tasks, skill in coping with them becomes a subgoal of organizational training. For example, resolutions to power struggles between generations or racial groups will usually require skill in both communication and listening.

Laboratory groups conducted among strangers can "loosen up" participants and enable them to participate in group exercises with less anxiety, but they do not give intact work groups practice in functioning more skillfully as teams. Organizational training does not exempt members from training on the ground that they have already "had that" elsewhere. It is the intact work group that must learn new ways and new norms, not individuals. This "subsystem rule" cannot be stressed too often. The consultant facing a work group that is missing one or two members faces an important decision: should he go ahead with the plan as if all members were present and hope the group can absorb the remaining members later without his help, or should he redesign the training to bring in the missing members immediately? In general, we recommend the latter course. An ordinary college class or workshop with a few members absent is no worry; a work group in a school trying to establish new group norms is often crippled when one or two members are missing.

Sometimes previous experience in laboratory training can hinder effective membership in organizational training. Many group laboratories which emphasize "personal growth" concentrate on freeing the individual from his fears about expressing emotions publicly, but do little else. A person with such an experience sometimes interprets serious attention to feelings in the group as a signal to enlarge on his own personal attitudes. In organizational training we encourage discussing feelings only when they are relevant to the work of the group. Furthermore, mere expression of feelings does not in itself lead to group growth; more important is accurate description of one's own feelings to others in the group so that the group can choose acts that are helpful to the aroused person. This kind of communication requires discipline, not abandon.

Levels of Intervention

Before elaborating further, we wish to place organizational training in perspective with other types of intervention to show how it differs from other approaches to improving schools. The following descriptions of interventions—classified according to level from most superficial to deepest—come from Harrison (1970).

1. *Rational assignment of tasks.* This strategy is to redistribute (by proclamation) the tasks, resources, and power among the jobs in the organization. The consultant can do this without knowing in advance who will be occupying the positions. This is the technique used by most private firms offering consulting services to management (referred to above as traditional consulting). The classic theories underlying this technique are the theories of bureaucracy and time-and-motion, and the classic theorists are Weber and Taylor.

2. *Direct influence on performance.* This strategy evaluates the performance of individuals and directly manipulates it. Particular techniques include appraising the skills an employee brings and placing him in an appropriate job, giving promotions, increasing or decreasing salary or wages, transferring employees, and using the techniques of management by objective. The classic theory underlying these techniques is "reinforcement" psychology and its prophet is B. F. Skinner.

3. *Direct influence on the interpersonal interactions through which work is accomplished*—for short, interpersonal instrumental rearrangements. This strategy opens to negotiation those instrumental (task-oriented) acts that individuals direct toward others: delegating authority or reserving decisions to oneself; communicating or withholding information; collaborating or competing with others on work-related issues. The consultant is interested in the organizational member primarily as a doer of work. Much of Douglas McGregor's (1967) theorizing deals with this level.

4. *Interpersonal emotional rearrangements.* At this level, the consultant deals with feelings, attitudes, and perceptions and the quality of human relations. "Interventions are directed toward helping trainees to be more comfortable in being authentically themselves with one another, and the degree of mutual caring and concern is expected to increase," says Harrison. Sensitivity training in the T-group is a typical technique, though not the only one. This kind of

intervention has been carried out in numerous industrial organizations; it has also been used extensively in the school districts in which Carl Rogers has worked.

5. *Therapy.* The deepest level focuses on the individual's relations with himself—and on increasing the range of experiences he can bring into awareness and cope with. This is traditionally the realm of psychological therapy and its patron saint is S. Freud. Religious leaders, historically, have also directed most of their efforts at this level of change.

Organizational training primarily centers at level 3, although it involves aspects of levels 2 and 4. We assume that improved instructional programs in schools require changing the interpersonal instrumental relationships among staff members. Moreover, we believe that interventions at other levels, such as Program Planning and Budgeting Systems (PPBS) (level 2) and T grouping (level 4), will *not* have sustaining payoff in terms of improving the school's culture unless they are accompanied by interventions to rearrange role definitions and norms for work. Changing the ways people relate to one another and work together in schools—from our point of view—requires staff members and ultimately students to learn new role definitions, interpersonal norms, and group skills. The best way to do this, we believe, is to intervene with techniques at level 3 and to branch out later to techniques at other levels as the intervention progresses.

Adaptability

The goal of organizational training for schools is adaptability. An adaptable or self-renewing school can cope with changes in its environment while maintaining an effective educational program.

A receptive and responsive organization cannot, in the long run, use any single organizational structure or procedure exclusively. While there is typically some formal hierarchy, form must follow function. People organize themselves into groups to solve specific problems; both the structure of the organization and the methods used in the groups change to suit the nature of the current problems. For example, a group with the goal of modifying curriculum might be highly structured, with a strict agenda, a designated leader, and a well-defined method of voting to make decisions; while a long-range planning department might be quite loosely organized to permit time for planning, allow further time for experts to pool their points of view, and allow for final decisions to be made through a process involving community groups, parents, and students.

School organizations become more responsive, we believe, when decisions are made by the persons who have accurate information. Instead of looking to those who have the legitimate authority, emphasis is placed on the best possible decision. Decision making requires adequate information and, unfortunately, too often those in authority lack such information or have it in a distorted form. In an adaptable district a group of students and parents might decide on dress codes; teachers and students might decide on classroom procedures; while some teachers, the principal, and the superintendent might decide on whether to involve principals in in-service leadership training. Since decisions are required from work groups at all levels in the adaptive school district, the intent of organizational training is not to restrict training in problem solving to certain parts of the district; rather it prepares groups at all levels for this vital and inevitable function. A truly adaptive organization has sensing processes and feedback mechanisms to tell when change is needed. There is open communication not only among those in the district but also between the district and the community at large. An adaptive educational organization further manages itself according to specified goals accepted by its members. It has systematic problem-solving techniques for surmounting obstructions to these goals. The district, naturally, is able to change the goals judiciously as inputs from the community change.

Finally, an adaptive organization has a culture characterized by open, direct, and clear communications which permits the processes mentioned above to take place. Members of the organization view conflict as inevitable and natural; they take occasion to bring conflict into the open so that it can be used to bring about creative change instead of impeding the work to be accomplished. Members exhibit creativity and, rather than suspecting new ideas and new persons of bringing trouble, welcome them as additional resources.

Organizational Training as Technology

Getting jobs done in any organization requires two resources: (1) information and skill concerning the task itself and (2) special information and skill to facilitate the work of people who do the task. In schools, for example, arranging classes and assigning duties require expertise in the logistics of scheduling. For full effectiveness, the task of scheduling also requires competence in arousing commitment from both those who will do the planning and those who will operate within the schedule.

The management of group processes, in other words, is a job in its own right. Organizational training aims to help school organizations develop increased competence in using group processes to accomplish tasks. Whatever the kind of work in which a group of educators may be engaged and whatever the condition consultants may be trying to improve, there are inevitably certain skills, exercises, and procedures that can be useful. These are the building blocks of organizational training.

Skills

We use the term *skills* to signify ways in which interactions with others can be executed in a group. Sometimes the skill is one of communication, such as paraphrasing what another has said so that the other can verify that he has been understood. Sometimes it is one of guiding a group through a survey of opinion. Sometimes the skill involves writing interview schedules to obtain diagnostic information about a school.

All these skills, it should be noted, are put to work only in reciprocal relations between persons; no individual can make use of these skills in isolation. Each skill is actually one person's part of a reciprocal role relation. Paraphrasing can only be done in conversation with at least one other person and is not a complete act until the other has verified the accuracy of the paraphrase. The skill of a pair or group, consequently, is often surprisingly independent of the skill of the individuals composing it. The convener can be skillful in conducting a survey only if the members know their parts of the role relation; an interview schedule can be prepared effectively only if the interviewers using the schedule act with the same goals and values as the writer and only if the respondents join the communicative act in the way the writer and the interviewers anticipate.

There are many skills useful in organizational life that organizational training typically does not touch upon. It ignores, for example, the skills of rhetoric, of making conference telephone calls, of using Robert's Rules of Order, of choosing what to include in the minutes of a meeting, and many others. In this book, we discuss those skills that we think are very useful for improving organizational processes and that cannot be got from the educated person's ordinary experience.

Exercises and Procedures

A useful distinction in organizational training can be made between *exercises* and *procedures*. An exercise (simulation) is a structured gamelike activity designed to produce interpersonal processes that participants can easily conceptualize because they are related to their own personal experience. Each exercise is designed to make salient a certain type of group process and thereby illustrate specific lessons so that they are easy to comprehend.

A procedure, on the other hand, refers to an interpersonal form for communication in a group without any particular content in itself. A procedure can be used for a variety of tasks or purposes. One example of a procedure would be voting and another would be the "fishbowl" procedure for sharing ideas and observations.

Exercises have two major advantages: they can be designed to produce specifiable learning experiences, and they typically have very different content from the day-to-day work of an organization. These strengths make possible very specific learning goals (for example, using more sources of information in decision making or encouraging more communication from faculty to administration) without having to deal with specific content, which may carry with it the barriers to reaching these goals in everyday organizational life. Through an exercise, participants can learn the advantages and deficits of one form of behavior over another and can make plans to establish more productive behaviors. Typical questions consultants ask in debriefing an exercise are, "How is the behavior exhibited in this exercise similar to or dissimilar from your behavior on the job?" and "What did you learn from the exercise that has application to your behavior on the job?"

While the content of an exercise is determined by the consultant, procedures are content-free and are used to work more effectively toward whatever goal the group has chosen. Under most conditions, intervening with an exercise takes a group away from a task and is used to produce a new understanding inherent in the exercise. Procedures, on the other hand, are typically introduced to facilitate accomplishing a task the group is already facing. They are steps or routines within which a group's business can be moved forward. In this regard, procedures are less obtrusive in the normal functioning of a group and less gamelike. Procedures such as problem solving and "process consultation" have been useful to schools, departments, and cabinets, and sometimes to teachers who have tried them in their classrooms to improve the learning environment (for the latter application, see Schmuck and Schmuck, 1971).

Sequence of Organizational Training

People in organizations often search for new ways of doing things when they are dissatisfied with present ways. It is in the hope of relieving their dissatisfactions that they attempt to work together in new ways. We think of discrepancies between unsatisfactory present states of affairs and ideal states as organizational problems. Organizational training attempts to resolve such problems by teaching working groups ways of reducing such discrepancies on a continuous basis. Accordingly, organizational training does not teach skills, conduct exercises, or display procedures as a mere string of lessons. Usually these activities are embedded in a design for solving problems, thereby helping the organization to behave more adaptively. . . .

Before the Training Starts

A school organization acknowledges a problem when some influential person or group within it conceives a state significantly more satisfactory than the present state. A superintendent may be plagued by subordinates asking him, "Who is supposed to do such-and-such?" A principal may read an article that shows him that the way he thinks of his school's goals does not enable him to ascertain whether he is approaching those goals. Problems can arise from interpersonal demands within the district, as in the above example of the superintendent. They can also arise from new ways of conceiving of things, as in the case of the principal. They can also arise from demands made by people outside the district, as when parents, legislators, or salesmen make demands; sometimes, for example, outsiders try to persuade a school district that it ought to undertake some innovation such as team teaching or organizational development.

In our experience, productive change is not likely to be achieved unless the persons who may otherwise stand in the way of change acknowledge the problems and become reasonably committed to solving them. A sizable portion of the organization, and especially the more powerful members, must accept the problem as "their" problem; they must not acquiesce to a project merely to help an outsider with an issue they perceive as the outsider's problem. For this reason, we think a project of organizational development usually has a dubious prognosis when it originates from the initiative of the outside consultant. If the personnel within a district do not acknowledge a discrepancy between ideal and actual states as an organizational problem before the outsider arrives on the scene, it is generally difficult for them to adopt that view soon enough in the sequence of training. The consultant will be safest if he adopts it almost as a rule to enter into contract only with those districts that are reaching out for help.

Entry

The organizational consultant does not begin with all parts of the district and all aspects of its functioning at once. He begins in one or a few places and branches out from there.

The traditional place to begin interaction with a district is in the office of the superintendent. Yet this is not as automatic a procedure as it once was in American schools. Many people who want to influence high schools nowadays, for example, do so by organizing teachers or even students first, just as, in earlier times, agents of change organized workers in factories. There are, nevertheless, obvious advantages in involving the superintendent of the district or the principal of the school at early stages of the intervention.

Often, when a school district approaches the outside consultant, the one who initiates the contact will be the top man or his appointed agent. This is not, however, always the case. In one of our projects, we were first approached by a counselor in a junior high school who wanted to explore the possibility of our offering leadership training for the building administrators in his district. After we discussed the possibility of carrying out a project in organizational development instead of just leadership training, he spoke on the subject with the superintendent. We did not act until the superintendent requested a first conference with us; then we began taking initiative when appropriate.

If the superintendent or principal approves the project at the outset, the organizational consultant can at least get the attention of other parts of the district. He will not get commitment or even acquiescence from the others merely through the approval of the top man, but he will at least acquire the legitimate power to call meetings and present the goals and techniques of organizational training. If the project is district-wide, the consultant will need to obtain acceptance for the project from every significant group within the district. Even if organizational training is limited to a single school, it will be necessary to get the powerful central figures of the school in support before proceeding very far into the training.

In first entering and at every subsequent step, the principle of working with an entire subsystem is vital. The organizational consultant should almost never accept a meeting with "whoever can come." At the outset, the crucial questions are "What is the problem?" and "Who is willing to commit himself to organizational training?" In considering both of these questions, a potential school participant in the training must consider the likely answers of those with whom he works. The organizational member will want to see and hear how the others in his work group react to the goals of organizational training. He will also want to ascertain how far they will commit themselves to it. This is one reason the consultant should, from the outset, deal with intact work groups within the district. The other reason, just as important, is that people who work together will at the later stages be trained in their intact groups, as we explained earlier in this chapter, and to begin dealing with them in groups will introduce that principle early and make later conceptualization easier.

Some parts of school districts are more powerful than others; usually, it is helpful to work first with the more powerful subsystems so that they become allies rather than enemies. Typical powerful parties in districts are the school board, the superintendent and his cabinet, the principals, teachers' organizations, and, in more and more districts, groups of students. In individual school buildings, the powerful parties can be the teachers, department heads, counselors, principal, and certain student groups. (Particularly powerful in many schools are teachers whose work is seen as having unalterable routines, so that the schedules of other teachers must defer to them: for example, athletic coaches.)

The consultant should not be slow in moving his attention from the more powerful groups to the less powerful; teachers and secretaries (and students, if they are to be involved) must not form the conviction that they are less important to the consultant than administrators. The final step during the first phase of organizational training, consequently, is to gain at least verbal commitment to the enterprise from all key groups that will participate in the training. The consultants should be explicit about their goals, their role, the project's budget, and the time they are willing to spend in the project.

Consultants are often tempted to give trainees a short, clear presentation of what the training will consist of. We have found, however, that the essential features of organizational training are very difficult to communicate in a lecture. We have found that no matter how detailed the description of what the training will be like, the actual training experiences will stir new insights in one participant after another. A typical comment to the consultant is: "I had no idea it would be like this! I would have been able to understand it so much more quickly and fully if you had told me at the beginning it would be this way!"

Chances are the consultant *did* tell the participant how it would be, but the words did not at that time mean at all what they mean after the experience—and the trainee, of course, remembers his expectation, not the consultant's words. Furthermore, the consultant knows that the experiences of individuals will differ. As we conduct it, organizational training is largely experiential, and experience is an individual thing. It does not help a particular person much to tell him that one of eight or nine kinds or degrees of experience may happen to him; he already knows that life is uncertain. In brief, the consultant should take a few minutes to describe what the training will be like, if only to show that he wants his listeners to know. But he should not expect them to get an accurate picture from his words. The quickest and surest way of conveying this information is to present a demonstration of the training.

It is also important to keep in mind that entry situations can be filled with various kinds of feelings. Issues of trust and suspicion, well-being and dissatisfaction, investment and cautiousness, and openness and closedness are very near the surface. We believe that direct acknowledgment of such prominent feelings is a prime requisite for good contract making. The hidden issues for both the school people and the consultants should be uncovered and discussed. Relationships of any sort cannot be forged from task agreements alone.

Diagnosing Present Functioning

Gathering information about the organization is vital to effective action by the consultant; he needs detailed information on which to base his training design. At the same time, this information-gathering phase is a part of the procedure of formulating the problem. Diagnostic data can ascertain, for example, whether the problem extends beyond the imagination of the persons who initiated the first contact with the consultant. It can reveal the different shapes the problem takes in the minds of educators in different parts of the district. Moreover, diagnostic data can later be compared with data collected after training, when the change can show evidence of profit from the training. . . . Some diagnostic data can be collected from members of the district without betraying confidentiality, and these data, if they portray a widely felt problem, can serve to motivate further effort if they are fed back carefully.

We think that communication, role definitions, goal setting, the realization of conflicts between groups, the study of processes at meetings, and the development of methods for reaching decisions are all important for the effective functioning of schools. But which should receive first attention from the consultant? In our opinion, the consultant should give first attention to those processes that

seem most to be impeding the proper functioning of other processes
—break the logjams first, so to speak. Another useful rule is to treat
early those impaired processes that the people in the organization
feel are most painful; success with these processes will produce motivation toward further work.

. . . Interpersonal communication . . . has been unclear and ineffi-
cient to a degree in every school district we have encountered; we
think efficacy of communication is probably below optimum in
more than 99 percent of human organizations everywhere. Since
poor communication can block every other process, it is usually
profitable to begin with this process. (Of course, the consultant
should gather careful diagnostic information to help him choose particular communicative links with which to begin.) Choosing goals . . .
must surely be done before goal-directed work can have any meaning. Even conflicts in the group . . . can be dealt with more intelligently if goals have been defined and enumerated so that methods of
dealing with a conflict can be judged on the basis of their effect on
the goals. More effective group procedures . . . , too, can be chosen if
the goals they are intended to facilitate are clarified. Consequently, it
seems to us that the process of selecting or clarifying goals should
usually be undertaken before the processes of bringing conflicts into
the open and improving group procedures.[4]

After the four processes already named have been re-examined and
altered, the organization is in a strong position to improve its daily
work: solving problems . . . and making decisions. . . . Finally, after
problem solving and decision making are being conducted in the new
ways, an assessment of the presumed benefits of the retraining can be
carried out. Of course, preliminary data for such an assessment
should be collected at the outset of the program.

Proposing a Training Design

After initial approval for the project has been obtained from the
appropriate parties of the school district and after the consultant has
carried out a diagnosis, the subsystem to receive the first training
must be recruited. This is the climactic stage of the entry process.

---

4. Sometimes it becomes clear to the intervener that strong conflicts and
distrusts exist but that members of the organization are hiding the fact from
themselves. Again, members may be aware of the conflicts but may suppose
everyone else has resigned himself to "working around" the conflicts instead of
dealing with them directly. In such cases, the consultant may judge it useful to
exhibit the true nature of the conflicts even before beginning work to clarify
goals.

The general rule here is the same as the rule for first contact with the organization: "Don't call them; let them call you." If the consultant has sufficient time, this is the strongest strategy to use. At some point, the people who initiated the contact between the organization and the consultant will ask him when he would like to begin training. The consultant can then negotiate directly a training schedule for those people and their immediate work group. If he is effective with them, the experience will arouse the interest of other groups in the district, and the program can continue.

If the consultant or the first people trained are not willing to wait for such communication to recruit further parts of the district, a more risky policy must be adopted. Under this policy, groups within the district invite others for recruitment. For example, the superintendent and his advisers can invite the principals to a meeting at which the project is described and the consultants invite not only the tentative approval of the principals but also their agreement to participate in demonstration of the training techniques. Similarly, a principal could ask his teachers to attend such a meeting.

It is very important, for ethical reasons, that final decisions in such meetings remain strictly voluntary. For example, persons who are absent from the meetings must not be punished. The consultant must make clear to the authorities and those present that he is not requiring attendance nor ensuring it by the use of any sanctions whatsoever. Furthermore, it should be clearly stated that approvals are revocable for cause in the future, and that agreement to attend a demonstration does not automatically ensure attendance at further demonstrations. After each agreement has been carried out, the consultant must engage in new negotiations concerning the next phase of the work. A request from the superintendent to a high school principal to cooperate with the consultant, for example, does not mean that the consultant should expect the principal to go along with any plans he may dream up. The consultant should expect only that the principal will give the consultant's offer of negotiation a fair hearing. We have found principals, incidentally, to be key figures in the success or failure of organizational training.

Aside from questions of ethics, people who feel "ordered" into a training event will be poor participants. Some will actively sabotage the consultant's efforts. Others, though they may acquiesce in their own districts, may pass the word to other districts that the consultant is one to be avoided. Teachers, especially, may acquiesce only halfheartedly and later talk critically of the project when the outside consultant is not present. Beyond this, the ethical side of the issue remains the important one, in our opinion. The consultant who values the free commitment of participants will not make the strategic error of coercion.

Demonstrations

A demonstration of organizational training can be useful as a first step in negotiations with an unsophisticated staff. By a demonstration we mean participation in laboratory training activities that communicate experientially the nature of organizational training to those who have previously had little experience in it. When a project is meant eventually to have effects throughout a large organization such as a large secondary school or an entire district, such demonstration of the nature of organizational training is a sufficient task for the initial event.

Within the context of a particular project in organizational training, of course, the material of which the demonstration is built can be the frustrations and conflicts actually existing within the district. Such a demonstration can have three important outcomes: (1) it can motivate the participants toward further work by giving them a small taste of success in dealing with one or more of their problems, (2) it can give them a more correct and complete conception of organizational training, and (3) it can make them into supporters or "public relations agents" for later events.

As an example, we undertook a fairly large demonstration to launch a two-year program of organizational development with the Kent, Washington, school district. The trainees included the superintendent and his cabinet, the elementary and secondary principals, and selected teachers who were leaders within the Kent Education Association. At least one teacher from every building attended the meeting, along with the key officers in the association.

The event lasted four days, but only the superintendent's cabinet was present all of the time. On the evening of the first day, before others arrived, the superintendent and his cabinet discussed ways in which communication had broken down among them, the lack of clarity in their role definitions, the ambiguous norms that existed in the cabinet, and, finally, their strengths as a group. The trainers gave structure to the discussion and kept it centered on organizational topics.

On the second day, the principals joined the cabinet in a specially designed confrontation that brought into the open organizational problems seen by each group as involving the other. First, the entire group divided into three units: cabinet, elementary principals, and secondary principals. Next, each of these units met separately to consider helpful and unhelpful work-related behaviors of the other two groups toward their own group. At the end of two hours, all perceived actions of the other groups were written in large letters on sheets of newsprint. Problems between groups brought to the surface were earmarked for future problem-solving procedures. The session ended with a brief period of training in the communicative skills of paraphrasing and behavior description.

Next, one group sat in a circle, surrounded by members of the other two groups. Participants sitting in the outer ring read aloud the descriptions they had written of the inside group. A member of the inner circle then paraphrased the description to make sure that his colleagues understood it. During this step, group members in the inner circle who were receiving descriptions of their own group were not allowed to defend their group against the allegations made by the others. After all items describing the inside group were read, the remaining two groups took their turns in the center circle.

After this step, the three groups again met separately to find evidence that would support the descriptions they had received; they were instructed to recall examples of their own behavior that could have given the other group its impressions. The three groups then came together once again with one group forming an inner circle. Each inner group told the others of the evidence it had recalled to verify the perceptions of the others. Once again, the inner group was discouraged from defending itself; members were asked simply to describe the behavioral events they thought supported the others' perceptions.

On the evening of the second day, teachers arrived to join the principals and cabinet, and for four hours all of the key line personnel in the Kent district were together. A modified confrontation design was continued, culminating in a meeting in which the three groups indicated the organizational problems they thought existed in the Kent district. Discussion was lively, penetrating, and constructive; most personnel had never before confronted persons in other positions so openly with their perceptions of district problems. The principals went back to their buildings the next day, leaving time for teachers and cabinet to interact with one another. On the fourth day, the cabinet met alone to schedule some dates for future problem solving.

Sequences of Training Events

After some members of a school district have experienced favorable outcomes from one or more demonstrations, the consultants will find it relatively easy to make entry into other parts of the district. One means of doing this is to hold a conference of appropriate people to discuss their own special problems as a group; from this may come a vision of the way organizational training can help in solving those problems. Sometimes a subproject can be started very rapidly in some segment of a district. This is especially true when the top man of that segment (principal, director of a division, head cook, or another) has the confidence of his staff. Whatever the mode of entry into the subsystem, the presence of persons in the subsystem who have participated in an earlier demonstration is very helpful, in that they can vouch for the consultant, a service the consultant cannot do for himself and which is suspect when administrators do it for him.

First Main Training Event

Once the demonstration stage has come to an end, the district or a subsystem of it is ready for its first main training event. This is the event in which a sequence of stages is set in motion to achieve a stated goal. The goal is known in advance to consultants and trainees, and the general nature of the stages by which it is to be reached, too, is shared as much as it can be. Some examples of particular goals that a project in organizational development might undertake are converting a school to differentiated staffing, aiding a school to achieve desegregation smoothly, reshaping the role of the department head, and improving the clarity with which the roles of the superintendent's chief lieutenants are understood throughout the district.

In subparts of districts we have conducted first main events lasting as little as three hours to as long as two weeks. We think a great deal of impact is lost, however, if the initial main event is shorter than two-and-a-half or three days. The chief weakness of short sessions is related to the fact that in the training session itself a period of time is needed to bring new norms into play. The direct experience of these new norms, in turn, is the glue that binds together later training events with earlier events. Later events can be much shorter than the first main event. For many purposes, a few hours can be productive. A good standard length for a first main event is five consecutive days. Under special circumstances, this time should be lengthened.

The first main event has chiefly the purpose of providing the participants with enough changes in norms and habits so that they will make efforts to continue the new ways in their natural work settings. The initial training does not guarantee, however, that the efforts of the participants will override the competing challenges of the natural work setting and become stable. Without further training, most groups and organizations will revert to the old ways. Most projects of any size, such as those influencing an entire school faculty, require periodic training events for six months or a year after the first main event.

The core ingredients of the organizational training sequence we have used fall generally into the following three stages.

Stage 1: Improving Communicative Skills—Building increased openness and ease of interpersonal communication among the district personnel by training them in such communication skills as paraphrasing, describing behavior, describing own feelings, and checking their perceptions of others' feelings. This stage develops constructive openness, increasing confidence among the staff that communication with colleagues can be worthwhile.

Stage 2: Changing Norms—Building new norms that support helpfulness among the staff. The consultant can use, as a lever with which to change group norms, the desires of professional personnel to ameliorate some of their actual problems. For example, the consultant can invite the educators to state some frustrations that they are encountering in their jobs and to practice a sequence of problem-solving steps to reduce these frustrations. (See Schmuck and Runkel, 1970.) Cooperative problem solving not only reduces frustrations but also yields the satisfaction of knowing that others value the contribution one has made to the solution. Changes in organizational norms of openness and candor occur when the consultant asks staff members to behave in new ways in their actual work groups, thereby enabling their colleagues to observe the new patterns of behavior in the school setting.

Stage 3: Structural Change—Building new functions, roles, procedures, policies, or subsystems. These new structures should become part of the basic fabric of the school district. They should be formal and institutionalized, and have budgetary support.

As the structural changes are being implemented, training events should be designed to shore up those processes that show weakening while at the same time enabling the daily work of the school to progress. It is equally important to carry through to a successful conclusion any new undertaking begun by the participants. Designs must be tentative because unforeseen events will inevitably occur. The goals of this stage will often (though not always) fit into a sequence such as this one:

1. Carry forward any subprojects undertaken at the initial training.

2. Conduct further group building and skill refurbishing with significant work groups.
3. Provide special training in leadership skills to groups containing high proportions of persons holding formal leader positions.
4. Collaborate (with initiative from the participants) in arranging further learnings in organizational development.

Assessment

Progress should be assessed not only through the impressions of the consultants, but also by formal data collection. These data will permit objective communication with the participants, but care must be taken so as not to create mistrust and distance between the consultants and the trainees during data collection. The data can be useful in communicating (once names and any other confidential information are removed) with the teachers and administrators in the district, with the community in which the district is embedded, and with the professional colleagues of the trainers. Rapport should be established before any formal data are collected, and the instruments should be shown to participants whenever they wish to see them, provided anonymity is protected. Formal data of this sort also enable the consultant to discharge his obligation to communicate accurately, succinctly, and objectively with professional colleagues and publics.

Withdrawing

Leaving a client system is as complicated as entering it. It is unavoidable that a certain dependency becomes established between consultant and trainee. Too sudden a departure can make trouble for both. The consultant should prepare the participants for his withdrawal by giving ample and repeated notice of the date of his final availability, and then sticking firmly to that date. He should also, of course, give the participants ample practice in taking over all his functions in one way or another.

References

Buckley, Walter (1967). *Sociology and Modern Systems Theory.* Englewood Cliffs, N.J.: Prentice-Hall.

Campbell, J. P., and Dunnette, M. D. (1968). "Effectiveness of T-group Experiences in Managerial Training and Development." *Psychological Bulletin,* 70.2:73-104.

Friedlander, F. (1968). "A Comparative Study of Consulting Processes and Group Development." *Journal of Applied Behavioral Science,* 4:377-399.

Gardner, John (1963). *Self-renewal: The Individual and the Innovative Society.* New York: Harper and Row.

Harrison, R. (1970). "Choosing the Depth of Organizational Intervention." *Journal of Applied Behavioral Science,* 6:181-202.

_____ (1970). "Role Negotiation: A Tough-minded Approach to Team Development." Unpublished manuscript.

Langmeyer, Daniel, Schmuck, Richard, and Runkel, Philip (1971). "Technology for Organizational Training in Schools." *Sociological Inquiry,* 41.2: 193-204.

Lansky, L., Runkel, P. J., Croft, J., and MacGregor, C. (1969). *The Effects of Human Relations Training on Diagnosing Skills and Planning for Change.* Technical Report. Eugene, Ore.: Center for the Advanced Study of Educational Administration, University of Oregon.

McGregor, Douglas (1967). *The Professional Manager.* New York: McGraw-Hill.

Schmuck, Richard A., and Runkel, P. J. (1970). *Organizational Training for a School Faculty.* Eugene, Ore.: Center for the Advanced Study of Educational Administration, University of Oregon.

_____, and Schmuck, Patricia A. (1971). *Group Processes in the Classroom.* Dubuque, Iowa: Wm. C. Brown Co., Publishers.

Leadership

15 The Principal's Role in Facilitating Innovation

Mark Chesler
Richard A. Schmuck
Ronald Lippitt

It is a unique school indeed in which teachers discuss their classroom problems, techniques, and progress with one another and with their principal. In most schools, teachers practice their own methods —rarely hearing, or even caring, if one of their colleagues is experimenting with some new teaching device or technique. We know that many teachers are trying out new ideas and experimenting with new practices and forms of classroom management, and we believe that teaching is improved when teachers share and evaluate new ideas and practices with their colleagues. Further, we maintain that teachers can learn from one another's experience, and any situation enhancing the interchange of ideas and practices should add to each teacher's repertoire of skills and techniques. Such sharing of information and experience should improve the character of education in a school and should be of vital concern to those interested in improving classroom education.

We assume that the kinds of interpersonal staff relations in a school will be important factors either encouraging or discouraging

Reprinted from *Theory into Practice*, 2(Dec. 1963):269-277. *Note:* The work reported in this paper is part of the Inter-Center Program of Research on Children, Youth, and Family Life of the Institute for Social Research at the University of Michigan. It was supported by grants from the National Institute of Mental Health (Grant OM-376) and the U.S. Office of Education (Cooperative Research Project No. 1167).

the sharing of educational insights and experiments. We also assume that the school principal plays an important role in directly or indirectly influencing this process. By direct influence, we mean the principal's role in encouraging or discouraging individual teachers to try out and report upon their new ideas. By indirect influence, we mean the principal's role in encouraging or discouraging the creation of a staff atmosphere that supports experimentation and sharing. The principal's indirect style may help create precisely those staff relations that help teachers feel comfortable when talking about their innovative efforts.

Research performed on industrial work groups supports the notion that peer groups set up pressures and establish standards of performance and communication that influence the productivity of individual members. So it is, we believe, with school staffs. In some teaching staffs, colleagues are encouraged to try new practices, to attempt to find out what others are doing, and to help new teachers by suggesting alternative ways of handling classroom problems. In such schools, the principal, together with his staff, creates a situation in which professional concerns and the quality of teaching are of prime importance. In other schools, however, teachers may lack standards of high professional purpose. They may shy away from discussing new ideas and personal classroom practices, and [they] may fail to be encouraged to evaluate their own teaching. The latter situation inevitably inhibits the development of creative teaching.

With the foregoing as background, we would like to review briefly the initial results of a pilot investigation designed to determine what influence the principal's behavior has on the developing and sharing of innovative classroom practices.[1] Our research dealt primarily with those variables leading to the identification and diffusion of teaching practices promoting subject-matter competence and pupil mental

---

1. By innovative classroom practices, we mean teaching procedures that are new to the teacher who develops or adapts them. For instance, role playing is not a new teaching practice, but, for the teacher who tries it for the first time or who considerably modifies it in order to solve a particular classroom problem, it is an innovation. For further clarification, see the following documents of the Inter-Center Program on Children, Youth, and Family Life: R. Schmuck and M. Chesler, *Solving Interpersonal Problems in the Classroom*, Number 12 (Ann Arbor: Institute for Social Research, University of Michigan, 1963). Forthcoming are "Classroom Study Tools for Improving Classroom Atmospheres," by R. Fox, M. Luszki, and R. Schmuck (Number 13); "Creative Practices Developed by Teachers for Improving Classroom Atmospheres," by M. Kaufman, R. Schmuck, and R. Lippitt (Number 14); "Role-Playing in the Classroom," by M. Chesler and R. Fox (Number 15).

health. The investigation included assessments of the "styles," or personal qualities and methods, of teachers and principals, and their interrelations within the school. We analyzed the system of staff communication and influence, and the priority given to professional growth, to determine their contribution to staff norms supporting the creation and dissemination of new classroom ideas and practices.

In the fall of the 1961-62 school year, we collected data from the entire staff in each of nine elementary and secondary schools. During that year, university consultants offered in-service sessions for those teachers who were interested in new ideas and practices. Complete data were again collected in late spring in order to determine what changes had occurred through the year. Follow-up interviewing in the fall of 1962 provided more detailed information on some of the new teaching practices that had been developed. Some of the early results of this research and the implications that these should have for school principals are presented in the following sections.

Factors Influencing Innovative Teaching

Why is it that some teachers create and try out new classroom practices, while others do not? The teachers in the schools studied indicated the factors most relevant to initiating their creative effort. The most important of these can be organized into three major categories. The first category includes teachers' feelings that new practices can help solve problems important to them and their pupils, that is, emphasis on statements such as: I feel that there are some problems which I need to do something about; I have a feeling that doing something in the class about these problems would make both the students and me more comfortable; and I feel that my pupils are ready to respond positively to these kinds of changes in my teaching techniques. The second category includes teachers' feelings that a given practice is easily adaptable to their own styles of teaching and does not demand a great investment of time or energy, that is, emphasis on statements such as: of the many things I do on the job, working on classroom problems is a priority for me to find time for; even with the many things I need to do away from the job, I can find time to work on professional problems which are important; and these kinds of techniques fit in easily with my style of teaching. The third category includes teachers' feelings that the school administration will support new teaching practices.

The last category is important in suggesting the direct influence the principal may exert by encouraging staff innovation. He can directly stimulate inventiveness by either suggesting or openly supporting new ideas. Moreover, the principal may exert indirect influence by making some of the other factors more salient. He may indirectly stimulate inventiveness by helping teachers see their classroom problems or by rearranging the teachers' time and energy commitments.

Our data substantiate the assumption that the principal plays an important role in stimulating creative classroom teaching. There is a high and significant correlation[2] between the amount of staff inventiveness, as measured by the mean number of new practices developed by each teacher, and the staff's perception of the principal's support for innovative teaching. There is an even higher correlation[3] between the teacher's perception of his principal's support and his perception of his colleagues' support of innovation. The first finding substantiates the notion that the principal can have a direct influence upon his staff. The second finding substantiates the notion of an indirect role—the principal may encourage an atmosphere where the entire staff publicly supports innovation. Thus the principal's attitudes influence staff norms, and both his orientation and peer standards combine to influence actual staff innovativeness.

To determine the interaction of principal attitudes and staff norms in jointly influencing creative teaching, we divided the schools in the study into four major types: schools in which the teachers perceive support for creative teaching (1) from both the principal and the staff; (2) from the principal, but not the staff; (3) from the staff, but not the principal; and (4) from neither the staff nor the principal. Our data indicate that schools of type 1 (most support from both) have the highest average number of innovations per teacher (5.2); while schools of type 4 (least support from both) show the lowest average number of innovations per teacher (3.5). Types 2 and 3, with mixed degrees of support, are between these two polar types with averages of 4.8 and 4.9. Note that a considerable number of innovations occurred for all staffs—probably because of their involvement in the in-service workshops—but that the degree of inventiveness tends to differ according to staff perceptions of the amount of support from both principal and colleagues.

The Principal as a Professional Leader

Our research shows that at least two major factors are operating in the case of a principal who encourages staff inventiveness. First, the

2. rho = + .65, p less than .05.
3. rho = + .73, p less than .05.

principal must have an accurate perception of the values and skills of his staff. Second, the staff must be aware of the priority that the principal places on the improvement of classroom teaching.

In order to assess the influence of the first factor, the principals were asked to judge each of the members of their staff on their enthusiasm for, and involvement in, innovative teaching. At the same time, the teachers rated their colleagues on the same dimensions. The similarity of the two ratings affords an indication of the principal's accuracy in assessing his staff. The degree of his accuracy indicates his sensitivity to the perceptions and interests of his teachers, and to the way in which they relate to one another. Our research shows that a principal's sensitivity is related positively to his staff's tendency to innovate. The mean number of innovations per teacher in schools with more accurate principals is 5.2, while that of schools with less accurate principals is 3.8.

Principals with innovative staffs were found to be in tune with their teachers' feelings and values about education and better informed about their informal relationships. Conversely, principals with less innovative staffs relate more formally to their teachers and fail to consider their values and emotional associations. Their perceptions of their staff's interrelationships and communication patterns appear to be less accurate, apparently because they are less concerned with individual teachers and classroom processes.

The data relevant to the second factor suggest that principals must act in ways that demonstrate their support of staff inventiveness. It is not enough that the principal be interested in staff innovativeness; his interest must be obvious to the staff. The principal who publicly supports new classroom practices is more likely to have innovative teachers than the one who does not.

Another important factor was revealed through interviews made during the course of our study: principals with the innovative staffs are more "professionally" oriented than those with less innovative staffs. The former are concerned with improving classroom processes, encouraging teacher growth, and continually evaluating pupil learning. The latter group, on the other hand, tends to be more "administratively" oriented. They are concerned primarily with achieving a smoothly running organization, and [they] are very responsive to the demands of their administrative superiors. They tend to regard the improvement of classroom practices and a concern with the more abstract purposes of education as luxuries that seem less important than keeping the school running efficiently. Quite often these administrative principals do succeed in effective organizational management. However, teachers in such schools are prone to allow organizational demands to precede those of the classroom and, consequently, are less apt to develop innovations.

Specific Suggestions for Principals

Our research has shown the importance of the principal in the development of creative classroom practices. What, then, can principals do? The principal's first task should be to secure accurate information about staff relations. Through the sensitive and diagnostic use of discussions and questionnaires, he can assess colleague relationships in his school. He can determine the social pressures that are brought to bear on his teachers and their own commitments and values. Further, he should be sensitive to indications of his success in relating to his staff.

As the principal learns where he stands with the staff and how each teacher views the school situation, he can begin to try new ways of influencing them to innovate and to share new ideas. There are two methods he might employ: (1) influencing the personal priorities and values of his teachers, and (2) influencing the peer culture to encourage teacher desire to support and share new practices.

Many of the teachers we studied had time commitments that interfered with their desires or attempts to develop and share new practices. The principal can help solve this problem by arranging released time for his teachers. He can make greater use of substitute teachers and explore the possibility of occasionally allowing the older pupils to lead the younger ones. To facilitate staff communications about new practices, he might use a tape-recording system; teachers could listen to recorded reports whenever they have free time. He could find consultants to guide his teachers to important literature in the field, thus saving them the time they would waste scanning irrelevant materials.

The principal can collaborate with university project staffs and resource personnel to develop in-service training programs. Further, he can arrange joint meetings with the staffs of other schools at which innovative teachers can describe and evaluate new procedures they have tried. Such meetings are particularly valuable because they not only examine alternative solutions to mutual problems, but they also help principals and teachers to see their problems, not as unfortunate idiosyncrasies of their schools, but as general professional problems.

If a principal finds that in his school there is little colleague support for innovation, he will want to encourage his staff to develop relationships based on mutual assistance and the sharing of ideas. He can encourage informal meetings among his teachers for the discussion of teaching techniques, thus letting them know that sharing and evaluating one another's practices is "the professional thing to do." He can attempt to improve teacher communication by encouraging teachers to observe one another's classroom procedures, by working out a written format for identifying and describing new teaching techniques, and by including descriptions and evaluations of such techniques in staff meetings. Above all, the principal must demonstrate his active support and concern for raising the level of his teachers' competence.

In all of these attempts to encourage innovation and improvement, the principal who is a professional leader will constantly evaluate the effects his behavior is having on his staff. Only by so doing can he remain sensitive to the needs of his teachers and the effectiveness of his performance in promoting innovation.

The Sociology of Institutions, or

16 Who Sank the Yellow Submarine?

Eleven Ways to Avoid Major Mistakes in Taking Over a University Campus
and Making Great Changes

Warren G. Bennis

*One cannot expect to know what is going to happen. One can only consider
himself fortunate if he can discover what has happened.* —Pierre du Pont

On December 19, 1966, I received a phone call from an assistant
to President Martin Meyerson [now President of the University of
Pennsylvania] at the State University of New York at Buffalo. The
assistant began the conversation with almost sinful empathy: "I bet
you don't know what's going on here at Buffalo, do you?" I allowed
that I did not, and he proceeded to describe an academic New Jerusa-
lem of unlimited money, a new $650-million campus, bold organiza-
tional ideas, a visionary president, a supportive chancellor and gov-
ernor, the number of new faculty and administrators to be recruited,
the romance of taking a mediocre upstate college and creating—well—
the Berkeley of the East. Would I consider taking part in the effort? I
was smitten by the verve, the *chutzpah*—and by the thought of having a hand in the transformation. S.U.N.Y. at Buffalo had been a
relatively unnoticed local college founded by the thirteenth U.S.
President, Millard Fillmore, "His Accidency." It had gained an uneven distinction between 1930 and 1962, the year it became part of
the University of New York.

Reprinted from *Psychology Today*, 6.6(November 1972):112-120. Copyright
Ziff-Davis Publishing Company.

New York wanted to create a multiversity and in 1966 had lured Meyerson from Berkeley (where he was the acting chancellor) to make the dream materialize.

Meyerson arrived with a monumental plan to redesign Buffalo's conventional academic structure. Within two months, the faculty senate had ratified the plan, which provided as follows:

1. The ninety existing departments would be restructured into seven new faculties, each with a provost as the chief academic and administrative officer. Each faculty would consist of the basic disciplines within the newly defined area, plus the relevant professional schools. (Meyerson wanted me to head the social science disciplines that included anthropology, psychology, and—to the chagrin of the Arts and Letters Provost—philosophy and history. My domain also would include the schools of management and social welfare.) The provosts would have ample resources and administrative leeway to create interdisciplinary programs and launch new education ventures.

2. The university would build thirty small colleges on a new campus. Each would house only four hundred students with up to six hundred day students as affiliates. Faculty and students would live and work together in the intimate atmosphere of these intellectual neighborhoods. Meyerson hoped the small college would offset the apathy and anomie that characterize enormous campuses. In addition, they would break the stranglehold that traditional departments traditionally leave on the university. Undergraduates would not get a watered-down version of what professors taught their graduate students; they would learn directly from their teachers in a communal setting.

3. Action-research centers and councils on international studies, urban studies, and higher educational studies would unite scholars and students from the entire university (and from the outside) for work on vital issues.

Esteem. Meyerson's overall concept impressed me. Several aspects of the plan were especially attractive: the decentralization of authority, the potential of the program (if you did not fit in with a department, you could always connect with a college, center, or council), and Meyerson's clear intent to raise the self-esteem of the university, the self-esteem of the faculty and students, and the self-esteem of the Buffalo community. Meyerson assured me that, with the new campus, there would be enough money to build quality on top of the university's inevitable deadwood.

I was sold on the man and his conceptual vision. The timing

seemed perfect, the new organizational design would go into effect on the same day my term of office was to begin. I arrived at Buffalo in the fall of 1967 and during 1967-68 I recruited nine new chairmen and two deans for the faculty, and changed about 90 percent of the leadership structure in the social sciences area. The faculty gained forty-five new full-time teachers. I spent almost three-fourths of my first year in recruiting.

Buffalo raided Harvard, Yale, and Princeton. Each new appointment increased enthusiasm, generated new ideas, and escalated the Meyerson optimism. The tiny, crowded campus barely contained the excitement. Intellectual communities formed and flourished.

Steam. The change was pervasive. Almost 75 percent of the present Buffalo faculty got their appointments under Meyerson.

The newcomers were eager recruits—committed to innovation and risk taking. The student body also was changing. By 1968, eight in ten of the entering freshmen were from the top 10 percent of their high school graduating classes, compared to only one in ten a decade before. Buffalo was regarded as one of the State University's radical campuses according to *Esquire* magazine (along with Stony Brook on Long Island). Meyerson's Berkeley-of-the-East approach may have had an appeal that he had not fully calculated. For one year, Buffalo was an academic Camelot. The provosts met around the president's conference table to work miracles. Occasionally I got signals that not everyone on campus took us quite as seriously as we took ourselves. One morning I found a Batman cape on my coatrack. The anonymous critic had a point: the atmosphere was a bit heavy with omnipotent fantasy.

Although construction had not started for the living quarters on the new campus, the six human-size colleges got underway at once. Almost immediately they provoked controversy. Rumors began to circulate that course cards for College A—the unit devoted to independent study and self-evaluation—were being sold, snatched up by students who did little or nothing and rewarded themselves with A's at the end of the semester. "Why do you think they call it 'College A'?" one cynical student asked. There were tales of credit for trips to Europe and the building of bird cages.

The master of College A regarded any impugning of its grading system as an antirevolutionary tactic. No one in the Meyerson administration, including myself, wanted to take a harsh public stand against this nonsense, particularly after College A and its master became the target of vicious community attack.

Status. There were other rumblings in paradise. The centers were not doing well. We learned that it was easier to break down barriers than to build bridges. For example, the Center for Higher Education did not generate new programs or attract faculty and students as planned. The Center for International Studies began to publish a newsletter—the only substantial sign of its new status. The Center for Urban Studies undertook a series of much-needed but thoroughly conventional projects in Buffalo's inner city.

In one form or another all the faculties had problems. Many departments raised questions about the new faculty structure. I felt that the many individual accomplishments, the promising new programs, [and] the appointment of a particularly good teacher or administrator did not add up to a significantly changed university. We were not consolidating our gains, and I feared that they might somehow slip away. These feelings were eventually confirmed. Camelot lasted barely a thousand days.

Setting. I took part in many of the crucial decisions that affected the progress of the Meyerson plan. And I now see, with all the unsettling clarity of hindsight, that we undermined many of our own best aspirations for the University. If I were asked today how to bring about change in a university setting, I would offer the following guidelines:

1. **Recruit with scrupulous honesty.** Most of the faculty who came to Buffalo shared the academic vision of its new president, Martin Meyerson.

Meyerson's gift as a recruiter was his ability to transmogrify all of the highly visible and terribly real drawbacks of Buffalo and make them reappear in the guise of exhilarating challenges. Those he attracted recruited others.

Sweetener. My personal recruiting at Buffalo depended on a falsely bright picture of the situation. It was not that I lied. But, consciously or not, I sweetened the package even when I was trying to be balanced and fair. Recruiting is a courtship ritual. The suitor displays his assets; the recruit, flattered by the attention and the promises, does not examine the assets closely. We were naive. The recruiting pitch at Buffalo depended on the future. We made little of the past and tended to deemphasize the present. Buffalo was the university of the future—of course, it would take time to catch up.

New arrivals had barely enrolled their kids in local schools before reality intruded. A labor union dispute delayed construction of the promised new facilities. Inflation nibbled away the buying power of the allocated construction funds at a rate of one and a half percent a month. It was easy to put up with the inconvenience of overcrowding when one was sure that the condition was temporary. But the dispute dragged on for months, and there was no room on the old campus. The situation might have been challenging if we had not led the new faculty to expect something magical. We had urged them to reveal their most creative, most imaginative educational thinking, then had assured them that their plans would receive generous support. In reality, money to staff new programs was difficult to come by. After one year, the state legislature began to pare the budget. Many new faculty members felt they had been conned. As recruiters, we had not pointed out our ultimate inability to control the legislatively determined budget. We had promised a new university when our funds could provide only an architect's model.

Shock. Inadvertently, we had cooked up the classic recipe for revolution as suggested by Aaron Wildavsky: "Promise a lot; deliver a little. Teach people to believe that they will be much better off, but let there be no dramatic improvement. Try a variety of small programs but marginal in impact and severely underfinanced. Avoid any attempted solution remotely comparable in size to the dimensions of the problem you are trying to solve. . . ."

The intensity of the disaffection felt by some of those I had brought to the university came to me as a shock. We had raised expectations as high as any in modern educational history. When our program met only a part of these expectations, the disillusionment that followed was predictable and widespread. The disparity between vision and reality became intolerable. No one had said a word during the seductive recruiting days about triplicate forms, resentful colleagues, and unheeded requests for help from administrative headquarters.

Support. Those who rose above the mundane annoyances provoked by university bureaucracy felt cheated in other ways. Recruits had joined our academic revolution because they shared our goal and wanted to participate. To keep such a cadre committed, an administration must keep them involved. But the warmth of our man-to-man recruiting interviews was not evident in later meetings with administrators. In fact, such meetings became fairly infrequent. The continuing evidence of personal support that might have overcome the unavoidable lack of concrete support was not forthcoming.

2. Guard against the crazies. Innovation is seductive. It attracts interesting people. It also attracts people who will take your ideas and distort them into something monstrous. *You* will then be identified with the monster and will have to devote precious energy to combating it. A change-oriented administrator should be damned sure about the persons he recruits, the persons who will be identified as his men or women.

A few of the persons who got administrative posts under the new administration were committed to change, but they were so irresponsible or antagonistic that they alienated more persons than they converted.

Sense. It is difficult to distinguish between agents of responsible change and those who rend all they touch. The most successful innovators often are marginal to the institution, almost in a geographical sense. They have contacts in other institutions, other areas. Their credentials are unorthodox. They are often terrible company men with little or no institutional loyalty. Change-oriented administrators must be able to distinguish the innovators, however eccentric they may be, from the crazies. An academic community can tolerate a high degree of eccentricity. But it will brutally reject an individual it suspects of masking mediocrity with a flashy commitment to innovation.

3. Build support among like-minded people, whether or not you recruited them. Change-oriented administrators are particularly prone to act as though the organization came into being the day they arrived. This is an illusion, an omnipotent fantasy. There are no clean slates in established organizations. A new president cannot play Noah and build the world anew with two hand-picked delegates from each academic discipline. Rhetoric about new starts is frightening to those who suspect that the new beginning is the end of their own careers. There can be no change without history, without continuity.

Stayers. What I think most of us in institutions really want—and what status, money, and power serve as currency for—is acceptance, affection, and esteem. Institutions are more amenable to change when they preserve the esteem of all members. Given economic sufficiency, persons stay in organizations and feel satisfied in them because they are respected and feel competent. They are much freer to identify with the adaptive process and much better equipped to tolerate the high level of ambiguity that accompanies change when these needs are heeded. Unfortunately, we did not attend to these needs at Buffalo. The academic code, not the administrative one, determines the appropriate behavior in the university. The president is a colleague, and he is expected to acknowledge his intellectual equals whatever their relative position on the administrative chart. Many old-guard professors took the administration's neglect as a personal snub. They were not asked for advice; they were not invited to social affairs. They suspected that we acted coolly toward them because we considered them to be second-rate academics who lacked intellectual chic and who could not cut it in Cambridge or New York. Ironically, some of the old-guard academic administrators who kept their positions were notoriously second rate. Meyerson extended the appointments of several such, perhaps hoping to avoid the appearance of a purge. Among the incumbents were a couple whose educational philosophy had rigidified sometime in the early 1950's. Instead of appeasing the old guard, these appointments added insult.

The old guard suspected that the new administration viewed them as an undifferentiated mass. They wondered why we kept these second-raters and overlooked a pool of potentially fine veteran candidates.

We succeeded in infusing new blood into Buffalo, but we failed to recirculate the old blood. We lost an opportunity to build loyalty among respected members of the veteran faculty. If veteran faculty members had been made to feel that they, too, had a future in the transformed university, they might have embraced the academic-reorganization plan with some enthusiasm. Instead the veteran faculty members were hurt, indignant, and—finally—angry.

4. **Plan for change from a solid conceptual base—have a clear-cut understanding of how to change as well as what to change.** Buffalo had a plan for change, but we lacked a clear concept of how change should proceed. A statement of goals is not a program.

The Buffalo reorganization lacked the coherence and forcefulness that would have guaranteed its success. The fault may have been that it was too abstract. Or perhaps it was too much a pastiche. A great many influences were evident: the late Paul Goodman and the community of colleges; the colleges and sense of academic tradition of Oxbridge; the unorthodoxy and informality of Black Mountain; the blurring of vocational-professional lives practiced at Antioch and Bennington; the collegiality of Santa Cruz; the college-master system of Yale. Each of these elements was both desirable and educationally fashionable, but the mix never jelled. No alchemy transformed the disparate parts into a living organism.

Students. We had no coherent mechanisms for change. Instead we relied on several partially realized administrative models. The burden of change fell upon the faculty senate, which emphasized the small-group model. Change depended on three things: 1) participation by the persons involved, 2) trust in the persons who advocate the change, and 3) clarity about the change itself. None of these conditions was fully present at Buffalo, and, as a result, the change was imperfectly realized.

Radical students utilized a revolutionary model. The students saw an opportunity for radical educational change in the Romantic tradition—the result was the College A controversy. The administration relied heavily on the model of successive limited comparisons, popularly known as muddling through. This is the model of most organizational decision making. It is a noncomprehensive, nontheoretical approach. Most administrators are forced to muddle through because the decisions they are called upon to make are simply too complex to treat comprehensively—even by committees. As a result, we neglected possible outcomes, overlooked alternative solutions, and could not predict the ultimate impact of the resulting policy on values.

Sensitivity. Ultimately the reorganization failed to concentrate its energies on the model that would have satisfied the ambitions of all parts of the university: an incremental reform model. Revolution inevitably produces reaction. All power to the French people one day, and to Thermidor the next. If change is to be permanent, it must be gradual. The incremental reform model depends on a rotating nucleus of persons who continuously read the data provided by the organization and the society around it for clues that it is time to adapt. These persons are not faddists, but they are hypersensitive to an idea whose hour has come. In a university such persons know when an idea is antithetical to the values of an academic institution and when it extends the definition of a university and makes it more viable. One cannot structure these critical nuclei, but an organization cannot guarantee continuous self-renewal without them. At Buffalo a few departments and programs developed these nuclei. Most did not.

5. Do not settle for rhetorical change. We accomplished the change at Buffalo by fiat. The faculty senate announced that the president's plan had been ratified. (This was a good beginning, but only that. Ratification occurred only two months after Meyerson arrived and almost one year before the plan was implemented. The senate was not exactly representative and the plans were barely understood. It was basically a paper plan with virtually no commitment except to a vague and poetic vision.) Significant change does not take place that way. An organization has two structures: one on paper and another one, deep, that is a complex set of intramural relationships. A good administrator creates a good fit between the two. We allowed ourselves to be swept along by our rhetoric and neglected the much more demanding business of building new constituencies and maintaining established ones.

6. Do not allow those who are opposed to change to appropriate

such basic issues as academic standards. I became Meyerson's academic vice-president in August of 1968. Members of the old guard soon began to accuse me of being soft on standards. I had refused to disavow some of the more flagrant abuses of self-evaluation in the new colleges, and I had failed publicly to chastise faculty who subverted traditional academic practices as part of the radical revolution (although I did so unofficially).

Silence. The problem of academic standards soon became a political issue. Privately we avowed our commitment to standards; publicly we were silent. The approach was notably unsuccessful. We did not want to undermine the fledgling colleges or violate the rights of radical faculty members. After "fascist," "McCarthyite" is the dirtiest word you can use on a liberal campus, and none of us was eager to hear it. We allowed the least change-oriented faculty members to make the issue of standards their own. They persuaded a great majority of moderate faculty members that administration was committed to change-for-change's sake, whatever the price in academic excellence. We made a mistake that no successful revolutionary ever makes: we did not make sure that respectable people were unafraid of what was about to happen.

7. Know the territory. A peculiar balance exists between the city of Buffalo and its one major university. Buffalo is not a university town like Princeton or Ann Arbor. The university is not powerful enough to impose its style and values on the city. Philadelphia and Los Angeles have several powerful universities that divide the city's attention and diffuse its rancor. Buffalo has a single target for its noisy anti-intellectuals. Two years ago some powerful forces in the town tried to close the university. I do not know of another campus in the country that has had to function with such constant unsympathetic pressure from the surrounding community. (The period I had in mind was the year of Kent State. From all I have heard about Meyerson's successor, he has worked hard at reviving a more sympathetic and supportive reaction to the campus.)

Meyerson barely had arrived in Buffalo when a group called "Mothers Against Meyerson" (MAM) began to petition for his removal. Their argument was that he was a Jew (a charge erroneously made against Meyerson's predecessor by an earlier group, "Mothers Against Furnas") and that the campus harbored such dangerous criminal types as critic Leslie Fiedler.

Buffalo blamed the disruptions of 1970 on the "permissiveness" of the new administration. I got mail recommending that Curtis LeMay succeed Meyerson as university president. The local exmarine who nominated LeMay believed that only the general's exotic blend of authoritarianism and right-wing values could undo the harm that we had perpetrated.

We never mastered the politics of local chauvinism. At the same time that the national press was romancing the university, one of the two local dailies was libeling her unmercifully. We devoted too little energy and imagination to public relations.

8. Appreciate environmental factors. Like any other human activity, change proceeds more smoothly in optimal environmental conditions. Buffalo's chief environmental problem was not its miserable weather. (Buffalo has two seasons—winter and the 4th of July. Residents recognize summer as three weeks of bad ice skating.) The problem at Buffalo was (and still is) overcrowding. The faculty we recruited expected to move their books into futuristic offices like those promised by the architect's model of the new campus. Instead, they moved in on top of the faculty already there. The university assembled some prefab annexes for the overflow. Barbara Solomon, writing on the paranoia at Buffalo, noted that we pursued the life of the mind in quarters so ugly as to seem calculated. (Her article, "Life in the Yellow Submarine," appeared in a 1968 issue of *Harper's*. It pictured S.U.N.Y.-Buffalo at the crest of the Meyerson dream, zany, careening, spectacularly lush, as played by the Marx Brothers in a World War II movie set of sallow, wooden barracks.)

The new university campus barely had begun to rise by the time we reached the originally proposed completion date of 1972. The university had to lease an interim campus near the new campus site. Eleven academic departments moved out to this temporary facility in the spring of 1971. The leased buildings had been designed for commercial and light industry use. The fifteen-minute bus trip is a drag for students and the isolation of the interim campus is contrary to the whole spirit of the Meyerson plan.

We neglected to protect new programs from external forces. College A began an experimental program in community action that was housed off-campus because of space priorities. College A is located directly across from a parochial grammar school and a diocesan center for retarded children. Every time a Scarsdale Maoist wrote "fuck" on the wall or a braless coed played her guitar in the storefront window, the residents of the neighborhood understandably reacted. Students of College A were determined to interact with their neighbors; mothers of the schoolchildren were equally determined not to interact. They picketed. The wholebusiness snowballed, increasing the community's normally high level of outrage against the university.

9. Avoid future shock. Buffalo aspired to be the university of the year 2000. The future limited the campus just as the past limits the neurotic. The future insinuated itself into every attempt to deal with current issues and distorted our perception of the present. The unfinished new campus became an albatross, reminding everyone of the limited progress that was being made toward limitless goals. We put so much stock in the vision of future greatness that our disillusionment was inevitable. The problem with planning for the future is that there are no objective criteria against which to measure alternative solutions. There is not yet a contemporary reality against which to test. As a result the planner generates future shock along with valid ideas, and there is no surefire way to separate the two.

10. Allow time to consolidate gains. The average tenure of an American university president is now 4.4 years and decreasing. It is impossible to transform a university in so short a time. Only a year after Meyerson assumed the Buffalo presidency, rumors began to circulate that he was leaving. Supporters of the new administration feared abandonment. Social critic David Bazelon commented to me, "In every other university I've been to, the faculty hated the administration. Here they worry about desertion." The changes proposed by Meyerson depended on continued presidential support for their success. The campus had, in effect, undergone major surgery and did not have sufficient time to heal before a series of altogether different demands, including a semester of unrest, a new president, and a major recession, were made on it.

When Meyerson finally did resign in late January 1970, it was as though someone had prematurely pulled out the stitches.

The last guideline I offer to the would-be university reformer is so basic that it might well come first:

11. Remember that change is most successful when those who are affected are involved in the planning. This is a platitude of planning theory, and it is as true as it is trite. Nothing makes persons as resistant to new ideas or approaches as the feeling that change is being imposed upon them. The members of a university are unusually sensitive to individual prerogatives and to the administration's utter dependence on their support. Buffalo's academic plan was not generated popularly. Students and faculty did not contribute to its formulation. People resist change, even of a kind they basically agree with, if they are not significantly involved in the planning. A clumsier, slower, but more egalitarian approach to changing the university would have resulted in more permanent reform.

Surprise. The problems surrounding innovation and change in an entrenched bureaucracy are not peculiar to universities. Every modern bureaucracy—university, government or corporation—is essentially alike and responds similarly to challenge and to crisis, with much the same explicit or implicit codes, punctilios and mystiques.

Bureaucracy is the inevitable—and therefore necessary—form for governing large and complex organizations. Essentially we must find bureaucratic means to stimulate the pursuit of truth—that is, the true nature of the organization's problems—in a spirit of free inquiry, and under democratic methods. This calls for those virtues our universities and colleges have proved so capable of inspiring in others: an examined life, a spirit of inquiry and genuine experimentation, a life based on discovering new realities, of taking risks, suffering occasional defeats, and not fearing the surprise of the future.

The model for truly innovative and creative organizations in an era of enormous change becomes nothing less than the scientific spirit. The model for science becomes the model for all.

Assault. Now, four years after the dream was born, the campus mood is dismal. Many of the visionaries are gone—those left must live with the wreckage. The spirit of change has been stamped out.

Meyerson has officially disappeared. The state considers his administration to have been the reign of an educational antipope. There is rarely mention of him or his works.

Last year the American Council on Education released its current evaluation of the nation's graduate programs. Buffalo had improved dramatically in the ACE ratings. The university proudly held a news conference at which campus officials announced that the upgrading of graduate education at Buffalo took place under the late President Furnas.

What saddens me is a suspicion that this gross assault would have been successful if we had been more effective. Meyerson wanted to transform the university, but the current administration resembles that of Meyerson's predecessor, Clifford Furnas. By all appearances, our efforts changed nothing.

Epilogue

I wrote the above several months after I resigned from Buffalo—an outsider, though still living in Buffalo, supported by a grant from the Twentieth Century Fund. Outsiders and expatriates adopt a more critical perspective, I suppose, than those who remain.

Perhaps this article is not "objective" truth but "exiled" truth, not especially appropriate for those presently at Buffalo. Still and all, I would hope that some external validation of their former plight will help sustain their vitality.

At the same time, I hope that this critique of the Buffalo attempts at change will provide a template of action—for myself and my new Cincinnati administration, for faculty and students as well—that will conform more closely to a humane and democratic effort at university reform. We begin with more total community support and involvement than is enjoyed by any other urban university.

Evaluation

17 On Neglect of the Independent Variable in Program Evaluation

W. W. Charters, Jr.
John E. Jones

A common practice in evaluating experimental programs in education is to rest the innovation's case on comparisons of student outcome data, using results of standardized achievement tests or specially designed measures of cognitive or affective attributes. Concern with such outcome measures is eminently reasonable, of course, since it addresses what is probably the most important question asked by educators and laymen about any new program: "Does it really make an appreciable difference for students?"

Pressed to answer this kind of question, evaluators expend considerable resources in developing appropriate outcome measures and in planning and executing elaborate research designs. Well-planned evaluation studies involve collecting outcome data in "experimental" schools or classes where the program has been introduced and in "control" situations, carefully matched with "experimentals," to rule out the effects of critical extraneous factors. Comparisons may extend to variations in the type of innovative program at stake. More

Reprinted from W. W. Charters, Jr., and John E. Jones, *On Neglect of the Independent Variable in Program Evaluation.* Project MITT Occasional Paper (Eugene, Ore.: Center for Educational Policy and Management, University of Oregon, 1974). An abridged version of this article appeared in the November 1973 issue of *Educational Researcher* under the title, "On the Risk of Appraising Non-Events in Program Evaluation."

advanced designs entail collecting the outcome data on a before-after basis so that gains in student achievement can be compared.

What is not standard practice in evaluation studies is to describe fully, let alone to measure, how the programs in "experimental" and "control" situations actually differ from one another—or even to certify that they do. As educational researchers well know, characterization of the independent variable is a major bugaboo of program evaluation. Except in tightly controlled studies conducted in laboratory-like settings, experimental programs rarely "hold still" for the evaluator; they are subject to modification, refinement, and reinterpretation as they are put into practice in the field. Beyond this, however, evaluators encounter difficulty in describing in principle the essential dimensions according to which a proposed program differs from a conventional one. Neither the analytical language nor measurement techniques are available.

A serious consequence of slighting the independent variable is that elaborately designed evaluation studies may sometimes end up appraising nonevents, with no one the wiser. There are certainly circumstances in which differences between what researchers regard as "experimental" and "control" programs are more fictional than factual, but in the absence of a measurement technology or tradition, such circumstances may well go undetected. Then the researchers' findings of no consistent differences in student outcomes between "experimental" and "control" programs can fundamentally mislead educators regarding the substantive worth of innovations.

These observations are far from original with us, but the apposition of two studies recently completed at the University of Oregon so aptly illustrates the point that we feel impelled to report them. The innovative program in question was differentiated staffing (DS, for short), and the first study to be described was a doctoral investigation seeking, in the candidate's words, "to assess the relative effects of differentiated staffing on elementary students' achievement."

Student Outcomes of "Differentiated Staffing"

The doctoral investigation had a commendable objective, given the wide popularity differentiated staffing has attained in the last several years. The candidate chose for his evaluative study an elementary school (we will call it Efstutt School) in which a DS program was to be installed in the 1970-71 school year and another school across town in the same district (Gordon School) that was not implicated in the district's federally funded DS Project. Restricting the study to fifth and sixth graders, his plan was to administer the Comprehensive Test of Basic Skills in the early fall in both schools and again, using the parallel form of the test, in the late spring of the school year. He obtained information indicating that the fifth- and sixth-grade pupils were closely similar in the two schools with respect to IQ and socio-economic status—two factors that might otherwise account for differences in achievement scores.

The investigator described in some detail the DS plan that was to be introduced in Efstutt School that fall, drawing for his descriptions on the proposal the Efstutt faculty had developed in the preceding spring. Briefly, his description was this. Efstutt's thirteen classroom teachers were organized into three instructional teams to conduct the teaching program for the first and second graders, the third and fourth graders, and the fifth and sixth graders. One teacher on each team was appointed team leader and paid an additional salary. Cross-cutting this arrangement were curriculum teams responsible for curriculum development in each of four teaching areas, again with appointed leaders. A high-level professional position was established in the school—that of instructional coordinator—whose occupant was to function in a supportive role to the teachers and teams. One teacher on each of the instructional teams was designated an associated instructor, thereby distinguishing him from the more senior teachers, or instructors. Additionally, twelve noncertificated personnel were hired in Efstutt to serve as teacher assistants, and the instructional teams had the service of part-time clerical aides. There were several other features of the DS plan, including job descriptions for the various positions that had been drawn up by the Efstutt faculty, but those we have reported represent the main ones.

Insofar as Gordon, the comparison school, was concerned, the investigator merely pointed out that it was staffed according to the "traditional elementary instructional model."

[What were the] findings for student achievement in the "experimental" and "control" schools at the end of the year? They were mixed: achievement score gains did not consistently favor either Efstutt or Gordon. There were no differences between the schools on the reading test of the Comprehensive Test of Basic Skills. On the language section, Efstutt's fifth graders showed greater gains than Gordon's, but Gordon's sixth graders gained more than Efstutt's. On arithmetic, there were no school differences at the fifth-grade level, but Gordon's sixth graders outgained Efstutt's.

Thus, a reader of the study would be tempted to draw the conclusion that, in this instance, at least, differentiated staffing failed to produce consistently and appreciably greater achievement outcomes than the traditional staffing pattern. Certainly, the two schools did not differ strongly on the dependent variable, but did they differ on the independent variable? Precisely what was the contrast at stake? The investigator, of course, intended the contrast to be between "differentiated" and "traditional" staffing, and the study's published conclusions are phrased in these terms, but a close reading of the dissertation reveals that no procedures were used to certify that the staff organization operated differently in the two schools.[1] The independent variable was neither described nor measured in regard to its actual manifestation.

That inattention to the independent variable can lead to mistaken inference is the point we now want to document.

Staff Organization—Behaviorally Described

The second study we will report was initiated and conducted independently of the doctoral investigation but, as chance would have it, in the same location. Efstutt had been one of four schools that researchers at the Center for the Advanced Study of Educational Administration (CASEA) had chosen during the summer of 1970 for in-depth investigations into the problems of implementing major organizational innovations. One researcher, the second author of this paper, virtually lived in Efstutt during the 1970-71 school year making detailed observations and records of the course of the DS implementation.

Simultaneously, another group of CASEA researchers was developing instruments for use in more extensive studies. The purpose of these instruments was to measure role behavior and relationships of school staffs. By asking teachers to describe what they do on the job, with whom they talk and collaborate in their work, what realms of discretion they do and do not have, and so on, it would be possible to measure the work operations of the school along a number of

---

1. At the end of the dissertation, the candidate reported some informal observations regarding the "attitudes" of teachers toward the DS project which would alert a careful reader to the possibility that differentiated staffing was not operational in Efstutt during the 1970-71 year. The study's findings, however, are unlikely to enter the archives of research on educational practice except through the summary in *Dissertation Abstracts,* where the comparison is flatly described as between "a differentiated staffing school" and a "nondifferentiated staffing school."

dimensions of organizational analysis. Differentiated staffing is supposed to replace the essentially autonomous work operations of teachers in conventional elementary schools with articulated work groups, differentiated by skill and responsibility, serving as the basic units for carrying out the instructional program. Organizational dimensions regarded by the researchers as particularly relevant included the division of instructional labor, degree of specialization, extent of task interdependencies and work-oriented interaction, and the locus of instructional decisions, to name a few. Thus, the measures could be used to determine whether or not a staff was organized, behaviorally speaking, in accordance with key features of the differentiated staffing model.

The main instrument was field tested in three of the case study schools, including Efstutt, in the late spring of 1971—toward the end of the first year of implementation efforts. Efstutt's case investigator, who, of course, had learned about the doctoral study, seized on an opportunity and arranged for the CASEA questionnaire to be administered to teachers in Gordon School as well.

Details of the Efstutt case study have been published elsewhere, as have the instrument data comparing Efstutt and Gordon Schools, but their combined findings can be quickly reviewed. (See Jones, 1973; also Charters, 1973.)

While Efstutt teachers had been assigned to cross-graded Instructional Teams for joint instruction, for all intents and purposes, the educational program continued to be carried out in self-contained classrooms. Each classroom teacher continued to teach all subjects to the same students (except physical education) just as in Gordon School, and although Efstutt teachers at certain grade levels occasionally attempted cross-classroom grouping of students, their efforts did not last. Indeed, by the end of the year, there were more instances of close teacher collaboration in Gordon than in Efstutt.

As for Efstutt's curriculum teams, they were virtually inoperative. They met twice during the year for the purpose of selecting teaching materials and ordering supplies.

The position of instructional coordinator was filled by a well-qualified, experienced person from outside the school system, but the position turned out to be an awkward one, and the incumbent did not function entirely as expected. She was shunted by the principal into peripheral activities associated mainly with training the contingent of paraprofessionals, and she had difficulty in working out a meaningful role with the teachers, who were reluctant to accept her on a collegial basis. In the end, she came to serve in a role much like that of a vice-principal.

The distinction between instructor and associate instructor was totally inoperative in Efstutt. While the job descriptions had indicated a limited and subordinate role for the associate instructors, in practice the tasks they performed were indistinguishable from those of any other teacher. They were on the same salary schedule as all other teachers in the district. Staff members themselves were never heard to use the term "associate instructor" throughout the entire year, and on one occasion, when the case investigator asked the principal to identify the associate instructors, he had to check his records to recall whom he had designated.

Profiles of task performance of teachers in Efstutt and Gordon were nearly identical, with only a few important differences out of sixty-seven items. There was no evidence of the emergence of specializations among Efstutt teachers, but they spent less time than the Gordon staff on clerical chores, due to the presence of clerical aids. At the same time, they devoted less time and effort to a series of tasks indicative of the individualization of instruction than was true among teachers in the so-called "conventional" school (like working with small groups, doing diagnostic work on learning problems, or holding remedial sessions). And at the end of the school year, Efstutt teachers were inordinately involved in pupil management tasks as a result of their large classes.

The presence of paraprofessionals created the most pronounced differences in staff organization, behaviorally speaking, between Efstutt and Gordon Schools. The differences were not always as expected. Teacher assistants were apportioned to classroom teachers on a one-to-one basis rather than to the instructional teams as such. The close relationship of the teacher and his classroom assistant brought an entirely new dimension into the Efstutt organization. The total volume of interpersonal communication increased dramatically as a result of the new dyads, and it was communication in which teachers (for once) talked to another adult about the intimate details of their classroom work.

Thanks to the DS plan, though, Efstutt's classes were unusually large for the district—averaging about thirty-seven pupils in contrast to Gordon's twenty-four—and the Efstutt faculty relied heavily on their assistants to carry the added burden. This did not work for several reasons. For one thing, the assistants were inexperienced in managing pupils and were unable to invoke the authority of a teacher. For another thing, the assistants were on a shortened daily schedule and did not arrive early enough to participate in planning the day's activities or work out their responsibilities with the teachers. (This was changed later in the school year.) In consequence, the presence of the teacher assistants failed to relieve teachers of the extra burden of large classes and, in fact, exacerbated the problems of instruction and of pupil control.

In sum, the CASEA case study information makes it clear that in many respects the Efstutt staff was not behaving as a "differentiated staff" by late spring of 1971, and the comparative measures taken at the same time indicated that on several key dimensions Efstutt's educational program was operationally organized in a fashion almost identical to Gordon's. That differences existed between the two schools, there can be no doubt. There were three dominating concerns among the Efstutt teaching faculty during the year that, insofar as our data can tell us, distinguish it from the Gordon faculty: how to cope with teaching oversized classes, how to establish viable work relations with teaching assistants, and, above all, how to regain the control the teachers felt they had lost over pupils in their classrooms. All three can be traced to Efstutt's participation in the DS project. These differences, however, can hardly be conceived as defining a "differentiated staffing" versus "traditional" staff organization, and they are certainly not conditions from which one would predict appreciably greater gains in achievement for the Efstutt case.

These are the reasons, then, that it would be wrong to attribute differences in student outcome measures, or lack of such differences, to an independent variable described as "differentiated staffing" versus "traditional" organization. The dissertation study that was designed to assess the effects of differentiated staffing turned out to be appraising a nonevent.

Levels of Reality in Program Description

Are we too hasty, though, in saying that Efstutt was not a differentiated staffing school? After all, a cadre of teaching assistants had been employed, the position of instructional coordinator had been created and filled, instructional and curriculum teams were formed and their leaders appointed, and so on. Formally speaking, there were sixteen faculty and staff categories listed for Efstutt School— twice as many as for Gordon. Even though staff members did not perform roles precisely as anticipated by the vision of differentiated staffing, Efstutt unequivocally was a different school from Gordon in a number of important respects, and it was different from what it had been the previous year. These differences can certainly be laid to Efstutt's participation in the Differentiated Staffing Project of the district, so in what sense was Efstutt not a differentially staffed school?

Our studies of the innovation process at CASEA have required us to grapple with the definitional problem time and again. At what point can one say, for example, that an innovation has been adopted? How does the investigator establish that a so-called new program is generically different from the one it replaced, other than the name by which it is called? In general, how is change in a school's educational program to be conceived and measured?

As a first step, we have found it useful to distinguish four levels of reality of a school's program. We refer to them as "levels" because they are ordered according to their proximity to the attributes of students which they are designed to affect—learning outcomes. In our listing, below, they run from the most remote, in terms of functional relationships with the covert psychological processes of learning, to the most proximal. We consider them levels of "reality" because, from an organizational point of view, they each carry distinct, observable social consequences, by deliberate intent and in fact.

It is most natural for us to discuss the levels from the standpoint of program change, but this should not obscure the fact that the discussion applies equally well to program differences, such as in the comparison of two schools. We are, after all, concerned with the independent variable(s) of program evaluation, and by *variable* we mean some identified property of an object that can take on different values, whether from one time to another or from one instance to another. It is not our present purpose, however, to suggest variables but only the levels at which they might be sought.

Level 1. Institutional commitment. A public announcement that a school intends to introduce such and such an educational program is an event of significance, especially as it emanates from an authoritative source and embodies a more or less binding commitment on organization members. It is intended to have consequences, and it does. An authoritative commitment is designed to set directions and goals for staff members, to legitimize the reallocation of resources, to elicit enthusiasm and support, and so on, and it often has other effects as well, such as arousing vocal opposition to the plan in various sectors of the community or school. If the commitment is binding, as may be the case of a contract with a funding agency, school personnel may find themselves under close scrutiny and may be called to account for their failure to deliver at some later date. In any event, an institutional commitment alters the field of forces governing the actions of organizational participants in and out of the school and introduces new conditions with which they must contend.

One level of program description, then, is found in authoritative pronouncements, statements of intention, promises. It corresponds to Smith and Keith's (1971, chapter 2) concept of the school's formal doctrine and is analyzable according to the dimensions they suggest.[2] Few eavluators, of course, would be content to end their specification of the independent variable at this level.

Level 2. Structural context. "Structural" alterations refer to those changes in formal arrangements and physical conditions that form the context within which staff members carry out an educational program. They are usually of the sort that can be effectuated by managerial directives or acts and include such things as employing people, establishing pay rates, changing job titles, forming and appointing committees, assigning responsibilities, purchasing instructional materials, making equipment available, knocking out classroom walls, scheduling classes, and so on. Level 2 changes usually can be easily documented. While structural supports are minimal for some types of programmatic innovation, extensive contextual alterations are essential for other types. Differentiated staffing is a case in point. Structural alterations can be seen as varying in the compellingness of their impact on staff behavior. A school faculty may readily ignore changes in job descriptions or titles, but the daily presence of a paraprofessional in a teacher's classroom has inescapable consequences for the teachers, whether as intended or otherwise.

While structural features are easily observed, the investigator's problem lies in having at hand few generic dimensions according to which the features can be ordered. Currently, our language for program description consists largely of ill-defined nominal categories, or trade names, designed to promote and sell rather than to classify and analyze.

Level 3. Role performance (staff perspective). In denoting the third level of program description, we come close to what Gross and his colleagues meant in their discussion of the "degree of actual implementation" of organizational innovations. (See Gross, Giacquinta, and Bernstein, 1971.) In their view, the behavior patterns of teachers must be observed to change, and change so as to accord with the role performance required by the innovation, before it can be said that an innovation is actually implemented. It is the teacher's use of new instructional packages, for instance, that constitutes an innovation, not the mere presence of the packages in the classroom. It goes

2. Besides proposing a number of dimensions of variation in formal doctrines, these authors postulate various organizational consequences that can be expected from them.

almost without saying that behavioral changes of teachers do not automatically follow from the structural alterations and institutional commitments that are designed to produce them; less apparent, though, is the possibility that structural changes may induce behavioral adaptations on the part of staff members that are contrary to intentions. The behavioral consequences that ensued from the presence of teacher assistants in Efstutt's classrooms is a case in point.

Again, the evaluator is hampered by the absence of an analytical language suited to describing a school's work system in behavioral terms, and the observational problem is more severe than in structural description. Measurement entails relational as well as individual-performance aspects or roles, such as patterns of task interdependence, which cannot be discerned from one teacher's behavior alone.

Level 4. Learning activities (student perspective). The manifest purpose of the teacher's role performance is to produce learning in students, but this cannot happen directly. The best the teacher can do is to induce students to engage in activities deemed instrumental to the covert psychological processes he hopes to affect. It is the student's own activities and experiences that are most immediately related to learning outcomes, albeit the teacher has an important hand in arranging them so that the link is made. Yet, the most skillfully executed science demonstration will teach nothing to the boy who is in the lavatory marking on the walls. Opportunities for slippage are enormous between the teacher's performance as an instructional agent and the student's performance of the activities that are supposed to be instrumental to learning, quite apart from the general uncertainties as to what activities are instrumental, and it is of no small importance for program evaluators to attempt to describe or measure the school's educational program as experienced and enacted by students.

Given the many contingenies and contravening circumstances between what a student does in school and what he learns from what he does, the evaluator (or school man) might consider himself fortunate if he found anything other than "no significant differences" between program variations at even this most intimate level. In fact, we are inclined to the view that the local school's responsibility for a child's education ends at Level 4—at the point where the student is found to be engaging in, and engaged by, sequences of instructional events which, according to the best contemporary knowledge of pedagogy available to the school, have a reasonably high probability of producing the desired learning outcomes. To hold a school system accountable for the measured outcomes, themselves, seems to be an unwarranted shift to one institution of the responsibility that more properly rests in the pedagogical sciences and the R&D community. In this view, carefully devised measures of variables at Level 4 would replace achievement test scores as the criterion variable in program evaluation. If the view be regarded as extreme, at least such measures should be developed and used as intermediate criteria of program impact, giving the educational innovator something more tangible, or less tenuous, than changes in achievement scores by which to gauge his progress.

Figure 17-1 depicts the four levels of program description we have discussed. It makes apparent the torturous path between an announced intention to change an educational program and demonstrable changes in students' psychological capacities. Not only is a time lag implied but each section of the path is endowed with equivocality. For one thing, the state of the educational program at each of the levels is the product of many forces, only a fraction of which are subject to intentional manipulation and rational planning. This is increasingly true as we move from Level 1 to Level 4 in the diagram. Just as school experiences determine a small part of what children know, so the structures created by the educational innovator only partially determine how the instructional staff behaves, and the staff, in turn, governs only some of what the child experiences in school.

For another thing, plans have a habit of going awry. When one sets out to alter the state of the educational program at one level with the

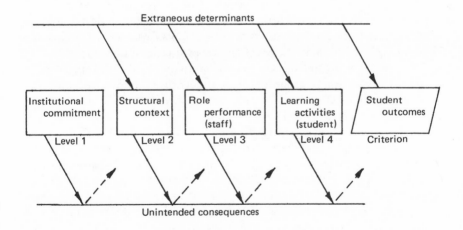

FIGURE 17-1
Levels of program description

intention of affecting the program at the next level in as complex a social system as the school, he can count on producing side effects and unintended consequences, and sometimes these work in opposition to the very effects he sought to bring about. We have alluded to a few of these in our discussion of the Efstutt case, and others could be cited. In the high school studied by CASEA investigators, for example, the human relations training given the staff to promote "openness" and readiness for change apparently crystallized among them a norm of equalitarianism that was in distinct conflict with the hierarchical features of the differentiated staffing plan. (See Wacaster, 1973.) In any event, each of the linkages in the chain of Figure 17-1 is problematic.

Our examination of the levels of program description helps put in perspective the question of whether or not Efstutt can be called a "differentiated staffing school." The answer depends on the level at which one chooses to describe the school. The doctoral investigator characterized Efstutt's program principally on the basis of documents accompanying the institutional commitment to differentiated staffing (Level 1), although taking account of the fact that the proposed alterations in structural context were, indeed, introduced (Level 2), while our measures and case-study data focused on the role performance of the staff (Level 3). There is no question but that Efstutt and Gordon Schools differed in commitment and structure during the 1970-71 school year, but the change in Efstutt gave rise to few of the behavioral consequences that were expected. Most of the Level 3 consequences were unattained or unintended, and some of the latter were counterproductive. Only with a Level 3 description in mind, then, is it fair to say that Efstutt was not a "differentiated staffing school" or that the investigator evaluated a nonevent.

Our analysis points up the essential futility of testifying to the worth of educational programs by comparing student outcome measures between classrooms, or schools, that differ only at the most functionally remote levels of program description. Not only is it futile, but it is seriously misleading to the field of professional education. Inherently valid educational ideas can all too readily be "proven" worthless by impressively designed statistical studies that, nevertheless, are remiss in certifying that program variation in fact occurred at a suitably proximal level of description. In our view, it is an abrogation of professional responsibility for program evaluators to collect achievement test data, as easy as they may be to come by, without simultaneously going to extraordinary lengths to document the program differences or changes at least at Level 3 and preferably at Level 4 of program description. Obviously, for evaluators to meet this responsibility, it is incumbent on the R&D community to develop the analytical language, the variables, and the techniques of measurement for establishing the state of the independent variable at one or another of these levels.

In closing, we would remark that each of the linkages shown in Figure 17-1 is worthy of detailed, extended investigation. Each is extremely complex yet essential to a full explication of the means by which the school is to achieve its prime mission. Thus, the study of the school's organization and management, though ostensibly dealing with matters peripheral to the core issues of instruction and learning, can be seen as helping to forge links in the causal chain connecting the goals we desire and seek through our educational institutions, on the one hand, with the goals we are able to attain, on the other.

References

Charters, W. W., Jr. (1973). *Measuring the Implementation of Differentiated Staffing: A Comparison of Two Elementary Schools.* Monograph No. 26. Eugene, Ore.: Center for the Advanced Study of Educational Administration, University of Oregon.

Gross, Neal, Giacquinta, Joseph B., and Bernstein, Marilyn (1971). *Implementing Organizational Innovations: A Sociological Analysis of Planned Educational Change.* New York: Basic Books.

Jones, John E. (1973). "A Case Study of a Selected Elementary School under Conditions of Planned Change." Unpublished dissertation, Syracuse University.

Smith, Louis M., and Keith, Pat M. (1971). *Anatomy of Educational Innovation.* New York: Wiley.

Wacaster, C. T. (1973). "The Life and Death of Differentiated Staffing in Columbia High School: Discontinuance of an Innovation." Unpublished dissertation, University of Oregon.

Political

18 Curriculum Change at the Local Level: A Case Study

David H. Hampson

Education and Politics

It has become a tradition in the field of education that schools could and should be separated from politics. Educators are becoming increasingly aware, however, that the practice of education cannot exist in a political vacuum. Leadership in education, be it in the school, the district office, or the university, includes a political dimension. Echoing this perspective, Sestak and Frerich (1968) have written:

> The public school can succeed only to the extent that it holds the understanding, interest, and confidence of the people. In a democracy the public school belongs to the people, and it cannot progress beyond the current level of public opinion. Educational policy is public policy, and only the citizens can make public policy in a democratic way [page 118].

However, as the Longstreth (1966) study corroborates, educational administrators are still relatively naïve concerning the power structure of their district. Of representatives of fifteen different sectors examined as to the identity of men in the power structure of the district, superintendents ranked fourteenth in their awareness of the power structure. This isolation of schools from the political system of the district does not bode well for school systems concerned with change. Failure to perceive relationships between education and political decision making can no longer be tolerated if educators are to play a leading role in the future of their profession and of the schools they serve.

Curriculum Issues and Political Processes

It follows, from this general aversion of educational systems for political processes, that both practitioners and researchers in the field of education have traditionally viewed curriculum issues as being separate from ordinary political processes and have regarded curriculum decisions as essentially "a professional matter to be decided on technical grounds by teachers, principals, supervisors, and directors of curriculum" (Kirst and Walker, 1970).

Any curriculum change process involves groups and individuals outside as well as inside the immediate school system, however, and the professional educator who only sees educational change as an internal concern ignores a broad range of forces outside the school environment that could easily overpower forces generated from within the system. Goldhammer (1965, page 1) stated: "It is evident that changes cannot be accomplished if they provoke rejection or broad-scaled dissatisfaction among either a policy-controlling or a consuming body." Brickell (1967, page 138), in reiterating this position, has argued that change cannot be accomplished unless "the learning goals of the school are acceptable to the external control and support system, i.e., the public in the case of the public school."

Gallup (1969) claimed that "there is a great interest in the areas that most school publicity presently neglects . . . [that is, in] the content of courses and the educational process versus school operations." The increasing interest and involvement of groups and individuals other than those traditionally associated with curriculum change process is a development that practicing educators must consider. Educators must become increasingly aware that they alone cannot make decisions based on the traditionally accepted professional standards; they must invite, and be prepared to accept, input from other sources.

This, then, forms the basis for a case study of curriculum change process at the local level, a study that traces the path of a single course change in the social studies curriculum within a selected school district. As the change process unfolds, there is an attempt to locate the *decision points* in the curriculum change process, the *actors* and their *modes of input* into the decision points, and, finally, the *change strategies* that emerge from the interplay between the actors and their modes of input into the decision points. While the event examined may be defined as an episodic issue in the life of the school district under examination, it does seem to highlight the problems, dilemmas, and interaction that local school systems face in planning and undertaking change.

The School District

Palo Alto nestles beneath the Stanford hills, in the shadow of a major university. With a high tax base and a population of 56,000, 98 percent of which is white, the district can be characterized as middle to upper class, with liberal leanings. The fact that over 80 percent of its operating income comes from local property tax, 17 percent from state funds, and only about 1.75 percent from federal sources is reflected in its demographic breakdown.

The first public school was built in 1893 by four volunteer carpenters. Now the district supports approximately 15,000 students in twenty-one elementary schools, three junior high schools, and three senior high schools. In nationwide achievement measures the students score high. In the Sequential Tests of Education Progress at grade 8, in reading, 85 percent of the students score above the median; in mathematics, 81 percent. Over 80 percent of the student population goes on to college.

The school district is perceived as successful by the community. The superintendent sees educational opportunity as an inducement for prospective employers and professional groups to come into the area. Similarly, many community members regard the strong academic pattern as a motivation for people to move into the district. As one community member put it, "People move into this town, sometimes at a substantial financial sacrifice, because they want their kids in the mold."

The Change Studied

The curriculum change process centered around the decision to adopt, within the social studies curriculum, a course entitled "American Political Behavior." The course had been developed by the High School Curriculum Center in Government at Indiana University.

The center had been established jointly by the Department of Government and the Indiana University School of Education in June 1966, with a grant from the United States Office of Education. The purpose of the center was to formulate a civics course for ninth-grade students based on the role of the individual in the American political system.

For one to understand and examine the change process surrounding the implementation of the American Political Behavior (APB) course, it must be viewed within the context of the historical roots of the wider social studies framework that the district hoped to undertake, at least until the specific change process involving the APB course emerged.

Groundwork

In social studies the bodies that make recommendations regarding the curriculum are traditionally steering committees. Two such committees exist, one at the elementary school level and one at the secondary school level. At the elementary level the committee is made up of people especially interested or trained in the social studies who volunteer their services. At the secondary level, with which this study is concerned, membership is more formal, usually consisting of the six department chairmen (see Figure 18-1). It was this committee that laid out the recommendations for course revision in June 1964.

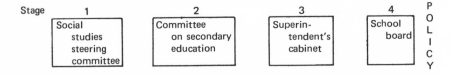

FIGURE 18-1
Committee stages through which a curriculum change has to pass
within the district (if the curriculum proposed is merely to
pilot a curriculum, the decision can be made at the
level of stage 3)

The committee (Palo Alto Unified School District, 1964) stated its intent as, "to chart a course of study, grades seven through twelve, for Palo Alto Secondary Schools. This is a long-range plan extending over five years." In their recommendations the steering committee stated their intention to look for "threads," representative of central human concerns, which would give meaning to factual content and offer unity to the curriculum as a whole. The first decision point in the change process had been reached.

The district social studies steering committee had been the actors at the first decision point. The decision to seek out and develop a new curriculum for grades seven through twelve was a "social process" type of decision. The steering committee had acted in an "authority" role, believing, as tradition provided, that such a decision was theirs to make. No external inputs had been called for or used. No change strategies are apparent, for none, it seemed, were needed. The decision to recommend a new curriculum approach to social studies and the opportunity to implement it fully were not, however, in accord. Two major factors, one internal and one external, impinged upon the ability of the social studies steering committee to develop and implement change.

Internally, the committee found the task of charting a new curriculum to be difficult. They found themselves on the growing tip of the "new social studies." While they were breaking fresh ground and developing new concepts, they produced some threads on which they were going to try and build, but the way proved difficult. Devising a new curriculum at the local level is extremely arduous. Only districts with a record of past success or with available resources—trained personnel, financial means, and willpower—should attempt the task. Even overriding these internal considerations is the question of whether somebody else is doing the same thing more successfully. Broad-ranging curriculum change at the local level is a major step, not to be undertaken lightly.

Externally, the committee found themselves hampered by state restrictions. The state code actually specified five out of six years of social studies in grades seven through twelve. Implementation of the recommendations of 1964 seemed a long way from realization.

Some isolated attempts had, however, met with limited success. One such development was at the ninth-grade level. In a letter to parents, dated October 12, 1966, six social studies teachers indicated that, though the course they taught was entitled "Modern European History 1500-1914," according to the state code, it had, in fact, "been evolving away from European history and toward a more unified social science approach" for three years. There were, it seemed, ways of getting around the state code.

External Influences and Opportunity

The school district's efforts to develop a new perspective and framework for the social studies curriculum received a boost in 1965. Almost one year after the district had made its "change" recommen-

dations, the State Board of Education established the statewide
Social Science Study Committee (Moody, 1968).

This committee was charged with four purposes:

1. to review the present (1962) social studies framework in the light of the new
   research in the social sciences . . . ;
2. to review and evaluate materials and data from the national social science
   projects . . . ;
3. to develop a new social studies framework; and
4. to identify activities needed for implementing the framework.

At approximately the same time, the school district was requested
by the State Department of Education to send an observer to the
state's social science committee meetings, which indicated that the
school district was soon likely to find support in the form of a state
framework.

Two significant actions undertaken at the state level had a re-
sounding influence upon curriculum change at the district level in
1968, a most significant year. The first was Senate Bill I (SBI as it
came to be known by opponents and supporters alike). It stated
that:

Because of economic, geographic, physical, political and social diversity, there is
a need for the development of educational programs at the local level, with the
guidance of competent and experienced education and citizens. Therefore it is
the intent of the Legislature districts to develop programs that will best suit the
needs and interests of the pupils [California, Education Code, 1968].

The bill, voted into law in May, had been delayed for two years by
a dispute over the mandatory inclusion of physical education in the
curriculum. The measure entitled the "George Miller, Jr., Education
Act of 1968," passed with only one legislator voting against it. One
district official called it "the Magna Carta of Education," and a member of the steering committee deemed it as "having a freeing effect
on the curriculum." Assemblyman John Know (D-Richmond) was
quoted as saying, "It gives local schools boards the tools to provide a
great revolution in education" (*San Jose Mercury*, 1968). Certainly it
"freed" the public schools from many of the chafing bonds of state
curriculum requirements. It also, as the *Palo Alto Times* (1968) espoused, "relieved the pressure of mandated subjects, which the legislature had loaded in the decade since Sputnik."

Amid the accolades, there was, however, one word of warning. It
came from Assemblyman Winfield A. Shoemaker (D-Santa Barbara).
A teacher by profession, he warned that giving power over curriculum decisions to local school boards "could lead to a 'political blood-

bath' in board elections between right wing and left wing groups" (*San Jose Mercury,* 1968). The warning was to assume greater significance in the coming years.

Senate Bill I had removed one of the major impediments to the development of a new social studies curriculum within the district. Freedom to implement without the necessary material or a workable plan was not very helpful to the district steering committee, however. The newly developed "Proposed State Framework" was to offer the skeleton upon which ideas could be fleshed, and it was this framework that was to prove the second significant external influence.

By fall 1968 the new state framework was ready to go to the State Board of Education for its approval. The district was, of course, aware of the form and direction proposed in the new framework. From copies circulated by the curriculum commission, the signs pointed to the framework as the very vehicle the district had lacked in their move toward curriculum change.

Not all the opinions being expressed about the new framework were positive. A letter exchanged between two members of the advisory team made the following recommendations on behalf of the State Department of Education:

Unfortunately, this proposed Social Science Framework, while it has some merit . . . fails to heed the mandate of the people . . . sets up its own criteria, . . . and concentrates on techniques of instruction, rather than on subject matter material . . . .

At a time when the whole nation is calling for a revival of moral principles . . . , of self discipline . . . , of values which govern all men . . . , there is too much lacking in this Framework to fulfill the needs of instruction in the Social Sciences. I strongly recommend against its adoption [Klotz, 1968].

The discussion of the proposed framework came to a head at a meeting of the State Board of Education on November 14 and 15, 1968. The board decided to recommend that the report of the social sciences study committee should be referred back to the curriculum commission (California, State Department of Education, 1968). For all intents and purposes, the 1962 framework still guided the school district, and the proposed framework was in limbo.

Search for a New Curriculum Leads to "American Political Behavior"

Meanwhile, the district social studies steering committee had been active. They had been impressed with what they had observed and had been told was coming from the Statewide Social Sciences Study Committee: "It gave a logical and spiraling look to the social studies."

The "proposed" state framework was to provide the lever that would enable the school district to overcome the second major impediment with which they were faced—that of the curriculum framework to be taught. In anticipation of the opportunities that the proposed framework would make available, the district steering committee had undertaken a series of steps to bring about curriculum change in the social studies.

First, they attempted to assemble a "bank" of information on social studies projects being undertaken across the nation. It was at this time that they contacted Howard Mehlinger and learned of the American political behavior course being developed at Indiana University. The project was just beginning, which would allow involvement from the ground floor onward, and Howard Mehlinger was looking for school districts in which to try his materials. The die was cast; the American political behavior course was to come to Palo Alto on a pilot basis.

Thus, in winter 1968 the second decision point was reached. This decision was again made at the level of the steering committee, though agreement was also obtained from the central administration —another example of a social-process-type of decision made by a steering committee as actors in authority roles. There was no opportunity for external input. Outside of the steering committee, not even teachers were consulted. Bolstered by their apparent position of authority, the steering committee adopted change strategy that operated from an established power base and used the power they saw as vested in themselves to implement change.

Pushing Ahead with the Change

After discussions with Indiana University and Mehlinger, it was decided that the American political behavior course would be offered on a pilot basis in two of the district's three junior high schools, Jordan and Terman, during the 1968-69 year.

During the summer of 1968, the Curriculum Center at Indiana held an institute for prospective teachers. Two teachers from the Palo Alto Unified School District went to Bloomington for eight weeks that summer. They joined forty-four other teachers, undertook a review of recent research in political science, studied the course, watched demonstration classes, critiqued the classes, and generally prepared themselves to teach the pilot courses within the district that fall.

All during the school year the course was taught to eighth graders in the form of a two-semester, thirty-six-week course. At the Palo

Alto preschool conference on social studies held in September 1969, the pilot course was described to other eighth-grade social studies teachers from the three junior high schools. Several teachers asked to be able to use the APB materials in their classes, expanding the total number of classes to six. The course was gaining teacher support.

The Administration Approaches the Board

In May 1969 the administration approached the district board of education for a study session. This was one year after Senate Bill I had successfully been negotiated through the legislature, six months after the state Board of Education had returned the "Proposed Framework" to the curriculum commission, and almost one year after the pilot program began.

Study sessions allow policy or other crucial district matters to be placed before the board for discussion. In the *Policy Manual* of the district these are included under the heading of "special meetings," and the description reads:

> No business shall be transacted at such a meeting except for that which is called. . . . Certain Special Meetings may be designated "Study Sessions." At such sessions no official action shall be taken [Palo Alto Unified School District, no date].

Though the session ended with some polite comments expressed by the board on the professional nature of the staff, and with general agreement that the framework would be favorable for the district, no definitive step was taken, or, indeed, could have been taken, owing to the rules governing such sessions. In light of the fact that decisions could not be made at such a session, it is a little surprising that so many of the participants, particularly within the district staff, came to assume that a decision had been made with regard to the social studies curriculum. Because the administration thought they had the green light to go ahead with the curriculum change, the ensuing controversy was a shock to the professional education community.

The District Moves Ahead

On the assumption that they had received a mandate to proceed with their plans for the social studies curriculum change, the administration, the steering committee, and the teachers began to put together a revised K-12 program. The American political behavior course was now into its second year as a pilot project. It appeared, both to the steering committee and to the administration, that it would become a regular course since it was gaining in teacher support and seemed to fit the direction in which the district had hoped to move.

Between December 1969 and February 1970 the District Second-ary Social Studies Steering Committee was extremely busy. On December 17, the members held an all-day meeting, during which they decided to recommend that the American political behavior course replace European history throughout all ninth-grade classes in 1970-71.

At this time the school district had no reason to feel their curricu-lum change plans might be challenged. In terms of curriculum change procedures, they had, as far as they understood, only assumed a role traditionally theirs. In addition, no indication of impending opposi-tion had emerged. In March the district had held a forum to acquaint parents with changes in the social studies program in the district and on a state-wide level, and there had been no apparent dissent. On July 6, 1970, therefore, a report on the state of the art was to be made to the school board. Given the preparedness of the administra-tion and the apparent lack of opposition, this seemed to be a routine step. It was, however, to prove otherwise.

The Administration Reports to the Board

The assistant superintendent for curriculum addressed the board first. He noted that the curriculum development efforts were influ-enced, though not limited by, the proposed state framework for so-cial studies. He was followed by teachers representative of the three levels of schooling: elementary, junior high, and senior high. The junior high speaker noted that, during the ninth grade, students would study how Americans behave politically. Their presentation complete, the steering committee representatives awaited the reac-tion of the board, but they were not prepared for the board's re-sponse, which was split: two positive, two skeptical. One member was absent. Community speakers also raised concerns. Would the stu-dents get a strong sense of the "American heritage"? Had parents been involved? On the latter issue, the assistant superintendent was forced to admit that there had been little parental involvement. No motions were offered, and no decisions were taken except to set a date for an in-depth study session in the first week of August, a meeting that would certainly not be routine in nature.

The next day, the *Palo Alto Times* (1970) ran an article under the headline, "Drastic New Social Studies Program Draws Mixed Reac-tion." Although the report quoted all the major viewpoints, there could be no doubt in the reader's mind that all was not well with the passage of the new social studies curriculum.

While members of the administration were preparing for the study session, they were rocked by an early attack on their proposals, an early disadvantage. Prior to the August 5 study session, a regular board meeting was held. A critique of the proposed curriculum developments had been submitted to the board by Dr. Lewis Gann (1970), a senior staff member at Stanford University's Hoover Institution and deputy curator of the institution's Africa collection. It was a critique that could not be passed over lightly.

Its criticisms ranged broadly from discussion of the style of certain materials, neglect of the role of personality in history, and lack of historical continuity through to the argument over contemporary versus traditional teaching. Essentially he was arguing for the development of historical facts and a historical frame of reference before encouraging analysis and criticisms.

The letter was important for two reasons. First, it had served to put the administration on the defensive (they were aware that the board and the community had opposing arguments on hand). Second, the author, being a scholar, represented intellectual opposition to the proposals.

The study session lasted for three and a half hours and was attended by some eighty people. Board members unhappy with the proposals centered their efforts on raising questions and asking for explanations. The reactions from the majority of the five-person board were not supportive. The meeting concluded with no action being suggested and no decisions made.

By midsummer, after the administration had come to the board with their proposals for curriculum change, the conflict was no nearer settlement. The general tenor of the two meetings had not been favorable. The board, for its part, had not made any decisions about the proposed changes; nor, indeed, had it been asked directly for such decisions. The members felt they had been sounded out about a "proposal," not asked to approve an implementation process.

The administration apparently believed it could proceed with curriculum changes, having been granted approval to move ahead at the May 1969 meeting. As a steering committee member commented, "I don't think it occurred to any of us that we had to go back again." Subsequent meetings with the board were viewed as merely keeping it informed.

In midsummer, after the board session, the assistant superintendent for curriculum authorized adopting an American political behavior course in place of a European history course throughout all ninth-grade district classes for the coming fall. He was later to say, "I certainly would not have authorized the department heads . . . to implement that program ... if I thought the community or the Board was going to polarize around it." The third decision point had come, and gone.

The decision to implement had been made by the assistant superintendent for curriculum. He was the sole actor with whom responsibility lay. He acted from the vantage point of an authority figure, believing that he would have the backing of the board, but he was to find his power base was nonexistent. The board reacted negatively to the move, feeling that their function had been usurped and that they had been bypassed. The assistant superintendent's strategy of change backfired as the district came to realize that it did not possess the power to implement change in this manner.

Fall Quarter: APB Replaces European History

Three issues were to develop out of the decision to offer the American political behavior course in the fall. The first was to center around the process by which the course was implemented. The second was to develop around the values perceived as being espoused in the course by some members of the community. The third, and the issue that was to emerge as central to the opponents of APB, was the fact that it replaced European history as the course of study.

The first indication that many students and parents had of the course change was when texts were issued or brought home for study. Criticisms were leveled that the administration had acted in a devious manner. One parental letter to the board charged:

It appears that the District saw the mounting concern of the School Board, parents, and influential people in the community, like Dr. Gann, and decided that the only way to make sure that the program would go through was to sneak it in and hope that nobody discovered it until it was too late to do anything about it [Palo Alto Unified School District, Board of Trustees, 1970].

Sensing the mounting opposition to the curriculum change and in anticipation of the first board meeting of the fall quarter, the assistant superintendent for curriculum prepared a memorandum for his superintendent. Pointing out the existing problems, he suggested that:

Comprehensive plans must be developed by which Board and other community members can become more knowledgeable of the staffs curriculum development ... and have opportunities to provide constructive criticism [Palo Alto Unified School District, 1970].

In the memorandum he went on to explain how such community participation might be accomplished. Recommendations ranged from scheduling board members for periodic observation sessions and urging parents to visit classes to offering adult education courses on the reform movement in the social studies. The administration had awakened, somewhat late, to their predicament.

The board did not favor the ninth-grade curriculum change that had been offered without their approval. Only one of the five members espoused no concern over the action of the professional staff. The board instructed the administration to send a letter to all ninth-grade parents informing them that their children were in an experimental program that had not received the board's approval, and making provisions for children who wished to take the original social studies program.

A letter inviting parents to a series of meetings at the junior high schools was duly sent out on September 25. Far from alleviating the problem, it only aggravated it in the minds of many community members. Two factors concerning the letter aroused community resentment. The first was the time allowed between when the letter was sent and when the meetings were scheduled. The letter was dated Friday, September 25, 1970; the meetings were scheduled for Tuesday, Wednesday, and Thursday of the following week. The earliest date the letters could have arrived in the homes of the ninth-grade parents was Monday, leaving some parents less than twenty-four hours to arrange to be at the meeting.

The second factor, stemming from the first, was that some community members perceived the action as an administrative ploy to railroad the new program through under the guise of following the board's directive. This perception was aided by the fact that the letter made no mention at all that this was not an approved course.

The rebuff of the district's curriculum change by the board and their demand that the community be informed of the board's concern may be noted as the fourth decision point in the change process. The board had emerged as the authority force, replacing the district administration and the district steering committee as the actors having input into the decision-making process.

The board's actions were also to have repercussions upon the strategies of change employed by the school district in implementing change. Until this decision point, the district had thought they possessed a mandate, based on the trust of the board and the community, to progress in this manner. Their strategies would require rethinking.

The subsequent lack of response from the community in requesting changes of curriculum (twenty-eight requested a change back to European history) might well have reflected the haste with which the meetings were called, rather than disinterest. It was this marginal result, however, that was subsequently transmitted back to the board at its meeting on October 5. The board decided the figure did not warrant setting up alternative classes. The administration, it seemed, could breathe a sigh of relief. Their curriculum change appeared to have surmounted the problem.

The respite was to be short lived, merely a lull in the interchange. An opposition community group was being organized and would soon be ready to enter the lists. The board, which still had not ruled on whether the course change was to be retained, preferred to see how the course was received over a trial period. They did not have to wait long.

The Community Opposition Group

Represented in the community opposition to the curriculum changes proposed by the school district were many philosophical and political perspectives. The group included university professors, lawyers, doctors, housewives, engineers, and an occasional teacher, certainly not the stereotype of a group developed to oppose educational change.

Just as the participants were diverse in background, so were they diverse in their philosophical orientation to the problem. Some approached the issue at hand feeling the proposed changes raised disturbing problems by "reason of its implicit assumptions, presentation and bias . . . ." (Gann, 1970). Others saw the curriculum change as an attempt to bring behavioral change into the classroom and eliminate individuality in the student. Yet others saw, in the elimination of European history from the curriculum, a move toward a "soft," undisciplined approach to curriculum.

The opposition group developed initially through interpersonal communication. Individual community members, some interested in the broad spectrum of the social studies changes and others specifically in the APB course, contacted each other by word of mouth. Founder members then assigned themselves tasks. One became the historian; others, investigators. They decided to concentrate on the APB course as an example of a change made without board approval.

The intention was to spread their "position" among other community members and in turn bring pressure to bear upon the school board. They started with small gatherings at private homes. At first they were not too successful, or polished, in their presentation. One community member who had attended an early session out of amused interest said later that he "misjudged the political import . . . substantially."

As the group expanded, they contacted teachers for information, wrote to the State Department of Education for rulings and materials, fed information to the newspapers, wrote letters to the board, attended and spoke at board meetings, met individually with board members, and, perhaps most important of all in view of the administrators' "authority" stance on curriculum matters, they brought in experts of their own. Law professors, history professors, and education professors, were approached to offer their opinions and appear before the school board. The community effectively opposed the curriculum change.

The Professional Element

The early part of the curriculum change process had seen the professional element within the district performing what they considered to be their traditional role—authority figure on curriculum matters. From this stance they had initiated proposals on curriculum changes, undertaken a search for relevant materials, piloted programs, and, where they felt appropriate, made choices. Until fall 1970 the administration had not been seriously questioned on its role as decision maker in the area of curriculum change. It was this role which was, however, to prove central to the controversy during the fall quarter.

At the board meeting on September 21, the administration recommended methods by which the board and the community might make inputs into the curriculum change process. These might well be interpreted as an attempt to offset some of the pressures that were mounting against the controlling role the administration played in curriculum change. This was the same meeting at which APB was officially adopted for all ninth-grade classes and board resentment began to manifest itself.

The administration's action gave the opposition element in the community a focal point for attack, but, perhaps more significant, the administration appeared to have usurped (in the opinion of the majority of the board) the board's prerogative with regard to curriculum change approval. The board wanted to recapture that prerogative, and, in the process, the administration was going to have to adopt a partisan role and compete with other groups for board approval. Temporarily, at least, the "special relationship" had been suspended.

The administration, forced into a partisan role, entered into it with a will. They had to bring influence to bear both upon the board and upon the community in order to sell their curriculum change. It was decided, as a steering committee member put it, that their approach would be "mostly a reeducation and an effort to reach people we hadn't reached."

By the end of October visitation opportunities were made available for board members to "sit in" and observe the course being taught. Study sessions were set up at which parents could examine, talk about, and criticize both the American political behavior course and the wider projected social studies changes.

The Forum for Education (FEE), an unaligned community group, was encouraged to sponsor a forum on APB, while on another occasion an education professor from Stanford was invited to speak on the "New Social Studies." One member of the steering committee did his own thing. He organized a series of informal gatherings at the "feed in" elementary schools to acquaint those who were interested with new developments in social studies at the junior high level.

An additional asset gained from these activities lay in the good press they developed. The *Palo Alto Times* (1973) article reporting the forum on the American political behavior course was headed "Parents Like Palo Alto Political Behavior Class." Such headlines were a relief to the beleaguered administration.

The Curriculum Controversy Moves Toward Resolution

By early November the controversy seemed to have quieted. The board had been satisfied that there was not enough demand from the community to warrant the setting up of an alternative course to APB, and they had resisted the demand by one community member for a district poll on the new curriculum, even though two board members supported the request.

The faux pas committed by the administration in adopting the course without board approval had receded as an issue, and opponents of the curriculum change were even beginning to soften their approach on it as an instrument of behavioral and value change. The argument turned, instead, to the issue that emerged as central to the debate: whether APB should replace European history as the course taught in the ninth grade. It was around this issue that the final throes of the controversy centered.

The European history argument had a great deal of support in the community. The chronological approach was a framework with which most community members were familiar. History offered the sense of an academic discipline some members found lacking in the American political behavior course. Others felt that it provided the students with insight into their cultural heritage.

November and December saw programs and activities initiated by both the professional element and the opposition group. As the board had not made any decisions with regard to the future of the curriculum change, both sets of activities were viewed as providing an input to the board. At the level of the board, the debate was low in profile. Apart from polite interchange about the success of board visitations and the study sessions, interchange was limited. The year ended quietly with no further developments. In the new year, however, debate was to reawaken. Both sides were keeping up their program activities, still canvassing the field. On January 11, the district held a social studies discussion in a local high school. Small presentations covering the spectrum of proposed social studies were the order of the day.

The opposition group was also active, particularly at board meetings. At a session of the board on January 12, three speakers representing the conservative position addressed the board. Once again, the plea was for the board to consider the offering of American political behavior as an elective, leaving European history as the mandatory offering.

The district had arranged a study session with the board for February 11. It was to be a grueling session. For the professional staff, it was their last chance to convince the board to move in their direction. For the community group, it was a time to sit and listen. The teachers withstood the discussion well, answering questions and clearing up misconceptions. There was one major difference in this meeting. They had learned from the session in August 1970 that they had to come to the board and present them with possible options.

As one steering committee member said, "We came to them and said these are the decisions we have to have at these grade levels." Three possibilities concerning the ninth-grade course of studies were offered: (1) to teach the American political behavior course and the Bay Area course; (2) to teach European history; (3) to offer an option between the two. One board member intimated that none of the options excited him; no one smiled.

General support seemed to develop for the third possibility, offering an option to students. A compromise, it seemed, was called for. Agreeing to make the social studies proposal an action item at the next meeting, the board agreed to adjourn.

At the board meeting on February 16, both sides of the controversial issue were well represented. In the call to order, the president of the board indicated that several persons in the audience wished to speak to the social studies item. He was right; sixteen people intended to speak. Eleven opposed the substitution of American political behavior for European history; four favored the third option in support of American political behavior; one person spoke on the history curriculum in general. The curtain had risen on the last act.

The opposition group mustered their strength for the final interchange. Among their speakers were several Stanford University faculty, who spoke in favor of the discipline of history. Much of what they argued, however, was undermined by the prospect of an option being offered to students. It therefore was not an either-or situation.

Other conservative speakers echoed arguments heard early in the controversy, which had lately receded from the opposition presentations. One parent objected to APB because it was "designed to change the attitudes and values of my children to that of the author's, the teacher or their peers" (*San Jose Mercury*, 1971).

Another parent said the American political behavior course should be "thrown out of our schools immediately" (*San Jose Mercury*, 1971) because it undermined belief in American society and tore down respect for authority.

After the speakers had concluded, a motion was passed by the board expressing appreciation for, and confidence in, the social studies steering committee. Then the meeting returned to the order of the day, a board decision on which of the three social studies packages to adopt. A supporting board member moved and was seconded that the third choice be authorized, with the addition of the American political behavior course as an option in the senior high schools.

Opposition was heard from two members who indicated they could only support the third alternative if American political behavior was made an elective, with European history still the requirement. Following from this position, a complicated substitute motion was offered. The motion essentially compromised regarding European history courses as well as the courses on American political behavior and the Bay Area, suggesting that the latter courses be continued as "experimental" and subject to yet further review.

For a brief moment it seemed to many observers that the whole process of interchange was to begin all over again. Two opposing members were in agreement, and a third board member who had indicated opposition to the program all along had yet to vote. It appeared as though a decision would finally go against the proposed curriculum changes, and that, at best, they would only continue on an "experimental" basis. When it came to the vote, however, the substitute motion was defeated, three votes to two. The supporting motion passed by the same margin.

The swing vote was not expected. As one observer noted, "it was a great surprise to everybody that he voted in that fashion." On being interviewed, the swing member stated that, having had the opportunity to view the curriculum being taught, he had been favorably impressed. He went on to say that "an evaluation and a reading of the materials only resulted in quite a mistaken impression of how the thing was presented and what it was all about." The reeducative program undertaken by the professionals had thus had a powerful influence on the decision outcome. The three-to-two margin was enough to make American political behavior a bona fide district course. It had been adopted. The fifth and final decision point in the curriculum change process had been reached.

The decision to approve the course had been made by the board as actors. They had made a social process decision from their reaffirmed vantage point as authorities. Influence had been brought to bear upon the board by both partisan groups, professionals and community opponents. The change strategy emerging from the agents of change, the professional group, had undergone drastic revision. Forced from their authority position, they had ceased to work from a lower position or from a position founded upon the self-evident worth of their change offering. They had adopted a series of reeducative activities, interacting directly with the community and the board.

The process had been longer, more trying, and more complicated than its initiators had estimated. The final position was a compromise one that had not been intended at the outset, but the process had been completed. As one steering committee member commented:

It seemed to me that the one thing we've learned out of this, and that we would not normally have done in past years, is that now we check base and ask, do we have the authority to move?

Almost one month later to the day, the board received a letter from the Social Studies Steering Committee members, thanking the board for the resolution of confidence (Palo Alto Unified School District, 1971).

Analysis

The curriculum change process related here was an episodic issue. For Palo Alto, both in terms of professional education and the wider community, it was a problem unique in its history. This does not, however, preclude a similar controversy erupting again either in this community or elsewhere. As Coleman (1957) notes,

It is in such a situation that social research can perform a valuable service, by speeding up the diffusion process so that the experiences of many communities become available to each. Case studies of individual communities perform part of this service, by providing examples which may correspond to the situation in which a community finds itself [page 3].

The forces involved as the curriculum change process can be broadly categorized as: (1) professional internal, (2) professional external, (3) nonprofessional internal, (4) nonprofessional external (see Figure 18-2). From the unfolding of the change process, it is possible to see the interplay of state guidelines and legislation with local direction setting, professional priorities, and community involvement. The forces are dynamic and cannot be neatly compartmentalized. Professional educators must strive to recognize these forces and be capable of dealing with them.

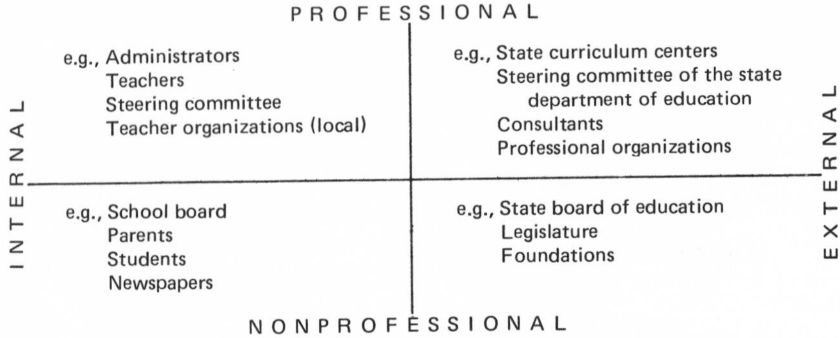

PROFESSIONAL

	INTERNAL	EXTERNAL	
INTERNAL	e.g., Administrators Teachers Steering committee Teacher organizations (local)	e.g., State curriculum centers Steering committee of the state department of education Consultants Professional organizations	EXTERNAL
	e.g., School board Parents Students Newspapers	e.g., State board of education Legislature Foundations	

NONPROFESSIONAL

FIGURE 18-2

A categorization of forces impinging
on the curriculum change process

From the five decision points identified in the body of the chapter, it is evident that the change process is not an overnight happening. The first decision point, identified in 1964, resulted in general direction setting, which was to lead to identification and use of the new curriculum. The last decision point saw the curriculum finally adopted as a regular course offering.

From an examination of the five decision points it is possible to note two significant factors. The first is the degree of authority possessed by the professional staff in the early stages of the change process. No matter who controls the final phases of the change process, it is clear from the study that the change process being acted upon was the choice of the professional staff. The second factor is the degree of control that the board of education can choose to exercise at the stage of closure, should they decree.

The most striking conclusion issuing from this study of a single educational community is that none of the major actors behaved as the literature commonly characterizes them as behaving. The school administration did not exhibit all the power commonly attributed to them, the school board exhibited more power than is commonly attributed to them, and the district community was more successful in bringing influence to bear than might have been expected.

It is apparent that administrators undertaking curriculum change must be sensitive to, and make provisions for, early community and board inputs into the change process. Communications from the administration need to be publicized.

It can be gathered from the controversy surrounding this particular curriculum change that some changes should be perceived as more sensitive in nature than others. Where changes can be expected to threaten perceived value stances held by segments of the community, particular care should be taken by professional educators in their negotiation of the change. The importance of external factors upon the change process was reiterated. The roles of the legislature and the State Board of Education were largely instrumental in bringing pressure to bear on the district. Such external factors will be more likely to increase in importance as federal and state monies are used to bring about educational reform.

Another external influence was the curriculum center at Indiana. The influence of the center was not as strong as it might have been. This is due to the nature of the district, its propensity toward innovation, its development as a "lighthouse" district, and its sophistication toward such external inputs.

The role of such centers in other districts not as familiar with curriculum innovation and change can be assumed to be more substantial. With the vast increase in federal expenditures on education since the mid-sixties, pressure has increased upon the educator to remedy, through educational programs, many of the ills facing society. One result has been to prompt districts to upgrade their curriculum offerings. In turn, this has necessitated the search and the need for new curricula. Curriculum change at the local level is an arduous process, even if the district possesses the talent and the financial resources to meet the challenge. Increasingly, therefore, it would appear that local districts must turn to national centers that possess the necessary talent and monetary resources.

An overriding issue is that of professional versus nonprofessional decision making. There was a basic questioning of the competency of the professional in making decisions, both by the conservative opposition members of the community and by some members of the board. If curriculum is to reflect a synthesis of the best community and professional viewpoints, then they must be heard. Certainly we will hear more of this issue as community participation and control of schools increase. The school administrator who wishes to effect change in the future must have both political sensitivities and professional expertise in order to provide the leadership necessary to continue to question and upgrade the quality of the nation's schools.

References

Brickell, Henry M. (1967). *Two Change Strategies for Local School Systems, Rational Planning in Curriculum and Instruction*. Washington, D.C.: Association for Supervision and Curriculum Development, National Education Association.

California, Education Code (1968). Sections 5001 to 12900, c 182 p 432 Sec. 31.

———, State Department of Education (1968). Minutes of the meeting of the State Board of Education, November 14-15, in the files of the State Department of Education, Sacramento.

Coleman, James (1957). *Community Conflict*. New York: Free Press.

Gallup, George (1969). *How the Nation Views the Public Schools*. Princeton, N.J.: Gallup International.

Gann, Lewis H. (1970). Letter from Gann, Senior Staff Member, Hoover Institution, Parent and Community Member, Palo Alto, July 30.

Goldhammer, Keith (1965). *Issues and Strategies in the Public Acceptance of Educational Change*. Eugene, Ore.: Center for the Advanced Study of Educational Administration, University of Oregon.

Kirst, Michael W., and Walker, Decker F. (1970). "An Analysis of Curriculum Policy." Paper prepared for the RAND Corporation Seminar Series in Education, Santa Monica, California, August 5.

Klotz, E. F. (1968). Letter to Dr. Eugene Gonzales, October 31; both members of the committee making recommendations on behalf of the California State Department of Education.

Longstreth, James (1966). "Guide for Administrators—Knowing Who's Who in the 'Power Structure' Can Pay Dividends." *The American School Board Journal* (August).

Moody, Charles O. (1968). "Relationship of the Emerging SSSSC K-12 Social Studies Framework to Local District Curriculum Development." Paper delivered by the Executive Secretary of the SSSSC before a meeting of the Palo Alto Unified School District Social Studies Steering Committee, February 27.

Palo Alto Times (1968). Issue of May 17.

Palo Alto Times (1970a). Issue of May 7.

Palo Alto Times (1970b). Issue of October 23.

Palo Alto Unified School District (no date). *Policy Manual.* Article I, Number 1030.4.

——— (1970). Memorandum from the assistant superintendent for curriculum to the superintendent, September 17, in the files of the school district.

——— (1971). Minutes of the meeting of the board of education, March 15, in the files of the school district.

———, Board of Trustees (1970). Letter from three sets of parents to the chairman of the board, October 1.

San Jose Mercury (1968). Issue of May 15.

San Jose Mercury (1971). Issue of February 17.

Sestak, Michael E., and Frerich, David D. (1968). "The Principal's Role in School-Community Relations," in *Selected Articles for Elementary School Principals.* Washington, D.C.: Department of Elementary School Principals, National Education Association.

19 Rules for a Machiavellian Change Agent: Transforming the Entrenched Professional Organization

J. Victor Baldridge

This is the age of the expert. The professional reigns supreme in many areas of life. Doctors heal our bodies. Teachers shape our children's minds. Lawyers handle our disputes. Professors create new generations of professionals. All are part of an intricate network of experts in modern society, and we have allowed them much power. They often control entry into positions of power; they certify who is educated and who is uneducated; they determine life and death on the sickbed; they turn the wheels of justice so that some win and some lose. Probably never before in the history of mankind have experts maintained such a stranglehold on the operation of society. The professionals are in many senses the gatekeepers to success, the wielders of power, and the deciders of right and wrong, truth and beauty. The claim to knowledge has become a claim to control.

The Problem: Entrenched Professionals

The dilemma has always been simple: Who guards the guardians? If modern society has relinquished all this power to professionals, it may have done so to its own peril. That professionals work more to benefit themselves than to serve their clients is a very real possibility. In many ways the professional groups have become an entrenched, privileged oligarchy that enriches itself at the expense of clients, all the while cloaking self-interest under the slogan of "service to mankind." A physician's first loyalty may be to the Hippocratic oath, but at least part of his loyalty is dictated by his pocketbook. A teacher may be dedicated to the education of children, but strong teachers' unions have not always sought educational gains as they struggled for bigger paychecks. A university professor may first seek truth as he goes about the business of shaping the minds of the youth, but there is a nagging suspicion that he is more interested in free time and his own esoteric research than his students. A lawyer may be concerned primarily with justice for all men, but he can become wealthy in the process.

Not only are individual professionals suspect, but they unite in powerful organizations to protect the privileges they have gained. The American Medical Association wages a war against a responsible national system of medicine more to protect the financial interests of physicians than to protect the public against poor health service. Bar associations rarely disbar members, even in the face of flagrant violations of the legal ethic. Teachers' unions, despite proclaimed objectives related to educational innovation and the welfare of children, seem more interested in money and benefiting the teacher. Associations of professors dedicated to the advancement of science are also very dedicated to the advancement of professors' financial and social status. In short, professional organizations reinforce the self-serving activities of individual professionals.

Finally, professionals control the organizations where they work. Hospitals are more responsive to the desires of doctors than patients; law firms are more sensitive to the needs of lawyers than clients; universities respond more to professors than students; schools are more in tune with teachers than pupils. In every case, the professionals have entrenched themselves behind strong organizational structures that enhance their status, reward them financially, and protect them from outside criticism. This is particularly true for older professionals, the aristocracy that controls power in the guild.

Storm clouds of criticism have, however, been gathering. Professors came under intense fire in the 1960's because of student revolts. Teachers are now feeling public hostility because of strikes that keep children on the street. Even the venerable and virtually untouched medical establishment is sensing tremors beneath it. Many of the moves to call the professions to account have come from outside pressure groups and legislatures. Outside pressure and legal moves can bring change in professional organizations, but equal attention should be given to change from within. Much of the power to change the professions still lies in the institutions or establishments where the work is done—hospitals, universities, schools, law firms, social work agencies. Levers of power are often lodged in the decision-making councils of these professional organizations. How can the levers of power within professional organizations be moved in order to change them? How can younger members of the professions get power to deal with oligarchies already established? How can the clients insist on more responsive organizations? These questions have political answers since they are essentially questions of power and its use within professional organizations. Let us assume the existence of some dedicated change agents who really want to change the professional organizations. How should they go about it? The first move is to be clear about the *goals* of change.

Vision: What Should Be Changed

Over the last few years planning committees for professional conferences have expressed deep concern about problems of "organizational change." Over those same few years I have discovered that the professionals who run organizations are not really interested in changing them, and especially not the aristocracies who plan such conferences! My suspicions regarding professional conservatism have been reinforced by the way people at such meetings have responded to one simple question: What would you change about this organization to make it accomplish its purposes better? The results have always been astonishing.

Typical replies from teachers included: make classes smaller, assign more aides to classes, increase salaries for teachers, and handle discipline problems outside the classroom. A group of professors wanted better-quality students, better pay, more participation in decision making, and fewer restrictions on tenure. Social workers would reduce the amount of red tape; eliminate supervision by superiors, encourage more participation of social workers in decision making, and increase pay. A group of doctors suggested that there be fewer Medicare patients, more efficient collection of bills, protection against malpractice suits, and greater participation of doctors in making policy for the hospital. These lists are not only representative; they are also remarkably similar.

Most of the changes listed would benefit the professionals, not the clients. There were four areas of concern. *Money* was a primary issue, and professionals seem to want more of it. *Decision participation* was an issue, and professionals express an insatiable urge to control the institution. *Decreasing the amount of evaluation* is consistent with the desire to ease tenure requirements on the part of professors, cut down on supervision on the part of the social workers and the teachers, and protect against malpractice suits on the part of doctors. Finally, *making working conditions easier,* or lightening the load of the professionals and in general making their lives more pleasant, is another persistent theme.

The "General Motors" assumption seems to pervade: Eisenhower's Defense Secretary, Charles Wilson, once stated that, "What is good for General Motors is good for the country." Professionals often use similar logic: What is good for the professional has to be good for the client. If professionals' lives are pleasanter, the client will somehow benefit. The changes requested by professionals, however, are usually self-serving, small in scale, and have little impact on clients' needs. This judgment of professionals may be overly harsh, but the vision of organizational change desired by core professionals is too often restricted and egocentric.

What should that vision be? Clearly, any serious change agent must propose changes that directly benefit the client. This is the only goal that seems worth fighting for. Making life easier for the professional may make the professional happier, but it is no guarantee that the client will also benefit.

In order to serve the client better, any vision of change must take into account political realities. First, it must allow for the *structure* of the organization, as well as the attitudes of the people involved. Altering structures without a corresponding change in attitudes will affect behavior only minimally; attitudes that change without accompanying structural change are quickly squelched by the system. Second, changes must be *politically feasible,* that is, they must be organized and implemented so that political support can be marshaled and professional leadership can be harnessed to help promote the changes.

If client service, structural as well as attitudinal changes, and political feasibility are goals, then what kinds of change efforts make sense? To answer that question requires a look at the *decision structure* of professional organizations. Unless we know how the organization operates, we cannot know how to change it.

Decision Processes in Professional Organizations

Professional organizations have a number of unique characteristics. Fundamentally, they are people-processing organizations, and, in order to handle that complex and delicate task, they usually have large staffs of highly trained professionals. Since people cannot be divided into segmentalized tasks in the same way that physical products can, professionals with a high level of expertise are needed to deal holistically with clients' needs. Thus it is that the first characteristic of professional organizations is that they are highly professionalized, client-serving systems.

Second, people-processing organizations have extremely ambiguous goals, and a list of legitimate activities for a university, a public school, or a social work agency would be extremely long. Because the goals are unclear, almost anything that serves the client is legitimate. On the other hand, the goals can be contested. Anything can be considered legitimate, but anything can also be questioned. Since the organizations themselves are not exactly clear about their functions, they are often racked with conflict over what they should or should not do. This is important for understanding change processes. If an organization does not know its specific objectives, then an individual with an idea and the energy can often bend the organization in his direction. Ambiguity and contest over goals pave the way for the skillful politician.

Finally, professional organizations are extremely vulnerable to outside pressures. Since the clients themselves—students, the physically or mentally ill, welfare recipients, law breakers—are relatively powerless, society generally demands accountability from the organizations. As a consequence, outsiders demand the right to influence internal decisions. The public's success varies considerably: in school systems outside voices are often influential; in hospitals or law firms the organization has generally listened with deaf ears.

What we see, then, is an unusual kind of organization that serves clients, has a highly professionalized staff, has unclear and contested goals, and is subject to much external pressure. It is fluid, complex, and changing. Sociologist James March has called it "organized anarchy." The decision-making process in an organized anarchy has some of the following characteristics:

Decision is by committee. Since expertise, not hierarchical office is the organizing principle, then committees of experts decide many of the critical issues.

Fluid participation. Many of the decision makers are amateurs, engaged in pursuing their professions, not in making decisions. As a consequence, they wander in and out of the decision process, and power belongs to those who stay long enough to exercise it.

There is an issue carousel. Issues have a way of always coming around again. Decisions are not made forever, because pressure from outside groups, from clients, and from professionals pushes the same issues full circle. Decisions are not made as much as they are pinned down temporarily.

There is a "garbage can" process. The longer it takes to make a decision, the more issues get piled onto the original subject. People, hoping to accomplish several things at one time, burden simple decisions with countless subsidiary issues.

Conflict is common. Professional groups, clients, and outsiders support divergent interests in setting the ambiguous goals of professional organizations. As a consequence, conflict over goals is common as decision makers cope with the pressures from diverse interest groups.

How can we summarize? The image that captures the spirit of the decision process in professional organizations does not resemble a normal bureaucracy; nor does it look like the "community of peers" that is often considered the model of professional management. Three images capture the spirit of the process. First, the structure of the organization does resemble March's organized anarchy. Second, within organized anarchies the decision process looks like a political system because of competing groups and the high degree of conflict. Finally, the fluid, unsettled character of the decision process can be captured by using the term *decision flowing* instead of decision making. Decision making has a final ring to it; decision flowing sounds like a never-ending process that must continue in order to make outcomes really work.

Rules and Tactics for the Change-Oriented Machiavellian

The problem is clear: entrenched professionals are more interested in serving themselves than in serving their clients. The vision is compelling: the organization has to be changed so that the client's needs are in the forefront. The decision process is complex: an organized anarchy with the political decision process is an ugly monster to alter. What tactics will work for the reformer who might want to tackle the dragon? It would probably be important to remember the following rules of strategy.

Rule 1: Concentrate Your Efforts

A basic mistake made by people interested in changing the system is that they frequently squander their efforts by chasing too many rainbows. An effective political change agent, realizing that change is really difficult, concentrates efforts on only the important issues.

Remember that most people do not care about most issues. If you care enough to concentrate, you have enormous power to win. The frustration caused by the resistance offered by an immovable system is usually the result of scattered and dispersed efforts. Remember, if "fluid participation" is the rule, then most people wander in and out of the issue. If you stick with one or two critical issues, you are more likely to win.

Rule 2: Know When to Fight

To concentrate is to choose a few issues, and a tactical genius knows which ones to choose. Most of the time it makes sense to support issues when you know you can win. If it is obvious that you will lose, wait. Remember, with the "issue carousel," the situation will probably return, allowing you time to muster your resources for the next battle. There are exceptions to the "fight to win" rule. Sometimes it is wise to fight because the moral issue is great, or because it is possible to make future martyrs. We do not always fight to win today; sometimes we fight today so that we can win tomorrow. Most of the time, however, the rule is to choose issues with high payoff. The sophisticated and astute observer can usually tell the difference between a winner and a loser.

Rule 3: Learn the History

Every issue has roots deep in the past. The issue carousel has trotted it past several times before. Consequently, the wise tactician searches for the historical bases of an issue. When was it around before? Who took what position? Who won? Who lost? Knowing the history can reveal what coalitions fight together and what tactics prove useful—information that helps in planning strategy. Under most circumstances the person who is historically naive about the issue is a loser.

Rule 4: Build a Coalition

Never go it alone. Good politicians know that much of their job is not influencing decisions as much as it is building a political base for influencing decisions. This means that a dedicated cadre of change agents must be formed, a committed group that exchanges ideas and reinforces each other's efforts. In addition, a strong change group needs equally strong links to those in viable political coalitions.

Rule 5: Join External Constituencies

As we noted earlier, professional organizations usually have strong external constituents who apply pressure to the decision-making process. The wise strategist uses support from these external constituencies to influence the internal process. In building coalitions it is useful to associate with outside groups as well as inside groups, particularly since major decision makers themselves are often tied to outside groups. Insiders, with their limited view of the outsiders' role, naively overlook the political strategy of cultivating external allies. Welfare recipients and legislators can be strong forces in changing social welfare agencies; parents, alumni, and foundations can help change universities; community groups can be marshaled to transform public schools. The potential power of external constituencies must never be neglected.

Use Committees Effectively

Most major decisions in professional organizations are made by committees of experts who combine their specialized knowledge to solve organizational problems. Therefore, organizational politics often center around committee politics. Having influence on a committee is frequently equal to having influence over the decision.

How can a Machiavellian change agent best use a committee to effect organizational change? First, get on the right committee by simply asking for an appointment from an incumbent official. If the organization has a "committee on committees" it is wise either to know someone on it or to be on it yourself. Such rule-making appointive committees wield power in large professional organizations, and this can be exploited to the best advantage. In addition, after acquiring membership it is critical simply to *be there.* Remember, fluid participation is a characteristic of professional organizations, and the person who sticks with the committee is likely to have enormous impact. In a recent study, for example, Steve Weiner of Stanford University analyzed decision making in a San Francisco school board committee charged with proposing plans for racial integration. He concluded that expertise, social prestige, and personality characteristics were important in the early stages of the committee's work. In later stages, however, those who had the most staying power had the most influence. The first move, then, is to get on the committee, to be there with great regularity, and to stick it out even when others drop off.

The second rule of committee success is to do your homework. Expertise is vital in a professional organization. If you observe the earlier rule of concentrating your efforts, you have more time to accumulate the knowledge that will put you ahead of others. In addition, it is always useful to make part of your homework the job of being secretary or chairman of a group. The chairman can set the agenda and often has the power to call committee meetings, while the secretary controls the memory of the committee. Committees are blessed with short memories since most members do not recall or care what is recorded in the minutes. Controlling the memory of a committee means reiterating the issues that you consider important, a definite advantage for political bargaining. Doing your homework— whether it is gathering knowledge, learning the history, being the chairman, or doing the secretarial chores—puts you in a strategically advantageous position.

Finally, a major tactical procedure in committees is to "fill the garbage can." Since decision issues, like garbage cans, attract various irrelevant material, they can be used to the change agent's advantage. Dump new garbage into the can, and then compromise readily on the unimportant issues. Helping to load the garbage can leaves plenty to bargain over when the deadlines are close and allows you the chance to insist stubbornly about retaining key issues.

Use the Formal System

Professional organizations, like other bureaucracies, have complex formal systems to carry out their activities. Often naive change agents are not aware that they can achieve a desired outcome simply by asking the appropriate official for it. This requires savvy. It requires experience within the organization. It requires knowing where the levers are, and which ones to push.

Inexperienced change agents may fail to realize that most organization officials are eager to please. Success is difficult to judge in most professional organizations because the tasks are too ambiguous to be assessed. As a consequence, most officials depend upon "social validation" for judgments of success. That is, they are successful if people are pleased and think they have done a good job. The ambiguity of the task, the lack of hard evaluation criteria, and the psychological need of most administrators for approval gives tremendous advantage to partisans who want to get something done. Do not forget a basic tactic: ask for what you want and you will be surprised how many times you get it.

Follow Through to Push the Decision Flow

We have said that the concept of "decision making" is a delusion. Decisions are not really made; instead, they come unstuck, are reversed, get unmade during the execution, or lose their impact as powerful political groups fight them. In real life decisions go round and round in circles, and the best one can hope for in the political battle is a temporary win.

As a consequence, the aware politician knows that he must follow important decisions even after they have supposedly been made. What do most people do after the committee has reached its decision? They evaporate. The person who traces the decision flow on through to execution, and who fights when issues are distorted is the person who really has the power. The truly dedicated partisan who wants to see changes really work will be a tenacious watchdog, monitoring the steps of the decision, staying on the backs of administrators, and calling public attention to administrative lapses.

There are a few tricks to the trade of following through on decisions. First, be sure to set deadlines in the process of making the decisions. Delay is the enemy of change; deadlines are flags that help call attention to stalling. Second, give the idea a sheltered start. If placed back into the regular routine of the organization, a new change will usually be smothered by the powerful old routines. As a consequence, the shrewd change planner builds a shelter around the change in its infancy. This often means giving the program a home under the wing of a strong, hospitable executive of the organization. Only later, after the new idea has established roots, should it be placed into the regular structure of the organization.

Several follow-through techniques involve people. It is always useful to place your allies in the vanguard of the people responsible for executing the decision. If people embodying your ideas are running the show, then the change is more likely to succeed. In addition, the reward system is very important. Do you want things to change? Then reward people whose behavior helps promote the change. Rewards can be straightforward in the form of money, or they can take the equally valuable form of prestige, status, and public acclaim.

A Glance Backward When the Change Is Completed

Let us assume the changes have really been made. The last piece of advice is the hardest to swallow: be skeptical about your own changes. Few good changes have eternal lives. A deep ego-investment can be made in a project that does not work. Don Campbell, a psychologist, once commented that the world would be better off if people could be dedicated to solving problems rather than to promoting particular projects or changes. In this sense, following through means evaluating, judging, and deciding whether the performance lives up to the expectation. If it does not, you must start all over. The problem is still there, but the solution did not quite make it. Evaluating your own idea as objectively as possible and listening carefully to the evaluations of others are valuable and necessary skills for true change agents.

Any organization's vitality and creativity depend heavily on the constant influx of new ideas. Even the bright, new change that you worked so hard to establish will, in time, be dull and old. The last step, then, is the most ruthless of all: kill your own project when it has outlived its usefulness. This is where most change agents fall down. After building their ego-investments they fight like stuffy bureaucrats to hang on to an idea long since grown old. The cycle must continue, and the change agent must once more struggle to infuse creativity and excitement into the professional organization.

In modern technological societies the professions and their elite organizations are the centers of much social power. Unfortunately, the professionals have learned too well to serve themselves, not their clients. The vision, then, is to change the professional organizations so that they really focus on client needs. Although it seems nearly impossible to make changes in those organizations, it is not out of the question. What is needed for successful organizational revolution?

First, it is important to understand the nature of the decision system. Most professional organizations act like "organized anarchies" with high environmental input, unclear technologies, high professionalism, and fluid participation. This is a messy, politicized kind of decision structure, best characterized as a miniature political network. Second, if the decision structure is political, then a Machiavellian change agent must learn a few basic tactics: organize, work through committees, do your homework, and follow through the change process to the end.

The task is not easy, and failure may be more common than success. Often these tactics will not work; nor may any others. Nevertheless, if professional organizations are to be called back to their prime goal—serving clients—then the effort must be made. Most important, the vision must guide the tactics, not the other way round.

PART THREE
CASE STUDIES

The two initial goals of this book have been to introduce some sociological perspectives and to suggest some strategies for change. If we have succeeded, then the readers can supplement an individualistic approach with complex, sophisticated conceptions of the various subsystems that comprise an educational organization. They recognize that subsystems interlock and that each may be the target of change as well as being affected by innovation in other subsystems, and they have been introduced to a repertoire of strategies from which they can draw when attempting change within their school district, school, or college. Armed with knowledge and strategies and sensitized to the pressing need for revamping educational organizations, our audience can, we hope, confront problems of educational innovation and change valiantly and enthusiastically.

But if we left this zeal untempered, we would be neglecting the third goal of this book: making readers vicariously realize, based on experiences of other administrators, just how difficult it is to change organizations. This final part contains case studies of changes in both new and established educational organizations. The case studies provide an opportunity to try out some ideas from the first two parts, and each can be analyzed using the five perspectives on organization. Each case also provides a chance to second-guess the administrator calling the shots and to Monday-morning quarterback without experiencing the consequences.

As we have mentioned previously, the case studies present a bleak prognosis for administrators who wish to change educational organizations. We have not purposely selected studies that represent only grim realities, difficulties, and minor successes. In fact, as we searched the literature we tried hard to find examples of successful educational change. The fact that we were able to locate only one provides additional evidence of the awesome task confronting a change-oriented administrator. But the hypothesis underlying this book is that the thoughtful analysis of where things went wrong will be an important administrative asset in overcoming obstacles to innovation.

The case studies in this section are arranged in two categories: those dealing with change in established institutions and those starting with a clean slate and a new cast of characters.

Established Institutions. Packard's "Changing to a Multiunit School" is a case study of a series in which the research staff of the Center for the Advanced Study of Educational Administration examined the implementation of differentiated staffing and the "multiunit school" concept in a variety of settings. Packard analyzes the implementation of differentiated staffing in four elementary schools. Although the experiences of the four schools are different, there are numerous similarities. Packard develops some generalizations about the sequence of events that led in each instance to insurmountable barriers in installing the multiunit concept. The study by Gross, Giacquinta, and Bernstein focuses on a single elementary school's experience when fundamental changes were made in the role of teachers in the school. The proposed new role prescription for teachers, which enjoyed general popularity among educators, had the following characteristics: teachers were to give students more autonomy, emphasize process over substance, and facilitate rather than direct. In spite of initial enthusiasm on the part of teachers, six months later the new role model was for the most part nonexistent. Gross, Giacquinta, and Bernstein describe the events that go nowhere and analyze post hoc where things went wrong.

Our rare and valued semisuccess study—Baldridge's investigation of a major change in direction for New York University—is particularly important since it is the only example of an educational organization which implemented a major organizational change without losing the innovation, the organization itself, or a top administrator in the process. The New York University study is clearly an example of the initiation of a new organizational "saga." Environmental and internal changes produced a set of circumstances that forecast organizational doom. Enter a new president with an image of the future. Allied against the new president is a powerful array of opposing forces; on his side is an equally formidable group of ardent supporters. After a vigorous political struggle, New York University emerged as a significantly changed organization with at least a fighting chance for its future.

Innovation is often viewed differently by various individuals, departments, or subunits within a school. The Bredos, for example, discuss a junior high school's adoption of the "house plan"—an innovation that involved teachers daily in counseling the same group of students. Six months after the adoption of the plan, the school was in political chaos. The internal disturbance was contagious and spread to the parents, the local community, and the district office. Their analysis shows dramatically the varied "reviews" of the innovations from different subject area departments. The tighter the subject matter taught by the teachers in the department, the more negative the reaction to the house plan. In the informal hierarchy the teachers of the tighter subjects were more influential and thus the political battlefront eventually brought about the demise of the plan.

New Institutions. Wacaster's study of Columbia High School, another series of case studies undertaken by the Center for the Advanced Study of Educational Administration, focuses on the implementation (or nonimplementation) of differentiated staffing. From all initial indicators, Columbia appeared to be an administrator's dream: sufficient lead time in planning; carte blanche to select an "innovative" faculty; ample resources; outside change agents; a clean slate; adequate environmental support; and participatory decision making. Wacaster follows the dream through to its transformation into an administrative nightmare and, finally, to its disappearance.

Deal calls upon direct experience when he examines the formation of two "alternative schools." He suggests that new educational organizations in the "alternative school" tradition ran into trouble because of the problem of revising the traditional authority relationships within schools, and he speculates that schools of the "do your own thing" variety, with a population of alienated students, experience a sequence of developmental stages that culminate in dissolution, a shift to more traditional models, or true experimentation. Few took the third route.

The final selection is from Smith and Keith's *Anatomy of an Educational Innovation.* It is the study, once again an unhappy one, of the inauguration of Kensington Elementary School, a grandiose educational experiment. Its similarity to the other cases is remarkable, and it is with the failure of Kensington School that we end this investigation of change processes in educational organizations. The note is sad, but, if the other goals of the book are met, administrators now have more conceptual tools and strategic skills with which to attempt successful educational change.

Established Institutions

20 Changing to a Multiunit School

John S. Packard

In reporting findings from CASEA case studies of the efforts of four schools to implement differentiated staffing, Charters and Pellegrin (1972) provide both fresh insight into the implementation process and tacit reaffirmation for other less novel, more broadly shared conceptions of innovation in schools. With regard to the latter, by implication, two impending axioms are once again brought into light: the probability of nonfulfillment is great, and knowledge of how to implement, if it exists, is a well-guarded secret. Sustenance for these conclusions is drawn from two major findings: Charters and Pellegrin report that all four schools fell considerably short of their own project goals, and they provide twelve generic implementation problem themes or barriers to explain why.[1]

The Charters-Pellegrin report of implementation labors and underlying problems will certainly aid further explorations of this little-known period in the life of an educational innovation. Yet their findings with regard to barriers are not surprising. Similar observations

Reprinted from *The Process of Planned Change in the School's Instructional Organization* (Eugene, Ore.: Center for the Advanced Study of Educational Administration, University of Oregon, 1973), pp. 105-121.

1. Implementation barriers include unclear goals, assumptions that appropriate behavioral changes will follow structural changes, statements of values and project objectives, unrealistic time perspective, untrained staff, role overload, lack of resources, lack of evaluation technology, and the ideology of teaching self-governance. See Charters and Pellegrin (1972).

have been recorded in other implementation studies (Gross, Giacquinta, and Bernstein, 1971; Smith and Keith, 1971); they match what logically follows from the knowledge concerning schools as an organizational type (Bidwell, 1965; Carlson, 1964), and reflect properties of the traditional school work culture (Pellegrin, forthcoming; Willower, 1970). That is, rather than being characteristic of just the implementation period, implementation barriers, as reported by Charters and Pellegrin, seem more like pervasive institutional features which become quite visible in times of stress.

That problems encountered in the implementation period might be thought of as steadfast barriers may be misleading. As noted, such properties seem to characterize most public schools, not just those which adopt differentiated staffing. Furthermore, implementation may be successful elsewhere in spite of these problems. Finally, because schools studied by the Charters-Pellegrin research team had not resolved their problems and either abandoned the project officially or had made little progress by the time the investigation had ended, the inability to overcome persistent problems may be the primary barrier and not the problems or their sources. More practically, due to the performance of these schools, factors which might facilitate the implementation of differentiated staffing could not be uncovered.

In response to these subsequent considerations, a more modest study was devised by CASEA staff members to begin to answer two pressing questions: "What were the problems of schools during the period in which they had implemented a collaborative staffing model? How were these problems solved?" The line of reasoning underlying these dual, guiding questions reflects the continued search for facilitators in the implementation process. If most schools experience similar difficulties while attempting to implement one or another model of collaborative staffing, then that which distinguishes relatively complete implementation may be that some significant number of key problems have been solved. The search for facilitators focused on the identification of problems and their resolution in schools where staff reorganization had taken place.

Investigators conducted weeklong retrospective case studies in four elementary schools which had made considerable progress in implementing a collaborative staffing model, the multiunit school.[2]

2. Multiunit structural characteristics include several teaching units of usually five professionals each and 150 students. Each unit has a lead teacher, and all unit leaders and the principal form a faculty council to coordinate school-wide affairs (Klausmeier, 1971).

This [chapter] reports the major findings of the four case studies by grouping observations in categories of central organizational changes conceivably implicated in the changeover to a collaborative teaching model. The delineation of implementation problems encountered by these schools occupies the major share of this [work]. Unfortunately, and for reasons to be discussed later, resolutions to specific problems are altogether absent here.[3]

Methodology

Multiunit (MU) schools are a fact of life in certain parts of the country, especially in Wisconsin, as a result of the efforts of the R&D Center in Madison (*Education U.S.A.*, 1972; *Multiunit Newsletter,* 1972). Through various procedures (Charters, Introduction; Carlson, forthcoming), four multiunit schools in Wisconsin were chosen for this study on the bases that sufficient implementation progress had been made and that recollections of the implementation period were still fresh. Each of the schools agreed to permit a researcher to "live in" for one week to interview staff and other personnel and to prepare case histories of their findings.

The Problem Pattern

With regard to the implementation histories unraveled, the four schools are impressive in terms of their dissimilarities. Each exists in a unique context, and each has its own story to tell. Had there been a broader search for causes of implementation, a major conclusion might have been: there seem to be at least four different ways to install the same staffing pattern. Even this is somewhat unwarranted in that the research resulted in the identification of implementation problems and not factors contributing to success. However, judgments about important facilitating factors have been made (Carlson, forthcoming).

The variety of implementation problems recorded gives rise to a common central impression even though there are not a great many specific parallels across all four cases. Problems come in waves depending upon the stage of implementation. Certain problems appear initially, while others lay further down the road. As time passes,

3. Members of the research team were Richard O. Carlson, Harry F. Wolcott, Robert B. Everhart, and the author. This summary report is singularly the responsibility of the author. Greater detail will be provided in a final report now being prepared by Richard O. Carlson (forthcoming).

implementation progress increases the variety and complexity of the problems which arise. Early failure probably would mean that problems would be reduced and that life would be simpler for lack of progress.

Apart from implementation progress, problems are tied to another major factor—the fragile status of the innovation. Though new ideas and novel practices undoubtedly seem robust enough to their advocates, when placed in the public education institutional setting, they are vulnerable and extinguishable. The merest trouble or the slightest mistake may squelch them. Problems arise because new practices require constant protection.

The following analogy may reinforce these points. Consider a man trying to light a fire on a cold, bleak, and windy mountain. Consider also that he is freezing, afraid of attracting wild animals and not quite sure how to build a fire. His implementation problems will be tandem. First, there is the problem of gathering kindling and then one of fashioning a gradation of fuel so that eventually large pieces will catch hold. Then comes the problem of igniting the kindling which entails waiting for the wind to die down, finding a protected spot, and making fingers work. If the fire is not started, implementation problems are over.

But suppose the kindling starts up. New orders of problems are created. He must protect and nurture the flame. He must not burn himself or attract too much attention from predators to whom he previously had been invisible. He must feed the fire and catch the larger pieces. Once underway, he must sustain a stockpile of fuel. He may even feel obliged to help others who wish to build fires of their own. Certainly they will ask for help.

Implementation Problems

The implementation activities of schools can be viewed in many ways. In this paper a nine-category classification model has been used primarily to show the relationship between implementation problems and major organizational changes implied by or observed in the transition from the conventional elementary school pattern to a collaborative teaching model. Seven rather well-known categories of the classification model denote the following organizational changes: (1) the redistribution of authority, (2) the redistribution of power, (3) division of labor, (4) teaming, (5) visibility, (6) shifts in the reward structure, and (7) changes in flow of communication. Two additional categories, which refer to organizational responses due in part to changes in the above areas, have been named (8) standardization and (9) incorporation.

Of the nine categories listed above, the first seven were chosen initially to serve as foci about which the many observations in all four case histories might be organized. They were flat categories in that all received equal conceptual weight before data were fitted into them. As the reader will see, each of the seven signals actual organizational changes. However, some changes did not result in implementation problems, and some categories are devoid of such problems. Generally speaking, problems located in these categories were relatively minor.

The final two categories are derived from observations which did not fit into any of the seven previous (originally selected) ones. These two, standardization and incorporation, catch the brunt of the two major problems faced by the four schools: the vastly increased work demands and task environment criticism. Standardization and incorporation also represent organizational responses to the two major implementation problems.

Redistribution of Authority

The locus of formal, binding decision making in MU schools shifts from individuals to groups, teaching units, and the faculty council and crosses traditional domains; unit leaders help make instructional as well as school-wide administrative decisions. These changes may violate the norm of autonomy-equality, severely alter the principal's conventional role, and create stress between unit desires and administrative concern for school-wide coordination. However, the establishment of units, unit leaders, and the faculty council did not result automatically in the above pattern.

Key differences among schools appeared to hinge on whether or not unit leaders were appointed. In the one school where unit leaders emerged following a year of experimentation, units were relatively self-reliant, conducted their internal affairs without assistance for the most part, carried out their external affairs without gaining clearance from the principal. The school abandoned the regular schedule of council meetings and replaced it with a deliberate system which handled "critical" issues raised by any staff member.

Conversely, where leaders were appointed, faculty council meetings were held on a regular basis, dealt with foregone and trivial issues, avoided or neglected troublesome topics, and were dominated by the principal who set the agenda and ran the show. Outside the council meetings, the principal was generally consulted to approve many of the activities which the units intended to perform.

This pattern affected the formal unit meetings. Self-reliant teams tended to deal with internal affairs, whereas teams with appointed leaders spent much time reviewing faculty council minutes and operated by the council's agenda. However, beyond these differences, internal decision making followed a consistent scheme across units. Joint decisions involving all members concerned orientation points and gross and general commitments (that is, to change the reading schedule or to adopt multiaged homerooms) and were "subject to change." Operational decisions, that is, whether and how to implement orientation decisions, were usually made by subgroups, often grade-level associates, and by individual teachers. Operational decisions were made outside the unit meetings, informally and independently. Teachers regarded implementation as more important than setting unit policy and frequently complained that unit meetings took time away from more useful work.

Most unit leaders were not objectionable to team members. Leaders played down their status by refusing released time or pay increases in some cases, and by coordinating rather than dominating unit meetings. Moreover, they often did much more work than other members. Teachers viewed the faculty council functions of the unit leader as extra duties rather than as special privileges.

Overall, there was little attempt by those occupying superordinate positions to impose their will on others. Although teachers continued to exercise much discretion, considerable influence was effectuated informally in interactions outside of scheduled meetings. Although principals saw their roles as changed, none reported feeling the loss of decision-making prerogatives.

After two or more years in the MU design, redistributed authority was not problematic. Only in one case, the school with "elected" unit leaders, where the self-reliance of units was most obvious, did problems emerge. Teachers in other schools in the district were openly critical.

Redistribution of Power

In conventional elementary schools independent teachers make uncoordinated demands upon organizational resources. In a collaborative arrangement permanent faculty groups may represent more powerful agents, not only with regard to making their demands felt, but also with regard to intergroup competition over limited resources and in setting school-wide priorities. However, neither the units nor the faculty councils in the case schools seemed especially alert to the influence they might muster. Resource allocation continued to follow some sort of equity logic and even minor skirmishes were not observed or recorded. Principals were neither insecure about their organizational status nor did they exhibit fear of emasculation.

While this lack of muscle flexing could be expected, there are at least two areas in which increased power or control over resources was indicated. In the more definite case, units exerted considerable influence in hiring new members. While in most schools, the unit leader and the principal collaborated in the selection of a team member, in at least one school the hiring process was carried out almost entirely by the members of the unit. As for the other, more speculative case, MU schools joined regional associations for mutual support. In one of these associations (it was reputed) bonuses for supervising student teachers were placed into a regional kitty. Otherwise, these networks had begun to function as informal job placement agencies for those experienced in the team approach. Should such trends continue, these associations may generate substantial commitments and be able to influence their members' organizations.

For the most part, it was not evident that power had become centered in newly formed groups. Nor was there much evidence to suggest that different parties sought to accrue power or thought in terms of increased organizational control. Instead, the fairness and equity educators typically espouse was practiced, at least with regard to other adults, and permeated most considerations of resource distribution and school-wide priorities.

Division of Labor

Major problems in the early stages following adoption have to do with developing the curriculum and implementing the instructional program. In the beginning both sets of tasks were faced by a scantily prepared staff at the same time students appeared. There were myriad details to work out, including setting up groups of students, developing class schedules and making and carrying out teaching assignments. Instruction was expected to show manifestly greater rationality consistent with a philosophy of individualization; diagnostic tests had to be prepared, administered, scored, and summarized; lessons appropriate to a variety of diagnoses had to be anticipated, readied, and implemented; the effects of instruction had to be assessed and new tests delivered, scored, summarized, and so on. In response to these markedly accelerated work demands, units had to hold an enormous number of meetings and divide the labor.

That new divisions of labor may be problematic in the first years of implementation seems somewhat irrelevant. Rather, dividing up the labor was a response to a great many problems. The alternative being to abandon the entire project, that teams divided the labor may be looked upon as an indication of effort and commitment on their part. There are two ways in which labor was divided in these schools: (1) departmentalization, each person developed and presented lessons in one subject area exclusively and (2) "prioritization," all members worked jointly on the development of lessons in one top-ranked subject area until it was reasonably polished. Otherwise, each teacher presented lessons in all academic areas.

While these two solutions were beneficial in that work was manageable, each led to problems. Departmentalization was boring, and, after two years in this mode, teachers gladly became generalists once again. Departmentalization led to conflict with special teachers of art, music, and physical education. Seeing their areas usurped in the units' curriculum development process, special teachers complained bitterly. This has yet to be resolved. Prioritization was a slow, tedious process where one subject area was out of line with the others. Instruction in other areas was thought to be either better or worse than in the developing one. This forced an uncomfortable reconciliation, making it difficult to actually prioritize. Work in other areas started ahead of schedule. However, prioritization avoided conflict with special teachers since these areas were ranked low.

Teachers did not specialize by student characteristics (other than by grade level), group size, or instructional tasks. When or if teachers do, the problems associated with divided labor might be studied fruitfully. For the present, divided labor is best viewed as a short-term solution to manage increased work demands. Seemingly, once curriculum development is over, teachers want to perform all tasks.

Visibility

Increased opportunities for faculty members to view one another is thought to be problematic primarily because teachers may be more vulnerable to professional criticism by colleagues. Indeed, the potential risks accompanying the absence or diminution of walls upset a substantial segment of at least one school's faculty, making them reluctant to begin the teaming operation. Yet, in this regard, increased visibility had not proved to be a serious problem. The reduction of physical barriers was in and of itself insufficient to make teachers more critical or vulnerable.

While, during the first weeks of teaming, the presence of others was felt acutely, many teachers maintained that they adjusted quickly to all the new sights and sounds. This is more than a shift in perception threshold or sensory adaptation, however. Certainly routine serves to blend many distractions into background noise. Particular distractions are not as easily handled, and areas of considerable student activity, the media center, the special education class, the physical rehabilitation group, and the kindergarten were located in separate rooms or sealed off by walls of "movable" furniture. Often "ordinary" classes were arranged so that teachers faced one another while the various groups of students were back to back.

For a number of reasons criticism of team members [and] their techniques and styles occurred infrequently, if at all. Class time observation was difficult. Since teachers were busy at the same time and separate, they did not attend to what others were doing. By the same token, teachers went to some lengths to avoid calling attention to themselves. Some teachers reported cutting out plays, singing, and games. Students were rarely disciplined by shouting. One unit took pride in the notion that in their area a pin hitting the carpet could be heard. The purpose of these mufflers, teachers said, was to avoid interfering with other classes.

As a result of these adaptations, the variety of experiences teachers normally provide (in conventional classrooms) may be reduced. Some recognized this, reporting they were less likely to try "new things." An educational problem with collaboration may be the low level of peer criticism. On the other hand, this feature may enhance implementation of a collaborative design since friendship and cooperation often thrive in the absence of criticism among group members.

Teaming

Both instrumentally and practically, teaming implies getting along well enough to work together. Teachers frequently championed the quality of interpersonal relations among unit members as the key to implementation. For many, collaboration was associated with personal cost as well as with personal gain. While most units had a history free from severe internal rupture and exhibited close interpersonal involvements and relatively intense work relations, some units suffered internal strife. When serious trouble occurred, minimal effort was given to collaboration, and the units existed in name only. The quality of interpersonal relations did, in fact, seem crucial in determining whether a team established itself.

The reasons given for interpersonal problems were many. The root issue seemed to be the degree to which unit decisions bound individual members or subgroups to definite behaviors and approaches.

When conflict arose, failure to reclaim the aggrieved party by expressing sympathy or argumentation evoked the time-heals-all-wounds strategy. When disharmony persisted, interest in fence mending diminished, team members drew back, and team operations lagged along until the dissenting member was replaced.

In silent testimony to the growth and course of interpersonal relations among unit members were the "moving desks." In some cases, upon forming new units members located their desks in separate corners. Over time, the desks moved progressively closer together, finally touching near the center of the instructional area. According to those who experienced this, the process was below consciousness; seemingly, the desks were self-propelled. When there was rancor, the desks separated, each retreating to a remote corner. When promise continued to grow, the cluster of furniture moved intact to the periphery of the instructional area.

Members of some units made a covenant to work together. Others displayed a united front on most matters. Units that ran smoothly invoked reputed expertise, experience, or hard work as a means to legitimate cooperation. "Being sensitive to the feelings of others," explained one unit leader, is the way to maintain pleasant relations in the team. Operationally, this appeared to mean careful avoidance of issues or statements which would cause hard feelings.

Rewards

In collaborative arrangements elementary teachers may be expected to share equipment, materials, lessons, space, and children with other unit members. In the shift from personal to group property, teachers may lack fulfillment and lose pride in ownership of, as well as feelings of responsibility for, classroom events. In addition, teachers may find in colleagues a relatively important source of reward. Drifting away from normal to somewhat novel means of fulfillment could be resisted by teachers as well as [be a] cause for parents and others to discredit the team approach. Our observations indicate some of these predictions are well grounded.

Many teachers in these schools said that they enjoyed relations with team members and at times displayed considerable loyalty to the unit. Since students moved among teachers for classes, the sense of owning children and the rewards from getting close to them seem diminished. Indeed, certain children went unnoticed until a colossal mistake or a parental complaint enlarged their profile. Naturally, such lapses were sources of frustration and embarassment. On the other hand, ownership of objects and areas was maintained. Within the unit's domain, space and equipment were reserved for teachers. Each operated in a fixed area with both physical and symbolic boundaries which, one noticed, other teachers usually did not cross unless children were absent. When children were present, teacher interactions took place in neutral or jointly owned areas.

Teachers collaborated in curriculum development efforts and in preparing new lessons for the unit, but did not freely part with personal, independently developed lessons. To illustrate, student teachers were able to use unit materials, but had to build their own lessons in areas the unit had not developed. As a token, one team gave its student teachers a portfolio of special lessons, for example, holiday activities, on the last day of student teaching.

As noted, one problem associated with the enlarged arena of rewards was losing track of children. This was often regarded as an unfortunate consequence of being too busy and out of touch with students. For some, these incidents illustrated the need to return to "the old way." For others, overlooked children were unfortunate mistakes but excusable in that "truly individualized instruction" was becoming a reality. Many teachers found work relations with colleagues to be both pleasant and beneficial—additional reasons for not abandoning the team approach.

Communication Flow

Our observations support earlier findings regarding communication patterns in multiunit schools (Pellegrin, 1969). Units were loci of comfortable and frequent work-related conversation; the principal talked with unit leaders more or less exclusively and thus was removed as the hub of the flow of much information. Loci of intense communication were unit-planning areas, the faculty lounge, unit and faculty council meetings. Informal links tended to parallel formal communication structures vertically (teacher-unit leader, unit leader-principal) and horizontally (limited interactions between and among units, but a relatively high volume of communication among members of the same unit).

That problems were associated with these patterns was not obvious. However, considerably limited information links may result in systematic misperception (Packard and Willower, 1972), and, indeed, unfounded rumors, jealousies and feelings of superiority characterized somewhat the feelings of unit members for other units. [Whether] these resulted from constrained channels of communication or only indicated a natural competitiveness between and among units could not be determined. However, competitiveness among units and systematic misperception of teachers in other units were noticed and might become foci of yet other studies. Then, too, in that unit leaders are major information links, the principal and unit members risk being vulnerable to manipulation and error by being badly informed. However, we have no evidence to support this proposition. In fact, some unit leaders tended to the other extreme—perhaps distributing more information than was sought.

Standardization

As used here standardization refers to the forces and the responses to forces which resulted in all units in a school adopting the same procedural characteristics. In a school all units employed the same report cards, lunch schedule, book lists, meeting routines, class schedules, and so on. Most had adopted the same curriculum development priorities and daily work models. While it may seem odd to attach significance to these facts, behind such "normal" behaviors may be something worthy of note. For example, during site selection, we found an energetic, enterprising unit unable to publish its own newsletter to parents until all other units agreed to do so. It was also noted that, while each school admitted to a wide range of instructional excellence among its units, at the same time it tolerated only limited variation in operating procedures.

Clearly, administrative problems are lessened and economies of scale are preserved when all units follow the same procedures. Naturally, the innovation embodies a new set of standard procedures which apply equally to all units. Yet there is a third pervasive, persuasive, and perhaps more basic standardizing influence: task environment criticism. Criticism comes up from under every rock, out from around every corner, and down from almost every high place. For schools, it is like a prevailing wind; though it may fluctuate, it rarely stops. For schools in transition, it can reach galelike proportions.

Not only were criticisms expected, but some teachers feared the worst. Indeed, certain faculty members seemed to feel guilty about "changing the system" and reacted noticeably to the merest hint of public displeasure. Then, too, as Hughes (1958) noted, schools and teachers adhere to safe, agreed-upon practices to avoid the charge of having made mistakes. In schools as elsewhere, service to clients is equated with following the proper procedure. For schools in transition, agreement about what are safe procedures is shaken until or unless criticism is felt and acted upon. Standardization is at least an adaptation if not a solution to, perhaps, the most severe implementation problem these schools faced—fickle, unremitting, intense task environment criticisms.

Incorporation

Here we refer to the implementation stage when the school decides it has achieved its goals and cuts back on its innovative efforts. The period preceding incorporation has been called the "intensive half-life" of the innovation (Wolcott, 1973), wherein great effort, vast amounts of time, and considerable money are poured into getting started. The "half-life" period also represents a level of exertion which many staff members cannot or will not sustain. Like the swimming champion who retires at the age of sixteen, so these faculties seem to have become emotionally exhausted and ready for a rest.

But, more than just exhaustion, there are other mechanisms which have the effect of reducing further innovative efforts. Teachers admitted to impending boredom, a feeling that all the excitement had drained away and no new worlds were left to conquer. In some schools when the powerful personalities who promoted change and expended as well as stimulated great effort—the "good" unit leaders or "super" principal—stepped down or moved on, no adequate replacements were visible. Others did promotion work for the innovation throughout the state: "Converts are called on to join the mission rather than come fully to grips with the meaning of their decision at home" (Wolcott, 1973). Indeed, the greatest efforts of the R&D center seem directed to the start-up phases. These schools noted that they did not get much help after the first year.

Public relations took its toll. Streams of visitors poured through the schools each year. Staff members were called in to give testimony in regional meetings. The innovation became a constant topic at monthly PTA meetings. After two years of effort, some schools seemed ready to claim complete implementation. Public relations occasions became episodes where such claims were advanced. Even in the face of criticism, the feeling of full implementation was enhanced. For example, in one PTA meeting the innovation became the fall guy in the staff's defensive reaction to parent critics. In arguing that MU was not for all students, the staff conveyed two messages: obvious blunders such as misplaced children were the fault of the new system and not the staff, and the innovation was set and could not be improved.

Otherwise, there was evidence that new unit members had difficulty in introducing changes they preferred or saw called for. Privately, some new faculty claimed their novel ideas were not welcome, that precedent, tradition, and status in the unit and school had been established along with a reluctance to adopt new ideas.

In brief, after two years or so, we found a novel implementation problem, incorporation—that is, ending implementation efforts too soon.

The Resolution of Implementation Problems

As mentioned, accounts of problem resolutions cannot be discussed in detail. The prime reason has to do with the lack of activity on the part of these schools which might conceivably qualify as solutions to problems. That is, there was little evidence to indicate that problems had been solved by the application of special techniques, logic, manipulation, or by systematic treatment. Moreover, although most problems received some attention by schools, there was little evidence to show that many had been solved.

A convenient way to deal with a problem is to dismiss or ignore it. Personnel in these schools evoked both of these strategies frequently, especially after attempted solutions had proven fallacious. In regard to specific events related to the two major implementation problems, increased work demands and task environment criticism, a number of corrective actions with short-term payoff were effectuated in response to almost every tiny, troublesome point in the myriad of related issues. The effects of these reactions, called here standardization and incorporation, can each be visualized in two ways: (1) as the sum of responses to an aggregated set of small changes and closely related troubles and (2) as a grand-scale problem resolution to a major implementation problem. Whatever, as one served to reduce variability by normalizing procedures and the other acted to inhibit continued implementation, each also can be thought of as a major implementation problem.

Conclusions

Considering both the Charters and Pellegin report (1972) and this paper, implementation problems appear to be related to three distinct sources: (1) the preexisting (in)capabilities of schools, (2) the vulnerability of new ideas and novel practices in schools, and (3) implementation progress. Roughly speaking, the three major implementation problems which can be identified by summing across the two papers appear to be independently linked to each source; the Charters-Pellegrin barriers to the first, task environment criticism to the second, and increased work demands to the third.

Finally, if these four multiunit schools are dependable representatives of implementation, then the search for facilitators to the implementation of collaborative staffing models must turn to other factors than the resolution of these three major problems. Prime candidates for future research focus are factors that operate such that the failure to resolve implementation problems does not prevent implementation.

References

Bidwell, Charles E. (1965). "The School as a Formal Organization," in J. G. March, ed., *Handbook of Organizations.* Chicago: Rand McNally.

Carlson, Richard O. (1964). "Environmental Constraints and Organizational Consequences: The Public School and Its Clients," in D. E. Griffiths, ed., *Behavioral Science and Educational Administration,* 63rd Yearbook of the National Society for the Study of Education. Chicago: University of Chicago Press.

_____ (forthcoming). Untitled final report of the Multiunit Project. Eugene, Ore.: Center for the Advanced Study of Educational Administration.

Charters, W. E., Jr. (1973). *Measuring the Implementation of Differentiated Staffing: A Comparison of Two Elementary Schools.* Eugene, Ore.: Center for the Advanced Study of Educational Administration, University of Oregon.

_____ , and Pellegrin, Roland J. (1972). "Barriers to the Innovation Process: Four Case Studies of Differentiated Staffing." *Educational Administration Quarterly,* 9.1(Winter).

Education U.S.A. (1972). Issue of September 18.

Gross, Neal, Giacquinta, Joseph B., and Bernstein, Marilyn (1971). *Implementing Organizational Innovations: A Sociological Analysis of Planned Educational Change.* New York: Basic Books, Inc.

Hughes, Everett C. (1958). *Men and Their Work.* Glencoe, Ill.: Free Press.

Klausmeier, Herbert J. (1971). "The Multi-Unit Elementary School and Individually Guided Education." *Phi Delta Kappan,* 53.3(November).

Multiunit Newsletter (1972). Issue for 4.1(October).

Packard, John S., and Willower, Donald J. (1972). "Pluralistic Ignorance and Pupil Control Ideology." *Journal of Educational Administration,* 10.1 (May).

Pellegrin, Roland J. (1969a). *Some Organizational Characteristics of Multiunit Schools.* Occasional Paper Series. Eugene, Ore.: Center for the Advanced Study of Educational Administration, University of Oregon, November.

_____ (1969b). *Professional Satisfaction and Decision Making in the Multiunit School.* Occasional Paper Series. Eugene, Ore.: Center for the Advanced Study of Educational Administration, University of Oregon, November.

_____ (forthcoming). "Schools as Work Organizations," in Robert Dubin, ed., *Handbook of Work, Organizations and Society.* Chicago: Rand McNally.

Smith, Louis M., and Keith, Pat M. (1971). *Anatomy of Educational Innovation: An Organizational Analysis of an Elementary School.* New York: Wiley.

Willower, Donald J. (1970). "Educational Change and Functional Equivalents." *Education and Urban Society* (August).

Wolcott, Harry F. (1973). "Three P's from a Pod: An Observer's Impressions of Staff Differentiation in a Multiunit Elementary School," in Mary-Margaret Scobey and John Fiorino, eds., *Differentiated Staffing*. Washington, D.C.: Association for Supervision and Curriculum Development. (An earlier draft of this paper constituted one of the four primary case histories on which this paper is based.)

21 Failure to Implement a Major Organizational Innovation

Neal Gross
Joseph B. Giacquinta
Marilyn Bernstein

In his incisive paper on "The Bearing of Empirical Research on Social Theory," Merton (1957, pages 85-117) points out that one of the ways in which empirical research invites the extension of theory is through observation of neglected facts. In his words (page 108), "When an existing conceptual scheme commonly applied to a subject-matter does not adequately take these facts into account, research presses insistently for its reformulation. It leads to the introduction of variables which have not been systematically included in the scheme of the analysis."

A case study we conducted of an elementary school attempting to implement a major organizational innovation led us to identify a set of facts that were of critical importance in explaining why the implementation effort failed; they appear to have been neglected in schemes of analysis proposed to account for the success or failure of efforts to implement changes in organizations. . . . We shall report selected findings of that case study and attempt to spell out their theoretical implications.

Reprinted from *Learning in Social Settings: New Readings on the Social Psychology of Education*, edited by Matthew B. Miles and W. W. Charters (Boston: Allyn and Bacon, 1970), pp. 691-705. Copyright 1970 by Allyn and Bacon, Inc., Boston. Reprinted with permission. Adapted from a paper read at the American Sociological Association meetings, Boston, August 1968.

The Implementation of Organizational Innovations:
The Way the Problem Has Been Conceptualized

In their attempts to account for the success or failure of deliberate or planned organizational change, social scientists have generally tended to conceptualize the problem as one of overcoming organizational members' resistance to change. (For examples, see Argyle, 1967, pages 87-101; Coch and French, 1948, pages 512-532; Lawrence, 1954; and Zander, 1961, pages 543-548.) Argyle's consideration of change in organizations provides a good illustration of this type of formulation. He states:

In the first place, there is usually resistance to change of any sort. . . . In social organizations, patterns of behaviour become established and are of great stability because individuals work out drive-reducing ways of adapting, and fear that any change will be to their disadvantage in some way. Changes in industry are resisted by workers because they are afraid that they will be paid less or will have to work harder to earn the same amount. Wage-incentive schemes have often foundered for this reason. Changes are resisted by managers because they are afraid that their position will be weakened somehow or that they will be further from the center of power. Current changes in prisons are resisted by prison officers and prisoners alike because they have no desire to be associated with each other . . . There is anxiety either about possible material loss or about the disruption of a well-established and satisfying social system.

As a consequence of this definition of the problem, many efforts to account for the success or failure of attempts to implement organizational change have focused on the ability of management or a change agent to overcome members' initial resistance to change.[1] Thus, Argyle, after his enumeration of a number of reasons why organizational members will resist change (1967, page 95), states, "It may be impossible to bring about change in the teeth of such resistance, and it is usually possible only if the new scheme can be shown to be advantageous. This may be achieved by means of financial

1. For example, see Warren G. Bennis (1966, p. 176). He views the following conditions as necessary elements for successful implementation. The client system needs to have as much influence as possible in developing and controlling the fate of change; it must have trust in the initiator; the client system must perceive the change effort as being as self-motivated and voluntary as possible; the change program must include emotional and value elements as well as cognitive elements. Bennis emphasizes that the quality of the relationship between the change agent and client system is "pivotal to the success of a change program" because the change agent "can be crucial in reducing the resistance to change by providing consultation and psychological support during the *transitional* phase of the change." (Italics ours.)

incentives, honorific ranks, training courses, or by sheer persuasive skill."

The premise of organizational members' resistance to change appears to be linked to the power-equalization concept,[2] which has been frequently invoked to account for the differential success of organizations in implementing innovations. This theory can be construed as assuming that members who must implement innovations will offer resistance to them unless they have been involved in formulating the innovation in the first place. It is further assumed that this resistance constitutes the major obstacle to the implementation of innovations. Thus, to overcome this resistance, management must share its power with those who must implement innovations by allowing them to participate in decisions about the change to be made. Implementers will then presumably perceive the innovation as self-imposed and thereby become committed to it.

Thus, in discussing styles of administration as they bear on organizational change, Argyle (1967, page 95) maintains:

The main principle here is that subordinates should be persuaded and motivated rather than ordered—so that they actually want to behave in the new way. This persuasive and democratic style means allowing people to take part in discussion and decisions.

And Leavitt, in his review of the power equalization approaches to organizational change (1965, page 1159) notes:

Power equalization has thus become a key concept in several of the prevalent people theories, a first step in the theoretical causal chain leading toward organizational change. It has been constructed as an initial subgoal, a necessary predecessor to creative change in structure, technology, task-solving, and the task implementation. Although the distances are unmarked, there is no obscurity about direction: a more egalitarian distribution is better.

The theme of resistance to change on the part of organizational members also is stressed in the body of group dynamics literature that deals with the problem of organizational change. It is asserted that through human relations training in sensitivity or T groups, organizational members' resistance to change can be "unfrozen" and a positive orientation to change can be instilled.[3] (Such training also

2. For a detailed discussion of this concept and its use in the planned organizational change literature, see Leavitt (1965).

3. For specific examples see Argyris (1962); Bradford, Gibb, and Benne (1964); Jaques (1951); Miles (1959); Lewin (1947); and Schein and Bennis (1965). For reviews of work related to this general area, see Greiner (1967); Katz and Kahn (1966, pp. 390-451); Leavitt (1965); and Miles (1965).

deals with other matters, such as efforts to improve communication, trust, and problem-solving skills. Resistance to change, however, never becomes a minor factor.)

Formulations that tend to view the problem of implementing organizational innovations as primarily one of overcoming organizational members' initial resistance to change appear to be too simplistic. Three general and interrelated conditions that they underplay, and that seem to us to be of critical importance, are: (1) organizational members who are *not* resistant to change may encounter obstacles in their efforts to implement an innovation; (2) individuals in organizations are in part dependent upon members of their role set to overcome these obstacles, and these members may or may not provide aid; and (3) members who are initially favorable to organizational change may develop a negative orientation to an innovation, as a consequence of the frustrations they have encountered in attempting to carry it out.

To explore these notions, we embarked on a study of an organization attempting to implement a major innovation in which members had an initial positive orientation to change. We reasoned that, if our reservations about the "resistance to change" explanations were groundless, then we should find that the implementation effort would be successful. If the implementation effort failed, then this might offer support for our contention that more complex schemes are needed to account for the success or failure of the implementation of organizational innovations. In this event, such a study also would provide evidence about the specific obstacles that confront organizational members as they attempt to implement organizational changes, and specific ways in which they are dependent on members of their role set.

An opportunity to conduct such a case study arose in the summer of 1966. We now turn to that study and its findings. In the final section of this paper we will propose a tentative theory of the implementation of organizational innovations, suggested by the results of our inquiry.

The Innovations and the Educational Setting

The innovation, a new definition of the teacher's role, was described by its originator to the teachers in an official document in November of 1966 as follows:

1. Teachers were expected to behave in ways that would assist children to learn according to *their* interests rather than in terms of a prescribed curriculum;

2. Teachers were expected to emphasize the process, not the content, of learning, and to allow pupils maximum freedom in choosing their own activities;
3. Teachers were expected to see that the classroom was saturated with a variety of educational materials, primarily self-instructional in nature, so that children could pursue their own interests;
4. Teachers were expected to act as facilitators of learning between children and materials and to encourage teaching of children by other children;
5. Teachers were expected to allow pupils to decide the materials they wished to work with, how long they would work with them, and with whom they wished to relate;
6. Teachers were expected to give pupils primary responsibility for directing their own learning and to assist them only when they perceived that their help was desired or needed.

The elementary school contained nearly two hundred pupils and eleven full-time teachers, and was located in a lower-class urban area of the central city of an eastern metropolitan area of the United States. Nearly 60 percent of the residents of this area were Negro, and they had encountered serious financial, housing, transportation, and educational problems. In 1965, in response to pressure from citizens in this and other sections of the city for new schools and improvements of the quality of education in existing schools, the Board of Education created a Bureau for Educational Change, financed by a large federal grant. It was charged with the responsibility of creating and administering laboratory schools; the school we studied was one of them. They were expected to focus primarily on developing and testing new programs to improve means of educating "disadvantaged students." An educational specialist brought from outside the school system was appointed as the director of the bureau, and became director of the school as well. He was the originator of the innovation.

The laboratory school into which he introduced the innovation in November 1966 contained a very positive external and internal climate for educational change. The parents and higher administrative officials had expressed a strong interest in obtaining improvements in the educational program of the school. The director was well known as an educational innovator and as a person who had strong beliefs about the necessity of educational change. He was given considerable autonomy in the operation of the laboratory school and freedom in selecting its faculty. He had attempted to secure a staff who were dissatisfied with the existing educational program offered to children in the ghetto and who had evinced a strong interest in educational change. Because of support by Title III funds, the financial and personnel resources of the laboratory school were substantially greater than those of other elementary schools. In addition to the teaching faculty, there were three subject specialists, student teachers, and teacher aides. Teachers received an additional payment of about 15 percent of their base salaries to compensate them for the additional time and energy they would be required to expend as members of a laboratory school staff.

In the fall of 1966, a basic norm of the school was that teachers should accept and promote educational change. Our interviews revealed that all teachers recognized and accepted the need for major educational innovations in slum schools, and our field observations showed that they were using new types of instructional materials and that the administration was rewarding innovative behavior. Therefore, it was not surprising that the interviews showed that no teachers were resistant to attempting to implement the innovation at the outset. When it was first announced, all indicated that they were willing to make efforts to carry it out, even though four of the eleven teachers in the school had negative reactions to the innovation.

In a forthcoming book, *The Implementation of Educational Innovations,* we present a detailed description of the research methods used in conducting the study, the problems that were encountered in carrying it out, and how we attempted to resolve them. An extensive body of data was collected on the basis of daily field observations conducted over nearly a seven-month period, the examination of public and private documents, and informal and formal interviews with the teachers, their administrators, and other school personnel. Evidence from several sources indicated that a high degree of rapport had been developed between the field worker and the faculty. The formal interviews with the teachers, averaging three hours in length, were carried out in the spring of 1967, just prior to three weeks of intensive daily classroom observations. These observations were conducted in an effort to assess the degree to which the innovation had been implemented.

Findings of the Case Study and Their Theoretical Implications

Despite the set of apparently positive antecedent and prevailing conditions that existed in the school system, community, and school in November 1966, when the innovation was first introduced to the teachers six months later, we found that practically no effort was being made to implement the innovation. In May 1967 all teachers were still behaving, for the most part, in accord with the traditional role model.[4] They were devoting very little time to trying to implement the innovation and, within that small period of time, their performance did not conform to key expectations of the new role model. We concluded that this was a case of a failure to implement a major organizational innovation.

A "resistance to change" explanation could not account for the failure of the teachers to implement the innovation; all the teachers had been positively predisposed to accept major organizational changes in the school when the innovation was presented to them.

The findings suggested that the failure of the teachers to implement the innovation in May could be traced to a set of unresolved problems or barriers to which they were exposed after they attempted to carry it out.

Barriers to Organizational Members' Implementing Innovations

One barrier to which organizational members can be exposed is *lack of clarity* about the innovation that they are being requested to implement. Our observations of teachers suggested that most of them

---

4. Our assessment of the degree of implementation focused on both the quantity and quality of the effort teachers made to carry it out in May 1967. To determine the quantity of staff effort, we observed and then calculated the proportion of (their) time that teachers behaved in accord with the traditional role model as compared to the new role model. This required the observer to make repeated "rounds" each day to check all classes and to keep running records of the amount of time teachers devoted to performance in line with each role model. Analysis of data collected for this aspect of the assessment showed that the staff overall during this period spent nearly 85 percent of the total time available to them in their classrooms behaving in accord with the *old* role model. To determine the quality of the teachers' performance during the time that they did devote to making "innovative efforts," the observer conducted in-depth systematic observations using an observation schedule of teacher performance in classrooms randomly selected for observation to guard against observer bias. Analysis of data collected for this purpose revealed that within the 15 percent of time which teachers allotted to "innovative effort," their performance typically did not conform to key expectations of the new role model (for example, their obligation to act as catalysts between children and materials, and among children). Moreover, interviews with many teachers, as well as teachers-in-training who were present in the classrooms and who understood the innovation, corroborated these two findings: (1) that teachers were spending most of their time in classrooms behaving according to the traditional role model and (2) that their relatively small amount of "innovative performance" had serious deficiencies. A detailed discussion of the rationale underlying the evaluation, the assessment procedures employed, and our analysis of the data are presented in chapter five of the previously mentioned book.

did not have a clear image of the role performance expected of them. Our formal interviews confirmed these field observations. They revealed that most teachers were confused about the innovation when it was first described to them in November, when they initially attempted to implement it in January, and just prior to our assessment of the degree of implementation in May.

In reporting our findings we shall present the responses of ten of the eleven teachers since the validity of the replies of one teacher to the formal and informal interviews is highly questionable.[5] When we asked the teachers, "After you first heard about the innovation did you have a clear picture of what you were expected to do in carrying it out?" nine of the ten responded in the negative. Here are some typical responses to the follow-up question, "In what respects was the innovation unclear?" One teacher replied, "At that time, *and still,* what methods would best implement it . . ."; a second responded, "It's unclear in most ways; how are you supposed to get a new idea across to children when he [the Director] didn't want us to call children together; I am unclear as to my role!" A third said, "How should the classroom teacher behave in this situation? The brochure never spelled out the teacher's job!" And a fourth replied, "What is the teacher's role? Should she outline daily activities? Should she spur children on? Would the activity period be all or part of the day?"

When these teachers were asked about their understanding of the innovation just before they were requested to make their first efforts to implement it in January, eight of the ten teachers again indicated confusion about it. As one teacher put it, "I still really don't have a clear understanding of the innovation, and I can assure you that I'm not the only one." Probe questions directed at the two teachers who felt they were clearer about the new role model in January than November indicated that they, too, had at best hazy notions about what was expected of them. And when we asked the teachers about the clarity of the innovation in May, just prior to our assessment of its degree of implementation, eight of the ten teachers indicated that they still had an ambiguous notion of what was expected of them.

Our findings suggest, in short, that the clarity of an innovation as

5. The decision was made for two reasons. First, several teachers reported in confidence to the field worker that this teacher was intentionally misinforming him. They quoted him as saying privately that he was telling the field worker what he thought the field worker wanted to hear. Second, there were serious discrepancies between what this teacher reported about his behavior and the field worker's observations of that behavior.

perceived by organizational members needs to be taken into account in conceptual schemes designed to explain the success or failure of implementation efforts.

A second potential obstacle to the implementation of an organizational innovation is that members may *lack the capabilities* required to carry it out. All teachers reported that serious problems arose when they made their initial efforts to implement the innovation in January. They all indicated that these problems persisted during the following months when they attempted to carry it out, and, furthermore, that new problems, with which they could not cope, also arose. In the words of one teacher, "I never was able to instigate enthusiasm in these kids while keeping the noise level down, and I never knew how to get them to use their time for learning instead of playing. The children were beginning to abuse freedom; they wouldn't do any work; they wouldn't record what they had done; many became discipline problems who weren't in the beginning. I just didn't know what to do." All teachers reported that they had encountered serious problems in maintaining discipline. Nine out of ten said that their pupils had "just played around with materials" or "made no effort to learn something from the materials." Eight out of ten mentioned related problems: difficulties in keeping children interested, in motivating them, in stimulating them to pursue their own interests, and in getting them to help each other with their learning problems. Most reported that large numbers of their pupils were continually demanding "direction" from them. This evidence, and much more that could be cited, indicates that the teachers were beset with a host of serious and unresolved difficulties during their attempts to implement the new role model. In this sense they were incapable of performing in accord with the new role model. We, therefore, concluded that their abandonment of efforts to implement the innovation in May was in part because they lacked the skill and knowledge to perform the new role.

A third obstacle is that organizational members may *lack the tools and equipment* required to carry innovations out. In a brochure prepared for the teachers by the administration, they were told that teachers should "transfer as much of the instructional and 'motivational' responsibilities as possible from the teacher to the total classroom environment—and to the greatly enhanced materials with which the room should be filled."

But our observations in the classrooms revealed that "highly motivating self-instructional materials" were never made available to teachers in their efforts to carry out the innovation. For example, the list of materials available to teachers in the primary grades for reading consisted of independent work sheets, word games such as "Spill and Spell," vocabulary flash cards, riddles, a set of telephones, and some library books. For mathematics, there were Cuisenaire rods, an abacus, "Count the Beads," a scale, math card games, math flash cards, a printing set for numerals; for art, the materials available consisted of paper and various media like crayons and water paints; and for writing, a typewriter was available.

Most of these materials represent the kind of supplementary materials that can be found in a well-stocked suburban elementary school. They did not appear to, nor did they in fact, represent instructional materials that permitted pupils to progress very far in a meaningful way on their own, that is, without instruction from the teacher. These materials were not only of dubious quality in terms of their intended educational objectives, but were also in short supply when the teachers attempted to implement the innovation. Eight of the ten teachers complained bitterly about the paucity of curriculum materials when they described their earlier efforts to implement the innovation. These findings suggest a third variable, the availability of tools and equipment, that needs to be taken into account in explaining the success or failure of efforts to implement innovations.

A fourth obstacle is *organizational conditions existing prior to and during an innovation's introduction that are incompatible* with the innovation. Although we were able to isolate many circumstances of this kind, we shall consider here only two of them.

The first is that, although the nature of the innovation required a highly flexible educational environment, most aspects of the rigid school schedule that existed prior to its introduction were retained. All children were kept out of the school building in the morning until the 8:30 bell rang and released in the afternoon by the 2:20 bell; a second bell rang in the morning before classes began. Bells were also rung for recess and lunch; all classes were expected to participate in recess from 10:30 to 11:00 and lunch from 12:00 to 12:30. Teachers were expected to adhere to this schedule. Children were taken in groups to lavatories at lunch and recess; they were required to walk up and down stairs in single lines, and were dismissed at the end of the day in a similar fashion. Moreover, children were required to participate in certain types of activities regardless of their interests. These included reading in the morning, art, music, sewing, gym, and field trips. The continuation of these school procedures clearly served to block the teachers' efforts to implement the innovation.

The second illustration is the retention of the old system of evaluating pupils. At the time of the announcement of the innovation, the school was using a report card system requiring teachers to "give grades" to each child for his mastery of different skills and subjects. However, the innovation specified that teachers should focus on the process of learning and the "operational competencies" involved, such as defining problems, organizing evidence and information, comparing and differentiating phenomena, and developing hypotheses. The system of evaluating pupils, therefore, would require alteration if teachers were to encourage these new types of behaviors in their pupils. However, the old report card system was retained. The teachers were not only acutely aware of the lack of congruence between the ostensible purposes of the innovation and the "outmoded" criteria they were being asked to apply to their pupils; they also became increasingly upset about this discrepancy over time. The extent to which organizational properties are compatible with innovations introduced into an organization, then, is a fourth important variable in explaining the implementation of organizational innovations.

Finally, our study suggested another important variable: the influence that management, as an important segment of the subordinate's role set, can have on the implementation process. We do not question the proposition that, if organizational members are resistant to change, power equalization efforts by management may be one means by which their resistance may be reduced. However, the performance of management can have a critical bearing on the implementation of innovations in other ways, most notably in establishing the conditions that will permit subordinates to implement innovations, and in rewarding them for their efforts.

In our case study, we asked why the barriers teachers encountered when they attempted to implement the innovations were never removed. The evidence indicated that the teachers' lack of clarity about the new role model could largely be attributed to the following conditions: ambiguities in the minds of the director and his administrative subordinates about the specific nature of the new role requirements for teachers; the failure of the administrators to provide effective mechanisms for teachers to obtain clarification about their role expectations; and the failure of the staff to secure clarification about the innovation, because of their lack of confidence in the capabilities of their administrators. In attempting to account for the staff's lack of capability in its attempts to implement the innovation, we concluded that this condition could be largely explained by the failure of the administration to recognize that the teachers needed to be resocialized if they were to conform to the new definition of their role, and its failure to provide them with the type of retraining they required. The lack of self-instructional materials which the teachers needed to implement the innovation was attributed in part to bureaucratic regulations about purchasing them. But more important was the unwillingness of the administration to face up to the reality that teachers had neither the skills nor time required to develop new instructional materials on the job. The failure to make modifications in organizational arrangements was traced back to the administration's unawareness that existing organizational elements were incompatible with the implementation of the innovation, and to a lack of commitment on the part of the director's key administrative subordinate to it.

These findings led us to conclude that teachers were unable to implement the innovation largely because the administration failed to recognize or to cope effectively with the problems to which it exposed teachers when it asked them to carry it out. This condition, we would contend, was a consequence of the director's simplistic view of the process of the implementation of organizational innovations and his lack of awareness of his role obligations to his subordinates when he initiated this process.

The director's view of the steps required to implement the innovation, as evidenced by the strategy he employed, may be described as follows: (1) explain the philosophy and objectives of the innovation through several written documents to the staff; (2) give teachers maximum freedom to carry it out; and (3) delegate responsibility to an administrative subordinate (the assistant director) to see that the innovation is implemented.

The director's strategy was inadequate, for two basic reasons. First, it failed to take account of difficulties to which teachers would probably be exposed when they attempted to implement the innovation. Second, it contained no provisions for mechanisms to identify and cope with unanticipated problems that might emerge during the period of attempted implementation.

The director's strategy for implementing the innovation gave practically no consideration to the kinds of obstacles that were likely to confront the teachers as they attempted to implement the new role model. Since the director's strategy essentially ignored these potential problems, no efforts were instituted prior to the introduction of the innovation to attempt to remove these barriers; nor was consideration given to ways to cope with them if they emerged during the period of attempted implementation.

The second major deficiency in the director's strategy was its lack of feedback mechanisms. The assistant director had a number of reservations about the innovation, as did the subject specialists and a number of the teachers. But the assistant director was never given adequate opportunity to communicate his feelings to the director about this matter, and the teachers and subject specialists never spoke frankly about them to their superiors. And, for still other interpersonal and organizational problems that occurred during the period of attempted implementation, open and frank discussion never occurred.

The director made numerous assumptions about the innovation and the operation of the school that were in fact tenuous. He assumed that the assistant director and he were in agreement about the nature of the innovation. He assumed that the teachers did not need outside assistance in coping with their classroom problems and that those that did arise could be effectively handled by the assistant director or the subject specialists. But these and other assumptions he made were in fact erroneous, and since he did not provide for feedback mechanisms in his strategy of implementation, he had no way of obtaining "the facts" and thereby could not identify or cope with these unrecognized implementation barriers.

This suggests that subordinates may be unable or find it difficult to make changes in their role performance unless management conforms to a set of expectations that subordinates "have a right to hold" for its performance. More specifically, subordinates have a right to expect management (1) to take the steps necessary to provide them with a clear picture of their new role requirements, (2) to adjust organizational arrangements to make them compatible with the innovation, (3) to provide subordinates with the resocialization experiences required to develop the capabilities needed to cope with the difficulties involved in implementing the innovation, (4) to provide the resources necessary to carry out the innovation, and (5) to provide the appropriate supports and rewards to maintain subordinates' willingness to make implementation efforts.

Furthermore, subordinates have a right to expect management to be committed to the implementation of the innovation, and to provide effective mechanisms and decision-making procedures to cope with anticipated and unanticipated problems that may arise during attempted implementation. Our findings, in short, suggest that the extent to which these expectations are recognized by management, built into its strategy, and conformed to will have a direct bearing on the degree to which subordinates implement organizational innovations. The role of management in the implementation process needs to be brought to center stage in theoretical formulations of the problem.

The Time Dimension

Our third reservation about "resistance" explanations was that they minimize the fact that resistance can develop over time among organizational members who are positively predisposed to change, as a consequence of frustrations they have encountered in attempting to implement an innovation.

As noted earlier, there was a general acceptance of the need for change at the school in November 1966, and a general willingness to make the efforts needed to carry out the innovation. Furthermore, the data showed that, although four of the teachers had negative reactions to the innovation at the time of its announcement, all reported a willingness to try to make implementation efforts.

The general picture, however, changed between the time of the innovation's announcement by management in the fall and our assessment the following spring. We found then that most staff members were no longer willing to make the necessary effort to try to implement the new role.

The following statements illustrate the reactions of teachers to the innovation at that time. After a brief absence from school, one teacher noted sardonically, "Ya know, I was sitting home the last two days saying that it can't really be that way, and that this school can't be as bad as I think it is; then I came back. Ya know, it really *is* that mixed up, confused, and nutty!" Another said, "I wonder whether it's worth the effort one has to put into it [the innovation] . . . . I can't really tell how much they're learning nor how many are learning. . . ." In a statement revealing more openly the frustrations teachers were facing with the innovation, a third exclaimed, "I'm just getting tired; I can't take it with the kids anymore; I can't see what good it's [the innovation] doing; it's not worth it. . . . I go home and I've got a headache; I bite my nails. . . ." A fourth teacher reacting to the lack of discipline in children, which she felt was caused by their response to the innovation, exclaimed, "The kids are getting really fresh now. . . . Yesterday I had to go home and take two tranquilizers. The worst class is the second grade . . . ; what one child said to me I couldn't repeat. . . . I really hated coming to school today; I am sick of this place. . . ."

Our findings thus suggest that resistance to making implementation efforts can develop over time among members originally positive to changing, because of problems and ensuing frustrations encountered during the period when they attempt to carry an innovation out.

A Tentative Theory of the Implementation of Organizational Innovation

The findings of our case study thus indicate a number of conditions and circumstances that appeared to account for the failure of the implementation efforts. These are not taken into consideration by theoretical formulations which define the problem of implementing organizational changes as primarily one of overcoming resistance to change.

We would suggest that an explanation of the process of implementation of organizational innovations needs, as a start, to be based on the five following assumptions:

The first is that the degree to which members of an organization have a clear understanding of the innovation will be positively related to their ability to implement it. If they have an ambiguous understanding of the innovation, then they will be unclear about what is expected of them. If they have an erroneous interpretation of the innovation, then their efforts at implementation will be misguided.

The second assumption is that a staff's ability to implement an innovation will be a function of its capacity to carry it out. If teachers lack the skills required to perform in accord with the demands of the innovation, then it will be impossible for them to carry it out.

The third condition is that their ability to carry it out will be a function of the availability of the tools and resources required by the innovation. The fourth condition is the compatibility of organizational arrangements with the innovation. If arrangements in existence prior to the introduction of the innovation are incompatible with it and are not changed, then it will be more difficult for organizational members to carry it out.

However, if all of these conditions are fulfilled, it does not follow that the staff will implement an innovation. Staff members must also be motivated to expend the time and effort required for implementation.

Our next assumption is that the extent to which these five conditions are fulfilled will be a function of the performance of management. If ambiguity or confusion exists in the minds of the staff, management is in the best position to clarify the situation. Furthermore, the authority to establish training programs and provide the materials and tools required for the innovation is lodged in management. In addition, only it has the power to make changes in organizational arrangements that are incompatible with the innovation. And management, too, is in the position to offer the types of rewards and punishments that can motivate the staff to expend the time and effort required to implement an innovation.

If, as we have assumed, the implementation by the staff of an innovation is a function of the degree to which the five conditions specified above are fulfilled, and if the extent to which these conditions are fulfilled is a consequence of management's performance, then it follows that the degree of implementation of an organizational innovation will be a function of the extent to which management fulfills these conditions.

Final Considerations

Until now we have stressed findings of the case study that suggest the need for the reformulation of "resistance" conceptualizations. Several additional reservations about these formulations can be made.

First, the assumption that organizational members are resistant to change may be tenuous in many empirical situations. It assumes that members are generally satisfied with existing organizational conditions and thus that any disturbance in them, such as a proposed change, will be met with resistance. We submit that in many organizations the empirical reality is that many members are exposed to difficult problems in their work situation, and would welcome innovations that would appear to offer solutions to their difficulties. The degree to which organizational members are resistant to change needs to be taken as problematic, rather than as "a given," in theoretical formulations of the successful implementation of organizational innovations.

Secondly, some existing conceptualizations assume that the nature or complexity of an innovation is irrelevant to its successful implementation. It may turn out, however, that different strategies of implementation tend to be more or less effective, depending upon such circumstances as the magnitude of change required of organizational members in carrying out the innovation, and the difficulties it creates for them. This suggests the need for a typology of innovations, and the possibility that different explanations will be required to account for the successful implementation of different types of organizational innovations. In this connection, it is important to note that the theoretical explanation we offer in this paper to account for the implementation of organizational innovations may be relevant for only certain kinds of major organizational innovations, for example, those involving radical changes in the role performance of organizational members.

Finally, we wish to emphasize that our reflections have led us to recognize the need to conceive of successful implementation as the result of a process which can be reversed or halted at numerous points in time. We suggest that this process must fulfill simultaneously the five conditions specified earlier if maximum implementation is to be achieved. Since these conditions are not likely to prevail in most organizations when the decision is made to introduce an innovation, they must be developed prior to or during the period of attempted implementation. It may well be that there is a sequence of stages involved in fulfilling the several conditions. Furthermore, because the conditions, even when achieved at one stage of the process, can be reversed, problems of their maintenance need to be considered as well as those of their development.

If this dynamic conception of implementation has merit, then management would need to develop a strategy which takes into account this processual view of the problem. One contribution of research could be the systematic isolation of factors in a variety of settings that block or facilitate management's efforts to lead organizations through such a process.

The implications or generalizations drawn from a single case study, of course, must be taken with many grains of salt. We would have greater confidence in our conclusions, if they had emerged from studies of both successful and unsuccessful efforts to implement organizational innovations. However, we believe our study does raise a number of basic questions that have been minimized or overlooked in schemes designed to account for the success or failure of the implementation of organizational innovations, and [it] suggests a number of variables that need to be taken into account in subsequent theoretical formulations.

References

Argyle, M. (1967). "The Social Psychology of Social Change," in T. Burns and S. B. Saul, eds., *Social Theory and Economic Change*. London: Tavistock Publications.

Argyris, C. (1962). *Interpersonal Competence and Organizational Effectiveness*. Homewood, Ill.: Irwin.

Bennis, W. G. (1966). *Changing Organizations*. New York: McGraw-Hill.

Bradford, L. P., Gibb, J. R., and Benne, K. D., eds. (1964). *T-group Theory and Laboratory Method*. New York: Wiley.

Coch, L., and French, J., Jr. (1948). "Overcoming Resistance to Change." *Human Relations*, 4:512-532.

Greiner, L. E. (1967). "Patterns of Organizational Change." *Harvard Business Review*, 45:119-128.

Jaques, E. (1951). *The Changing Culture of a Factory*. London: Tavistock Publications.

Katz, D., and Kahn, R. L. (1966). *The Social Psychology of Organizations*. New York: Wiley.

Lawrence, P. R. (1954). "How to Deal with Resistance to Change." *Harvard Business Review*, 32:49-57.

Leavitt, H. J. (1965). "Applied Organizational Change in Industry: Structural, Technological and Humanistic Approaches," in J. G. March, ed., *Handbook of Organizations*. Chicago: Rand McNally, pp. 1144-1170.

Lewin, K. (1947). "Frontiers in Group Dynamics." *Human Relations*, 1:5-41.

Merton, R. K. (1957). *Social Theory and Social Structure*, rev. ed. Glencoe: Free Press.

Miles, M. B. (1959). *Learning to Work in Groups*. New York: Teachers College Press.

Miles, R. E. (1965). "Human Relations or Human Resources?" *Harvard Business Review*, 43:148-157.

Schein, E. H., and Bennis, W. G. (1965). *Personal and Organizational Change through Group Methods*. New York: Wiley.

Zander, A. (1961). "Resistance to Change—Its Analysis and Prevention," in W. G. Bennis, K. D. Benne, and R. Chin, eds., *The Planning of Change*. New York: Holt, Rinehart and Winston.

22 Organizational Change: Institutional Sagas, External Challenges, and Internal Politics

J. Victor Baldridge

For decades New York University's uptown Bronx campus, with its excellent liberal arts college, had been the pride of the university. In summer 1973 the university took a drastic step and sold the entire campus to the state of New York for the modest sum of $62,000,000. The storm clouds of financial crisis that had threatened the very existence of NYU had finally reached their darkest point. This event, the culmination of dramatic changes that had shaken NYU for fifteen years, provides a focal point for analyzing a major organizational change.

Organizational Change Themes

Although organizational theory has spawned a large amount of literature about organizational change, most of those studies are part of the organizational development group and its "human relations" approach to organizational changes. (See the excellent review of the literature in Katz and Kahn, 1966, chapter 13.) The development group's strategies typically focus on small-scale changes involving intergroup relations, communication patterns, and authority relationships between subordinates and superiors. Although this literature is

This chapter, completed with the editorial assistance of Jeanette Wheeler, was prepared under the sponsorship of the Stanford Center for Research and Development in Teaching, Stanford University, Stanford, California.

rich in its implications for some kinds of organizational change, it is not always useful for those concerned with large-scale organizational dynamics, institutional survival, and the relationships between institutions and their environments.

This study concentrates on the major organizational change of a massive university during its fight for survival. It was a situation charged with major shifts in organizational mission and goals, with heavy threats from outside forces, and with conflict-filled plays for power. Three intellectual themes interweave as they form a framework to examine the problems of organizational change.

The Organizational Saga Theme

Burton R. Clark (1970, 1972) has argued that some organizations develop deeply rooted institutional missions and mythologies. The "organizational saga" encapsulates the *content* of an institution's missions and goals. What does the institution believe in; what are its major guidelines; in what direction is it moving? Knowing the direction of an institution's mission is especially necessary to understand large-scale organizational changes because missions that shift or are attacked by outside forces demand major adjustments within the organization.

The Environmental Theme

Many theorists have concluded that the prime impetus for large-scale change in organizations usually comes from external forces. (See Katz and Kahn, 1966.) This is an interesting shift in perspective since most change-oriented literature examines small-scale human relations problems within an organization and ignores the massive organizational changes that occur under powerful external pressures. This research analyzes the external environment, the *source* of the forces for change.

The Political Conflict Theme

While the saga theme focuses on content and the environmental theme focuses on the source of change, the political theme, in turn, examines the *processes* of change. (For a development of the political process in organizations, see Baldridge, 1971.) These processes include the responses of organizational interest groups to external pressures and their attempts to influence decisions during change. Rarely are organizational responses to external threats rationally planned. Instead, the conflict-filled process pits competing blocs within the institution against each other to gain the power to protect their threatened domains.

This study, then, is about a series of large-scale changes that affected New York University. The three themes blended together help to interpret the process. NYU had developed an institutional saga, a set of beliefs and mission statements that guided its actions. The viability of the institution and its missions were threatened by a series of massive external changes. In response to these changes, heavy organizational conflict and political activities emerged as the institution tried to revitalize its saga. This case study demonstrates the usefulness of the three themes for the study of large-scale organizational change.

Methodology

Two methodological thrusts are made. One has been widely used (case studies); the other has been largely neglected (historical analysis). The case study approach focuses on events within a single institution, a strategy common to organizational research. In 1968-69, eighteen months were devoted to an analysis of change processes at NYU. The principal research techniques were interviews with eighty-one faculty and administrators, a survey of all faculty, and participant observation in executive decision councils. In 1974 follow-up visits were made to update the materials.

There was a major attempt to assemble a historical study of the institution, primarily through the use of document analysis. This strategy is too often omitted in organizational analysis. Sociologists, in general, and organization theorists, in particular, tend to ignore the historical roots of a social system: tradition, culture, ethos, and deep-rooted values. It may be, in studying organizational change, that attention is on immediate interventions and findings that can be quickly translated into administrative policies. The neglect of history may also stem from the fact that most sociologists lack training in historical analysis. The case study technique, coupled with serious attention to organizational history, does, however, provide a depth and richness that highlights many problems of organizational change.

Organizational Saga

The study of organizational goals and values has often been the subject of theorizing and research, but one of the most penetrating studies was Philip Selznick's *TVA and the Grass Roots* (1948). Selznick recounts how the original institutional mission of TVA gradually eroded as powerful interest groups from the local community were co-opted into the decision councils. The mission became sharply redirected.

Following in Selznick's tradition, Burton R. Clark has always been fascinated by problems of institutional values, goals, and missions. His early work, *Adult Education in Transition: A Study of Institutional Insecurity* (1956), examined the "precarious values" of an organization that was lodged in a hostile environment. Later Clark looked at the consequences of the "open door" mission statements of community colleges and how that philosophy produced major changes in the San Jose Community College (1960). Clark develops the notion of "organizational saga," a belief system that provided purpose and direction for the three elite colleges he studied: Reed, Swarthmore, and Antioch. Clark defines an organizational saga in the following terms:

An *organizational saga* is a collective understanding of unique accomplishment in a formally established group. The group's definition of the accomplishment, intrinsically historical but embellished through retelling and rewriting, links stages of organizational development. The participants have added affect, an emotional loading, which places their conception between the coolness of rational purpose and the warmth of sentiment found in religion and magic. An organizational saga presents some rational explanation of how certain means led to certain ends, but it also includes affect that turns a formal place into a beloved institution, to which participants may be passionately devoted . . . .

The study of organizational sagas highlights nonstructural and nonrational dimensions of organizational life and achievement. Macroorganizational theory has concentrated on the role of structure and technology in organizational effectiveness . . . . A needed corrective is more research on the cultural and expressive aspects of organizations, particularly on the role of belief and sentiment at broad levels of organization . . . . With a general emphasis on normative bonds, organizational saga refers to a unified set of publicly expressed beliefs about the formal group that (a) is rooted in history, (b) claims unique accomplishment, and (c) is held with sentiment by the group [Clark, 1972, pages 178-179].

Clark seems to imply that an organization either has a saga or it does not, and he picks small, elite colleges that have clearly articulated, rich cultural belief systems—attitudes intensely held by the faculty, the students, and the community at large.

A Continuum Formulation of Saga

It probably would be an improvement on Clark's notion if we saw the structure of organizational beliefs as a continuum varying on the dimensions of clarity, degree of cohesion in accepting the beliefs by organizational participants, and environmental reinforcement. At one end of the continuum would be organizations with sharply defined sagas, widely shared among participants and reinforced by the environment. At the other end would be organizations with weak sagas or flabby fragmented beliefs, poorly articulated, that produce many subunit goals that have no unifying effect. Environmental support of the values in such cases is low.[1]

If we use the continuum concept, then we can propose some hypotheses about conditions that promote strong sagas:
- the smaller the size, the more likely the acceptance of the saga by most participants;
- the older the organization, the more likely a strong saga will develop;
- the more organizations screen entry, the more likely participants will share the saga;
- the fewer the tasks of the organization, the more likely it will articulate a clear, cohesive saga;
- the more homogeneous and stable the environment, the more likely a cohesive saga will develop and persist;
- the more insulation the organization can build (for example, reserve resources, physical isolation, rigid entry requirements) against environmental opposition, the more likely the saga will persist.

These are only suggestive hypotheses, but they illustrate the potential theoretical value of understanding organizational saga as a continuum and of proposing hypotheses that explain why a given organization may be located at some position on the continuum.

NYU's Traditional Role

What kind of saga could an organization as large and fragmented as NYU muster? Obviously, it might not be as clear or intensely held as that of small, elite institutions such as Reed or Swarthmore. Fragmentation and massive size certainly dilute intensity of feelings about any single institutional mission and probably lead to the development of miniature sagas around organizational subunits. On the other side of the balance, however, was a fairly clear set of institutional goals articulated by a broad spectrum of the institution and supported by a significant segment of its salient environment. Thus, even an institution as complex as NYU had all-encompassing mission statements and values that to some extent directed the organization's future. It probably had a medium-strong saga.

The role that a university plays in society is both planned and acci-

---

1. Clark would probably wish to reserve the term "saga" for only those belief systems at the clear, cohesive end of the continuum. However, this leaves the difficulty of identifying the other points on the continuum with other labels. Thus I suggest we simply use "strong-weak" sagas instead of restricting the term.

dental, both deliberate and a whim of fate. The role that NYU plays as an institution of higher education, for example, is shaped by a mixture of historical events, deliberate planning, and pressure from many sources. For many years NYU had a consistent interpretation of its role in higher education in New York. From its founding the university offered educational advantages to all types of people, including underprivileged minority groups. NYU accepted students with relatively low academic scores, allowing them entry into the world of higher education as part of the long-standing philosophy that it was a "School of Opportunity"—in the best tradition of the "Great American Dream." This philosophy became an organizational saga, a belief that faculty, students, and outsiders held firmly.

This orientation was more than idle rhetoric; it was an operating principle of the university that gave the campus a distinct institutional character. Generations of students testify to the importance of that philosophy in their lives, and many a Wall Street businessman and New York teacher gives credit to the chance afforded him by NYU. Large groups of the faculty, dedicated to this ideal, were willing to fight when that saga was threatened.

Times were changing, however, and this image of NYU was challenged. Not all members of the university community were happy with a philosophy that accepted large numbers of relatively poor students and then failed many of them. As one professor said during the case study field work:

Sure, we were the great teacher of the masses in New York City. In a sense this was a good thing, and we undoubtedly helped thousands of students who otherwise would never have had a chance. But we were also very cruel. We had almost no admissions standards and we were brutal about failing people. There were many years in which no more than 25-30% of an entering class would graduate. Sure, we were the great "School of Opportunity" for New York, but the truth of the matter is that we were also the "Great Slop Bucket" that took everybody and later massacred them.

From the inside, there was mounting opposition to the "School of Opportunity" philosophy, with its low admission standards and its high failure rates. At the same time, professors, particularly from liberal arts and graduate units, objected to lowering standards. Pressure was slowly building internally that would produce a different saga for NYU, even as events on the outside also indicated change.

The Environmental Threat

A number of major organizational theorists have suggested that the impetus for large-scale change almost always comes from outside an organization (for reviews, see Katz and Kahn, 1966; Thompson, 1967). Katz and Kahn state the environmentalist theme very clearly:

The basic hypothesis is that organizations and other social structures are open systems which attain stability through their authority structures, reward mechanisms, and value systems, and which are changed primarily from without by means of some significant change in input. Some organizations, less open than most, may resist new inputs indefinitely and may perish rather than change. We would predict, however, that, in the absence of external changes, organizations are likely to be reformed from within in limited ways. More drastic or revolutionary changes are initiated or made possible by external forces [Katz and Kahn, 1966, pages 448-449].

Certainly the events at NYU show the impact of heavy environmental influences, for external events were pressing the university toward a reevaluation of its mission, image, and saga. NYU exists in an environment in which other universities are competing for resources, students, and social influence. For many years NYU was the major "service university" in New York that took the masses of students. High admission standards at both the City University of New York and Columbia excluded most of the student population.

In the late 1950's, however, both the state and the city assumed more responsibility for educating the masses. A rapidly expanding network of junior and senior colleges caused public university enrollments to skyrocket. Public institutions charge little tuition. Even though privately supported NYU raised its fees until they were among the highest in the nation, it still lacked the resources to compete with public colleges and universities, and public institutions began usurping the role of educating the city's student population.

The effects of the shift in student population were rapid and dramatic. In 1956 NYU published *The Self-Study*, a major attempt at long-range planning that predicted many of the coming changes. The authors of that farsighted document were aware of the impending threat, but it is doubtful that they understood how immediate it was. In fact, they stated, with some confidence,

Even the enormous expansion of the tuition-free city college system with its excellent physical plan has not as yet substantially affected the character of NYU. . . . [New York University, 1956, page 11]

The Self-Study also predicted increasing enrollments for NYU from 1955 to 1966. By the early 1960's, however, it was obvious that the expected growth was not materializing. Thousands of students who previously would have attended NYU were going to public institutions. Figure 22-1 compares *Self-Study* projections with actual enrollments for the period 1955-1973. By 1966 the actual figures

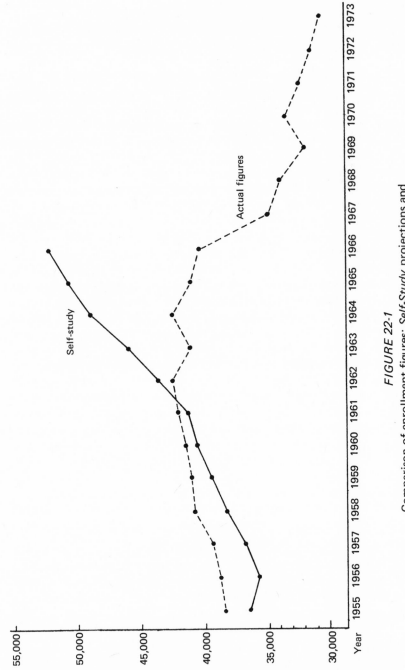

FIGURE 22-1

Comparison of enrollment figures: *Self-Study* projections and
actual figures, 1955-1966; actual figures extended to 1973
(New York University, 1956, page 9)

were running a full 20 percent, over 9,000 students, behind the predictions. As one administrator viewed it, "We certainly anticipated pressure from the City University, but frankly the pinch came ten years ahead of our expectations." Throughout the 1960's and into the 1970's, enrollments fell well behind the number needed to sustain the university's operation, and the situation grew progressively worse.

NYU was not alone in facing the threat from the public universities. Throughout New York State in the 1960's enrollment in the public institutions shot from a relatively small percentage to over 60 percent of all students by 1973. During that period private colleges and universities closed their doors as more and more students attended state institutions.

NYU did not die, but it was certainly sick. The financial impact was alarming. From 1964 to 1973 NYU accumulated deficits of over $32,000,000 that ate away a significant portion of its $62,000,000 endowment. In 1970, in a desperate attempt to gain more revenue, the university's undergraduate tuition went up to $2,700, a figure that exceeded even Harvard's. The financial picture was overwhelmingly bleak.

Burton Clark suggests that often during periods of crisis, when the established organization proves inadequate, organizational sagas are attacked, making way for change. Those in charge, after years of attempting incremental adjustments (Lindblom, 1959), realize finally that they must either give up established ways or the organization will fail. In order to survive, they may:

relinquish the leadership to one proposing a plan that promises revival and later strength, or they may even accept a man of utopian intent. Deep crisis in the established organization thus creates some of the conditions of a new organization. It suspends past practice, forces some bordering groups to stand back or even to turn their backs on failure of the organization, and it tends to catch the attention of the reformer looking for an opportunity [Clark, 1972, page 180].

NYU was an institution almost overripe for a new saga. Seriously weakened by competition from public universities, it was losing students, and its financial stability was being undermined by the loss of vitally needed tuition. It was a question of how to meet the challenge —how to frame a new saga that would serve the educational needs of the community and the survival needs of NYU. The changes that resulted were the source of intense political controversy.

Political Controversy and the Emergence of a New Saga

Once the saga of the institution had been challenged and external pressures had forced the university into a crisis condition, a series of essentially political processes began. Several organizational theorists have looked at decision processes as political activities (Cyert and March, 1963; Thompson, 1967). In an earlier work, I argued:

When we look at dynamic processes that explode on the modern campus today we see neither the rigid, formal aspects of bureaucracy nor the calm, consensus-directed elements of an academic collegium. On the contrary, student riots cripple the campus, professors form unions and strike, administrators defend their traditional positions, and external interest groups and irate governors invade the academic halls. All these activities can be understood as political acts. They emerge from the complex, fragmented social structure of the university, drawing on the divergent concerns and life styles of hundreds of miniature subcultures. These groups articulate their interests in many different ways, bringing pressure to bear on the decision-making process from any number of angles and using power and force whenever it is available and necessary. Once articulated, power and influence go through a complex process until policies are shaped, reshaped, and forged from the competing claims of multiple groups. All this is a dynamic process, a process clearly indicating that the university is best understood as a "politicized" institution [Baldridge, 1971, pages 8-9].

A political image brings with it a number of basic assumptions about decision-making processes, all of which definitely apply to the NYU situation.

Basic Assumptions of a Political Model

The political model assumes that complex organizations can be studied as miniature political systems, with interest group dynamics and conflicts similar to those of cities, states, or other political situations. All stages of the political model center around policy-forming processes. Policy formation becomes a focal point, for major policies commit the organization to definite goals, set the strategies for reaching those goals, and determine the long-range destiny of an organization. Policy decisions are critical, not merely routine; they are decisions that have major impact and mold the organization's future.

Since policy decisions bind the organization to important courses of action, people in the organization use their influence to see that their special values are implemented. Policy becomes a major point of conflict, a watershed of interest group activity that permeates a university's life. In light of its importance, policy becomes the center of the political analysis. Just as the political scientist may select legislative acts in Congress as the focus of his analysis of the state's political processes, organization theorists may select policy decisions as the key for studying organizational conflict and change. Some basic assumptions about political processes in organizations are:

Inactivity prevails. Policy making may be a political process, but not everyone becomes involved. On the contrary, policy activity generally follows a "law of apathy," that is, much of the time the process is an uninteresting, unrewarding activity avoided by most people. Both in the world of academia and in the larger society, administrators are allowed to run the show. Voters do not vote, people do not attend city council meetings, and, by and large, the decisions of society are made by small elites.

Fluid participation. Even when people are active, they move in and out of the decision-making process, not spending much time on any given issue. Decisions are usually made by those who persist, those small groups of political elites who govern most major decisions.

Fragmentation into interest groups. Like most social organizations, colleges and universities are split into interest groups with varying goals and values. These groups usually exist in a state of armed coexistence. High resources and benevolent times create minimal conflict; tight resources and attacks from pressure groups act to mobilize interest groups to defend themselves and their own causes.

Normalcy of conflict. In dynamic social systems such as colleges and universities, conflict is natural and expected. Instead of indicating breakdown in the academic community, conflict can be vital to promoting healthy organizational change.

Limitations of formal authority. Formal authority, as prescribed by the bureaucratic system, is severely limited by the political pressure and bargaining power of interest groups. Decisions are not simple, bureaucratic orders. Often they are negotiated compromises between competing groups. Officials are not free to issue a decision; instead, they must jockey between interest groups, building viable positions between powerful segments.

External interest groups. Academic decision making does not occur in a vacuum, for external interest groups exercise much influence over the policy-making process. External pressures and formal control by outside agencies, especially in public institutions, are powerful shapers of internal governance processes.

Challenges to the Old Saga

Political processes accompanied the struggle at NYU for institutional viability in the face of massive external threat. By the end of

1961 a debate about the university's future was raging behind closed doors, with disagreements going far deeper than the question of how to recruit more students. The essential issue concerned NYU's total educational mission. Could it continue with business as usual, or was this a critical turning point? Many top administrators felt that it was time for a sweeping evaluation of NYU's destiny, particularly in light of the financial crisis facing the institution.

The debate at this point involved the goals and long-range commitments of the university. The assessment was not only that the university should adopt new management techniques to solve its financial crisis, which it did, but that it would also have to develop new goals and new orientations toward the future to survive as a significant contributor to higher education. Confronted with multifaceted pressures, university leaders deliberately "tinkered with the future." NYU consciously sought to change its saga by creating and projecting a revised self-image, a new institutional character.

Several events accelerated the changes. In 1962 James Hester, former executive dean of the liberal arts units, was selected to be the new president. He was acutely aware of the problems facing the university and made it his first order of business to confront them. In addition, the Ford Foundation invited NYU to apply for a comprehensive development grant. This opportunity was seized as a means of providing financial support for the planned changes, and eventually the Ford Foundation granted $25 million to NYU.

In early 1962 several committees were appointed to formulate plans for the Ford request. It became progressively clearer that NYU's problems had to be faced if the grant was to be educationally meaningful. Although faculty bodies were asked to prepare plans to be included in the Ford proposal, many faculty members claim that the critical decisions were really made by a small group of administrators. Some administrators claimed that the faculty's contribution was limited because of their inability to look beyond individual departments to the needs of the entire university.

In any event, it is fascinating to observe the conscious efforts of the university community as it planned its future. The debates, factfinding, and committee work for the Ford requests continued for more than a year, one of those rare periods when an organization really maps out its destiny and redesigns its saga. Rather than responding impulsively to the pressures of the moment, the university attempted to realistically plot a future based on a careful study of its needs, and then to engage in explicit decision making.

By fall 1963 the Ford report was completed, and the foundation responded generously, expressing strong confidence in the plans for the reshaping of NYU. The university was challenged to raise $75 million from other sources to match the $25 million grant. A complex, interconnected series of changes to promote NYU's new saga emerged from the Ford report. They included:

1. Undergraduate admissions standards would be raised substantially.
2. The fragmented undergraduate program (with Education, Commerce, Washington Square College, Engineering, and University College each having separate programs) would be unified.
3. An "urban university" orientation would be developed.
4. More full-time faculty and students would be recruited, and more on-campus residences would be provided.
5. More energy would be directed toward graduate and professional training, so that direct undergraduate competition with the state university would be avoided.

It is important to note several things about these decisions. First, they represented a basic, far-reaching transformation of the very nature of NYU. Second, the relation to the external social context was particularly critical, for, in large measure, these decisions represented a "posture of defense" for NYU. Third, the posture of defense allowed a confrontation with reality and the development of new future images that could turn NYU from potential disaster toward a revitalized educational role. A crisis situation had promoted the birth of a new saga.

From a sociological perspective it is important to realize that the resultant plans were framed by a context of conflict and that pressures were impinging on the decision makers from many sides. Although the forces for change were great, both inside and outside groups had strong vested interests in the status quo. At least two major units, the School of Education and the School of Commerce, as well as many influential alumni, were committed to the "School of Opportunity" image. It was, of course, exactly this philosophy that was being challenged as the university searched for its revised educational role. A confrontation was virtually inevitable.

The Role of Strong Leadership in Developing a New Saga

Burton Clark argues that major changes in organizational sagas, while often provoked by crisis circumstances, are usually fulfilled through strong institutional leadership. In fact, one could almost argue that the crisis produces a hero to make the decisions. The early presidents at Reed (William T. Foster), Antioch (Arthur E. Morgan), and Swarthmore (Frank Aydelotte) capitalized on critical situations to build new organizational sagas.

NYU had its aggressive leadership in James Hester and the chancellor, Allan M. Cartter, a noted economist specializing in higher education. The central administration team took strong action. In fact, most people at NYU felt that a small group of top administrators made critical decisions with little faculty consultation. To be sure, the University Senate was consulted about most of the plans, but at that time it was believed that the relatively weak Senate merely rubber-stamped decisions. As one member put it:

We were "informed" about these matters, and we were asked to vote our approval, but I wouldn't say we were actually "consulted" in any meaningful way. It was a one-way street—they told us what they were going to do and we said "OK."

In addition, faculty committees were working on the Ford report, but many people suggested that the critical decisions were not actually made by these committees. Instead, most of the faculty learned about the decisions when they were publicly announced. One rather bitter professor in the School of Commerce commented:

The School of Commerce was about to have its throat cut and we didn't even know about it until after the blood was flowing! Sure, Hester came over and gave us a little pep talk about how much this was going to improve things, but he didn't really ask our advice on the issue. He didn't exactly say it was going to be his way "or else," but we got the point.

From their perspective, the administration clearly saw the threats facing NYU from the public universities and knew that something radical had to be done—quickly. Administrators, disappointed in the faculty's conservative contribution to the Ford report, felt that their broader perspective gave them the duty to act as the key "change agents." It is also clear that they knew some moves would be vehemently opposed, and extensive consultation might arouse enough hostility to kill the whole matter. As President Hester explained it:

The University was confronted with critical conditions. We had to undertake action that was radical from the standpoint of many people in the University. Some of these changes had to be undertaken over strong opposition and were implemented by administrative directives. In two of the undergraduate schools a number of faculty members had accepted the "school of opportunity" philosophy as a primary purpose of their school. This had been justifiable at one time, but no longer. Many faculty members simply did not recognize that circumstances had changed and did not accept the fact that the service they were accustomed to performing was now being assumed by public institutions at far less cost to the students.

At this point the administration had to be the agent for change. It was incumbent upon us to exercise the initiative that is the key to administrative leadership. In the process, we did interfere with the traditional autonomy of the schools, but we believed this was necessary if they and the University were to continue to function [personal interview].

It might be helpful to examine some of the factors that enabled the administrators, as a critical leadership group, to execute this change so successfully. Strong opposition to the planned changes could be expected from those adversely affected. How did the policy succeed despite this opposition? What factors were working in favor of the central administration as it moved to implement these transformations?

First, the central administration's power had been greatly enhanced through centralization under the strong leadership of President Henry Heald. Before Heald's administration in the 1950's, NYU had been a loose collection of essentially autonomous schools. President Hester's success, then, was very dependent on Heald's earlier preparations.

Second, Hester, as a new popular president, could still rely on the "honeymoon effect" to win support from both the trustees and a substantial part of the faculty. As one professor of commerce noted, "He's as close to a popular president as any you'll find, and that makes him a hard man to beat on most issues." In 1969, for example, the general faculty indicated their "General confidence in the central administration of the university" on a questionnaire. Compared to the identical question on a Faculty Senate Survey for 1959, this represents a sharp increase in the level of confidence (see Table 22-1).

Third, large segments of the faculty supported the changes. Cross-pressures from various interest groups can allow decision makers

TABLE 22-1. Degree of confidence in the central administration

Survey	Degree of confidence				Number of cases
	High	Medium	Low	Total	
		(percent)			
1959 (Faculty senate)	40	18	42	100	(596)
1968 (Baldridge)	47	32	21	100	(693)

more freedom than would be possible if most groups lined up in opposition. In the NYU case, many liberal arts professors favored raising admission standards, and they were joined by graduate-level professors who felt that higher undergraduate standards would indirectly improve the graduate programs.

Fourth, the decisions were successful because of the obvious bureaucratic weapons controlled by the central administration. The centralized admissions office, for example, could be instructed to raise standards, thus effectively bypassing the opposition. In addition, the twin powers of the budget and personnel appointments were brought to bear often in the struggles that followed the decisions.

Finally, one of the most important reasons that these dramatic changes could succeed was the external threat from the public institutions. A common finding of sociological research states that groups threatened by outside forces will tolerate internal changes that they otherwise would oppose. The administration recognized that NYU was truly under attack and fought to implement changes that would protect the university. The trustees, convinced that these changes were imperative, stood solidly behind the administration in the struggles that erupted—as they did all over the campus!

The Political Conflict: One Example

There is no question that NYU was in a crisis, demanding a strong leadership to make radical changes. The inevitability of conflict over the changes is especially clear in the issues provoked in the School of Commerce, a school dedicated to the "School of Opportunity" saga, and a large core of its professors fought to retain that concept.

The situation is complicated, however, because not all the business education faculty was opposed to the changes. The Graduate School of Business (GSB), a separate unit for graduate and advanced professional degrees in business, allied itself with the central administration. GSB wanted to become a major research center and a nationally reputable business education unit. Its professors were more interested in scholarly research on industry and business, and they feared that the undergraduate School of Commerce was damaging the reputation of business studies. Thus, the business education professors formed two distinct interest groups with two different emphases, each fighting for their image of NYU's future.

Most of the commerce professors believed their jobs would disappear if the changes were instituted. They feared reduced enrollments, a loss of the night school program, decreased faculty size, and a general weakening of their influence in the university. It is now clear that what they feared most was to happen in a short time!

Probably the majority of the commerce faculty opposed any major changes in their basic philosophy and admission policies. Moreover, the administration's chief representative, Dean John Prime, was not totally convinced that the changes were desirable. A power struggle developed, but the administration had most of the weapons. As one professor said in a personal interview:

I guess now that it's all over these changes were good for us, but we fought it all the way; there was a fantastic battle. Actually, I'd say it was rammed down our throats. Several foundations made reports which suggested we were too "provincial," and we needed to upgrade standards and eliminate the duplication in our undergraduate programs. But remember, this was done by academic types, who really didn't understand a professional school and were prejudiced against us. This would not have happened a few years ago when the whole University lived off Commerce's surplus money. It is only our growing weakness which made this change possible. The various schools are always competing and at this moment we are in a bad relative position.

For many months the task of convincing the faculty to cooperate with the changes continued against strong opposition. Finally, two key appointments were announced. First, in April 1962 an "executive dean" was appointed to supervise both the School of Commerce and the Graduate School of Business. Second, in September 1963 Dean Prime resigned, and Dean Abraham Gitlow became local dean of the School of Commerce. To no one's surprise, both deans favored the administration's plans to upgrade quality in the School of Commerce, and a major breakthrough in faculty cooperation came at about the same time.

By almost any yardstick the School of Commerce is radically different from what it was a few years ago. By deliberate policy decision, S.A.T. scores went up, and enrollment figures went down. Of course, the cut in enrollments caused an equally drastic decrease in faculty positions. From a high of nearly three hundred members in the late 1950's, the number of faculty dropped to sixty-one in 1967-68. Many part-timers were dropped, many nontenured people were never tenured, a few senior men were "bought off" to retire early, few new people were hired, and many current faculty members left. Although NYU lived up to its contractual obligations, professors had to find positions elsewhere.

These changes hit the School of Commerce hard, yet the quality of the students, the faculty, and the program vastly improved. Those at NYU today, including members of the original faculty, now believe that the changes were necessary.

The Political Process: Summary Comments

The struggle over the School of Commerce only illustrates the larger political process occurring throughout NYU as it struggled over its new saga. Some characteristics of that general process can be summarized:

1. Many interest groups were threatened by the changes (in the Schools of Commerce and Education).
2. Influence was exercised by whatever weapons the interest groups could muster (threats of faculty resignations or withdrawal of alumni support).
3. Strong leadership was demonstrated from the top, and administrative authorities mustered political support from change-oriented groups (the liberal arts faculty).
4. Administrators were caught in a complex set of cross-pressures coming from different groups (the School of Commerce and the Graduate School of Business demanded different things).
5. Coalitions were formed to fight or press for the changes (the Schools of Commerce and Education united to fight changes; the School of Liberal Arts and the Graduate School united to promote them).
6. Bureaucratic mechanisms—budget, early retirement policies, reorganization of departments—were used as political weapons by administrators.
7. Outside pressure groups were often involved (alumni of the School of Commerce).

In short, the formulation of a new institutional saga for NYU was an eminently political process involving high conflict, influence tactics, and coalitional behavior. It reflected the general political dynamics outlined earlier.

The New Saga in Action

From the mid-1960's on, the decisions based on the new saga were carried out at NYU. The effects were dramatic and had repercussions throughout the university. First, undergraduate admissions dropped sharply—a stunning 20 percent from 1962 to 1965. This sharp dip was largely due to raised admission standards. At the very moment when a sum of approximately $10 million above normal costs was desperately needed for quality upgrading, the drop in enrollment cut off vitally needed tuition funds. From 1962 to 1973 the total number of students gradually decreased in the face of higher tuition, an expanded network of state institutions, and the same overall decline in enrollment that affected all of higher education.

A second indication that the planned changes had a strong impact was the tremendous rise in freshman S.A.T. scores, an increase of nearly one hundred points in the years 1961 to 1966; after that the scores once again leveled out at a higher plane.

A third indicator of the changes is related to student housing. The school's new role emphasized recruiting more students from outside New York City, and more full-time resident students. The university was forced to provide both housing for students on a large scale and residences for the full-time faculty. New housing units were constructed as part of a $75 million capital improvement program that spanned the 1960's. From 1960 to 1974 the number of on-campus students increased by over 500 percent.

A fourth change that accompanied the reconceptualized saga occurred in the composition of the graduate student enrollment. There was a shift toward more full-time graduate students, while the number of professional students remained relatively constant. In 1960 only 23 percent of the graduate enrollment was full-time, while by 1967 the percentage increased to 55. This meant that the absolute number of full-time graduate students had tripled in only seven years. This pattern continued into the early 1970's. In fact, the commitment to graduate and professional education is shown by the fact that, of the total number of degrees granted in any given year, nearly two-thirds are either graduate or professional.

The Crisis Continues: The Politics of Survival

To many observers it appeared that the drastic changes planned in the early sixties and implemented during the last half of the decade would solve most of the university's problems. Unfortunately, the rosy predictions were overly optimistic. City and state institutions in the area continued their phenomenal growth, and NYU still faced difficulties with student recruitment. In turn, deficits continued to mount so that, by the early 1970's, the institution seemed ready for bankruptcy. By this time the faculty opposing the administration's changes had realized that the university's survival was at stake, and more and more senior faculty rallied to the administration's support.

In 1972 a series of severe measures was taken. First, there was a university-wide freeze on salaries. Second, many nontenured faculty were fired. Third, a university task force was set up to make emergency recommendations toward controlling the financial crisis. The task force proposed a number of stringent changes:

1. Every School in the university would operate on a strictly balanced budget, or cut back their programs to fit their budgets. Except for the College of Arts and Sciences, which was allowed an annual $1,000,000 subsidy, no help would come from the central endowment for the schools that exceeded their income.
2. The university campus in the Bronx was to be sold. Subsequently, New York State bought the campus for $62 million, a sum desperately needed to shore up the shrinking endowment.
3. A sharp cut of $10.5 million in instructional costs was begun.
4. It was recommended that the School of Social Work be phased out. (It would be interesting here to expand on the political controversy around the School of Social Work as we did with the School of Commerce, but space does not permit it. The School of Social Work was not willing to give up; in fact, its faculty and students mobilized to raise $1,000,000 and the campaign successfully bought additional time for the school.)
5. The mandatory retirement age was reduced from 68 to 65, and people were encouraged to retire at 62. Over 100 faculty and staff were pushed out because of this move.

As these radical proposals were implemented, the faculty casualty toll was high. Many members supported the administration and its tough but necessary action; others were bitter and anxious to fight back with whatever political weapons they could muster. The controversies that raged around attempts at organizing unions would fill a book, but by 1974, when the issue was presented, the majority of the faculty still voted "no bargaining agent."

In spite of all the problems confronting NYU, a new spirit has begun to pervade the institution. Recently an enormous $300,000,000 fund-raising campaign was initiated, enrollments have taken a slight upturn, and the deficits plaguing the school have been reduced so that a break-even budget is anticipated for the 1974-75 school year.

Most important, in the face of disaster NYU has struggled to change its image and to develop a new organizational saga. It is unlikely, of course, that an institution as fragmented and as complex as NYU will ever exude a simple, cohesive saga. But this massive institution seems to have captured some direction in its drift, seized opportunities in the midst of crises, and created the self-image of a high-quality private institution.

Just as dynamic presidents led the moves toward new sagas at Reed, Swarthmore, and Antioch, much of the credit for NYU's rising hopes can be attributed to the capable leadership of President James Hester. A recent editorial in *Change* magazine paid tribute to Hester's leadership:

One is left with the impression that, even in this very large place, the influence and contribution of its president are unique and life-size. He is a capable, agile administrator and a consummate fund raiser finely attuned to the sensitivities of his faculty. In these days of tight finances he could carry a big stick, but he does not. Instead, he gives much of each day to the infinite process of consensus building among his 5,450 full- and part-time faculty, and in doing so he seems to be succeeding where many others have failed. It may be the new miracle on Washington Square, and an eloquent testimonial to the ability of complex universities to spring back to life [*Change*, 1974, page 13].

Summary

The story is obviously not complete. NYU's new institutional saga is only partly fulfilled, and devotion to the revised image is largely untested as yet. Although NYU often seems to be going in every direction at once, the notion of saga has some usefulness, even in the face of such diversity. A new belief, a renewed spirit, and a rekindled hope are placed in plans that emerged from fifteen years of crisis.

Impetus for change came largely from outside the institution. It is doubtful that NYU would have undertaken such severe transformations had it not been confronted with survival in a changing environment. The external threats were real; the internal responses were drastic.

Finally, the imagery of politics and interest group dynamics are particularly useful to an examination of major organizational changes. At NYU different groups had different goals. As external pressures buffeted the institution, powerful interest groups maneuvered to protect traditional activities and domains. Only the interference of strong, able leadership from the central administration was able to contain the conflict and move the institution toward survival.

This has been a study of massive organizational change. By using the case study method and a historical framework, we have tried to show how three themes in organizational literature can be enlightening for the study of institutional change. The notion of saga gives insight about the *content* of the changes; the environmentalist themes are powerful in showing the *sources* of change impetuses; the political theme is helpful in analyzing the *processes* necessary to institutionalize a new saga.

References

Baldridge, J. Victor (1971). *Power and Conflict in the University.* New York: John Wiley and Sons.

Change (1974). April issue.

Clark, Burton R. (1956). *Adult Education in Transition: A Study of Institutional Insecurity.* Berkeley: University of California Press.

_____ (1960). *The Open Door College. A Case Study.* New York: McGraw-Hill.

_____ (1970). *The Distinctive College: Antioch, Reed, and Swarthmore.* Chicago: Aldine.

_____ (1972). "The Organizational Saga in Higher Education," *Administrative Science Quarterly,* 17.2:178-184.

Cyert, R., and March, James (1963). *A Behavioral Theory of the Firm.* Englewood Cliffs, N.J.: Prentice-Hall.

Katz, E., and Kahn, R. (1966). *The Social Psychology of Organizations.* New York: John Wiley and Sons.

Lindblom, C. E. (1959). "The Science of 'Muddling Through.' " *Public Administration Review,* 19:79-88.

New York University (1956). *The Self-Study.* New York: New York University Press.

Selznick, P. (1949). *TVA and the Grass Roots.* Berkeley: University of California Press.

Thompson, James (1967). *Organizations in Action.* New York: McGraw-Hill.

23 Effects of Environment and Structure on the Process of Innovation

Anneke E. Bredo
Eric R. Bredo

One of the most distinctive features of educational innovations is the rate at which they fail. If proposed, they often are not adopted; if adopted, they frequently are not fully implemented; if implemented, they rarely last. The history of educational innovation sometimes seems like the case of the desert straggler pursuing a mirage; in spite of great effort, he never seems to reach his objective.

In this chapter we attempt to analyze some factors that may lead to the failure of educational innovations. Our analysis is based on the case study of a junior high school, where attempts to implement changes met with notable lack of success. While it is difficult to generalize from a case study, a detailed analysis of internal processes may make some contribution to current thinking on organizational innovation.

The process of innovation in the school is described in considerable detail, and the description serves as a base for the more theoretical discussion that follows. Five main areas are covered: environmental pressures, response to the pressures, implementation of the innovation, teacher reactions, and administrative response. Discussion centers on the interrelationships of the environmental and structural factors that helped determine the process of innovation, and this is followed by consideration of some practical and theoretical implications for educational innovation.

The original study was done in collaboration with Paul D. Chapman. A different version of this chapter appeared as R&D Memorandum No. 132, "A Case Study of Educational Innovation in a Junior High School: Interaction of Environment and Structure," published by the Stanford Center for Research and Development in Teaching. This research was conducted at the Center pursuant to contract NE-C-00-3-0062 with the National Institute of Education, Department of Health, Education, and Welfare.

The Setting

Hillview Junior High School,[1] located in a middle-class suburban community, is a fairly large school that has more than a thousand students. The faculty is divided into eleven subject-area departments, the larger ones having department chairmen who handle a variety of administrative chores. The school is regarded as a desirable teaching location, and faculty turnover in recent years has been extremely low. Prior to the innovative period discussed here, most teachers were apparently quite satisfied with both the school and the way it functioned.

The Process of Innovation

Pressures to Innovate

Pressure for innovation at Hillview came from three main sources: public criticism, student unrest, and district views. The intense public criticism of schools in recent years, together with widespread student unrest during the late 1960's, gave rise to a demand for "relevant" educational programs that would more closely approximate students' needs. At Hillview student pressures were a major factor in triggering emphasis on innovation. The fundamental nature of the criticism implied that major changes were required, but opinion was divided on what the nature of the changes should be. In many ways, the issues could be reduced to the question of more student freedom versus greater constraint, and there were strong proponents of both points of view.

Similar conflicting pressures came from the district's central office. Perhaps in response to public criticism and student unrest, several administrators began to emphasize innovativeness, especially in the junior high schools. Both the elementary schools and the high schools were seen as being far more flexible and receptive to change than the junior high schools in the district, Hillview among them, which were considered "bottlenecks" with respect to educational innovation. Some officials, therefore, began to advocate innovation with considerable enthusiasm. At Hillview, a district administrator exhorted the faculty to make changes, saying, "Don't be afraid to fail!"[2] Other central office members were more conservative, especially the curriculum head, who insisted that academic standards

1. A pseudonym.
2. Several faculty members subsequently remembered this as the "Go out and fail" speech, perhaps an indication of their bitter experiences later.

must be maintained and discouraged the dropping of requirements. These somewhat divided views led to confusion over just what kind of support to expect from the central office. Junior high schools were encouraged to relate better to their students, but not to sacrifice academic standards or change their requirements. As one Hillview faculty member bitterly put it later, "The District was speaking out of both sides of its mouth." Overall, the message communicated by the school's environment was that major change was desirable, but the nature of the change was left ambiguous.

Response to the Pressures

Increased Search

Organizations facing problems are likely to search for new ways of doing things, and Hillview was no exception. The faculty was quite receptive to the idea of innovation. Their school had a record for academic excellence, and it was reputed to be the most innovative of the junior high schools. Anxious to retain this image, Hillview teachers began an informal search for innovative educational practices. When one faculty member gave a glowing report of an innovative program in a school he had happened to visit, it was received with considerable interest, and several committees, including district representatives and faculty members, were sent to investigate the program further. Their reports were generally favorable, though some members had reservations.

The school they visited had provided students with a greater choice of courses and teachers by means of Arena scheduling. They also had a House Plan, whereby students met regularly with a teacher in a modified homeroom situation to work out scheduling problems and to provide for casual, friendly student-teacher interaction in an informal environment. It was a relatively small school, and, since all required courses were dropped, students had a great deal of autonomy in deciding their own program. The visitors on the whole were very impressed with the way the innovation seemed to be working.

Differing Perceptions and Preferences

The reports on the program were generally well received by the Hillview faculty, but different members were impressed by different aspects. For some, the new form of scheduling, which included quarter courses and double-block periods, was most attractive; for others, the greatest appeal lay in the emphasis on affective relations with students; still others found increased student autonomy to be the outstanding feature.

To a great extent these differences could be related to differences in departmental preferences (Table 23-1). By nature of its subject matter, a department such as social studies could far more easily adapt its courses to students' interests than a department with a more structured curriculum such as math, where courses had to follow a certain sequence and requirements seemed essential. Similarly, changing students every quarter would be more problematic for more structured subjects. Even differences in the extent to which faculty members felt comfortable with students in informal situations, which influenced their attitudes toward the House Plan, could be related to departmental differences, as Table 23-1 shows. These differences in

TABLE 23-1. Rankings of departments by mean reported preferences: A. balance between required and elective courses; B. length of time to keep students; C. comfort with students in informal situations[a]

	Rankings		
Department	A. Required versus elective courses[b]	B. How long to keep students[b]	C. Comfort in informal situations[b]
	(1 = more required)	(1 = longer)	(1 = less comfortable)
Foreign language	1	1	3
Math	2	2	1
Physical education	3	6	4
English	4	3	5
Science	5	5	2
Social studies	6	4	6

Computation of Spearman's rho shows that rankings on preferences of A and B above are quite similar (rho = .80), as well as rankings on A and C (rho = .77). Relations between rankings on B and C are not quite as strong (rho = .63).

[a]Not included are the very small departments having only a few members.
[b]The question was:
A. "In your subject area, how do you feel about the present balance between required and elective courses at Hillview?"
B. "For most of your courses, how long would you prefer to keep students?"
C. "Compared to teaching in a more structured classroom situation, how comfortable would you say you are with students in an informal situation?"

Response categories were:
A. Many more requirements, more requirements, present mixture, fewer, many fewer requirements.
B. Year or more, semester or more, semester or less, quarter.
C. Much less comfortable, somewhat less, equally comfortable, somewhat more, much more comfortable.

orientations were relatively consistent across departments. Thus, the structure of the school, highly differentiated into formal departments, helped promote different interests, subgoals, and the formation of different perceptions as to what innovations were desirable. In addition, outside expectations and pressures facing the departments reinforced these differences. A department like social studies, with its more diffuse subject area, was expected to relate to current events, but the more structured math curriculum, being specific and abstract, would not be expected to be "relevant"; rather, its aim was to maintain rigorous standards.

Early Participation and Planning

In light of these differences, it is not surprising that support of the innovation varied, and different departments were differentially represented in the committees and interest groups formed to study the innovations. Participation was influenced by interest in the proposed changes and available time; those with the greatest interest or the most time participated most. As a result, many of the most influential faculty members who were most pressed for time, including several department chairmen, did not attend the sessions. The house committee set up to study the House Plan (predictably including many social studies members) soon became the most active and controversial of the committees. When its representativeness was questioned, the principal responded in a memo that anyone concerned about the issue should attend the meetings and make his views heard; the exact legitimacy of the committee was never made clear.

The house committee was largely responsible for planning the innovation. These plans were remarkably imprecise; they were full of ideals, but contained few specifics. This may have been due in part to a need to persuade others of the innovation, an idealistic oversell required by the committee's perceived lack of legitimacy, which made it vulnerable to criticism. Concrete proposals would have made apparent the conflict between different interests; ideals were more easily agreed upon. Strong time pressures also prevented working things out in detail, for scheduling changes had to be made far in advance if the innovation was to be adopted for the coming school year.

Selling of the Dream

As a result of time pressures and poor planning, faculty members were obliged to make decisions under very confusing conditions. It was not clear what was involved in supporting the innovation since plans were vague, and participants were given no clear alternatives from which to choose. Whether the innovation was a "package deal," so that supporting one component implied support for all, or whether active support of the House Plan would be voluntary was never made explicit. In addition to uncertainty over the extent of their commitment, the faculty lacked information on many specific issues, such as the precise nature of the new scheduling or the exact obligations connected with having a House class. However, in part because of the laudable goals of the proposed innovation and in part because of strong administrative approval, most faculty members came to feel that disagreement was equivalent to disloyalty, and they expressed support for the changes to be made. One teacher later said, "We were told to think big and not worry about the future"; another admitted, "The school went into the changes with an 'it will work out' policy."

Implementation of the Innovation

Nature of the Innovation

The changes adopted at Hillview involved a major reorganization of the school as a whole. The innovation was systemic rather than localized, so that it affected all departments and almost all individual roles. Moreover, it implied a complete revamping of the school program all at once, rather than a few minor changes at a time. Scheduling was changed to a quarter system, and was to allow for increased student choice (although many requirements were maintained); it also included double-block periods for all subjects, which were new to most departments. House periods were planned for alternate days, and were to provide counseling on students' programs and schedules as well as affective relations between teachers and students. The student composition in each "House" was to be as varied as possible, representing both sexes and all grade levels. In addition, changes were made in the counselors' roles, report cards, and in the attendance system. In short, few areas of the school program were left unaffected by the innovation.

Technical Difficulties in Implementation

When faculty members returned to school in September, they still had no clear image of what to expect, but it did not take them long to discover the extent of their difficulties. Many specifics of the innovation had not been worked out over the summer, notably the scheduling system. The increased technical complexity of the new scheduling system created problems in programming, and, as a result, Hillview began the school year with only 40 percent of its students properly scheduled, which meant that House periods during the first month and even part of the second were fully taken up with individual scheduling difficulties. This was not a propitious beginning for creating an affective atmosphere. Teachers, untrained in scheduling techniques, often felt awkward and incompetent at this new task. Moreover, when they did get around to other activities in House, they found they had almost no guidance at all on what to do. Apart from a poorly attended voluntary workshop given a few afternoons in the week before school started, no further support or extra materials were forthcoming. Many teachers soon came to look upon House as an unwelcome extra course in an unstructured situation that they often found uncomfortable.

The school's policy during this period may best be described as a "seat of the pants," day-to-day kind of adjustment to immediate contingencies; the whole atmosphere became that of a crisis situation. Teachers overwhelmed with scheduling problems faced an unstructured House period they somehow had to lead; students, often bored by lack of direction in House, responded by cutting it. Both the administration and the teachers were concerned with the growing lack of discipline, and the school schedule was constantly being adjusted as meetings were called almost daily in an attempt to retain command of the situation. The innovation had gotten off to a very rocky start.

Conflicting Goals

Not only were there technical difficulties. Some problems arose because the innovation seemed to be aimed at a number of conflicting objectives simultaneously. Increasing student choice is difficult to reconcile with creating a warm social environment in a school as large as Hillview. When students change teachers more frequently, they do, indeed, get more choice, but it is unlikely that they can get to know the teachers as well. At the district's insistence, most requirements were still maintained, so that student autonomy was in fact severely curtailed. Finally, while House was intended to provide a warm, supportive environment, it was also compulsory, and students had little choice as to which teacher or students would be together in a House unit. This often precluded the formation of a cohesive group. Moreover, incentives that could promote cohesiveness in House, such as valued activities, were not provided, in part because no extra support or materials for such activities were given to the teachers, and they received no special training for their new role.

Teacher Reactions to the Innovations

General Reactions

Many Hillview teachers, probably a majority, were extremely up-set and complained bitterly about the new innovation. The new scheduling system had created unprecedented technical difficulties, and the House Plan led to a lack of role clarity. (Should House teachers be schedulers, counselors of individual students, minicourse specialists, group therapists?) Moreover, many felt that House imposed the burden of an extra course period without extra compensation. To add to their rancor, a few teachers managed to avoid getting a House because they had not supported the idea in the spring, and their comparative freedom increased House teachers' feelings of injustice. Decision making became much more difficult in the general confusion; faculty meetings, often ad hoc, increased in frequency and required more time and effort from teachers already irritated by the innovation. Many felt that they had seen the future, and it did not work. They would have been glad to return to the tried and true ways of the past.

Departmental Differences

In many ways attitudes toward House were indicative of faculty members' more diffuse feelings of support for the innovation as a whole. Again, there were dramatic differences by departments; the more structured departments were least favorable to House (Table 23-2). Across departments, there were quite strong relationships between attitudes to House and preferences on balance between required and elective courses, length of time to keep students, and comfort in informal situations with students. The strongest predictor of attitudes to House appeared to be preferences on the balance between required and elective courses; these preferences varied system-

TABLE 23-2. Departmental differences in mean reported attitudes to House[a]

Department	Ranking on satisfaction with House
Foreign language	1 (least satisfied)
Math	2
English	3
Physical education	4
Science	5
Social studies	6 (most satisfied)

[a]Major departments only.

atically by department with attitudes to House, and the rank orders are almost identical to those shown in Table 23-1 (rho = .97). Preferences on how long to keep students also showed similar rankings (rho = .89), as did comfort with students in informal situations (rho = .74). It seems that teachers in the more structured, sequenced curricular areas were least favorable to this type of innovation. Table 23-3

TABLE 23-3. Departmental rankings on mean self-reported influence[a]

Department	Influence ranking
Social studies	1 (highest)
Math	2
Science	3
English	4
Foreign language	5
Physical education	6

[a]Major departments only.

shows the rankings on the mean self-reported influence scores of the major departments. When we compare these rankings to rankings on attitudes to House in Table 23-2, it is interesting to note that the most influential departments (math and social studies) are practically at opposite ends in their attitudes toward the innovation. Not surprisingly, this led to considerable tension and conflict between members of different departments. The vehemence of many teachers' reactions to House suggests how much some faculty members disliked teaching in an unstructured setting ("My House should be called 'zoo' "; "It should self-destruct"; "House is just another confrontation in a day filled with confrontations.") Other teachers, while often critical of some aspects of the innovation, were unwilling to admit defeat; a theme frequently heard was, "I am very supportive of the original ideas behind House, and unwilling to give up." These teachers were harking back to the original idealism attached to the proposed innovation; they continued to support the ideals despite the problems created in implementing it. Perhaps this is an effect of selling an innovation idealistically; some support persists since ideals are never wrong.

Criticism of the Administration

As the crisis continued, more and more teachers began to be critical of the way the innovation was being implemented, and to direct their criticism to the administration. Their statements convey a sense of being imposed upon. ("In previous years changes seemed to have a sense of legitimacy, but this year's innovations have a sense of imposition"; "The administration's lack of success in planning has increased. Those in charge of the innovation . . . have presumed too much on the goodwill of Hillview teachers to help them out of the crises that the innovations have created.")

There were apparently conflicting views on what the principal's role should be, however. For some, the current predicament seemed directly related to a need for greater faculty participation in decision making, so that such injustices would not be perpetrated again. Others felt that the principal should be stronger in dealing with the problem, rather than leaving decisions to the teachers. ("There is too much decision making. Somewhere in the administration some decisions should be made for us"; "Planning is too democratic. Are not administrators trained to organize schools in efficient patterns? Why let staff vote itself into a noose?") Sometimes a single statement expresses both views at the same time. ("We are lacking a quality of leadership. The faculty doesn't have any sense of participation in the decisions that are made.")

Administrative Response

Dilemma in Leadership

For the principal, the conflicting expectations posed a difficult dilemma. Since the faculty was not united in its views but represented different interests, it was difficult to exert strong leadership; no matter what position he took, he was bound to offend some teachers further, something he could ill afford to do. On the other hand, the greater the chaos, the greater the need to make decisions that would resolve the difficulties. For a man who until this year had been a highly respected, well-liked principal, the unaccustomed criticism was a shattering experience.

Response to the Dilemma

By this point the principal had lost his credibility with the faculty and felt unable to take a strong public stand for or against the innovations. Instead, he responded with a number of interim measures intended to avert criticism and to help him "ride out the storm." His efforts were largely directed at strengthening his perceived legitimacy and diverting attention away from himself. They included seeking hierarchical support, increasing participation, co-opting powerful faculty members, and focusing attention elsewhere by calling for an evaluation.

By getting stronger support for the innovation from district administrators, the principal hoped to increase their legitimacy in the teachers' eyes. He met with little success, however. District backing was confined to encouragement and verbal support. As an alternative approach, to increase the perceived legitimacy of decisions made at Hillview, he extended participation in the decision-making process to all fronts, including parents and students, and he was very careful to consult the faculty in making every decision. While this made decision making more representative, it also took an inordinate amount of time. Decision making became even more confused than before, and demands for stronger leadership intensified.

In an additional effort to spread the responsibility for making decisions and also to gain the approval of influential faculty members, the principal extended the power and prominence of the faculty senate. Because he remained ambivalent about his own role, however, that body was never fully certain of the full extent of their powers. His apparent role conflict and uncertainty were also evident in his ambivalent attitudes toward teachers; he was alternately threatening ("Transfer to another school if you don't like it here"), conciliatory ("I would never have started this if I hadn't thought you wanted it"), and retiring, reducing his visibility by avoiding contact with many school personnel. These ambivalent attitudes made it difficult for the faculty to know what to expect, and they continued to criticize his lack of leadership.

A final means of focusing attention elsewhere was by calling for an evaluation of the innovations. In so doing, the principal hoped to divert attention away from the school's immediate problems and his own role in them, as well as get an outside view of how the school "got itself into this mess."

End of the Innovation

The evaluation established the fact that most of the faculty members were weary of the innovations, although they were still strongly divided in their views over the value of the intended goals. The general reaction was a shift to greater conservatism, and a "never again" attitude toward radical, system-wide change. By the following year, the school had almost completely returned to its old ways; teachers were happier, and it almost seemed as if the innovation had never taken place.

Discussion

This study suggests that the interaction of environmental pressures with the organizational characteristics of a school may have a profound effect on the process by which an innovation is planned and implemented, and on its eventual success or failure. In the case of Hillview, environmental demands were directed toward fundamental changes, but the demands were vague, ambiguous, or even contradictory, leaving it to school members to decide on the nature of the changes. If the external forces had been united in demanding a specific change, the school would not have faced as difficult a problem in deciding what kind of response to make.

Two organizational characteristics of the school affecting its response to ambiguous and conflicting stimuli were the limited power of its chief administrator and its differentiated (departmentalized) structure. These together served to rule out a uniform, harmonious reaction to the pressures. Like most school administrators (though unlike head administrators in some other types of organizations), the Hillview principal was quite dependent on the goodwill of his faculty and could not simply impose his ideas upon them. Nor could he fire those who might oppose him, and, since the school was a desirable place to teach, faculty members were loath to transfer. Because he had limited administrative power, decision making had to be opened up to wider participation, including teachers who did not necessarily share common views.

A differentiated organizational structure, exemplified by the departmentalization at Hillview, is frequently associated with the development of differences (Lawrence and Lorsch, 1967; March and Simon, 1958). This was certainly the case at Hillview, where very different preferences existed between departments on a number of issues quite closely related to the innovations (Table 23-1). Potential differences may not become activated under some conditions, however. When the external problem is ambiguous, as when an unfamiliar, rather vague issue is being confronted, the implications for existing interest groups may be unclear, and the effect may be to mute potential differences. On the other hand, when the issue is familiar and clearly specified, it may be seen as partisan and as pitting one department or interest group against another, accentuating the differences between the groups.

At Hillview, the diffuse, ambiguous pressures for change led to relatively diffuse agreement to "go along with the changes," and did not activate potentially conflicting interests. Thus, rather than resulting in a bargaining situation between articulated and recognized interest groups, the diffuse pressures prompted a generally receptive, if unfocused, response from the Hillview faculty.

The vague and idealistic plans that were developed seem to have been a product of the environmental pressures and the organization's structure, combined with limitations on time. Strong pressures to reach some kind of agreement in time to implement the innovation by the following school year meant that faculty members developing the plans had little time to work out specifics. Moreover, to do so might have resulted in making differences between them more obvious, particularly in light of different departmental preferences, thereby threatening agreement. The end product was a vague plan couched in idealistic terms. Few could disagree, and the plan would "sell" to the whole of the faculty. The faculty in effect made a symbolic agreement to "go with the plan," even though it was not at all clear what this entailed.

Symbolic agreements of this type, in which vague ideals are agreed upon in lieu of a more specific plan, appear most likely when there are potentially divergent interests, with tenuous bonds between participants loosely allied in a common endeavor, and where time for reaching agreement is limited. Under such conditions, specific details are avoided and potential differences smoothed over in the hope that the flag of common ideals will draw participants to a common allegiance. Such agreements are vague enough to allow latitude for each participant to imagine that his own preferences are represented. Rather than reconciling divergent interests, symbolic agreements thus tend to defer the time when differences have to be resolved. Similarly, the vague and general nature of symbolic agreements makes them capable of tolerating considerable inconsistency with respect to means or procedures, an inconsistency that only becomes apparent when there is an attempt to put the vague plans into operation.

Two types of difficulties are likely to emerge when symbolic agreements are made the basis for action: unsolved technical difficulties and unresolved goal conflicts. Technical difficulties place additional burdens on members and add to the confusion in their work, which often makes an innovation less desirable. Attempting to resolve these difficulties involves making decisions that were previously deferred, which often brings out latent conflicts. At Hillview, implementation difficulties produced interdepartmental conflict and a sense of injustice over unexpected burdens. Many of the participants withdrew support feeling that they had not realized what they were getting into. The difficulties also caused participants to question the legitimacy of the process by which the decision to innovate was made in the first place. Deferring decisions until an innovation is under way usually means that time pressures increase since the luxury of a planning phase no longer exists. Time limitations, then, have the effect of reducing participation in decision making, thus strengthening the sense of injustice felt by many members. At Hillview, this resulted in a seemingly paradoxical call for both stronger leadership and more participation, and, ultimately, the collapse of the attempt at innovation. This argument can be summarized as shown in Figure 23-1.

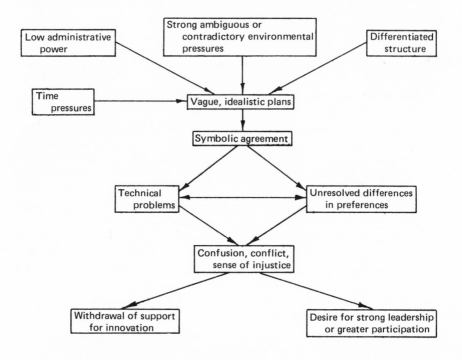

FIGURE 23-1
Interaction of environmental pressures with organizational characteristics
in the process of innovation

Implications for Educational Innovation

The failure of Hillview's attempt at innovation may in large part be attributed to two factors: they tried to introduce a major innovation all at once rather than introducing changes incrementally, and the change was introduced system-wide, rather than on a more local-ized basis affecting only a part of the school. When major changes are made that affect all of the subunits in an organization, the degree of felt interdependence is often increased, and problems of coor-dination and conflict are likely to result. At Hillview, these problems were neither foreseen nor adequately resolved, and the process of the innovation, outlined in Figure 23-1, may be regarded as a "recipe for failure."

Alternative Approaches to Innovation

Incrementalism

One alternative approach to innovation is to introduce changes more gradually, on an incremental basis. When only minor innova-tions are made at any one time, more time and resources are available to deal with difficulties as they arise. At Hillview many facets of the school were changed, and problems of all kinds emerged at the same time. Small changes also are less difficult to sell, so that the cycle of exuberant early idealism and subsequent disappointment can more easily be avoided. External pressures for major change easily lead to overreaction, which, in retrospect, seemed to be true at Hillview. The school would probably have done better with a series of successful small changes than with one large failure.

Incrementalism seems a particularly useful strategy in situations where the environment demands specific changes, where future con-sequences of proposed changes are unknown, or where time pressures preclude careful planning. When specific changes are implemented one at a time, adaptation is made easier, and the likelihood of major confusion and conflict is reduced. If the future consequences of the changes cannot be ascertained in advance, incrementalism is safer, for the success of each minor change can be evaluated, and, if the results are unexpectedly negative, they are at least limited in scope. When time pressures are too great to work out careful plans for a major change, especially in cases where divergent interests and potential conflicts are involved, incrementalism again seems preferable since less time is required to plan for a few minor changes at any one period.

Localized Change

Another alternative to major systemic change is the strategy of localizing the change to apply to only a part of an organization or to a subset of its members. Even major changes can be made much more easily if only small units are involved, since coordination and decision-making difficulties are reduced by more efficient communication between participants. Localized change also means that different preferences and commitments can be taken into account—only those who want the change need to be involved—and potential conflict can be avoided.

Localized change would seem to be a useful strategy in situations where there are external demands for fundamental change, where the organization is highly differentiated and composed of relatively strong interest groups, and where there is insufficient time to work out the differences between different interests. At Hillview, where all three of these occurred at once, systemic change magnified different preferences into major conflicts of interest, antagonized those adversely affected by the innovation, and created major rifts between opposing factions. If only those committed to making a change are included as participants, such conflicts are less likely to arise. Moreover, it allows for a "trial" of the change on a smaller scale. The rest of a school faculty could, for instance, adopt a "wait and see" attitude while some of their colleagues tried out a new innovation.

Ways to Reduce Problems of Coordination and Conflict

Both of the strategies outlined above represent ways of minimizing interdependence between organizational members or subunits: incrementalism limits the total number of task areas affected, and localized change limits the number of members or subunits affected. At times an organization may decide to go ahead with major, system-wide changes in spite of the difficulties that this implies, either through ignorance of the potential problems or from a conviction that pressure for change is so great as to allow no other choice. If such a decision is made, the problems of coordination and conflict resulting from increased interdependence could still be reduced by means of increased planning, strengthened hierarchical leadership, or increased lateral participation and communication.

Increased Planning

Planning can simplify the implementation process of innovation by providing procedures and programs to deal with contingencies before they occur, so that the need for spur-of-the-moment problem solving and decision making is reduced. In addition, clear plans make explicit the commitment or contract of each participant, so that later questions over legitimacy or perceived injustice are less likely to arise. The limitations to this approach are that a great deal of time is often required to work out detailed plans for a major change and that the implications and consequences of the change must be clear before adequate provision for contingencies can be made. If time is short or outcomes are difficult to anticipate, as was true at Hillview, planning is less likely to be effective.

Strengthened Hierarchical Leadership

Strong administrative leadership may be an effective approach to implementing major change, particularly in the case of resistance from some of the organization's members. Administrators can bolster their position by enlisting increased support from superiors (in the case of schools, from the district office), in the form of policy commitments, resources, or enhanced formal powers. If such support is not forthcoming, and if an administrator is weak or, like the Hillview principal, has used up much of his "credit" with his staff, attempts to impose changes are not likely to meet with success.

Increased Lateral Participation and Communication

Increasing participation in the decision-making process often has the effect of making the decisions seem more legitimate to participants. When individuals have taken part in a decision to make a change, they are less likely to oppose the change later, and the chance of conflict is reduced. Increased participation also has some drawbacks, however. It tends to make the decision-making process rather cumbersome. With an increase in the number of individuals participating, the extent of communication and the number of different opinions also increases, and a great deal of time may be needed to take all the different views into account, resolve the differences, and reach a solution. At times, as in the Hillview case, such a solution may not be reached at all.

Conclusions

Many studies have examined the effects of environmental pressures or of organizational structure on innovation. While our study deals with both of these factors, it is less concerned with their independent effects than with the way their interaction may help to determine the process of innovation. This interaction can determine the type of innovation that is adopted and the way it is implemented. This study has documented in considerable detail an example of an innovation process that was strongly, and adversely, affected by the interaction of environmental and organizational factors. Diffuse pressures for major change were imposed upon a differentiated structure with weak leadership, resulting in a poorly articulated response, and, ultimately, in the rejection of the innovation. A similar interaction may have led to the failure of many other educational innovations.

References

Lawrence, Paul R., and Lorsch, Jay W. (1967). *Organization and Environment.* Cambridge, Mass.: Harvard University Press.

March, James G., and Simon, Herbert R. (1958). *Organizations.* New York: John Wiley and Sons, Inc.

New Institutions

24 The Life and Death of Differentiated Staffing at Columbia High School

C. Thompson Wacaster

In Overland District, differentiated staffing (DS) was claimed to be "helping to steer the way to improvement in the education process in view of growing student enrollment, disenchanted students, disillusioned teachers." DS was lauded as "a relatively new idea in American education," which would make "better use of better teachers on a professional career ladder," and provide new sources of "individualized instruction and guidance" and "energy to meet particular needs."[1]

However, less than a month after these claims were voiced in the Overland District, staff members of the district's differentiated staffing pilot high school voted to discontinue their DS model. An innovation process that included over two years of planning and training prior to eight months of attempted implementation had ended.

Why did the staff vote to discontinue the DS model? Some answers to this question emerged from clues contained in the story of differentiated staffing at Columbia High School (Wacaster, forthcoming).

Reprinted from *The Process of Planned Change in the School's Instructional Organization* (Eugene, Ore.: Center for the Advanced Study of Educational Administration, University of Oregon, 1973), pp. 35-51. The research was done as part of CASEA's Program 20.

1. These quotes are taken from a pamphlet published under the auspices of the federally-funded Overland District Differentiated Staffing Projects in late March 1971 [hereafter cited in text as Overland District Memo].

Life and Death of an Educational Innovation

Starting up a new high school can be exciting business. It offers an opportunity to begin again, to chart new directions, to right present wrongs. Or so it seemed in September 1967 to the principal-designate and the committee appointed to plan the yet-to-be-built, yet-to-be-staffed Columbia High School. They wanted to "enrich and individualize" student learning. They wanted to reward good teaching, thereby encouraging competent teachers to stay in the classroom and not move into administration or out of the profession. They wanted to design a school plant that would facilitate individualization of learning and make the educational experience an enjoyable one for both students and teachers. They wanted, finally, a staff utilization pattern that not only permitted the flexible use of teacher time and talent—a condition perceived by them as necessary for individualizing instruction—but one that also permitted reward for good teaching.

During the fall of 1967 and winter of 1968, the committee decided that some form of differentiated staffing would be an appropriate staff utilization pattern and that the specific Columbia DS model should be planned by the "high school staff and other district personnel" (Overland District Memo, n.d., page 6). To secure funds for the formulation of such a model and the training necessary for its implementation, the committee prepared an Education Professions Development Act proposal. It was submitted to the U.S. Office of Education in the late spring of 1968.

Also during the spring of that year the Columbia principal began recruiting faculty members. Since the committee had decided to staff the school with "renegades and innovators," he was seeking persons who had "proven innovative talent in prior positions" and "strong personal motivation and self-assertion" (Overland District Memo, n.d., page 6). In addition, he tried to give each applicant a picture of the goals of DS although, as he said, there still was no final DS model or even an established process at this stage for developing one. He was sure, however, that each person hired knew about DS and was "acceptive of its goals" at the time they were hired.

The 35 Columbia staff members met as a group for the first time in August 1968. The principal had arranged for a two-week "training laboratory in interpersonal relations and theory of organizational structure" to be offered by a staff member of Northwest State University (Overland District Memo, n.d., page 6). At the end of that workshop, staff members prepared a "Philosophy, Policies, and Procedures" document that began with the following statement: "We the Columbia staff agree that there will be an equal sharing of responsibility by the staff, including the departments, department chairmen, and administration, for the decision making and the functioning of the school."

In early September the school opened in temporary quarters with 587 students. No word had been received from the U.S. Office [of Education] concerning DS project funding and indeed little was done by the staff during the 1968-69 school year to develop a DS model. The staff, however, operated under a consensus decision-making model in that period, deciding issues ranging from assembly attendance policies and the content of a staff in-service program to early dismissal of student government officers for an out-of-school trip.

At the district level some activity relating to the project occurred during the 1968-69 school year. The school district received notification from Washington in December 1968 that Overland's proposal had been approved. A $10,000 planning grant was immediately made available to the district with the remainder of the proposal funding to be forthcoming at an unspecified later date.

Upon receipt of the planning grant, the Columbia curriculum vice-principal, who had been a member of the committee that planned Columbia, was appointed DS project director. Because the project now was envisaged as ultimately being extended to other district schools, his position was attached to the district personnel department with his office located in the district headquarters building.

The rest of the federal funding was received in the spring of 1969. It was used primarily to finance a DS workshop the following summer. This workshop was intended to prepare the Columbia staff to devise their DS model and to give them time to get on with the actual formulation of the model.

Prior to the workshop, the project director proposed that the following planning procedure be followed by the Columbia staff in developing their DS model:

Step 1: Make an education needs assessment.
Step 2: Define and list appropriate behavioral objectives for students.
Step 3: Define the skills, competencies, tasks and vehicles necessary to implement step 2.
Step 4: Define the responsibility levels required of personnel to implement step 3.
Step 5: Write job descriptions which satisfy the responsibility levels defined in step 4.
Step 6: Employ or train personnel to fill positions defined in step 5.

Step 7: Use the personnel so employed or trained.
Step 8: Evaluate, redesign as needed.

The Columbia staff accepted this planning procedure.

The Northwest State University faculty member returned to open the workshop with a week's training in interpersonal relations. A decision model also was devised for the workshop with all policy issues requiring consensus for passage while procedural matters needed a two-thirds majority. Then a variety of resource people were brought in to provide background for the staff to use in determining objectives for the Columbia program in general and the DS model in particular. The staff decided Columbia should both individualize education and educate "the whole child." The criteria of individualization and wholeness would require a wide range of specialists, given the perceived diversity of student talent and interest. Wholeness would also require, somehow, the integration of the learning experiences offered at Columbia.

The staff decided that the best way to bring about such integrated learning was to have an interdisciplinary curriculum. They subsequently discovered that the educational objectives they had been formulating during this time fell "naturally" into three categories: *Man and the Social World, Man and the Physical World,* and the *World of Work and Leisure.* They then decided to organize their curriculum around these three broad areas.

As a means to generate the interdisciplinary courses to be included in each area, the staff decided to split into three groups called domains. Each domain was to assume the name of one of the three broad curriculum areas and be responsible for curriculum development in that area.

Departments were to continue to exist but only as "service units" to domains. That is, departments were to supply members for domains, with each department charged to see not only that each department member was also a member of a domain, but that the department was adequately represented in all domains. Additionally, departments were to supply teachers and necessary materials for the interdisciplinary courses offered by the domains. Underscoring the notions that departments were to be service units to domains was the decision to phase out gradually the presently existing, departmentally offered, single-discipline courses.

With these general plans having been prepared, the workshop ended with neither DS positions identified nor job descriptions prepared.

The new $4.5 million Columbia building was ready for occupancy in September 1969. There were 982 students and 51 teachers, counselors, and administrators. Of thse 51, 28 had been on the staff the previous year, and these 28, plus 2 new staff members, had participated in the 1969 DS summer workshop. The staff voted to continue to operate under the previous year's decision-making model. Two other innovations were introduced for the first time that fall. Students were not assigned to homerooms, but met once a week in "Rep Rooms." This hour was to be used as a vehicle for student participation in student government and as a "care group" for students. PREP time was that portion of a student's day not scheduled into classes and was to be used for independent study, conferences with teachers, or recreational activities in the physical education or fine arts area. In short, when not in class, the student was on his own to pursue his individual interests.

During the fall, domains met at least eleven times and generated thirty-nine one- and two-page proposals for interdisciplinary courses. Of these, thirteen were selected to be opened to student registration in the spring and, if enough students signed up, offered in the fall of 1970, which was the target date for implementation of the first portions of the interdisciplinary curriculum and the DS model.

In the late fall the project director became alarmed. He wondered if there were a Columbia DS model. Plans were afoot in the school for domains, departments, and interdisciplinary teaching teams, but no DS positions had been identified and, as a consequence, no job descriptions for these positions had been prepared. The project director sent the Columbia staff an ultimatum: Write the DS job descriptions or get out of the DS project! He also conveyed to them the recently received U.S.O.E. criteria for DS models developed in federally funded training projects. One of these requirements was that the maximum salary of the highest-paid certificated position in the model be at least twice that of the lowest-paid certificated position.

The staff protested being dictated to by the project director and was not pleased with the U.S.O.E. criteria, especially the provision concerning pay. They decided for a variety of reasons, however, to go along with his demand. In a space of two weeks in early January 1970, the staff and committees thereof held a series of meetings in which they prepared and approved a set of DS job descriptions. In turn, these were forwarded to the project director.

The project director approved the descriptions and sent them along to the district's administrative cabinet: the superintendent and assistant superintendents. The members of the administrative cabinet rejected the job descriptions. They claimed "authority" and "responsibility" had been ignored and demanded that an organizational chart be prepared in which positions were ranked by levels of authority and responsibility.

When the job descriptions were returned to the Columbia staff with the administrative cabinet's specifications, the typical staff reaction was reported to be: "We're not that way! We don't want a hierarchy at all!" Nevertheless, such an organizational chart was approved by the staff, but only after a stormy faculty meeting was resolved by an impassioned plea from the principal, which was reported by others as follows: "We know how we work here. We have a very flat organization. So let's just submit the damn thing . . . not on the basis of this is the way we'll operate but because the central administration wants this chart. So we'll provide one for them." The chart [see Figure 24-1] which was approved by the staff depicts the structure of the DS model that they were to implement during the 1970-71 school year.

The chart was sent back to the administrative cabinet, who approved it and forwarded it along with the job descriptions to the school board. The school board said filling all the positions in the model and paying the salaries attached to those positions would cost 8 percent more than if the school were traditionally staffed. This cost figure was unacceptable to the board. After some negotiations with the Columbia principal, however, they permitted a 3 percent cost overrun, a figure they subsequently stood by in the face of two unprecedented budget defeats at the hands of the district voters.

During the spring the project director sent a memo concerning the 1970 summer workshop to the Columbia staff and the staffs of two other schools recently added to the DS workshop. Staff attendance at this workshop was to be mandatory and, in line with U.S.O.E. policy, workshop time was to be used for training *only*, with no curriculum or instructional development work of any sort permitted.

The Columbia staff exploded—but to little avail. Protests, meetings, and negotiations resulted in a week's instructional development time for teachers of the interdisciplinary courses, but no other concessions.

In the spring and early summer of 1970 persons were selected to fill the DS positions. The DS workshop began in the middle of June and ran for six weeks. The Columbia principal resigned effective July 1 to accept a district administrative position in another state. He was replaced by the acting district director of personnel.

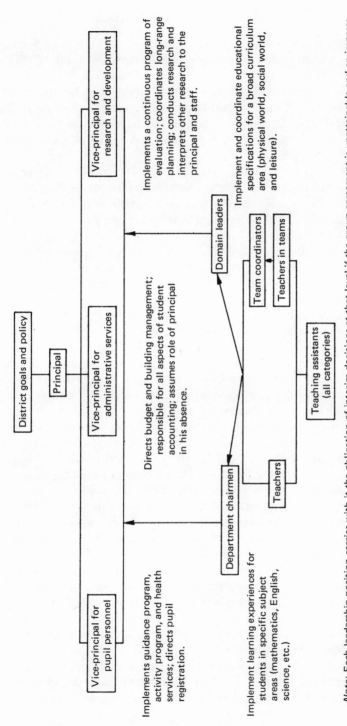

FIGURE 24-1

Organizational chart—differentiated staff experiment:
Columbia High School

Note: Each leadership position carries with it the obligation of interim decisions at that level if the group agreement is unattainable and an impasse obstructs the educational program.

Labor Day arrived and with it the start of the school year. Forty-five teachers returned from the previous year with the total full-time certificated staff in 1970-71 numbering fifty-five. This, too, was the implementation year for the Columbia DS model and for the interdisciplinary courses. A modular schedule was in use for the first time. PREP time and Rep Rooms were continued from the previous year as was the Columbia decision-making model. A move also was afoot to initiate an open campus.

Things didn't go well during that fall of 1970. Problems arose initially with the modular schedule. Students began to abuse PREP time and not to attend Rep Rooms. With late September and early October came unanticipated problems for teachers in the interdisciplinary courses. Because only brief outlines had been prepared when these courses were initially proposed and little time was allowed for instructional development during the previous summer, these teachers had to write their own courses of study as they went along, a task some found complicated by the fact that it had to be done cooperatively with other teachers on a team. Also, some instructional materials ordered for the new course had not arrived. Procedures for taking attendance at the large group sections of these courses hadn't been devised and skipping was becoming a problem. Additionally, as of October 15, over one hundred sophomores had requested transfers out of the interdisciplinary courses, usually citing the excess difficulty of the work as their reason.

In mid-October the issue of whether to have an open campus also provoked much controversy. The staff participated in a U.S.O.E. site visit regarding the DS model and sought to accommodate the flood of other visitors who came to view a DS model in operation. In addition, many of the above issues were dealt with by the faculty through the school's participative decision-making process. Difficulties also arose in that regard since it became difficult not only for the staff to secure consensus on solutions to problems but even to identify what the problems were in the first place.

Finally, domains did not function. Only four meetings were held during the fall and these were poorly attended. By mid-December just four new interdisciplinary courses had been proposed for the following year.

At the district level other significant events were transpiring. Prior to the Christmas break the DS project director noted in a progress report to the school board that costs for the next year's staffing of the DS schools would "not exceed traditional staffing expenditures." The 3 percent overrun for staffing was not to be allowed the following year. Indeed, in mid-April 1971 the district personnel department officially so informed the Columbia principal.

The principal subsequently took this information to the staff, indicating that as he saw it there were two courses of action open to them. They could decide to keep the present DS model and its salary differentials, although to do this under a condition of reduced funding would necessitate teachers having larger class sizes in order to create sufficient slack in the budget to pay the DS increments. Alternatively, they could decide to do away with the DS model, although this would entail a return to a departmentally organized school.

On April 23, 1971, the staff voted to discontinue the Columbia DS model.

As the story of differentiated staffing ran its course at Columbia High School, what were some of the factors along the way that may have influenced staff members to vote for discontinuance of the innovation?

The Setting: Norms and Values at Columbia

The administrators, counselors, and teachers brought together in 1968 as the initial Columbia staff members were for the most part strangers. These persons presumably were selected, however, because they were "renegades and innovators"—persons of "proven innovative talent" and "strong personal motivation and self-assertion." Such selection criteria may have resulted in the persons recruited into the organization having similar values concerning authority, the exercise of authority, and equality. The interpersonal relations training subsequently experienced by them at various times, then, may have operated to convert these similar individual values into group norms. That training, with its emphasis on participative decision making, equality, and open relationships may also have operated independently to instill values pertaining to those issues in individual staff members and build related norms into the group. At any rate, what does seem clear is that the criteria employed in the staff selection process and/or the interpersonal relations training received by the staff resulted in a set of individual values and group norms that appears to have had an important part to play in the story of DS's discontinuance at Columbia High School.

One such value was a belief in governance by the governed. It manifested itself in a number of forms, one being a norm that was formalized as an organizational rule: all policy and procedural issues affecting the staff were to be decided by the staff.

Staff members also seem to have held a belief that *all* persons—

teachers, students, members of the community—were of equal value. Certainly a norm of equality emerged at Columbia. While an administrator or science teacher or English teacher performed different jobs, the jobs were to be viewed as of equal value, as were the persons performing the jobs. There was to be no ranking of staff members in relation to each other.

What part did these staff norms and values, for the most part, intentionally built into the setting for Columbia's attempt at planned change, play in this story of discontinuance?

Incompatibility: Expectations for Project Control

Their belief in governance by the governed and faculty decision making appears to have been taken by some Columbia staff members to include the right to determine the nature of the preparation activities they would undertake in regard to the formulation and implementation of their DS model. They also expected to be the determiners of the dimensions of the Columbia DS model.

On the other hand, by the fall of 1969 the project director had come to believe that any U.S.O.E. guidelines for DS projects should be accepted unreservedly in Overland. Also, he felt any agreements made between the school district and the U.S. Office [of Education] concerning the local project should be adhered to strictly. That he assumed the right to undertake whatever action [was] necessary to enforce these guidelines and agreements is indicated by his insistence that the Columbia staff keep its previously made agreement to write their DS job descriptions, that these descriptions incorporate dimensions included in U.S.O.E. criteria, and that the 1970 summer workshop be for training purposes only.

Similarly, the district's administrative cabinet members indicated by their actions in February 1970 that they expected not only to have the right of review and veto for any DS model devised by the Columbia staff, but to specify some dimensions the staff should build into the model. The project director and the administrative cabinet, then, appear to have believed that control of various aspects of the Columbia DS project lay ultimately with them and not with the Columbia staff.

Given these incompatible expectations, it is not surprising that attempts at control by the project director and administrative cabinet typically provoked protest from the Columbia staff and other actions intended to thwart or at least modify such attempts. In each instance, however, the staff ultimately had to undertake whatever action was necessary to accommodate the various district-level personnel.

The expenditures of time, energy, and emotion required for protest and accommodation appear to have taken their toll at Columbia. The words of a domain leader make the point. When asked why the staff voted to discontinue their DS model, he replied, "There was no real benefit . . . and possibly some real hassle from staying in" and trying to meet the various guidelines.

Another consequence of the staff's subordination to the control of district-level personnel was that the dimensions desired by the latter were built into the Columbia DS model. These dimensions also had a part to play in the story of discontinuance.

Incompatibility: Dimensions of the Model—Staff Values and Norms

The Columbia DS model, as it finally emerged in February 1970 in response to U.S.O.E. criteria and the expectations of the project director and the administrative cabinet, was characterized in part by a hierarchy of positions ranked along dimensions of pay and authority. A staff member reports, however, that in the fall of 1969 and winter of 1970: ". . . red flags flew whenever anyone suggested pay differentials or authority differentials or anything to do with hierarchy." Another staff member, commenting on the controversy surrounding the preparation of an organizational chart for the DS model specifying levels of authority, stated: "In building a house you have carpenters and plumbers. They're doing different jobs, but have equal status . . . We were getting back to the old idea of horizontal structure in the building."

These statements, exemplifying available evidence, indicate that the Columbia DS model was strongly opposed by a number of staff members because it violated values and norms they held. A hierarchy of authority does not square with individual beliefs in governance by the governed or a norm of staff decision making. Pay differentials and the notion of individual ranking implied by hierarchy run counter to a sense of the equal value of persons. The vote over a year later to discontinue the DS model, then, might well have been an expression by some staff members of residual resistance rooted in such incompatibility of norms and values with dimensions of the innovation.

The incompatibility of expectations for project control, along with the incompatibility of staff norms and values with the DS model, however, may have contributed to the vote to discontinue in another more immediate manner, as will be seen in the next section.

Nonfunctioning of Key Positions in the DS Model

The Columbia DS model primarily was intended by the staff to serve as a mechanism for the development and implementation of a school-wide interdisciplinary curriculum. This curriculum, in turn, would accomplish the "education of the whole child." At the time the model was formulated, the staff apparently perceived the positions of domain member and domain leader as central to the model. Domain members were to generate proposals for interdisciplinary courses to be included in the curriculum. Domain leaders were to facilitate generation and arrange for implementation of that curriculum.

During the fall and winter of the model's implementation year, however, "the domains were not working successfully. The positions were there but not much activity was attached to them." This assessment was made by the English department chairman and was one of the reasons she cited when asked why the staff voted to discontinue the DS model. Domain leaders, other department chairmen, and the administrative vice-principal also cited this reason. Apparently the perceived nonfunctioning of key positions in the DS model was taken by a number of persons to indicate the entire model was not needed and should no longer be continued.

Some staff members attributed this lack of activity on the part of incumbents of domain positions to "busyness" and "fatigue." The fatigue was, in turn, attributed by them to two sources: the DS project preparation activities engaged in by the staff over the past two years and to the "busyness" of the staff during the fall of 1970 as it sought to cope with the anticipated and unanticipated demands of the overall Columbia educational program, especially its new components. Observational data and document analysis support these staff members' contention that busyness and fatigue existed and lend credence to their perception as to the sources of those phenomena. It would seem likely, though, that an additional source of fatigue might well have been the energy-consuming conflicts over control of the project and nature of the DS model.

A direct relationship of fatigue and busyness with the nonfunctioning of key positions in the DS model seems somewhat questionable, however. These two factors could be expected to operate equally to diminish job performance of staff members not only with regard to domain positions, but with other positions they occupied as well.

The problems with the interdisciplinary courses in the fall of 1970 may account in part for the domain positions being more susceptible to nonfunctioning than other positions. The desirability of the end—the interdisciplinary curriculum—that justified the existence of the domain positions could have been perceived by staff members as subject to question. Given conditions of fatigue and busyness, and thus the necessity to get priorities for the expenditures of time and energy, staff members would be less likely to perform jobs the ends of which have come to be perceived by them as of low desirability or of less desirability than ends of other jobs.

Other factors that might have made domain positions susceptible to nonperformance under conditions of fatigue and busyness include the newness of the positions, with all that could entail: vague job descriptions; lack of behavioral precedents for the job; lack of organizational mechanisms to monitor the performance of the job; and lack of formal rewards and punishment to be awarded on the bases of the monitoring, and so forth. Also, the nonfunctioning might somehow be a consequence of residual resistance of staff members to the DS model as a whole, with busyness and fatigue used to justify nonperformance because they were "socially acceptable" reasons. Space, however, prohibits a thoroughgoing discussion of these issues.

The Life and Death of an Educational Innovation (Concluded)

In April 1971 the Columbia staff learned formally that its certified personnel allotment for the following year did not include the 3 percent overrun permitted in the current year. Maintenance of the salary differentials in the DS model, the staff was told by the principal, would necessitate larger class sizes the following year. The staff was asked if they wished to continue the DS model.

Staff members, then, were being asked if they wished to continue a DS model, the dimensions of which apparently ran counter to some members' norms and values. Key positions in the model, too, had not functioned. The interdisciplinary curriculum (the primary goal of the model and one which may have served to diminish initial resistance to the model's dimensions) may have been viewed by a number of staff members as a less desirable end than previously. Finally, staff members were being told that to continue the model at a red[?] level of funding would necessitate larger class sizes—a conditi[?] likely to be accepted with equanimity, given the fatigue and b[?] experienced by the staff.

With only two dissenters, staff members voted to disco[?] DS model. The following day the principal conveyed this o[?] the project director and the district's administrative ca[?] project director wanted Columbia to continue in the proj[?] ministrative edict." The cabinet, however, accepted the[?] the staff. More than three years of effort had come

Differentiated staffing at Columbia High School had been laid to rest.

Some Implications for Policy and Research

The story of DS at Columbia High School raises a number of issues that might be of interest both to the educational practitioner who must manage the planned change process and the educational researcher studying educational organizations and their attempts to innovate.

One intriguing point emerges out of the analysis of staff members' values and norms, expectations for project control, and dimensions of the Columbia DS model. If the interpersonal relations training received by the Columbia staff were at least in part the origin of the norms and values that proved incompatible with dimensions of the innovation, then the anomalous situation existed in which the training activities included in the preparation phase of the innovation process produced intended outcomes (some norms and values) that, in turn, had the unintended consequence of contributing to the discontinuance of the innovation. In short, training activities believed to facilitate implementation of the innovation apparently proved to be inimical to such implementation. The question should be raised, then, as to whether any one preparation strategy, such as the widely used interpersonal relations training, can be considered an appropriate strategy to use with all innovations. Might one type of preparation strategy or activity be more appropriate with one type of innovation than another?

The earlier discussion of the nonfunctioning of key positions in the DS model suggests two other points that may have some interest for persons who manage or study educational change. The domains, it will be recalled, were initially established to generate the interdisciplinary curriculum. Teachers attempting to implement the interdisciplinary courses comprising that curriculum, however, encountered a [...] of operational difficulties. These difficulties may have been [...] nough to cause some staff members to question the desira[...] he interdisciplinary curriculum. Such questioning, in turn, [...] rompted these persons not to participate in domain activi[...]us, along with other factors, may have contributed to the [...]ning of key elements of the DS model, namely domain [...]d domain leader positions. That nonfunctioning may have [...] the extension of the interdisciplinary curriculum and the [...]t of departmental courses. It also apparently contributed [...]s decision to junk their DS model.

This all suggests the possibility of the occurrence of a "house-of-cards" phenomenon when multiple implementation of innovations is attempted. Some of those innovations may be functionally or ideologically dependent upon others in the "package." In the above case the interdisciplinary curriculum cannot be made functional on a school-wide basis if domains do not operate to generate and make arrangements for the implementation of the interdisciplinary courses. On the other hand, if the interdisciplinary courses are discredited, for whatever the reason, the ends for which the domains were set up are discredited. Domain members thus have no justification for expending their energy; domains have no raison d'être. In short, if one innovation falls, other innovations dependent upon it may fall in part or in toto—like a house of cards.

The second point that emerges from the discussion of the non-functioning of key positions in the DS model also has to do with the consequences of the multiple adoption of innovation and focuses on the concept of "competition." The multiple adoption of innovations, among other factors, appears to have contributed to the existence of fatigue and busyness among Columbia staff members. These conditions, in turn, seem ultimately to have induced competition of one innovation with another and with previously existing practices for the time and energy of the staff. Such competition had consequences for the degree of implementation of an innovation into the school's ongoing body of practices. It would be interesting to know what factors prompted one innovation or practice to be chosen over another for expenditure of time and energy. Also, if "reversion to type" occurs in attempts at innovation as often as it is reported, then one might wonder why previously established practices appear to have some edge over newly introduced practices in the competition for time, energy, and other resources.

At any rate, the "house-of-cards" phenomenon and this occurrence of competition for resources may have some implications for the "strategy of grandeur" or "wholistic approach" to educational change embodied, for example, in the experimental schools and, to a lesser degree, in the multiunit school-individually guided education programs.

25 Alternative Schools: An Alternative Postmortem

Terrence E. Deal

Five years ago, alternative schools gathered enough momentum for some educators to predict that the movement would supplant conventional secondary schooling within a decade. Since that crest, however, the wave of educational reform has receded, leaving in its wake disillusioned and frustrated educational idealists, a large graveyard of experimental schools, and many schools, still alive, that disguise conservative practices under a cloak of innovation. Only a handful of schools continue in the spirit of the original break from tradition. A number of on-campus versions have resulted from the co-optation of alternative ideas by public high schools. But, with these exceptions, another educational revolution has come and gone, leaving as its main legacy a reinforced set of conventional beliefs about schools and learning.

Why did so many of these experiments in secondary schooling fail? Several different explanations have been offered. One is the process of natural selection, where the strong survive and the unfit are discarded: innovative, humanistic schools did not achieve important educational goals nearly as well as schools following a more traditional pattern. Another is that the downfall was economic in origin: alternative schools withered away because of sporadic or insufficient income. A third explanation emphasizes politics: alternative schools fell victim to pressures exerted by the "establishment" whose vested interests are protected by conventional schooling. A fourth

A different version of this chapter appeared as R&D Memorandum No. 133, "An Organizational Explanation of Alternative School Failures," published by the Stanford Center for Research and Development in Teaching. This research was conducted at the Center pursuant to contract NE-C-00-3-0062 with the National Institute of Education, Department of Health, Education, and Welfare.

explanation is anthropological; alternatives were linked to the humanistic revolution or the "counterculture," and, as it waned, so did support for more humanistic schools.

There is another appealing explanation that has never enjoyed the popularity of the other four: alternative schools failed for internal reasons. They were unable to cope with the organizational problems produced by new authority patterns and by highly complex educational processes. In this view, the general development of past alternative schools showed the following pattern. Alternative schools attracted alienated students and teachers. The schools were designed so as to radically alter authority relationships among all participants, particularly those between teachers and students. Individual students were granted considerable autonomy in choosing their own activities and in making decisions for the school as a whole. This produced a very diverse, individualistic pattern of learning activities and a highly egalitarian and informal structure of governance. As the schools entered their initial phase, these two characteristics triggered a series of developmental stages that led ultimately to dissolution, a reversion to more conventional education, or, in a few cases, novel compromises in the educational process or in the distribution of authority. In the sociological literature, the stages encountered in alternative schools bear a striking resemblance to those experienced in other new educational institutions (Smith and Keith, 1973) or in leaderless small groups (Bennis and Shepard, 1961; Mills, 1964).

This organizational view of alternative schools suggests that the alternative ideology of autonomy, democracy, and "do your own thing" contained the seed of its own destruction. Alternative schools tried to accomplish a highly sophisticated educational task with underdeveloped and nearly anarchic structures for decision making and problem solving.

The educational issue this final explanation raises is whether many interesting and important educational ideas underlying alternative schools ever received a fair hearing. Without divisive internal problems, would they have fared better economically and politically? With some knowledge of how to solve internal problems, would these schools have provided new models for teaching and learning in secondary education? If alternative schools failed because they were unable to develop an organization suited to their complex aims and problems, then we need to give the movement a second look, and perhaps a second chance. If we can distill from their earlier difficulties some general guidelines for avoiding organizational difficulties in the future, then we may be able to test other aspects of teaching and learning that alternative schools proposed but were never able to implement. And if another widespread interest in alternative schooling should swell, then we could use these guidelines to build new strong and viable experiments.

The main purpose of this article is to provide some insight into alternative schools that may revise our sense of their past, help with problems they face in the present, and, finally, rekindle an interest in their future if accompanied by sound guidelines for more effective organization. To accomplish this primary purpose, we draw on two case studies of alternative schools and develop more fully the thesis that the authority patterns in these schools, combined with other innovative characteristics, led to a fairly predictable series of events, ultimately resulting in either the school's dissolution, the school's conformation to traditional guidelines, or the school's survival as a fairly stabilized alternative to conventional schools.

First, however, there must be a definition of alternative schools, along with some evidence that they did, indeed, attract an alienated clientele. This is followed by a brief description of the two alternative schools from which a stage model is abstracted, after which developmental stages and alternative outcomes are described and illustrated by anecdotal material from the two case studies. These steps finally lead to speculation about some of the processes underlying the stages and the practical implications of the model for alternative schools.

What Are Alternative Schools?

One of the difficulties in discussing alternative schools is in determining which schools can legitimately claim the title "alternative." There is wide diversity among schools calling themselves "free," "experimental," or "alternative." Even among those actually claiming to be alternative schools there is enormous variation: public versus private, on-campus versus off-campus, academic versus vocational, intellectual versus growth-oriented. One characteristic claimed by all alternative schools, however, is some sort of departure from the educational status quo. The word *alternative* actually means a choice, which implies that there must be some deviation from what already exists. In the case of alternative schools, the benchmark is conventional schooling. A simple, useful way to conceptualize schooling for determining either "conventionality" or "innovativeness" is to use six important dimensions of learning: *who* is involved in the learning process, *what* is learned, *why* it is learned, *how* it is learned, *where* learning takes place, and *when* learning takes place. Using these six dimensions, we can construct six separate scales with purely conventional characteristics on one side and purely alternative ones on the other. Of course, with each dimension, a particular school could fall anywhere between the two.

On the basis of this scheme, alternative schools can be defined as those which differ from conventional secondary schools in all six learning dimensions. It is possible to think of lesser degrees of

TABLE 25-1. Differences between conventional and alternative secondary schools on six important dimensions of learning

| Dimension | Secondary schools | |
	Conventional	Alternative
Who is involved in the learning process (roles)	Certificated teachers, counselors, administrators, and students. All roles have well-defined expectations	Teachers, administrators, parents, community members, students. Anyone who has something to teach. Certification requirements relaxed. Role distinctions blurred
What is learned (curriculum)	State- or district-prescribed curriculum. Knowledge is broken into subject areas, with special programs for noncollege bound or other "special" students	Wide variation in educational substance dictated largely by interest of students. It may encompass areas usually taught in school, but it can also extend into many other areas
Why it is learned (authority)	Extrinsic motivation. Learning is intended to fulfill requirements and pass tests. Authority is vested in teacher: "Do what you are told" is the teacher's directive	Intrinsic motivation. Learning results from interest or need to know, to learn a skill, or to develop knowledge. Authority is vested in student; the student chooses
How it is learned (methods)	Emphasis on reading, writing, listening. Group presentation by teacher is common, with some audiovisual aids and some discussion	Methods vary as widely as the curriculum. Reading, writing, and listening are not excluded, but emphasis is on doing and experiencing. All senses are involved
Where learning takes place (location)	On campus and in the classroom. There are some field trips, but they are exceptional	Wide variation in location of learning: private homes, beach, forest, libraries, businesses. Instruction in formal classroom is the exception rather than the rule
When learning takes place	Instruction typically occurs between hours of 8 and 4, day segmented into periods or modules	Learning takes place anytime, depending on the nature of the learning task, with infrequent scheduling and no time segmentation

"alternativeness" that would be produced by varying less than six, but at least one, but this would not constitute an alternative school for our purposes.

To some extent the six learning dimensions are probably interrelated and, therefore, changes in any one dimension undoubtedly cause changes in others, also. Giving students more autonomy widens the range of subject areas, and changing the location of learning to the community increases the likelihood that other members of the community besides teachers will be involved.

In point of fact, many experimental secondary schools did change all six learning dimensions although perhaps the most popular practice among them was to change the "why" dimension of learning from telling students "do what you are told" to offering them an opportunity to "do what you want." The importance of this shift is not to be underestimated as it transferred authority, or the right to make instructional decisions, from the teacher to the student. It also involved students in determining policy for the school as a whole. Evidence from Spellman (1971) and the few empirical studies that took a hard look at the authority differences between conventional and alternative schools lend some strength to the assumption that egalitarian, antiauthoritarian structures were prevalent (Bredo-Riemersma, 1971; McCauley, 1971).

What Kind of Students Did Alternative Schools Attract?

By and large, the clientele of alternative schools was white and middle class. Exceptions to this were special-purpose secondary schools and ethnic schools that included minority students. Although such schools would be considered alternative according to some definitions, most did not increase student autonomy in making decisions; instead, they varied other learning dimensions. The alternative schools which served the white, middle-class population, on the other hand, almost without exception changed the structure of authority dramatically.

Most students attracted to alternative schools shared more than a socioethnic background; they were alienated from the authority system of the traditional school. Spellman's (1971) absorbing study of a suburban high school revealed that 23.1 percent of the student body scored high on her composite index of alienation from the high school's authority system. By comparison Spellman and Deal's (1971) study of students selected for alternative high school in the same community showed that, on the same scale, nearly 60 percent of the students were alienated from the authority system of the conventional high school. Beyond this one comparison, little is known about the alternative school population; it seems reasonable to assume that most of the students who attended these schools were white, middle or upper-middle class, and alienated.

Case Studies of Two Alternative Schools

Two important points now limit the secondary schools to be discussed. First, those schools called alternative are secondary schools that differ from conventional schools along six learning dimensions, with changes in the "why" or the authority dimension being crucial. Second, the clientele of such schools comes primarily from the white, middle, or upper-middle class and tends, for various reasons, to be alienated from the typical authority structure of a conventional high school.

Both of the case studies presented meet both of these conditions. The first was a high school (1970) within a suburban public school system; the other a privately funded school (1971) located in a large city. In the second school the program lasted for only a semester, not a full school year. Since an entirely different student body was involved each semester, the program actually provides two separate case studies, making the total number studied three.

In both schools, observations during the inaugural year used the full repertoire of field methods available to a participant observer: observations, questionnaires, interviews, and some standardized instruments. Notes were made sporadically, and tentative conclusions were pulled together at the end of each program. During the middle of the first semester in the private school the pattern of developmental stages, which will be discussed later, emerged as a tentative hypothesis. In the final semester of the private school program it was these stages that were focused on specifically and explored in depth.

The public alternative school, which we will call Community School, had a student body of thirty, and a teaching staff of three. The school was financed by public funds and was located in two rooms above a town bakery. The students were volunteers from the traditional high school, selected because they had rebelled against the conventional high school and because there was no other district program to provide their education. As an interesting twist, the students were identified first, and, with the exception of the principal or head teacher (who was selected by the superintendent), selected their two teachers from among one hundred and twenty applicants. In all respects the school's program was an alternative to the conventional high school. The entire community was considered the classroom, and all citizens were considered potential teachers. Learning activities ranged from ceramics to logic, cooking to communications, dome building to American history. Students determined what they wanted to study, with their own immediate interests being the most important criterion. They were also collectively responsible, with the teachers, for setting school-wide policy. The entire community was used as a learning laboratory, and learning activities occurred around the clock on a random, unscheduled basis.

The second school, which we will call Urban School, was located in a large city. It was comparable to Community School, but it had a residential dimension since the twelve students and three staff members lived together in a large old Victorian house. The school was a pioneer offshoot of an elite private boarding school. It attracted older secondary students from wealthy families. The thrust of the school was to involve the students in the life and work of a large city, and internships in various city organizations were the formal mechanism for involving them. In most respects, the curriculum, methods, and authority structure of Urban School were comparable to that of Community School. The curriculum was more focused and the methods more systematically emphasized, but the students were responsible for choosing their instructional program and for making school-wide decisions. With certain limitations they structured their life style within the school's residential center. Once again, learning could take place anytime, anywhere.

A Stage Model of Alternative School Development

During the first months, Community School and Urban School (both semesters) passed through distinct stages. The sequence was remarkably similar in all instances, and from it a developmental model can be abstracted. It may apply to other alternative schools and may help to account for the rate of failure as well as the tendency to return to traditional programs.

The developmental stages are shown in Figure 25-1. The model assumes that newly formed alternative schools combined alienated students and an educational structure in which all six dimensions of learning were altered. The initial result of this combination, we suggest, is euphoria. In the first stage all participants in an alternative school—students, teachers, and parents—are extremely happy and enthusiastic. The dominant theme is "things were never so good."

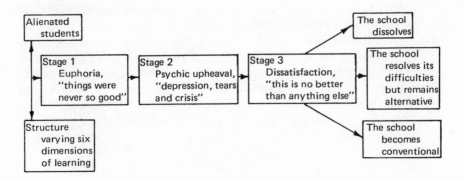

FIGURE 25-1
Model of alternative secondary school development

As the school progresses, however, the bliss and excitement give way to individual gloom and depression in the second stage, one of psychological crisis, which is marked by depression, sickness, emotional outbursts, and erratic behavior on the part of students. There is a tendency for the school to become more of a crisis center than a school at this stage.

About the time the school has stabilized in the second stage, the third stage, one of rampant dissatisfaction, begins. Students, teachers, and parents all agree that the school is experiencing great difficulties, is not accomplishing its purposes, and is failing to provide a satisfactory substitute for conventional schooling. Often, two subgroups form, one favoring the original "innovative" charter of the school and the other pressing for a more conventional program and more traditional patterns of organization. Whether or not such subgroups form the dominant theme of the third stage, there is a pervasive sense of dissatisfaction among all members of the school.

The third stage appears to be critical for alternative schools. They are faced with a level of organizational instability that must be resolved in one of three ways: by refusing to alter their course and either literally falling or splitting apart or voluntarily disbanding, by becoming highly conventional in their governance and approach to learning, or by stumbling intuitively into some form of compromise in their authority structure and educational program.

This development sequence, which was abstracted from the buzzing, confusing reality that two particular alternative schools faced, has been sharpened and refined through the simplifying filter of hindsight. The model is based on three separate case studies. For the most part, the stages capture the central development of each case. In each situation, of course, a welter of other complex processes, pressures, incidents, and events occurred simultaneously. The specific events or manifestations of each stage differed in the two schools. Anecdotal material from the individual case studies illustrates and amplifies the three stages of euphoria, psychic upheaval, and dissatisfaction and identifies the course of resolution taken by Community School and Urban School.

The Euphoric Stage

The beginning days of an alternative school are filled with excitement, romance, and adventure. Brief anecdotes from Community School and Urban School highlight this stimulating and blissful beginning.

Community School

At first, students resembled prisoners released from bondage who have spent long hours tantalizing about what life outside is like. Students plunged energetically into many atypical educational enterprises: planting organic gardens, building geodesic domes, planning how to refurbish the schools headquarters, walking on the beach, discussing the true meaning of life, delving deep into each other's personal motivations, discussing at great length the evils of conventional school and other "establishment" institutions.

Teachers, seeing ideal and long-wished-for teaching conditions, implemented and developed premature images of being pioneers in revolutionizing and humanizing modern secondary schooling. Prospective journal articles were outlined, and larger schemes to reform the town's main high school were developed.

One parent, ecstatic about her son's new glow and overwhelming interest in school, donated $50 to the school district. The superintendent was hard pressed to figure out the machinery to process such an unusual donation.

Invitations for teachers and students to speak at parent and community groups were numerous.

The teachers from the traditional high school were the only ones not excited; they were depressed because "a school like that should not work."

Urban School

In the residential center the first meals were festive banquets, often by candlelight. Everyone participated in buying the food, preparing it, and cleaning the kitchen following the meal.

Frequent shopping forays into the city were common. Students spent considerable time fixing their individual rooms into the resplendent environments they had always wanted to create.

One student during a collective dinner remarked that this was the finest school he had attended and the finest educational process he had experienced. He went on to say that he did not ever imagine that "things could ever be like this." His statement was loudly and wildly cheered by the other students.

The Psychic Upheaval Stage

The euphoric period ended abruptly, after lasting from two to four weeks. The transition into the second stage was rapid, and the plunge was dramatic and widespread. The main scenarios of this psychic upheaval stage included: individual depression, lethargy, sickness, crying, and erratic behavior.

Community School

It was not at all uncommon during this time for students to burst into tears in the middle of a conversation. A student walked into the headquarters one day, burst into tears, and was joined by four other students.

Two students locked onto one another, began to talk to each other in "baby talk," and were often seen skipping arm-in-arm through the town.

One subgroup which had formed in the school's beginning started to split apart. The coup-de-grace came one day when, during one of their meetings a girl burst into tears saying that "she could not stand it any more." The group fell apart shortly thereafter.

During this period, one student tried to take his own life.

Parents remained happy that the students were enjoying school and seemed to be getting help in resolving their emotional difficulties. But, parents too were occasionally depressed, and the teachers often received calls from parents asking for help with the parents' own emotional problems.

Urban School

Since the students and staff lived together, the staff served a parental function. During this period students often complained of insomnia, backaches, nightmares, and headaches. Drinking and drunkenness increased as did crying and other emotional outbursts. Students began to go home frequently on the weekends.

The Dissatisfaction Stage

The psychological crisis period lasted four to six weeks giving way quickly to a period of general disgruntlement and negativism. The dissatisfaction was shared by anyone involved with the school—teachers, students, parents, and the general community.

Community School

Students spent considerable time on the campus of the conventional high school seeing friends, eating lunch, even attending classes.

Absenteeism rose considerably. It was not at all uncommon for only a few students to even stop by the school's headquarters during an entire week.

Students were vocal in their criticisms of the school and of the staff for not doing something to make the situation better. But it was impossible for students to describe how they might like to see things changed.

Parental complaints both to the teachers and the district administration increased. Parents threatened to have students transferred to the traditional high school because "in the community school students were not accomplishing anything worthwhile."

The staff was torn between relying on the democratic decision-making process to develop a direction for the school or taking over as a way of preventing the school from falling apart.

Urban School

Long-distance calls from parents begin to flood the staff. One parent said, "What is going on there. I have lost all faith in private education and I never had any faith in the Urban School."

Students frequently returned to the parent school campus, often spending an entire day and even the night.

One contingent of students at the Urban School felt the director was not doing his job and complained formally to the founder of the private school supporting the Urban School program.

Resolution in Urban School and Community School

After a period of dissatisfaction it became quite clear in all three instances that three alternative courses of action were possible: avoid the problem by disbanding the school or allowing it to fold, return the staff's authority to make decisions about instructional as well as school-wide matters, or find a way to confront and solve the difficulties and problems.

Both Urban School and Community School took the third option. In both cases the choice was more intuitive and accidental than rational and planned. It was heavily influenced by a strong staff commitment to "failing for the right reasons." By gathering information through questionnaires and interviews and meeting in large and small groups to identify, discuss, and analyze problems, both schools hammered out a course of action that resulted in a shared set of goals. This involved adopting an authority position somewhere between the "do what you want" and "do what you are told" poles. This new position gave teachers the active role of developing and expanding alternatives, but allowed students to retain final decision-making rights about their own learning activities. It also gave the staff more responsibility for making school policy. The new structure, stated simply, was "do what you and I have jointly established."

In Community School the staff temporarily took a firm stand, interjected conventional high school requirements, and scheduled courses. Most students grabbed at the opportunity, and others, while shying at requirements, voluntarily pursued highly traditional learning objectives in mathematics, reading, and language arts. But this return to conventional schooling was viewed by the staff as a stopgap measure to stabilize the school temporarily until some common goals and a compromise in the authority structure of the school could be worked out.

Resolution in Other Alternative Schools

Faced with the same stage of general dissatisfaction, many other alternative schools fervently committed to the equalitarian and individualistic ideology of the counterculture refused to alter authority relationships. We suggest that this was the group of schools that dissolved and joined the alternative school graveyard. They were unable to identify options or to solve their internal problems because of ideological commitments. A well-accepted statistic was an average eighteen-month life span for an alternative school. Our model suggests that authority issues and the attending consequences contributed to the short longevity.

A second group of schools took another direction. At the height of dissatisfaction there was a dominant cry for someone to take over and restore order to the educational chaos. Interestingly, this plea was often from students who had previously clamored loudly for student autonomy. These students were now willing to sell their decision-making rights to anyone who would tighten the ship. Into this leadership vacuum moved one teacher or an entire staff that generally supported more hierarchical decision making. Shortly after, perhaps because the six learning dimensions overlap and flow together, such schools shifted from alternative patterns to conventional ones in other areas such as curriculum, methods, community involvement, and scheduling. Authority changes had an effect on all areas of the school. The schools thereafter operated as alternatives only in name. Many such schools continue as alternatives, although the distinction between their program and that of a conventional high school is very subtle.

A few other schools, like Community School and Urban School, emerged from the developmental stages as stable, viable alternatives. Most of these probably engaged at crucial points in systematic, collaborative, problem-solving efforts. Exactly why they stabilized remains a question. But it is highly possible that most successful schools reached a compromise in their authority structures or in other ways reorganized the school. These organizational compromises often continued student autonomy in making decisions about their own instructional program and school-wide matters, but also gave the staff an active role in defining boundaries and suggesting alternatives. Schools of this type often experimented with student contracts and some form of negotiating process, or developed student projects to set specific instructional tasks.

Possible Explanations Underlying the Stages of
Alternative School Development

Thus far, we have relied on Urban School and Community School to develop a descriptive model of alternative school development. We have speculated that alternative schools with an alienated student body and an innovative program (using the six learning dimensions as criteria) experienced specific stages in sequential order and resolved the final stage in one of three ways. We have hinted at organizational causes of the stages, but what are some possible explanations for this developmental sequence?

First, we can explain the stages as a process involving the expectations of the participants. Students and teachers began the schools with highly idealized, unrealistic expectations; individual disappointment and depression resulted when these were not met; individual disappointment gave way to a general dissatisfaction with the entire situation; and, finally, hard reality reduced the willingness to continue to work for the original dreams of what the school could be.

Another way to explain the stages is to emphasize the impact of the school on the identities of the participants. The schools attracted students and teachers who often reacted negatively to the conventional school structure. When that target was removed, the basis for identity was also removed. This caused students and teachers to search for a new way to define themselves and resulted in psychic distress. As they turned inward, they found a conservative side of the self. The way out of the swamp was thus to restore the old basis for identity by creating a conventional structure to which they, once again, could react, or to satisfy the newly found conservative side of the self by creating or returning to a conventional secondary school program.

We can borrow a third explanation from personality theory. Students and staff were placed in a situation different from that they had known previously. They did not have the skills, abilities, and attitudes to deal with the new situation, and they were forced to develop new skills and attitudes, making their personality structure more differentiated and, probably over time, more integrated. But because in many cases the situation was so overwhelming, students and teachers regressed and reached back for childish, defensive responses to the situation, thereby avoiding personal growth.

This does not, of course, exhaust the many conceivable explanations of what caused the stages in alternative schools. We could draw additional explanations from philosophy, anthropology, social psychology, and sociology. Our own bias, however, is to stress organizational explanations.

Viewed organizationally, alternative schools were new institutions with vague, diffuse goals and an underlying ideology that emphasized individual freedom, unique experience, and humanistic values. The schools often existed in hostile "establishment" environments and, because of frequent criticism, closed themselves off except to that sector of the environment that believed as they did. The educational program of these schools, following the goals and ideology, was highly individualistic and discontinuous, and both the techniques of teaching or learning and ways to judge progress and success were underdeveloped or nonexistent. The authority granted to students in selecting learning activities, the "do your own thing" character, increased the diversity of curriculum and instruction and made it difficult for teachers to have much of a role in student learning. Instructional tasks of any one student often involved input from several teachers, and, as a result, the efforts of teachers, as well as students, were highly interdependent.

The combination of organizational features required of these schools a highly developed structure to coordinate, support, evaluate, and deal with a highly complex instructional program in an often hostile environment. Yet structurally alternative schools were primitive, undeveloped, fragmented, and highly informal. The counterculture ideology abhors organization, routinization, and bureaucracy, and, as a result, decision making in alternative schools was participatory, consensual, cumbersome, burdensome, and ineffectual. Problem solving was laborious although enough problems existed to keep a well-oiled system working at full capacity. Using the organizational character of alternative schools as a framework, we would explain the developmental stages as follows:

In alternative schools experiencing the bloom of stage one there was no need for organization. Students and teachers were busily engaged in living out personal and educational fantasies. Students were able to do what they had formerly dreamed of in classes where instructional activities were meaningless. Teachers were able to provide instruction without the constraints of the conventional system. But, as time passed, there was no formally recognized standard to judge such activities; nor was there any feedback for highly individualistic accomplishments.

Stage two was a normless, listless, confused, anomic reaction to the lack of feedback for the learning activities of the first stage. Remember that the goals of alternative education were vague and diffuse. In living out their personal fantasies, students and teachers soon began to look for formal validation that their direction was "appropriate." But, as they looked for such recognition within the schools, they found no goals nor any real consensus so they turned their attention outside, where, again, they found little, if any, support for their activities. This threw students (and teachers) back on their own resources, and they looked inside themselves for the validation they expected from without. This introspection produced the predictable trauma and, as its intensity increased and extended to many of the students in the school, the "organization" began to reward disturbed students by giving them feedback about personal difficulties through the teachers or the formal system of evaluation. This, in the absence of other feedback, quickly led to a negatively based system of evaluation and rewards. Having a personal problem was formally recognized and rewarded.

At the same time, teachers were overloaded. They were required to provide counseling, to provide educational leadership for a school whose leadership was supposed to flow from the collective, and to develop and coordinate numerous and highly diverse instructional activities, many of which were not routine and many of which teachers were not professionally prepared to handle. Yet, at the same time, teachers were faced with the reality that collective decision making was insufficient and frustrated by the power of an ideology suggesting that this was the only way in which problems could legitimately be resolved. Few activities were routinized, yet the decision-making apparatus was cumbersome and often overlooked, making it difficult for any problems to be solved. Teachers were overworked, but unable to make needed changes since their proposals were modified or aborted by the consensual decision-making process.

Students, receiving little feedback from teachers, turned to their peers who were also too absorbed in personal problems to offer support or assistance. In frustration, students (and teachers) increased their reach outside to parents and others for some assurance that they were achieving educational goals. But, in this relatively "hostile" and unsupportive environment, they found only criticism and an exhortation to return to conventional patterns. This led quickly to stage three.

Stage three pressed upon alternative schools the realization that their organizational shift to a counseling or crisis center was insufficient. For some students, they provided a temporary "way station."

But, it was clear that other students were requesting, even demanding, some highly conventional instruction. How could this be provided when the demands were so diverse? How could the school become both a crisis center and a conventional high school? Even if this
were organizationally feasible, how could consensus be reached in a
highly pluralistic setting when the determination of policy was in the
hands of the entire population of the school?

Clearly, continuing the status quo would result in severe internal
splits or in destruction. On the other hand, if the faculty or someone
in the school took over, would not that act, in itself, destroy the
integrity of the school? In the absence of clear goals, in an environment that rejected the main learning activities, without a history,
without clear means for accomplishing learning or measuring success,
without the internal support of individual or informal group norms,
without adequate time for the professional leadership to develop
directions, how were alternative schools to maintain their organizational integrity?

For many schools the answer was clear. They either went down
without striking their colors, or they returned to the safety of a familiar and friendly port. These were the alternative schools that dissolved or reverted to a highly centralized and conventional system.

Those schools that "made it" did so because they were able to
find a middle ground organizationally by maintaining a highly differentiated structure that was also well integrated and formalized. There
was a division of labor. Roles were clarified. Students were still given
considerable autonomy in choosing learning activities, but now
teachers were given formal responsibility for expanding the base of
alternatives. Goals were specified, evaluation processes were regular-
ized, and decision rules were established to centralize some decisions,
while keeping others decentralized and consensual. Boundary maintenance activities were developed to control and process the flow of
negative information from the environment, while specific attempts
were made to persuade the parents and the community that the alternative program was highly desirable educationally—by any standards.
In short, the successful alternative schools developed a well-knit,
sophisticated organization capable of supporting the highly complex
instructional program they had chosen to operate. They compromised somewhat their original participatory, democratic, "hang
loose" approach to organization, but were able to maintain the integrity of the other elements in their alternative approach to instruction.

Some Implications for Alternative Schools

This organizational explanation is particularly appealing because of its concrete implications for present or future alternative schools. It provides a framework for raising questions and identifying solutions that teachers or students can really do something about. Using such a framework, they will have some basis for designing an organization that facilitates rather than impedes their educational aims. They will be able to seek an equilibrium or compromises in authority patterns or other organizational properties that will enable them to avoid falling apart or returning to a highly centralized system.

What is most important, perhaps, is the prior knowledge that these developmental stages may occur in the formative months of alternative schools. It may prevent the teachers and the staff from rising and falling with the natural development of the school. It will bring some degree of rationality to the situation and allow manipulation of aspects of the structure to minimize the effects of the various stages.

Whither Alternative Schools?

We have suggested an alternative explanation for the difficulties of the alternative secondary school movement. We contend that alternative education was denied the opportunity to test its basic ideas because schools organized in such fashion could not cope with the consequences of a revised authority structure. Alternative schools were initiated mostly by educational idealists who assumed that a new path to learning was traversed easily by removing barriers encountered on the old one. They did not, in their worst moments, ever conceive that the removal of the barriers would have such overpowering consequences. Neither did they have the understanding, the skills, or the organizational sense to cope with the problems they encountered without returning to the system they wanted to revise. We are older now, however, and certainly wiser about educational experiments. Despite the fact that former educational critics are now repudiating their first books on the merits of alternative education, this seems an interesting time to continue to experiment with new learning techniques, but in schools staffed with people whose zeal is matched with knowledge of how complex social systems and organizations work.

References

Bennis, Warren G., and Shepard, H. A. (1961). "A Theory of Group Development," in W. G. Bennis, K. D. Benne, and R. Chin, eds., *The Planning of Change.* New York: Holt.

Bredo, Anneke E., and Bredo, Eric R. (1975). "Effects of Environment and Structure on the Process of Innovation," R&D Memorandum No. 132. Stanford, Calif.: Stanford Center for Research and Development in Teaching.

Bredo, Eric R., and Riemersma, Anneke E. (1971). "A Study of Authority Relations in Three High Schools." Unpublished paper, Stanford University.

McCauley, Brian L., Dornbusch, Sanford M., and Scott, W. Richard (1972). "Evaluation and Authority in Alternative School and Public Schools." Stanford Center for Research and Development in Teaching, Technical Report No. 23, Stanford University.

Mills, Theodore M. (1964). *Group Transformation, an Analysis of a Learning Group.* Englewood Cliffs, N.J.: Prentice-Hall.

Smith, Louis M., and Keith, Pat M. (1971). *The Anatomy of Educational Innovation: An Organizational Analysis of an Elementary School.* New York: Wiley.

Spellman, Judith Blair (1971). "Alienation from High School Authority and the Counter-Culture." Paper presented at the Annual Meeting of the American Educational Research Association, New York, February.

―――― (1971). "The Relationship between Middle-Class High School Students' Educational Aspirations, and Their Attitudes toward the Authority Structure of the School." Unpublished Dissertation, Stanford University.

――――, and Deal, Terrence E. (1971). "An Evaluation at the Community Center High School." Paper presented at Pacific Grove District, Pacific Grove, California.

26 Formal Doctrine: Manifestations, Content, Dimensions, and Consequences

Louis M. Smith
Pat M. Keith

Sometimes a picture of social reality becomes clearer by stepping back from the concrete images of day-to-day activities and events and by viewing the larger context into which the particulars fit. One part of this frame of reference is what we have called the "formal doctrine."[1] ... All groups and organizations, in the course of their development, build a point of view or perspective about themselves, their problems, and their environment. These points of view vary in the degree to which they are visionary, conscious, and codified. ... The term "formal doctrine" [is used] to represent the complex combination of a point of view that is visionary, ... highly conscious, and ... highly codified. Ideology, a visionary theorizing, could serve about as well, although it tends not to emphasize the conscious and codified aspects. The doctrine includes an elaborated system of concepts, spelling out the entire structure of means and ends within an organization.

At Kensington, a number of events took place that demanded additional labels. These include mandate, institutional plan, and facade. A mandate is the formal charge or directive given by the

---

Abridged version of Louis M. Smith and Pat M. Keith, *Anatomy of Educational Innovation: An Organizational Analysis of an Elementary School* (New York: John Wiley and Sons, 1971), ch. 2. Reprinted by permission of John Wiley and Sons, Inc.

1. This is an adaptation of Selznick's (1949) concept of "official doctrine."

legitimate authority. In the case of Kensington, it is the superintendent's directive.[2] The Institutional Plan is the particular conception of the doctrine as the principal, Mr. Shelby, had developed it. ... In its most articulate form, it appeared as a mimeographed document titled *Kensington Elementary School: Design for Individualized Instruction.*

In addition, Kensington's formal doctrine was codified in three other major documents: (1) the *Educational Specifications* developed for Kensington's architect, (2) a proposal to the Olds Foundation that was written by the curriculum director, and (3) a published document from the Architectural Design Institute (ADI) that described Kensington as an innovative school. In general, a high degree of consistency existed among these statements; however, each carried the slant of its particular purposes and authors.

An additional and important phrasing of the formal doctrine occurs in what we have called the facade, the formal doctrine as it was presented to the public. Even here, further distinctions are required. The "public" is multiple; it includes the parents who are the immediate patrons of the school, the residents of the Milford school district, the broader audience of the subcommunities in the metropolitan area in which Milford exists and to which it compares itself, and, also, the national community. ... In addition, one can discriminate between the lay audience and the professional audience, the latter being the numbers of educational personnel who visited Kensington, who heard about the school from the many spokesmen connected with it, or who read about it in the numerous professional articles that have been printed about the school.

Finally, one must speak of individual faculty member's conceptions or schemata. The school was many and sometimes different things to individual faculty members. As we shall learn, [for] some it was a reason for being, a total existence; for others it was mainly team teaching, or ungradedness, or individualized instruction. In effect, particular elements were abstracted and focused on by particular staff members.

... "Why make such distinctions?" ... First, the doctrine varied in the world of Kensington. Second, the facade, that part which appeared in the national magazines, was often a series of special in-

---

2. This might be pursued further in the sense that a superintendent has a mandate from the school board and, in turn, the board might have a mandate from the residents of the community. In the Milford district these two additional linkages contained complexities of prior political conflict.

stances and fond hopes rather than the reality of the new school. Third, the principal's Institutional Plan was a culmination of considerable personal thought and was his image of what the school was to be made into through day-to-day interaction. It was not to be changed easily. Fourth, the doctrine served to buoy up spirits when the reality flagged. Fifth, the mandate from the superintendent to the faculty, "build a school," was in partial conflict with the principal's Institutional Plan. . . . Sixth, the individual staff conceptions, in accenting specific elements, often raised issues of conflict with the totality or other specific but different elements that another accented. Finally, and perhaps most important, the formal doctrine, especially in a new and developing school, suggests the means-means and means-ends relationships that become the structure of the school. In one sense, it is through varying interpretations, perceptions, and adaptations of doctrine that organizational structures are elaborated and changed.

Sources, Manifestations, and Content of the Doctrine

The Mandate

In our theoretical analysis the initial mandate, or general set of directives issued to the principal and faculty, precedes the formal doctrine of the school and also specifies elements in the doctrine. The mandate was characterized, as observed in the superintendent's statements, by its long-range goals. Both in substance and goals, the mandate reflects what might be called the "new elementary education" of the 1960's. The doctrine developed and adopted by the Kensington school faculty was geared somewhat more to immediacy and to effecting a program at the beginning of the school year in September.

Much of the broader mandate of the Milford school district was presented by the superintendent at a total Kensington school faculty meeting on August 18. Some of the points noted below form a major part of the doctrine that was propagated and that performed various functions for the school. The ideas were a part of a five-year plan that contained several points. In outline form, . . . the superintendent says:

Curriculum. The curriculum is all pupil experiences while under the direction and supervision of the school. It depends on the goals and the kinds of adults we want: . . . adults who have developed effective language techniques, life-long habits of continuous learning, and values which guide them as individuals and as members of society. We need communication and computation skills. . . . There is no instructional curriculum. . . . The curriculum is determined by the needs of pupils. We don't need a crutch such as a text. . . . The faculty is the curriculum.

Methods. (1) Individualize, (2) humanize, (3) dramatize, (4) socialize. Under the category of individualize, one must decide how to set objectives, plan, prepare, communicate, and evaluate, and, in doing these, decide whether or not one is operating within the framework of the group or individual. Item two, humanize, refers to getting to know the students and respecting them. Included in dramatizing, one emphasizes creativity, divergent thinking, and devices for handling wrong answers. Socializing deals with the learning of various roles for working in groups. . . .

Time. (1) The school day—There should be varied lengths of time in the school day. In the elementary school some should come at 7:00, 8:00, and 9:00 and leave at 2:00, 3:00, and so forth. It is hoped that in the Kensington school there will be no bell, and pupils can come when they want. We hope everyone will not leave at 3:30. (2) The school year—The twelve-month school year is advocated. The three months' vacation has outlived its usefulness. As an example, parents' vacations fit individual wants; they are able to resume their work when they return.

Student ages. Two-, three-, and four-year-olds should be able to come to and leave the school at varied times. All should not remain in school the same number of years.

Personnel. (1) Teachers—The teachers are to break down walls and become learning consultants rather than the traditional dispensers of information. (2) Pupils—Instead of classroom units, there will be pupil units. There will not be 18 units of 30, but 550 units. It is to be a completely individualized program. There are to be multilevel materials.

Protected subculture. The idea of the Kensington school as a protected subculture. If we are to be change agents, we must develop subcultures. Group norms and pressures influence teachers. This subculture will protect good teachers from being influenced by group norms. By protecting subcultures, we may help the spread of ideas. . . .

Behind the superintendent's words of August 18 were earlier aspects of the intellectual content of Kensington. In January, the year before the opening of school, a district-wide proposal of the Milford schools was submitted to the Olds Foundation. Broadly stated, it was a three-year "comprehensive project for developing a design for learning." Although Kensington was a protected subculture and had a mandate of its own, the district also was assumed to be ready for change, and Kensington was to be a vital part of that plan.

. . . The mandate is a concrete and tangible part of Kensington's environment, . . . important information for the organization and for its administrator. It ties an organization or system to the larger organization. Furthermore, . . . the mandate aids in clarifying the "supportive-nonsupportive" dimension of the environment. As organizational alternatives are raised, explored, and evaluated, the mandate is the template indicating which alternatives will be supported, which will be rejected, or which will be responded to with lukewarm interest. . . . This is an important specification of Simon's (1957) point that the next higher level of the larger organization specifies the decision premises of the immediately lower level of the organization. The implications for hierarchical control, for democratic school administration, and for teacher-pupil relations are quite real and quite important.

The Building Specifications

Another aspect and source of the doctrine of the Kensington school developed from . . . *Building Specifications* reflects the special concern of the architect who is aware of the open-system qualities of an educational organization and the closed-system qualities of a structure made of concrete and steel. Even so, further ambiguity is introduced because of professional education's inability to speak precisely about the ends of educational endeavors.

Objectives. The general objectives are stated and restated a number of times in the *Specifications*. The words used vary considerably: (1) ". . . all the children of all the people to develop to the limits of their potentiality" (p. 2); (2) ". . . complete living in all phases of life" (p. 10); (3) ". . . become the architect of his own character" (p. 10); (4) ". . . self-realization" (p. 10); (5) ". . . development of the child intellectually, socially, emotionally, and physically" (p. 12). . . .

If the analysis is correct, the difficulty in specification of goals in time and concreteness by the original planning group, by the superintendent, and by the principal has [permitted] only tentative . . . comparabilities in discussion of the building structure, the program of educational activities, and the structure of interaction among the significant participants. Educational and social theory have important problems that remain to be solved.

Physical Facilities. In our analytic framework the statement of general and specific objectives must be accompanied by a statement of means that have high probabilities of reaching the ends. The program of activities, the interactional structure of pupils, teachers, and staff, and the building facilities provide a simple taxonomy for the analysis of means. The most general statement of the building dimension appears in the *Specifications*: "Consequently, a physical plan which is considerably different from and more comprehensive than the traditional elementary plant is required" (p. 12). The specific elaboration of this as a taxonomy of facilities in the *Specifications* does not suggest . . . more comprehensiveness or greater difference from most school plant specifications. In outline form the statement is as follows.

1. Educational spaces
   a. General purpose classrooms
   b. Special instructional areas
2. Auxiliary spaces
3. Special facilities
4. General environment . . .

Flexibility is stated as a key dimension in the Kensington school specifications. . . . A flexible building, then, is a building that can be changed easily. . . . The prospectus speaks of four kinds of flexibility: (1) daily flexibility, (2) frequent flexibility, (3) infrequent flexibility, (4) long-range flexibility. . . .

Social Structure. Social structure, in its initial formulation, is primarily an activity structure and an interactional structure. Certain kinds of tasks are carried out and certain relationships exist among the persons involved. The building specifications suggest at several points the nature of the dimensions involved and their presumed interrelationships. . . . A half-dozen more specific interpretations are made that define the social structure of the school:

1. . . . a program flexible enough to provide for individual differences of pupils.
2. . . . schedules arranged according to needs and interests of each pupil.
3. . . . guidance of pupils into experiences of successful living.
4. Purposes and methods will be shared by pupils and teachers.
5. Pupils will carry out projects individually as well as in small groups and large groups.
6. Learning assignments will be individualized . . . [pages 10-11].

Notice that organizational structures such as team teaching receive no mention in the *Specifications.* . . . Guides for teacher activity and interaction structures that presumably would facilitate planning and development of flexible programs, schedules, grouping of pupils, and individualized learning were not explicit in the *Specifications.*

The Institutional Plan

Introduction. The Institutional Plan was the design of the school in the mind of the principal. . . . [The following is] a resumé of the content of the Institutional Plan of the Kensington school [as it] was presented to visiting educators, parents, reporters, and other interested persons. . . . This particular document served as the staff's first formal contact with the new school's program.

Objectives and assumptions. The general objectives for the elementary school formulated in the plan were these:

1. To assist pupils to become fully functioning mature human beings.
2. To meet the needs of individual differences by providing a differentiated program (rather than merely a differentiated rate for progressing through a uniform program).
3. To provide the skills, the structures, and the understandings which will enable pupils to identify worthwhile goals for themselves, and to work independently toward their attainment [page 4].

The school's function, according to the plan, was to establish and to implement a program that would assist in reaching the goals or objectives. Accordingly, the instructional program was based on two assumptions. The first idea was that learning results only from experience. Experience was defined as "what happened within an individual as a consequence of his living in or transacting with his environment." A second assumption was that it is impossible to structure a particular experience; only the environment can be structured in such a way that the desired experience is likely to occur. These assumptions implied that the Kensington school had a two-fold task: decisions must be made as to experiences considered desirable for the pupil, and ways must be located for structuring the learning environment so that these experiences are likely to evolve. The pupils at the Kensington school were to take active parts in both of the processes.

There was to be no one central focus such as textbook-centeredness, pupil-centeredness, or teacher-centeredness; instead, numerous facets of the school were to shape the learning environment. Learning was viewed as an interactive process that varied from individual to individual. These ideas were a part of the rationale utilized in decision making as it related to curriculum, teacher-pupil roles, the organization of the school, the building and facilities, and the instructional materials.

Curriculum. The Kensington school placed primary emphasis on process development as opposed to content development. What was designated as the "spiral curriculum" in which concepts, skills, and values were the central elements aided in this shift in emphasis. . . .

Redefinition of teacher-pupil roles. The document emphasized that more was involved in accomplishing the objectives of the school than just slicing subject matter in a variety of ways. . . . Human factors such as motivation, perception, discipline, communication, and thinking were designated as important in the acquisition of knowledge as well as in the development of the pupils into fully functioning human beings, which it will be remembered was one of the general objectives. The application of these processes brought about the recognition of a need for a change in the traditional teacher-pupil roles and in the organizational climate in which this interaction occurs. The following listing (from page 8 of Institutional Plan) shows the change in emphasis in teacher-pupil roles:

From	*To*
Passive, reactive pupils	Active, initiating pupils
Pupil followership	Pupil leadership
Restriction of pupils	Freedom for pupils
External discipline	Self-discipline
External motivation	Self-motivation
Group activities	Individual activities
Restricting pupil interaction	Encouraging pupil interaction
Teacher responsibility for teaching	Pupil responsibility for learning
Teacher planning	Teacher-pupil planning
Teacher evaluation	Teacher-pupil evaluation
Teacher as a dispenser of knowledge	Teacher as catalyst for inquiry
Teacher as controller of pupils	Teacher as organizer for learning
Identical roles for teachers	Differentiated roles for teachers
Closed, rigid social climate	Open, flexible social climate

... The doctrine surrounding the organization stresses flexibility. Teacher-pupil organization has as its base "planned flexibility." "Both horizontal and vertical organization of the school are, therefore, designed to provide the framework within which is possible the frequent reorganization of pupils and teachers for meaningful instructional activities" (page 9). Vertical organization is considered as referring to the sequence of progression through the school and is closely related to the concept of gradedness. In the past, in most schools sequence has not been viewed as problematic; however, the failure elsewhere to recognize that there are numerous sequences is pointed out in the document. The Kensington school avoids organizing on the basis of "rigidly defined 'levels' " or six lockstep grades. The vertical organization has three basic divisions, and there is opportunity for flexibility within and between divisions. The three divisions—basic skills, transition, and independent study (ISD)—are planned to perform differentiated functions. The organization within, horizontal organization, is also differentiated for maximum effectiveness. Much of this is summarized in Figure 26-1, a summary table from the Institutional Plan.

As has been shown, much of the doctrine emphasized the flexibility of both the building and the instructional program. The provision

Kensington Elementary School			
Function of the elementary school	Designed to develop the learner as an individual and as a member of society		
Means of fulfilling function	Focus on learning generalizations basic to the disciplines and on ways of knowing and thinking. Emphasis on the individual		
Organizational structure	Vertical organization consisting of three sequential divisions: basic skills, transition, and independent study		
	Basic skills division	Transition division	Independent study division
Distinctive function of division	To provide the basic communication, computation, and social skills essential for acquiring knowledge and for developing as mature human beings	To teach pupils to work within the structure of the school to pursue knowledge independently	To assist pupils pursue meaningful knowledge about the world in which they live
Means of fulfilling	Through the use of sequential learning activities and materials	Through the development of the classroom group as an effective social system for attaining institutional goals	Through the provision of a systematic framework that allows pupils to utilize extensive human and material resources for learning
Basic unit of organization	Classes within the division (self-contained classrooms)	Small groups within classes within the division	Individuals within the division
Organizational structure of the division	Vertical (sequential levels), with intraclass flexibility for instruction	Horizontal, with flexible vertical organization for instruction in skill subjects	Complete horizontal and vertical flexibility for instruction
Pupil progress	Differentiated rates of progress according to individual needs and abilities. Reassignment of pupils within division and to next division whenever appropriate	Provisions for variations in program according to individual needs and abilities. Reassignment of pupils within division and to next division whenever appropriate	Provision for variations in program according to individual needs and abilities. Reassignment of pupils to secondary school at end of fifth, sixth, or seventh grade

FIGURE 26-1

Summary of Kensington's Formal Doctrine (page 10 of Institutional Plan) for individual differences of students to the extent of schedules arranged according to the needs and interests of each pupil, which represented the "highly individualized" program, was descriptive of the school's intentions.

Schemata of Individual Faculty Members

... A number of instances of the formal doctrine [have been presented] as individual conceptions, since the mandate reflected the superintendent's position, the foundation request was written primarily by the curriculum director, and the Institutional Plan was the principal's formal statement of his view of the doctrine. However, ... each faculty member held his own view or schema of Kensington. Typically, each schema seemed to be generated out of personal needs and goals, early conversations about the school, ... and early documents. ... As the divisions and teams went their individual ways, both geographically and instructionally, individual members were privy to only partial experiences of the totality. ...

Perhaps the most critical doctrinal outcome for the organization was the inability of a number of the individual conceptions to become merged into a common enough framework, an agreed-on interpretation of the doctrine. Individual and subgroup interpretations of this doctrine were involved ... in the early schism between the two teams in basic skills, in the coalition aspects of transition, and in the continuing conflict in ISD. Differences as to teaching methods, materials, pupil control, and staff organization were prevalent. The staff was verbal and articulate in isolating and elaborating "reasonable but incompatible" individual interpretations of what Kensington should stand for. As these intertwined with other personality variables and with episodes in the school's evolving social processes (such as the T groups), they contributed to the complex puzzle that was Kensington. ...

Summary

In a sense, we are caught between these different but highly overlapping statements. On the one hand, they were sources of the formal doctrine; on the other hand, they were statements of it. In effect, there was no one clear and totally accepted statement of the doctrine. As we cite in other parts of our analysis, even more variety occurred in the conceptions of the doctrine as they were held by individual staff members. As in the parable, the elephant was less than an elephant as the five men clutched it in the dark, and thus it was [that] faculty members viewed the Kensington school.

Structural Dimensions of the Doctrine

As we analyze the doctrine apart from its substantive content, several structural dimensions seem significant. They include the degree of formalization, the degree of abstractness, the degree of consistency, and the degree of affectivity.

Formalization. . . . The rephrasing as formalized doctrine, the degree to which the "point of view" is systematized and codified, seemed significant. Kensington had a high degree of this formalization. . . .

The antecedents of this high degree of formalization seem to focus on a number of conditions. First, that the school was new and had an innovative thrust seemed crucial as . . . data [were examined]. Because it was different, it had to explain itself. In trying to explain itself, a formal statement of its point of view developed. The Milford school district also sought outside funds continuously, . . . [and such requests] demanded written statements, [which] enhanced the formalization of "what one is trying to do."

Within the Milford leadership, for example, the superintendent, the curriculum director, and the Kensington principal, a strong desire existed to have an impact on American education. . . . Not only did they seek to put [educational improvements] into practice, but also they talked and wrote about their ideas. Such behavior helped to shape a more formalized doctrine. . . .

Finally, . . . the community conflict [was] an important aspect of the move toward a formalized doctrine. . . . The superintendent's early attempts to build a social base at the district level pushed him to verbalize and codify his position. . . .

Although he was commenting on TVA, Selznick (1949) seemed to capture the interrelationships among the several sources of the doctrine as they were part of Kensington.

This quest for an ideology, for doctrinal nourishment, while general, is uneven. Organizations established in a stable context, with assured futures, do not feel the same urgencies as those born of turmoil and set down to fend for themselves in undefined ways among institutions fearful and resistant. As in individuals, insecurity summons ideological reinforcements.

The TVA was particularly susceptible to this kind of insecurity because it was not the spontaneous product of the institutions in its area of operation [page 48].

. . . Figure 26-2 [sketches the relations and shows] some of the consequences of a formalized doctrine. It provided a guide to action.

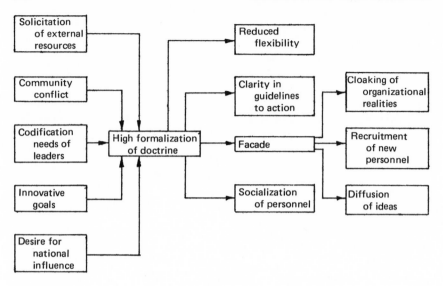

FIGURE 26-2
Implications of the formalization of the doctrine

It aided in socializing new members. It told them what the school was all about. . . . As the formal doctrine departed from the reality of the organization and was presented to the public, it became what we have called the facade. This facade became a cloak or screen covering the realities of organizational practices. This, too, had some exceedingly important implications. Finally, the doctrine and its counterpart, the facade, had implications in recruiting new staff.

Affective tone. Doctrines can be analyzed, irrespective of their content, in terms of the degree to which they have affective or emotional qualities. . . . (See Figure 26-3). Operationally, we presume one might measure doctrinal documents on this affective tone dimension by engaging in content analysis, using as a format the usually described propagandistic emotional appeals.

In the Institutional Plan, the principal's document, the affective tone is present, but moderate, at least, in comparison to the Architectural Design Institute's account. . . . [The earlier listing of the change in emphasis in teacher-pupil roles] contains a number of affectively oriented educational statements. The document from ADI contains even more significant attempts to excite the reader. . . .

In short, the affective tone, especially as . . . seen . . . in the ADI publication, and later with the appearance of the facade, suggested

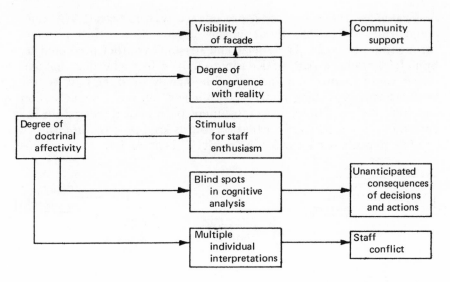

FIGURE 26-3
Implications of the affective tone dimensions of the formal doctrine

two important cautions: . . . renewed suspicions of written accounts that seem to strive to excite the reader . . . [and] renewed . . . concern regarding potential incongruencies between the doctrine in its many forms and the organizational reality lying beneath it.

Integration. The degree to which the content of the formal doctrine is consistent or integrated seems another dimension worthy of further investigation. . . . One of the major goals was individual pupil decision making. A major subgoal was an organizational structure that involved team teaching. The experienced teachers reacted frequently and spontaneously that they were able to provide more individual pupil decision making in their self-contained classrooms of prior years than they could in a team where their behavior was contingent on their teaching peers instead of upon their pupils. . . .

Another illustration of inconsistency within the doctrine appears in the deification of the group and of the individual. The doctrine argues for group consensus as an ultimate goal and individual development as an ultimate goal. The point [made] here is similar to Spindler's (1955) analysis of the transformation within American culture from traditional to emergent values. Kensington had internalized within its doctrine intense commitments to values of individuality and social processes. On what occasions and in what situations one value or the other took precedence was not clear. The rules about rules or norms about norms remained a critical problem throughout the year. The social and personal conflict predicted by Spindler became a part of Kensington. In effect, the doctrine was giving simultaneous and incompatible signals or directions to the teachers and provoking conflict within and between them. Neither the staff nor the broader establishment of American education has entertained strong analytic attention to this kind of issue. In terms of testable hypotheses, we offer the model in Figure 26-4.

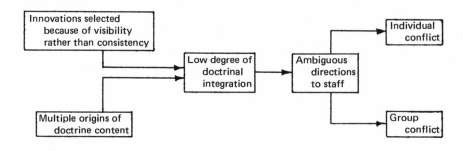

FIGURE 26-4
Hypotheses surrounding doctrinal integration

Abstractness. Doctrine may vary also in the degree to which it is abstract or concrete. Kensington's doctrine accented the abstract. Issues were treated at a lofty and general level. For instance, explicit concrete definitions of "individualized instruction" and "fully functioning pupils" did not receive final or agreed-on concrete operational definitions. Individualized instruction could be a carefully guided tutorial experience in which the teacher communicated specific concepts to a single pupil, or it could be a self-selected learning experience engaged in by one or more pupils. As a language system is abstract, it permits legitimate but varying concrete interpretations. A doctrine with considerable abstractness hypothetically can provoke a wide range of these interpretations. This problem arose even when it seemed that considerable specificity had been obtained with respect to teaming, resource specialists, and academic counselors.

. . . Kensington had a further complication in terms of the individual faculty member styles of problem solving. . . . The doctrinal content contained abstract statements of teacher power to make educational decisions but little specificity regarding means for doing this.

In addition, the peculiar quality of educational methods having little concrete evidence of effectiveness played into the abstract quality of the doctrine also (see Figure 26-5).

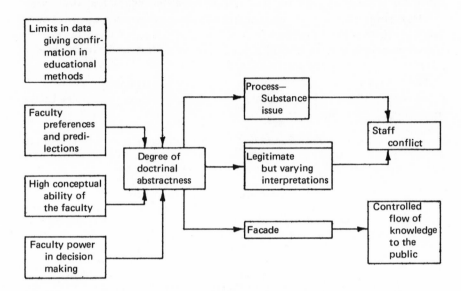

FIGURE 26-5
The relationships of the abstractness dimensions of the formal doctrine

Complexity. Doctrines vary in the degree to which they are simple . . . or complicated. . . . Increasing intellectual ability and increasing compulsivity of influential group members produce an organizational point of view that has many parts, elements, and nuances. Kensington's doctrine had a number of elements and each element, for instance, the nature of pupil-teacher interaction, had a series of components listed [earlier] in great detail.

Scope. Related to the complexity of the doctrine is the doctrine's pervasiveness or scope, that is, how much of organizational life is covered by the doctrine. In Kensington's case it was large. Specification in goals covered the total child and specification in procedures covered the whole day and a multitude of ways of behaving—teaming, ungradedness, no textbooks, and the like. This quality of doctrinal scope has implications for personal commitment to the organization by its members. . . .

Flexibility. Flexibility has at least two kinds of subissues connected with it. One of them is the flexibility or rigidity with which individuals hold to the specific content of the doctrine. . . . The other subissue . . . is the degree of changeableness of the doctrine. . . . Doctrines vary in the degree to which they are changeable, and this has important consequences for the organization whose social structure and activities are changing rapidly as was that of Kensington.

The issues in the relationship between administrative behavior and the doctrinal flexibility are highlighted in Selznick's (1949) comment:

Among the many and pressing responsibilities of leadership, there arises the need to develop a Weltanschauung, a general view of the organization's position and role among its contemporaries. For organizations are not unlike personalities: the search for stability and meaning, for security, is unremitting. It is a search which seems to find a natural conclusion in the achievement of a set of morally sustaining ideas, ideas which lend support to decisions which must rest on compromise and restraint. Organizations, like men, are at crucial times involved in an attempt to close the gap between what they wish to do and what they can do. It is natural that, in due course, the struggle should be resolved in favor of a reconciliation between the desire and the ability. This new equilibrium may find its formulation and its sustenance in ideas which reflect a softened view of the world. The ethic of revolt, of thoroughgoing change, assumes that human and institutional materials are readily malleable and that disaffection from current modes of thought and patterns of behavior can be long sustained in action. But leadership must heed the danger of strain and disaster as recalcitrance and inertia exert their unceasing pressures; in doing so, it may see wisdom in the avowal of loyalty to prevailing codes and established structures. The choice, indeed, may often lie between adjustment and organizational suicide [pages 48-49]. . . .

Uniqueness. Doctrines vary along a dimension of "run-of-the-mill" to uniqueness. As one looks at a number of schools, one can observe an important variation on this dimension. Kensington's ideology was not commonplace; its point of view was unusual in [various] ways. . . . A unique doctrine along with other aspects of uniqueness, for example, the physical structure of the building, makes the school visible, attracts a particular kind of staff, mobilizes energies, and may well evoke a higher ratio of unanticipated to anticipated consequences of purposive organizational activity.

Consequences of the Doctrine

As with all of our analyses, the models specifying antecedents and consequences indicate multiple hypotheses. These relationships seem viable in [the] data, and [they are offered] as testable propositions for the realities of other educational organizations. . . . Developed further, the analysis of the formal doctrine . . . seemed to fall comfortably into the context provided by our general conception of manifest and latent functions and dysfunctions.

Manifest Functions

Guide to action. A formal doctrine contains statements of goals and objectives toward which one strives. Also, it contains subgoals to be approached "on the way" toward the more general and ultimate objectives. Similarly, it contains specification of means, that is, alternatives of action, of social structure, and of procedures that contain high probabilities of attaining the goals. In effect, it is a plan—a guide to individual action and group activity. Kensington's formal doctrine possessed this manifest function. The building was built according to the building specifications. The August workshop was run according to the Institutional Plan. Although school was opened in temporary quarters, the dimensions of the beginning, as we shall describe shortly, occurred in terms of divisional and team understandings and interpretations of the doctrine. The doctrine had a potency that could not be denied. . . .

Group norms. Formal doctrine in its ultimate sense becomes the codified policies and rules of the bureaucracy as stated in the manuals of standard operating procedures. Group norms reflect the same kinds of issues, except that they usually are the informal statements of "the way we do things around here." The congruence of these two systems has been the subject of . . . research and discussion. Relatively less has been said of the interdependency in the development of each. . . .

At Kensington, we have the exciting case of multiple statements of the doctrine prior to the interaction of the staff and students who were to be the incumbents of the organization. These statements, especially the Institutional Plan, and the forcefulness of the principal as author of the Plan and as the central and most powerful member of the staff provided the basic framework in which norms were to develop. The issues in the doctrine were the issues with which the faculty struggled throughout the year.

In Jackson's (1960) terms, norms did not crystallize within the staff. Staff turnover was at a high rate even before the end of the first year. . . . The conflict and interpersonal difficulties contributed heavily to this lack of norm crystallization. Some subgroups did work well together and friendship groups developed also. They tended to give a picture of norm ambiguity, a special case of low crystallization.

Latent Dysfunctions

Cloaking of organizational realities. A well-codified and an abstract doctrine has a number of dysfunctions. One of them is the cloaking of organizational realities.[3] In this usage we argue that every organization to some degree masks its internal functioning to its public. . . . The more formalized the doctrine becomes and the more internal problems that exist the greater the degree of masking that will occur. . . . Internal problems . . . at Kensington [were]: the severe staff conflict, especially in the Independent Study Division, and the difficulties the divisions had in implementing the program as defined initially. Additional impetus to the cloaking of activities was the continuous "battle" with, at least, a minority of vocal parents and district residents whose biases toward traditional education were in conflict with one or more of the innovative elements of the program.

As consequences, inaccuracies in perception of the realities of the school and parental frustrations developed. This, in turn, prevented the building of long-term support for the school as well as for the district leadership. These implications are diagramed in Figure 26-6.

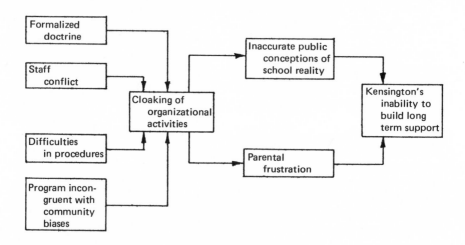

FIGURE 26-6

The antecedents and consequences of cloaking organizational activities

3. This point is essentially Selznick's (1949). Corroboration in the Kensington case extends the generality of the argument.

Self-deception. . . . Language systems have been viewed as possible vehicles for self-deception, rationalizations. An ideology or group belief with its concomitant social support possesses the increased strength to carry out consequences such as self-deception. In his trenchant style, Hoffer (1951) draws the picture of the extreme condition in the relation of doctrine to self-deception:

> All active mass movements strive, therefore, to interpose a fact proof screen between the faithful and the realities of the world. They do this by claiming that the ultimate and absolute truth is already embodied in their doctrine and that there is no truth or certitude outside it. The facts on which the true believer bases his conclusions must not be derived from his experience or observation but from holy writ [page 75].

The modal member of Kensington was not this extreme, although some individual staff members were. . . . Kensington did have such a quality about it. The formal doctrine seems to contribute to the masking of reality with regard to the members of the system. . . . Strong belief, commitment in action, specific implementation or ties to the real world, disconfirmations, and social support were critical elements. . . .

The Facade: Functions and Dysfunctions

The events that determine major aspects of an organization's social structure vary in the degree to which they begin as fortuitous and mundane conditions. Also they vary in the degree to which they are outside the immediate control of the participants in the system. The dislodged pebble that cumulates into an avalanche is not a bad analogy. . . .

. . . Facade refers to the image that the school presents to the several publics. Kensington was a highly visible school. Prior to our study, the board hired a superintendent who . . . held strong interests in developing in the Milford school district a unique, novel, and ultracontemporary educational program. Kensington was a major part of this. Through the consultants at ADI, and their publications, the school attained an initial visibility. Thus, the first image of the school was projected. As this attracted increased attention, further aspects of the formal doctrine were needed, were available, and were utilized to present the image of the school. As awards were won for architectural design, popular news media began to describe the program, which was equally unique. . . .

Theoretically, the uniqueness of the physical structure of the building and the superintendent's intentions for national leadership by Milford created an initial visibility. With this visibility came increased attention and the need for a codified point of view—the formal doctrine. However, . . . the day-to-day functioning reality was not totally congruent with the doctrine. This led to the special "public face" which centered on intentions, . . . and on special atypical concrete instances that illustrated these intentions.

The facade produced many important outcomes. On the one hand, the local and national acclaim was a hearty stimulant to flagging faculty spirits. The newspaper and magazine accounts brought commentary about "our school" from parents, relatives, and friends. The complex process of social approval and identity development for the individual staff member in relationship to his occupation of teaching seemed highly significant. . . . By the cloaking of organizational realities, we have reference to a biased or partial picture of the organization. . . . Other critical comments . . . on the public image are: inadequate discriminations between intention and reality in the program, the isolation of atypical teachers who were not representative of the majority, and inadequate normative data to make comparisons of such items as frequency of discipline problems. Hypotheses concerning the sources and consequences of the facade are presented in Figure 26-7.

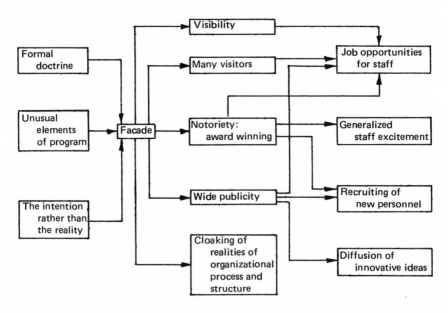

FIGURE 26-7
The implications of the facade

Conclusions

Our conclusions follow simply from the description and analysis. One needs a concept such as formal doctrine to talk fully and incisively about Kensington. Presumably, schools will vary in the degree to which they possess a visionary, conscious, and codified ideology. Second, in some instances, antecedents to the doctrine will exist in the form of mandates, as with Kensington. Other schools, especially new ones, will have building specifications that play dual roles—as antecedents of doctrine and later as another manifestation and sometimes contending operational definition of the doctrine. Third, organizational positions soon possess incumbents who interpret mandates, building specifications, and foundation proposals in terms of their own cognitive maps and professional schemata. In some situations this may be formalized to the point of a written "Institutional Plan." In the instance of Kensington this was a forceful and potent position paper. . . . It was a major determinant of the principal's decision making, a guide to the faculty, a source of conflict, and a major issue in the dilemmas of democratic administration.

To complement our observations and analysis . . . a brief summary of Selznick's position on "official doctrine" . . . in his study of the Tennessee Valley Authority [is] codified in Figure 26-8. Such a model indicates similarities across organizations and [suggests] a

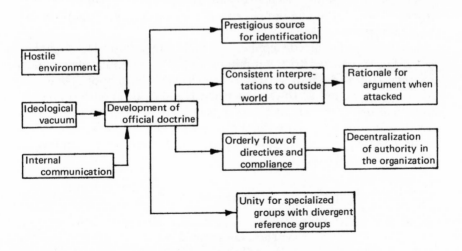

FIGURE 26-8
Model clarifying Selznick's (1949) reasoning concerning
TVA's official doctrine (pages 47-52)

more extended comparative organizational theory. The genesis of his "official doctrine" lay in a hostile environment, an ideological vacuum, and a need for communication within the organization. The antecedents of Kensington's formal doctrine overlapped only partially. The consequences, too, seem only partially common.

Perhaps schools differ from regional governmental organizations, or perhaps it is innovative schools that differ from innovative regional governmental organizations. Or maybe it is just Kensington and TVA that we are contrasting. Nonetheless, the doctrinal functions of internal communication and orderly flow of directives did not occur at Kensington. The abstractness of the formal doctrine—even when these abstractions were specified as carefully as the principal tried in the Institutional Plan—still could not communicate. The laments of the proponents of behavioral objectives (Bloom *et al.,* 1956) and operational definitions (Boring, 1945) were not heard. Even the voice of the tired traditional teacher saying, "This year we are going to go through the text from page 1 to page 250," has its own kind of concrete appeal. In spite of prodigious effort, common guidelines that guided did not exist; the language of school organization, teaching, and goals for pupils remains metaphorical and literary but neither practical nor scientific.

Our attempt to sketch dimensions of the doctrine has been exploratory, yet influential. . . . As . . . stated at a number of points our models seem to reflect well many of the specifics of [the] case. The degree to which they are more generally true awaits systematic verificational research. . . .

Finally, . . . the facade concept is most important. The organizational face presented to the public—especially in popular newspapers and magazines—did not reflect the reality of the school. These discrepancies have led us toward skepticism and caution with respect to any "feature" story about educational matters. Administrators who seriously try to keep up with the Jones district—or its facade—seem to be creating a new kind of problem while they are attempting to solve the original one.

References

Bloom, B. S., *et al.* (1956). *Taxonomy of Educational Objectives. Handbook I: Cognitive Domain.* New York: Longmans, Green.

Boring, E. G. (1945). "The Use of Operational Definitions in Science." *Psychological Review,* 52:243-245, 278-281.

Hoffer, E. (1951). *The True Believer.* New York: Harper and Brothers.

Jackson, J. M. (1960). "Structural Characteristics of Norms," in National Society for the Study of Education, *Yearbook*. Chicago: University of Chicago Press.

Selznick, P. (1949). *TVA and the Grass Roots.* Berkeley: University of California Press.

Simon, H. (1957). *Administrative Behavior*, 2nd ed. New York: Macmillan.

Spindler, G., ed. (1955). *Education and Anthropology.* Palo Alto: Stanford University Press.